Literary Lives

Founding Editor: **Richard Dutton**, Professor of English, Lancaster University

This series offers stimulating accounts of the literary careers of the most admired and influential English-language authors. Volumes follow the outline of the writers' working lives, not in the spirit of traditional biography, but aiming to trace the professional, publishing and social contexts which shaped their writing.

Published titles include:

Clinton Machann
MATTHEW ARNOLD

Jan Fergus
JANE AUSTEN

John Beer
WILLIAM BLAKE

Tom Winnifrith and Edward Chitham
CHARLOTTE AND EMILY BRONTË

Sarah Wood
ROBERT BROWNING

Janice Farrar Thaddeus
FRANCES BURNEY

Caroline Franklin
BYRON

Sarah Gamble
ANGELA CARTER

Nancy A. Walker
KATE CHOPIN

Roger Sales
JOHN CLARE

William Christie
SAMUEL TAYLOR COLERIDGE

Graham Law and Andrew Maunder
WILKIE COLLINS

Cedric Watts
JOSEPH CONRAD

Grahame Smith
CHARLES DICKENS

George Parfitt
JOHN DONNE

Paul Hammond
JOHN DRYDEN

Kerry McSweeney
GEORGE ELIOT

Tony Sharpe
T. S. ELIOT

David Rampton
WILLIAM FAULKNER

Harold Pagliaro
HENRY FIELDING

Andrew Hook
F. SCOTT FITZGERALD

Mary Lago
E. M. FORSTER

Shirley Foster
ELIZABETH GASKELL

Neil Sinyard
GRAHAM GREENE

James Gibson
THOMAS HARDY

Linda Wagner-Martin
ERNEST HEMINGWAY

Cristina Malcolmson
GEORGE HERBERT

Gerald Roberts
GERARD MANLEY HOPKINS

Neil Roberts
TED HUGHES

Kenneth Graham
HENRY JAMES

W. David Kaye
BEN JONSON

R. S. White
JOHN KEATS

Phillip Mallett
RUDYARD KIPLING

John Worthen
D. H. LAWRENCE

Literary Lives
Series Standing Order ISBN 978–0–333–71486–7 hardcover
Series Standing Order ISBN 978 0–333–80334–9 paperback
(outside North America only)

You can receive future titles in this series as they are published by placing a standing order. Please contact your bookseller or, in case of difficulty, write to us at the address below with your name and address, the title of the series and one of the ISBNs quoted above.

Customer Services Department, Macmillan Distribution Ltd, Houndmills, Basingstoke, Hampshire RG21 6XS, England

---

John Keats

A Literary Life

R. S. White
Australian Professorial Fellow and Professor of English and Cultural Studies,
University of Western Australia

First published in hardback 2010
First published in paperback 2012 by
PALGRAVE MACMILLAN

Palgrave Macmillan in the UK is an imprint of Macmillan Publishers Limited,
registered in England, company number 785998, of Houndmills, Basingstoke,
Hampshire RG21 6XS.

Palgrave Macmillan in the US is a division of St Martin's Press LLC,
175 Fifth Avenue, New York, NY 10010.

Palgrave Macmillan is the global academic imprint of the above companies
and has companies and representatives throughout the world.

Palgrave® and Macmillan® are registered trademarks in the United States,
the United Kingdom, Europe and other countries.

ISBN 978–0–230–57263–8   hardback
ISBN 978–1–113–703047–4   paperback

This book is printed on paper suitable for recycling and made from fully
managed and sustained forest sources. Logging, pulping and manufacturing
processes are expected to conform to the environmental regulations of the
country of origin.

A catalogue record for this book is available from the British Library.

Library of Congress Cataloging-in-Publication Data

White, R. S., 1948–
     John Keats: a literary life / R. S. White.
          p. cm. — (Literary lives)
          Revision of the 2010 edition.
     Includes bibliographical references and index.
     ISBN 978–0–230–57263–8 (cloth) 978–1–113–703047–4 (pbk)
     1. Keats, John, 1795–1821. 2. Keats, John, 1795–1821—Criticism and
interpretation. 3. Poets, English—19th century—Biography. I. Title.
     PR4836.W46 2010
     821'.7—dc22
     [B]
                                                                    2010011561

10 9 8 7 6 5 4 3 2 1
21 20 19 18 17 16 15 14 13 12

'A great strength of this impressive biography is the way it accompanies Keats's life narrative with critical and interpretative passages on the poetry – there is much in these pages that will provoke thought for students and more experienced Keatsians. Keats's childhood, school years and medical career are exceptionally well done, and among many highlights the account of Keats's plays, letters, and Endymion are especially rewarding.' – Professor Nicholas Roe, University of St. Andrews, UK

'... makes significant contributions at the most advanced level of research and, at the other end of the scale, would be an excellent introduction for college undergraduates and general readers ... a fine piece of research and writing ...' – Jack Stillinger, *New Books Online*

... White's *John Keats: A Literary Life* allows us to see Keats as an active/ creative agent, forging an identity *between* the competing demands of the actual and the imagined. This places Keats firmly within his own time, but it also brings his life into fascinating dialogue with the present. The book, a most welcome addition to the literature on John Keats, is certain to draw a wide and appreciative audience.' – Peter Otto, *Australian Book Review*

'R.S. White has written a focused, concise and perceptive biography of John Keats for Palgrave Macmillan's Literary Lives, which will stand readers of the poetry in good stead for years to come ... As a Renaissance scholar, White brings a thorough understanding of other literary periods to bear on the Romantics, and as a result offers some original commentary demonstrating the influence on Keats of Edmund Spenser, John Donne and, above all, William Shakespeare. He is also sensitive to the sense in which Keats regarded his second profession, poetry, as a continuation of his first – that of medicine. Both were concerned with the healing of mind and body, and that goes some way towards explaining Keats' change of career.' – Duncan Wu, *Times Higher Education*

'Elegantly written and expertly crafted, R.S. White's *John Keats: A Literary Life* aims to redress just this kind of imbalance between biography and critical commentary, not only managing to synthesise the most innovative current criticism on Keats's life and work in less than 300 pages, but also establishing a fresh set of contexts with which to read them ... Indeed, it is the insightful commentary that White repeatedly brings to apparently well-established events, ideas, and contexts that makes this book so valuable ... Academic readers will be glad that White has chosen to incorporate so much new material into his concise Life, but this is nonetheless one of those rare books that will appeal to both the general and the specialist reader: students requiring either a short biography of Keats or a critical overview of his major works will still find this book an invaluable starting point for further study. Considering the amount of material already published on Keats, it is a major achievement that White's Life is both accessible to students and an essential addition to our knowledge of Keats's life and work.' – Porscha Fermanis, *British Association for Romantic Studies*

'Students and scholars alike will find that White's discussion of contextual material about the Hunt circle and Keats's medical training, along with the author's extensive knowledge of Shakespeare's works, will enrich their understanding of specific passages in both letters and poems.' – Grant F. Scott, *The Keats-Shelley Review*

Contents

Acknowledgments

Writing literary biography has been a new and alien discipline for me. Whereas a critical book may pursue a single theme like playing a melody on a single instrument, a life-story is multi-layered and symphonic in the sense that the writer's life, friendships, career 'false starts' and the literature are inextricably linked in equal complexity. At times I have taken liberties in sacrificing strict chronology for thematic continuity, though I hope it will be clear when and why this happens. Generally speaking I have tried to read Keats 'forwards' rather than with a sense of tragic hindsight, giving him the space to be young and full of schemes and hopes rather than doomed from the start. Since Keats is a writer who draws any reader very close into a kind of warm sense of intimate kinship through his letters as well as poems, my prime acknowledgment must be to him, and also his loyal friends who ensured the survival of his 'priest-like' words.

More formally, I thank Nicholas Roe, not only for ongoing support for this book and for his own immensely important research, but also as current editor of *The Keats-Shelley Review* for allowing me to ransack my own two articles on Keats's medical training, first published in that journal: '"Like Esculapius of old": Keats's Medical Training', *Keats-Shelley Review*, 12 (1998), 15–49 and 'Keats and the Crisis of Medicine in 1815', *Keats-Shelley Review*, 13 (1999), 58–75. In researching those pieces, I acquired an early debt of gratitude to the archivist at Guy's Hospital Library, to the staff at the Library of the Wellcome Institute, and to Gareth Evans then working at the Chelsea Botanic Garden. The staff at the Reid Library at the University of Western Australia have many times satisfied my curiosity. The Keats House library in Hampstead gave me the opportunity to find books all in one inspiring place and the Houghton Library at Harvard opened my eyes to Keats's own handwriting, during a memorable, flame-coloured autumn period.

This book in particular has forced me to dig down through various archaeological layers of my own life since in very real senses it has been gestating for over forty years. I only hope its scholarship has not dated so visibly as I have. To be asked to write it was a kind of fairy story. Long ago I wrote my undergraduate dissertation at Adelaide on Keats's poetry and ideas in the context of philosophies of organic unity in Romantic literature and art (all in 15,000 words!) and I was shepherded through this absurdly grandiose terrain by John Colmer whose supervision enforced on me the realisation that scholarship is not only an exacting craft but it can also be an elegant art. At the same time the brilliant critic and poet Geoffrey Thurley with infectious enthusiasm introduced me to a whole galaxy of modern writers many of whom were Keats's heirs, and he made me feel that literature matters in a profound sense. I shared my own youthful excitement most often with Olga Marek (now Sankey). A little later, encouragement and help were offered by J. C. Maxwell, Barrie Bullen, Paul Hamilton and Ian Donaldson in my 'first go' at writing on Keats in a book which appeared as *Keats as a Reader of Shakespeare*, while Cathy Davidson who was all-important then, has also as Cathy Mulcahy been invaluable in her support now. During the fourteen happy years I spent lecturing at the University of Newcastle upon Tyne, I shared mutual enthusiasms for Keats and other things with many people whose friendship has continued much longer, in particular Desmond Graham, John Pellowe, Ernst Honigmann, Nicola Fletcher, Rosie King (who discovered at the time that she is related to Keats), Bruce Babington, Peter Regan, Terry Norman and Jane Whiteley. More specifically, it was a joy to teach as 'Special Authors' first Blake and then Keats with Claire Lamont whose erudition matches her delighted affinity with the Romantics. Our classes were remarkable for attracting a group of students whose interest extended into their later professional lives with great distinction, in particular John Goodridge and Jon Mee. Both have sustained a close interest in this book to the very end. So has Rebecca Hiscock who shared with me the 'Keats Walk' in Winchester and has continued to guide me along that memorable path in imagination. I followed in Keats's footsteps through most of his journeys, beginning with Wentworth Place, now Keats House in Hampstead, the Isle of Wight, Winchester, the north and Scotland, to the moving experience of standing in the room where Keats died in Rome, now the Keats-Shelley House. The Lake District is for me identified not only with Wordsworth and the 'Lakers' but also with Keats and the 'Lavers' – the wonderful Pete Laver and Mags – as well as Sally Woodhead. Their friendship has been as glowing in my life as the fires we used to warm ourselves beside on winter nights in Sykeside Cottage, Grasmere. Robert Woof always offered affectionate strictures that no matter how ingenious an interpretation of lines of poetry may be, it has to take into account the specific circumstances of where a poet was and what he was doing and thinking at the time. Later Michael Rossington has shared his voluminous knowledge of Shelley and he, together with Deirdre Coleman and Clara Tuite, has encouraged me to think of myself as not only an early modernist but also a Romanticist.

At the University of Western Australia I have once again found sympathetic souls willing to share their thoughts about Keats: Hilary Fraser, Dennis Haskell, Judith Johnston, Veronica Brady, Andrew Lynch, John Kinsella, Emma Rooksby, Chris Wortham, generations of students, and more recently Danijela Kambascovic-Sawers and the maestro of editing Roger Bourke. Michael Levine is a philosopher who profoundly fuses expertise in the history of ideas with an urgent moral and political concern for the present, and he reassuringly finds this combination in Keats. Many other friends have offered not only decisive help in particulars but heart-warming intellectual support, especially Maurice Whelan (child psychiatrist, biographer of Hazlitt, novelist, and poet) and Sam Pickering, the most distinguished and original essayist since Hazlitt. Thanks are also due to Christabel, Steven and Paula at Palgrave Macmillan for inviting me to write this book which, for all its deficiencies, has been a labour of pure love. The list could go on endlessly and I apologise for the many omissions but no acknowledgments would be complete without thanking once again Marina and Alana White and Pippi the pup, for invigorating every day for me with the simple joy of living.

Abbreviations

Allott	*Keats: The Complete Poems* (London: Longman, 1970)
Barnard	John Barnard (ed.), *John Keats: The Complete Poems* 2nd edn (Harmondsworth: Penguin Books, 1977)
Brown	Charles Armitage Brown, *Life of John Keats*, ed. Dorothy Hyde Bodurtha and Willard B. Pope (London: Oxford University Press, 1937)
CCC	Charles and Mary Cowden Clarke, *Recollections of Writers* (repr. Fontwell, Sussex: Centaur Press, 1969)
Chronology	*A Keats Chronology*, F. B. Pinion (London: Macmillan, Macmillan Author Chronologies, 1992)
FB	*Letters of Fanny Brawne to Fanny Keats [1820–1824]*, ed. Fred Edgcumbe (Oxford: Oxford University Press, 1936)
Gittings	Robert Gittings, *John Keats* (Harmondsworth: Penguin Books, 1968)
Heritage	*Keats: The Critical Heritage*, ed. G. M. Matthews (London: Routledge & Kegan Paul, 1971)
JKL	*The Letters of John Keats 1814–1821*, ed. Hyder Edward Rollins in 2 vols (Cambridge, MA: Harvard University Press, 1958)
KC	*The Keats Circle: Letters and Papers and More Letters and Poems of the Keats Circle*, 2nd edn, 2 vols (Cambridge, MA: Harvard University Press, 1965)

Note: Quotations from Keats's poetry are from Barnard, and those from Shakespeare, apart from ones directly quoted in Keats's words, are taken from *The Complete Works of Shakespeare: The Oxford Edition*, ed. Stanley Wells and Gary Taylor (Oxford: Oxford University Press, 1986).

Most of us, indeed, know little of the great originators until they have been lifted up among the constellations and already rule our fates ... Each of those Shining Ones had to walk on the earth among neighbours who perhaps thought much more of his gait and his garments than of anything which was to give him a title to everlasting fame: each of them had his little local personal history sprinkled with small temptations and sordid cares, which made the retarding friction of this course towards final companionship with the immortals.

George Eliot, *Middlemarch*, ch. 15

[Writing biography] taught me at least two things. First, that the past is not simply 'out there', an objective history to be researched or forgotten, at will; but that it lives most vividly in all of us, deep inside, and needs constantly to be given expression and interpretation. And second, that the lives of great artists and poets and writers are not, after all, so extraordinary by comparison with everyone else. Once known in any detail and any scope, every life is something extraordinary, full of particular drama and tension and surprise, often containing unimagined degrees of suffering or heroism, and invariably touching extreme moments of triumph and despair, though frequently unexpressed. The difference lies in the extent to which one is eventually recorded, and the other is eventually forgotten.

Richard Holmes, *Footsteps: Adventures of a Romantic Biographer*, 208

... axioms are not axioms until they are proved upon our pulses: We read fine – things but never feel them to thee [sic] full until we have gone the same steps as the Author.

John Keats, letter to John Hamilton Reynolds (*JKL*, 1, 279)

1
'He could not quiet be'

Keats reveals little information or even curiosity about his childhood. This is surprising. Many of his contemporary poets and writers were idealising childhood and exploring the links between the child and the adult. Jean-Jacques Rousseau saw the study of children as unlocking information about their later behaviour and personalities. Wordsworth in 'Ode: Intimations of Immortality From Recollections of Early Childhood' constructs a psychological model of a life cycle conceiving of human growth as a process of leaving a natural state of perception which will die away 'And fade into the light of common day'. William Blake in his *Songs of Innocence* and *Songs of Experience* explores the moral implications of naïvety and corruption in the passage from childhood to adulthood, while Coleridge in 'Frost at Midnight' in his words to 'My babe so beautiful, it fills my heart / With tender gladness thus to look at thee' anticipates a new 'poetics of parenthood'. Even Hazlitt, whom it is hard to imagine ever having been a child, was so deeply influenced by the experience of losing a child that he was conscious of its effect on his adult perspective on death.[1] The few passing references Keats makes to children, apart from his own niece whom he never actually met, are quite dismissive and he makes almost no mention of his own childhood. It is possible that the phenomenon of publicly acknowledging the importance of childhood, which had never until the late eighteenth century been manifested, may have been a result of the likelihood of losing children, though the odds were steadily diminishing: 'For example, the London Quakers kept careful track of infant mortality rates, and while the years 1725–1749 saw 341 deaths in infancy for every thousand births, by the same period a century later this number had fallen to 151.'[2] Before this time it must have been an emotional risk for parents to bond deeply with a child, or to spare much thought to continuity of life when the links seemed so fragile and loss so complete. Relief at having simply survived childhood must have been a common feeling.

If John Keats was born 29 October 1795 in a coaching inn, the Swan and Hoop at 24 The Pavement, Moorgate, this would establish his credentials as a kind of 'working-class hero', the lowest born of the group later to be derisively called Cockney Poets. No doubt this was the impression the radical Leigh Hunt wished to convey of his younger friend, saying that Keats's origin was 'of the humblest description ... He never spoke of it', though the latter phrase seems motivated by a psychological reticence about Keats's early experiences rather than expression of any embarrassment over class origins. Unfortunately, most of these details are far from certain. For example, the date of the baptismal entry for Keats is 31 October, but he and his family seem to have accepted the 29th as the day of his birth. His friend Charles Brown was to mention Keats's reluctance in adulthood to celebrate his birthday so the lack of clarity persisted. Nor is it clear that his parents were less than middle class, or even whether they were living at the inn at the time. His father, Thomas Keats, at some stage became the head ostler and the 'principal servant at the Swan and Hoop stables' (CCC, 121) and his mother, Frances Jennings, was the daughter of the relatively affluent proprietor of the inn, which seems to have been a successful business. They married on 9 October 1794 at St George's, Hanover Square, apparently in some haste since there were no family witnesses and the groom was only 21, the bride 19. We know nothing for sure of Thomas's family background – he was rumoured to have lived in the west country, in particular Devonshire, and family tradition suggested origins in Land's End, Cornwall – or of his economic circumstances, although the account which seems plausible is that when they met he was working as an ostler at the inn and that marriage to the daughter of the inn's proprietor improved his station. Frances's father, John Jennings, was a man of influence and some wealth. Master of the Innholders Company and a senior churchwarden, he had purchased the leasehold of the Swan and Hoop in 1774 and its neighbouring property in 1785, rather than letting the lease run out and having to move. Keats's mother's side of the family was, then, modestly wealthy, and Charles Cowden Clarke recalling this, admittedly seventy years later, placed the family among 'the upper rank of the middle class'. We simply do not know where the young couple began their married life, and it may not have been at the Swan and Hoop at all. Where they lived before 1798 is not known but we do know at least that the family, after living since Christmas 1798 on Craven Street, off the City Road, did indeed move to the inn in December 1802, where Mr Jennings at this time appointed Keats's father as head ostler, manager of the stables. This was an event which must have been interpreted optimistically by the family as evidence they were destined for financial and emotional stability.

Oddly enough, if we assume John's birth date was 29 October, the one thing we can be certain about is the weather in London on that day. According to the *Meteorological Journal Kept at the Apartments of the Royal Society by Order of the President and Council*, the day in London was fair with a south-south-westerly wind blowing and at seven in the morning the temperature was a cool 48 degrees Fahrenheit outside (rising to 54 at two in the afternoon) and a barely comfortable 60 degrees inside (rising only to 62 in the afternoon).[3] The previous day had been cloudy and fair but with 'much wind last night' – enough to be remarked upon in the official weather report. Cloud set in for a few autumn days and there was some rain on 31 October, the date of birth entered in the baptismal entry. John was baptised at St Botolph without Bishopsgate on 18 December 1795, another 'fair' day without rain, with a maximum temperature of 61, in a period of unusually clement weather for days so close to Christmas.

The political and social climate, however, was not so settled and 1795 was a tumultuous year in which the British government spied upon and prosecuted men perceived as radicals and dissidents plotting for the kind of republic instituted in 1789 in France.[4] *The Times* which appeared on Thursday 31 October gives a snapshot of the nation's preoccupations. An editorial laments the dispersal by heavy gales of a fleet bound for the West Indies under Rear Admiral Fletcher Christian (who had in 1787 gained fame as the master's mate in the mutiny on the *Bounty*), and although the ships were reported safe they were now at risk of marauding French vessels. The revolutionary, republican government instated in Paris in 1789 after the French Revolution, had declared war on Britain in 1793, and signs of hostility and fear recur in many of the news items. For the next twenty years or so England was to be on an alert war footing, and in his adult years Keats was to lament the obtrusive presence of 'the military' and its garrisons wherever he went, from the Isle of Wight in the south to the Lake District in the north. The prosecution of several men in Dublin for high treason under the controversial law which had just been passed into legislation, criminalising 'encompassing and imagining the King's death' is reported, and they are accused of 'deliberating and contriving to overturn the King's Government ... conspiring to aid and assist the French at open and public war, in case they should land for the invasion of the country'. The increasingly paranoid Tory government under its Prime Minister Pitt had suspended in 1794 (and was to do so again in 1798), habeas corpus, a time-honoured legal action accepted as a bastion of the English law which protected the individual from prosecution without an allegation and proof. At the same time, and reported more benignly, Britain's maritime supremacy is reflected in notices of ships leaving for various fledgling colonies in the expanding British Empire. The King himself is 'with infinite satisfaction' reported to have 'never appeared in better health, nor in higher spirits, which very agreeably disappointed many of his friends, who did not expect to see him so well'. 'Never was his Majesty observed to be in more perfect recollection of himself than yesterday', writes the official reporter who is clearly intent on countering the increasingly public rumours that George III was insane. A serious problem confronting the nation was a shortage of wheat, leading to plans and pleas to cut down the consumption of bread and pastries in the nation; while the most common ailment, the subject of many advertisements for medicines such as Cundell's Balsam of Honey, Dr James's Powder, Doctor Solander's Tea and Greenough's Tinctures (all made subject to stamp duty under a new law), was infection of the lungs evidenced in coughs, asthma and consumption – ominous for the Keats family in particular. Doctor Douglas, a self-professed specialist in treating venereal disease, proclaims his skills to potential patients who can expect to be examined 'with the utmost secresy'. Meanwhile, the Theatre Royal at Drury Lane was playing *First Love* and that at Covent Garden Shakespeare's *Comedy of Errors*. At the same time, a long and lugubrious letter in the newspaper warns innocent lads coming to the alleys and winding streets of London for work, against the temptations of the play-house, 'a rendezvous of intrigue and intemperance, where he soon acquires an intimacy with the idle, the profligate, the gambler, and the prostitute, who eye him as their lawful prey', leading him 'from one crime to another'. The sad example is given of one 'young spark' who 'smoaks, swears, and carouses', leaving himself prey to more vicious habits. Such was the London and England John Keats was born into.

Peering back towards the childhood of people, especially in days before photographs and copious public records, is as uncertain as gazing into a crystal ball to divine their futures. We know that the Keats household was undeniably urban London bred, Cockney according to the official definition of that word (a person born within sound of Bow Bells, the bells of St Mary-le-Bow in Cheapside), and that John as eldest child must have been increasingly surrounded by siblings. George was born on 28 February 1797, Thomas on 28 November 1799, and Edward on 28 April 1801. George, Tom and Edward were baptised at St Leonard, Shoreditch, on 24 September 1801, but Edward died before the end of the following year and was buried in Bunhill Fields on 9 December 1802. Keats's sister Fanny, presumably named after her mother, was born on 3 June 1803 and baptised at St Botolph's. John's schooling began at a 'dame school', as was customary in the days before universal state education. Charles Cowden Clarke recalled that he physically resembled his father, 'short of stature and well-knit in person ... with brown hair and dark hazel eyes' although with his mother's 'wide' mouth, while his brothers looked more like their mother, 'tall, of good figure, with large, oval face, sombre features, and grave in behaviour' (CCC, *passim*). Others said John's hair was reddish or 'auburn'. Despite his mother's aspiration for him to go on to Harrow, in August 1803 when he was 7, John, followed by his brothers, went as a boarder to Clarke's School in Enfield, which Frances's brothers had attended in the 1780s, and to which we shall shortly return. But less than a year later another tragedy struck the family, with far-reaching consequences that were to haunt Keats, both psychologically in ways he never reveals, and more conspicuously financially, throughout his life.

At 1 a.m. on 15 April 1804, according to the coroner's inquest, a watchman who saw a riderless horse galloping past, traced back along the City Road and found outside the cemetery at Bunhill Fields the unconscious body of Thomas Keats, bleeding from a deep wound in the right side of his head. The watchman dragged the body to the nearest surgeon and they took him back to the Swan and Hoop, but on that morning the father of 8-year-old John Keats, barely 30 himself, was dead. The nocturnal ride was occasioned by a visit to see his sons at boarding school, but no explanation has been found to account for the accident to a professional ostler and expert horseman on his 'remarkably fine horse'. Thomas was buried in the Jennings family vault on 23 April. Then something astonishing happened. Keats's mother, Frances, simply disappeared from the records, perhaps with the 11-month-old baby, Fanny. A person called Elizabeth Keats, presumably Thomas's sister, seems to have stepped in to care for the children at the stables to the inn. She stepped out again when Frances returned to her four young children, and with her late husband's small inheritance took a short lease on the stables of the Swan and Hoop. Then, only a little more than two months after her husband's death and in a position of financial precariousness, she remarried a man called William Rawlings, apparently a minor bank clerk about whom nothing is known. Since we know nothing of the circumstances we should be wary of devising theories about Keats feeling deserted by his mother, but these events must have influenced his adult attitudes towards women.

Soon after this, John Jennings died, leaving confusion over his inheritance since, although clearly a generous man, he was also (perhaps as a consequence of his magnanimity) somewhat unworldly about money affairs (George said he was 'generous but gullible'). The extraordinarily tangled financial history of the Keats and Jennings families is traced with scrupulous care by Robert Gittings in his book-length study *The Keats Inheritance*, showing how family members were turned into hostile antagonists during Keats's boyhood.[5] Andrew Motion's brutally concise summary of Jennings's unintentionally divisive legacy is probably the clearest on offer:

> He had been in poor health since his retirement, receiving regular visits from the local doctor, Thomas Hammond, and on 1 February 1805 he made a hasty will. His total savings amounted to £13,000. He left half to his wife, a third to his son Midgley, and annuities of £50 to his daughter and sister. His grandchildren were bequeathed £1,000 to be divided among them equally.[6]

The money to the grandchildren could not yet be paid because they were all minors. The figure in theory left to them was to swell substantially after their grandmother's death. These were not insignificant amounts, and to give some indication, £1,000 in 1800 would have the purchasing power of about £50,000 today. To anticipate (and to cut short a very convoluted story), John Keats always seemed to act on the reasonable assumption that eventually, on turning 21, he would be financially comfortable and even quite wealthy by the standards of his society, but in the meantime the reality was very different and more tangled. In the short run, after her father's death, Keats's mother Frances initiated acrimonious lawsuits over the will, accusing of duplicity both her own mother and brother Midgley, who soon after died of tuberculosis leaving the picture even more complicated. Others challenged the will over a period of years, not surprisingly since it was vague and involved a substantial amount of money. The domestic situation grew worse. Frances's gamble did not pay off. After lengthy legal proceedings she was left even worse off, with only an annuity of £50 and a portion eventually paid from Thomas Keats's intestate legacy of £2,000. The rest was left to her children in trust until the majority of each, though they never knew of this until after John died since it was known to nobody except their mother's lawyer who died during the interim period. Most of her available money was eaten up by debts attaching to the inn. In May 1805, Frances's mother, Alice Jennings, took over guardianship of the four children. We know she disapproved not only of her daughter's first marriage to Thomas Keats but also her swift remarriage to Rawlings, but we do not know whether she actively took control or whether Frances, realising her limitations, willingly put the children into her care. Admittedly, by the end of 1805 John, Tom and George were all at boarding school and Fanny may have stayed with her mother, so Alice's tasks could not have been especially onerous. In the middle of 1806, Frances was to separate from Rawlings and for the next three years she again effectively disappeared, according to Abbey to live with a Jew called Abraham, though Abbey's dislike of her makes this story untrustworthy. Once again the children went to their 69-year-old grandmother, now living in Ponders End, Edmonton, which is near Enfield.

Whatever happened in the sequence as a whole, the distilled facts were that in a very short period, after losing a young brother, and when he had barely started school, John Keats had lost his father and in the following two months acquired a stepfather, twice been separated from his mother, and was embroiled in extreme family tensions that ended up with he and his brothers and sister living with their grandmother. Child psychologists may offer clues as to the emotional consequences, but the fact is that we have no evidence recorded by Keats himself concerning his mother, father or grandparents. Whether he avoided or repressed the subject, or whether he controlled and overcame his feelings which must have included extreme grief, anger and, as the eldest child, a sense of vicarious responsibility, we can never know. All his later 'philosophising' is motivated by a desire to understand how loss and adversity can be part of a maturing process lying at the heart of individuation and unique creativity. He may have rapidly acquired an advanced sense of responsibility towards his younger siblings. Robert Gittings suggests the whole experience helps to explain Keats's later expression of mistrusting people's reliability, as he wrote 'I scarcely remember counting upon any Happiness ... I have suspected every Body' (*JKL*, 1, 186 and 292). *Hamlet* was to become one of his favourite plays of Shakespeare, and the similarities in personal circumstances cannot have escaped his recognition, not only because Rawlings so quickly supplanted his father in his mother's affection but also since that man was immediately given his father's job as manager of the stables, for which he was singularly unqualified and incompetent and which he eventually abandoned. The comparison between heroic father and despised surrogate must have seemed to the bewildered stepson like Hamlet's comparison, 'Hyperion to a satyr'.

It is often said that being sent to boarding school can be psychologically dislocating, but in Keats's case it surely sheltered him from the domestic upheavals after his father's death. He was with his brothers there and while alive his father was assiduous in visiting them regularly. Whether from innate aptitude or a desire to avoid problems, he was an extremely conscientious student, 'a most orderly scholar' according to Charles Cowden Clarke, and one who read so voraciously that he exhausted the school library. He started schoolwork before classes and 'occupied the hours during meals in reading. Thus his *whole* time was engrossed', even in recreation hours (CCC, 123). As a consequence, Keats won prizes for his work, receiving books which, although factual in basis – for example, John Bonnycastle's *Introduction to Astronomy* and books of voyages and travels – opened up his already impressionable intellectual horizons and imagination. He read many books on history and travel, including histories of France, Scotland and America by William Robertson, himself a political liberal and progressive thinker whose books Keats came back to later in his life. Gilbert Burnett's *History of his Own Time* was based on an insistence on religious tolerance and praised the Protestant heroes Milton and Algernon Sidney as great English republicans. Although Keats may not have gone far past Virgil's *Aeneid* in Latin, classical literature was favoured in his reading by Andrew Tooke's *Pantheon* and by Lemprière's *A Classical Dictionary*, which Keats virtually learned by heart. Clarke mentions Maria Edgeworth's novels but otherwise there was little weighting towards fiction or poetry in Keats's reading, or indeed imaginative literature in general. This interest he developed and shared with Clarke after his school days. But perhaps most significantly, the Clarke family were avid readers of the journal edited by Leigh Hunt, *The Examiner*, which they loaned to Keats, and through this he became aware not only of radical ideas which, in Clarke's opinion, 'no doubt laid the foundation of his love of civil and religious liberty', but also must have alerted him to the revolution in poetry heralded first by the controversies over Chatterton and the *Lyrical Ballads* by Wordsworth and Coleridge, first printed in 1798. He was to read it throughout his life.

One of the early and unfortunate effects of the traumatic losses sustained in his family may have been the exacerbation of a tendency towards childhood violence, which runs through many of the memorial anecdotes of the young Keats, and even if individually unreliable they are recurrent. One which seems to have been indirectly reported from his brother Tom as an adult suggests that John was 'violent and ungovernable' as a child while another, reported much later by Haydon but perhaps on Keats's information, was that he once held his mother prisoner in the house 'with a naked sword'. If this actually happened, we do not know whether it was before or after his father died, and if it was his own recollection then it must be admitted that a child's viewpoint may have exaggerated an innocent prank into an unreliable memory. Other such stories persist and in particular are confirmed by his teacher and later friend Charles Cowden Clarke who said the boy reminded him of the actor Edmund Kean whom Keats later admired. Some stories suggest that he fought either against bullies or to protect those weaker than himself, and even when he was much older he admires the 'energy' involved in fighting. Keats was interested in boxing, as Cowden Clarke reports: 'Keats also attended a prize fight between the two most skilful "light weights" of the day, Randal and Turner; and in describing the rapidity of the blows of the one, while the other was falling, he tapped his fingers on the window-pane' (CCC, 145). Prizefighting in its heyday at just this time, between 1800 and 1824, commanded considerable interest as 'the English sport', appealing to many contemporary writers such as Hazlitt, whose essay 'The Fight' appeared in 1822, Reynolds, Byron, Lamb, Cobbett and John Clare. Along with Hazlitt, Tom Moore and Reynolds, Keats was as an adult to dine with Pierce Egan, 'author of the four volume definitive edition of *Boxiana* the history of Regency prizefighting'.[7] Pugilism in the form of boxing and wrestling did not arouse the same liberal squeamishness as it does today, and it even carried an association of proud nationalism.

As a boy Keats was certainly far from effete or timid. We cannot entirely discount the significance of the fact that he must have been short as a child, as he certainly was in adulthood, and may have been a target for bullying or provoked to prove himself in a world of boys growing up at that time. But Cowden Clarke, who knew him better than most, although admitting that Keats's 'passion at times was almost ungovernable' also adds a comic image of 'wisp-of-straw conflagration[s]', given his small stature and affectionate nature. Clarke reports his 'terrier courage; but his high-mindedness, his utter unconsciousness of a mean motive'. Even the headmaster noticed Keats's sudden and unexpected 'moods'. Obviously we should remain nonjudgmental about his reputation as a fighter, and besides, if we were to replace the word 'violent' with 'spirited', 'rebellious' or 'self-willed', then we can infer a family likeness in temperament to what we hear of his mother's. While his father was described as simply 'a man of good sense and very much liked', John's mother acquired a reputation for 'saturnine' appearance, lively independence and vivacity, and she does not seem to have been universally liked though she was clearly admired as a woman aware of her female charms. Admittedly the more negative claims about her are mainly retailed by witnesses biased against her, but they are perhaps not entirely inconsistent with her marital record. Even if the stories are calumnious and wrong in detail, the impression remains of an undeniably forceful character who bequeathed this trait to her eldest son and to a lesser extent Tom, but not, it seems, to George who was described as 'a child of rather pacific nature', nor to Fanny who was very passive. His mother's personality must also have been an influence in Keats's later ambiguous feelings for and relationships with women.

At least in 1809 there seems to have been some kind of reconciliation, if one were needed after her abrupt disappearances, when she returned to her mother's home, though now crippled with rheumatism and very ill. In his school vacations and after he left school John cooked and cared for his mother through her terminal illness in the same year. To add to the ill-starred family's woes, Frances died of tuberculosis in March 1810, when Keats was 14. He was still at boarding school, where he gave way to a helpless grief which was reported as 'impassioned and prolonged', to the extent that during lessons he was given permission to hide 'in a nook under the master's desk' – as a modern biographer, himself a poet, has remarked, 'as if to return to the womb source of life in order to start over'.[8] After the death, all four children, who at least had created a remarkably strong and enduring bonding with each other in response to their tribulations, were then left by their grandmother in the care of two guardians, John Sandell and Richard Abbey, a tea merchant. After Sandell's death in 1816, Abbey was sole guardian and unfortunately, as we shall see, had complete control of the substantial amount of money inherited by the children. He will reappear later in this book since he has sometimes been accused of withholding the Keats children's inheritance, but for the time being it should be said that he seems to have been a fit person to be chosen by Mrs Jennings to act as guardian. He was a respectable businessman with a reputation for propriety and financial probity.

After reporting all these tempests in Keats's family life, it seems almost an anticlimax to return to his schooling, but here his experiences were more tranquil and lucky, and they must have provided some stability to his life at a time when everything else was shifting. Clarke's School in Enfield was named after its co-founder and headmaster, John Clarke, who had set up the school in 1786 with Baptist minister John Ryland, 'an ardent friend of liberty' and a staunch supporter of the Protestant cause in the 'Glorious Revolution' of 1688, and who was to become Clarke's father-in-law. The site is now Enfield Station, and in fact it was the arrival of the railway line in 1849 that turned Enfield from a quiet village which in Charles Lamb's words was 'cut off by country lanes', into a main-line suburb of London. Charles Cowden Clarke, son of the headmaster and a teacher in the school, recalls the building as dating from the late seventeenth or early eighteenth century:

> It was of the better character of the domestic architecture of that period, the whole front being of the purest red brick, wrought by means of moulds into rich designs of flowers and pomegranates, with heads of cherubim over niches in the building. (CCC, 120)

A drawing made in about 1840 exists (Motion, plate 7). The choice of school was a stroke of great luck in Keats's otherwise fraught childhood, whereas at Harrow he would certainly have suffered all the difficulties inherent in a large and expensive boys' school dominated socially by the sons of aristocrats, notorious for bullying, draconian punishment, regimentation, and educationally and politically conservative. Lord Byron was a pupil there (and was expelled for general troublemaking and later readmitted) and between him and Keats there later developed a mutual dislike expressed in terms of class antagonism between the effortless aristocrat who attended one of England's 'great public schools' and the petty bourgeois Cockney whose school 'catered for the sons of the trading and business classes' (Gittings, 51). At Clarke's School Keats was more fortunate in almost every way than he would otherwise have been. With only seventy-odd students it was possible for Clarke to fulfil the promise he offered of getting to know the boys personally and providing something of a family atmosphere. Educationally, whereas Harrow was built around the needs of the small minority who would go on to read Classics at Oxford and Cambridge, Clarke's was progressive. It was about as close to a modern 'alternative school' as one could find in the early nineteenth century, set up by religious Nonconformists on grounds of tolerance, a belief in individual self-development, without corporal punishment, and based on liberal principles. It was the kind of school set up in the wake of Locke's and Rousseau's pioneering educational principles which saw children as indviduals in their own person rather than as mere 'pre-adults', who had rights and were born innocent rather than burdened with original sin. Of particular value to the future poet was the headmaster's belief in nature as an educative force and example, and here he was supported by the local environment. Enfield was semi-rural, well away from the City Road in Moorgate, full of country lanes, woods and farms, and bordered by New River in which the schoolboys swam. The school itself was a 'hallowed old arbour' to Keats, containing gardens which the pupils were encouraged to tend. There was a large pond and 'a magnificent old morello cherry tree' where nightingales were to be heard at night. Both Ryland (who died in 1792, before Keats arrived) and Clarke were religious Nonconformists and politically progressive, as was at least one of the assistant masters, George Dyer, the well-known poet especially committed to issues like the rights of slaves and the poor. Famous (or infamous, in government eyes) radicals visited Ryland and Clarke – Joseph Priestley, John Cartwright, and other dissenters and liberals. Nicholas Roe has traced the culture of the Enfield school at the time, and has found that it was not just 'liberal' but radical and republican, and he concludes that even in his schooldays Keats was made aware of the politically progressive thought of his age.[9] The future guardian of the Keats children, the conservative Richard Abbey, told Keats that 'if he had fifty children he would not send one of them to that school' (CCC, 124), but for Keats it must have been a protective and secure place, and even a mental blueprint for the secluded, natural bowers that frequently appear in his poetry.

Keats was doubly fortunate in finding at Enfield school a kindred spirit in his tutor, Charles Cowden Clarke, who was the headmaster's son and seven years older than his student. His anonymous obituarist was to describe his 'cheerful face, broadly and brightly beaming with the best of good humour'. There was clearly a genuine and mutual affection between the two, despite the difference in age. Keats was later to write a verse letter to Clarke thanking him for his kindness and for supplying 'my enjoyments in my youthful years', and addressing him familiarly as 'My daintie Davie', 'C.C.C.' and 'My dear Charles' whereas he wrote to his other male friends by their surnames (*JKL*, 1, 71–2). Clarke befriended another contemporary student, Edward Holmes, who went on to become Mozart's biographer, while Keats himself chose as a friend William Haslam, a boy in his own year who was to become a staunch, lifelong companion. Clarke shared his father's political radicalism, and he was also a gifted pianist and singer, and would walk ten miles into central London to attend theatres. We should be immensely grateful to 'C.C.C.' since it was he who nurtured the literary interests of the future poet. Under Clarke's influence, the stories of Keats's fighting seemed to abate, to be replaced by reports of prodigious hard work and voluminous reading. Keats's determination to win prizes was rewarded when he won an award for French and Latin in 1809, and before he left he also won a prize for translating an awesomely large chunk of Virgil's *Aeneid*. Although they were destined to grow apart, Clarke retained a lifelong admiration for Keats and supplied to his later biographer, Richard Monckton Milnes (later Lord Houghton), generous recollections of Keats at school. Clarke introduced Keats to Chapman's translation of Homer, which led in 1816 to the sonnet, 'On first looking into Chapman's Homer', to Shakespeare (on whose work Clarke published books later in his life, *Shakespeare-Characters: Chiefly those Subordinate* [1863] and *The Shakespeare-Key* [1879]), Spenser and many other poets and books from his father's well-stocked library. In the 'Verse Letter', Keats defers to Clarke's classical learning, while thanking him for introducing him to English poets.

Clarke also created the first auspicious meeting between Keats and Leigh Hunt in October 1816, a 'red letter day' for Keats, Clarke reported, since he was the notoriously republican and pacifist poet and editor of the radical journal, *The Examiner*. Hunt and the young man he dubbed 'Junkets' found immediate affinity which was to prove enduring though the relationship was in some ways close to that of father and son with its ups and downs. Some biographers have noticed a tendency for Keats to bond with older men such as Hunt, Haydon and Hazlitt, perhaps as a need acquired after the early loss of his own father, though these men were just as attracted to Keats. Hunt's own 'Commonplace Book' collected mainly in the years 1810 to 1814 show that Clarke's values, which he must have freely shared with Keats at this time, were consistently libertarian, dwelling on such themes as 'the constitutional liberties of England ... religious toleration, the tyranny of the Stuarts, admiration for seventeenth-century radical heroes ... an opposition to war and violence, and belief in liberty'.[10] Such themes were to recur in Keats's letters throughout his life. Ironically, Clarke's only book to have a readership continuing into the twentieth century, apart from the sections on Keats in his *Recollections of Writers* (1878), was only ghost written by him. He 'collected and edited' *The Young Cricketer's Tutor* (1833) by the amiable chronicler John Nyren, a colourful reminiscence of players in the Old Hambledon Club which was the cradle of cricketing history (though the game itself went back to the fifteenth century).[11] Nyren was another member of the group that formed around Leigh Hunt, who reviewed the book, and he attended the musical evenings where Hunt and Vincent Novello presided, so Keats probably met him.[12] We know Keats played cricket as late as March 1819 in Hampstead, since he records suffering a black eye which required a leech on his eyelid: 'the ball hit me dir{ectl}y on the sight – 't was a white ball – I am glad it was not a clout' (*JKL*, 2, 78). Although he says it was his first game, it seems likely he played at school, given Cowden Clarke's passion for the game, and he may have meant it was the first occasion since school days. We can, incidentally, owe to cricket the composition of 'Ode on Indolence', since it was during his convalescence from the black eye that he wrote it.

It was Leigh Hunt who, after Keats's death, virtually constructed a familiar but inaccurate mythology of Keats as coming from impoverished stock but there is less reason to doubt his vivid pen-picture of Keats in his twenties, though by that stage very ill:

> He was under the middle height; and his lower limbs were small in comparison with the upper, but neat and well-turned. His shoulders were very broad for his size: he had a face, in which energy and sensibility were remarkably mixed up, and eager power checked and made patient by ill-health. Every feature was at once strongly cut, and delicately alive. If there was any faulty expression, it was in the mouth, which was not without something of a character of pugnacity. The face was rather long than otherwise; the upper lip projected a little over the under; the chin was bold, the cheeks sunken; the eyes mellow and glowing; large, dark

and sensitive. At the recital of a noble action, or a beautiful thought, they would suffuse with tears, and his mouth trembled. In this, there was ill-health as well as imagination, for he did not like these betrayals of emotion; and he had great personal as well as moral courage. His hair, of a brown colour, was fine, and hung in natural ringlets. The head was a puzzle for the phrenologists, being remarkably small in the skull; a singularity which he had in common with Lord Byron and Mr Shelley, none of whose hats I could get on.[13]

Keats would have appreciated Hunt's tactfully worded 'under the middle height'. In fact he was always self-conscious about being 5 foot 2 inches or less, and as he himself quipped, with a clear tinge of regret, 'I do think better of Womankind than to suppose they care whether Mister John Keats five feet hight [sic] likes them or not' (*JKL*, 1, 342). His friend Charles Brown was to describe him as 'small in stature, well proportioned, compact in form, and, though thin, rather muscular; – one of the many who prove that manliness is distinct from height and bulk'. The word he used to describe Keats's personality was 'ingenuous', and Keats was to return the compliment to Brown.

Although Keats may not have talked or written of his childhood and schooling, he carried with him the consciousness of being a child. When in 1818 he embarked on a walking tour with his friend Brown, he wrote a comic poem with signs of infectious haste:

> There was a naughty boy
> A naughty boy was he
> He would not stop at home
> He could not quiet be –
> He took
> In his knapsack
> A book
> Full of vowels
> And a shirt
> With some towels –
> …

And so the jaunty poem goes on in its whimsical, rhyming way: 'nothing would he do / But scribble poetry'. There are small autobiographical touches. The boy lives with his 'granny-good' and 'He kept little fishes / In washing tubs three' mentioning specific species. Keats was to recall, in a letter to his sister in 1819, a childhood fondness for 'Goldfinches, Tomtits, Minnows, Mice, Ticklebacks, Dace, Cock salmons, and all the whole tribe of the Bushes and the Brooks', and he even confesses an adult 'partiality for a handsome Globe of goldfish – well ventilated they would preserve all their beautiful silver and Crimson – Then I would put it before a handsome painted window and shade it all round with myrtles and Japonicas' (*JKL*, 2, 46). The poem, known as 'A Song about Myself', was written to amuse Fanny (*JKL*, 1, 312), to whom he always maintained a protective, playful and sometimes childlike tone, and his words to her even as late as 1819 seem to hold a delighted nostalgia for simple delights:

> I should like now to promenade round you[r] Gardens–apple tasting–pear-tasting–plum<b>-judging—apricot nibbling—peach sc[r]unching—Nectarine-sucking and Melon carving—I have also a great feeling for antiquated cherries full of sugar cracks—and a white currant tree kept for company—I admire lolling on a lawn by a water-lillied pond to eat white currants and see gold fish: and go to the Fair in the Evening if I'm good ... (*JKL*, 2, 149)

His younger sister repeatedly stimulated in Keats memories of some happier times in a shared childhood, which must in reality at best have been an oscillation between often deeply troubled and occasionally tranquil times.

2
'Aesculapius'

Seven years is a long time in a young man's life, and those from the ages of 14 to 21 are arguably the most impressionable of all, especially to somebody just orphaned. During this period of his youth (August 1810 to March 1817) Keats was qualifying himself to be a doctor. Since these are in some ways his 'lost years', seen by only a few critics as significant to his later career as poet but by most as a 'false start', I make no apology that this chapter is longer than some others in the book.

Whether by coincidence or not, it appears that his initial decision to enter a profession dedicated to the alleviation of physical pain came almost immediately after the death of his mother, whom he had nursed through 'consumption' (tuberculosis), with a touching solicitude reported by Haydon, 'allowing nobody but himself to administer Hammond's medicines'. 'He cooked for her and sat up long hours at night reading to her',[1] and it is legendary that he guarded her door so nobody could enter. This was over the Christmas of 1809 and into 1810, when he was 14 years old. There is another, less romantic but perhaps more plausible, explanation for his first choice of career. If Robert Gittings is right in his hypotheses about Keats's ancestors, then there was a strong and clear medical tradition in his family. A Dr William Keate(s) (born c. 1708–9) was an apothecary in Wells in Somerset in 1733 and later Mayor of Wells; Thomas Keate was house surgeon at St George's Hospital in 1767, later Surgeon to George, Prince of Wales, afterwards George IV, Surgeon General to the Army, and three times Master of the Corporation of Surgeons; his son, Robert Keate (1777–1857) was also a distinguished and successful surgeon attached to the army.[2] As Gittings suggests, if these were relatives then it would help to explain John Keats's rapid advancement from pupil to dresser under Sir Astley Cooper when he took his final year's training at Guy's Hospital in London. Nicholas Roe points to a personal and political intermediary between Keats and Cooper, Joseph Henry Green,[3] suggesting also that medicine was virtually the only profession not subject to the Test Acts and therefore open to religious dissenters and political reformers.[4] There was also a nexus between the various lecturers at Guy's and some of the most radical activists in England like John Thelwall, Horne Tooke and others. Astley Cooper in the medical 'Note Book' from which Keats studied, refers to one of his acquaintances, 'The Patriot K', who was the Polish republican Kosciusko to whom Keats in December 1816 addressed a sonnet which was printed in *The Examiner* on 14 February 1817.

In the summer of 1811,[5] Keats was apprenticed to the very apothecary who had tended his mother, Thomas Hammond, moving in to a room above the surgery at 7 Church Street, Edmonton, which was a few miles from the Swan and Hoop, and close to the Enfield school where his father had used to ride diligently to see his sons. Some time around 1813 Keats quarrelled with Hammond, whose status over his apprentices was *in loco parentis*, and moved out (whatever the cause it made him clench his fists to recall in later years [*JKL*, 2, 208]), perhaps to live with his brothers in St Pancras. George had been removed from school early to work in Abbey's counting-house as a clerk, where he would shortly be joined by Tom. Despite his differences with Hammond, John continued his medical apprenticeship, and on 1 October 1815 he began as a student at Guy's Hospital in London, funded posthumously by the philanthropist Thomas Guy and built alongside St Thomas's Hospital, with which Guy's is now merged. Keats shared lodgings, found for him by Astley Cooper personally, with other medical students, beside the hospitals at 28 St Thomas Street in Southwark. In those days doctors, although their profession was respectable, did not have particularly high status unless they had graduated from one of the 'great' universities in Britain, Oxford, Cambridge and Edinburgh, while surgery in particular had been traditionally carried out by barbers. Guy's was set up as a teaching hospital with a social mission to treat the poor, and it was always desperately full of patients. Keats's decision was at best indulged rather than approved by his guardian Richard Abbey who encouraged him to follow his own footsteps and become a tea merchant, instead of spending much of his inheritance on a medical training. A tea merchant, by contrast, was a steady and respectable job. Keats's schoolboy friend, Cowden Clarke, described the period of apprenticeship as 'the most placid period of his painful life'.[6] He remained in it for the obligatory five years, and what he learned is summed up by Hermione de Almeida:

> Keats would already have had the requisite training in surgery, diagnosis, and prescription deemed necessary for a provincial doctor, and his familiarity with the full complement of common diseases, injuries, and the complications of childbirth would have far exceeded the range of the specialised London physicians or surgeons.[7]

Keats did not waver in his pursuit of the qualification which, under the new Apothecaries Act of 1815, would enable him to become what we would today call a general practitioner, or if he wished to continue his study (as his teachers clearly encouraged), a full surgeon at a teaching hospital. The regulations were stringent, requiring a knowledge of Latin, five years' apprenticeship to an apothecary, attending lectures at a teaching hospital, and six months' experience in hospital work, all of which Keats fulfilled.

On 1 October 1815 Keats undertook the last stage of a year's 'internship' at Guy's Hospital. He enrolled for a full year which would have led to membership of the Royal College of Surgeons, though he chose not to stay for the final requirements. Since the expense charged against his inheritance was very large – about £1,500 – all the signs were that he was fully sincere about his future vocation and that his mind changed only in the very final stages. He attended lectures by, amongst others, the most famous surgeon-teacher in all Europe, Sir Astley Cooper. That he registered (and stayed) for a full year is significant, since it indicates that his initial intention was to aim eventually for the full status of surgeon. He could have opted for a six-month qualification as 'licentiate of the Society of Apothecaries', and in fact this is the qualification he finally emerged with, since he did not seek the usual certificate of proficiency for which his full experience qualified him.[8] But he did continue to work at Guy's after this period, holding open his options. That Guy's Hospital believed in his talents is evidenced by the fact that only twenty-eight days after his enrolment he was appointed a dresser to one of the surgeons, the cavalier Billy Lucas. According to Donald Goellnicht, he was 'the first member of his class to be so honoured'.[9] One unusual fact is that Keats was appointed as a dresser on 29 October 1815, just one month after entering Guy's, although he did not take up the position until 3 March 1816. Another is that he maintained the position not for the minimum six months but the maximum of one year, continuing until March 1817, even after he had gained his licentiate. For this privilege he would have paid 50 pounds to the surgeon (20 or 30 pounds more than the fee paid by a Walking pupil, House pupil or House surgeon). This meant he acted as a kind of resident *locum* at the major hospital, authorised to exercise independent judgment, prescribe medicines, change bandages, dress wounds and perform minor operations – although in a time before anaesthetics apart from opium and alcohol (chloroform was used instead of the dangerous ether first in 1847 to alleviate pain in childbirth by James Young Simpson) very few operations, even routine tooth-pulling, let alone amputations of limbs, would have been 'minor' by our standards. He would have kept records on patients, made preliminary diagnoses, accompanied surgeons on their daily rounds of patients, and commented on their condition. After his statutory six months' term, Keats was offered further employment for a full year until March 1817 as a 'dresser' after his graduation on 25 July 1816.[10] On this date Keats passed his examinations at Apothecaries' Hall for the Licentiate of the Society of Apothecaries, thus becoming fully qualified as apothecary, physician and surgeon, his name listed in December in the *London Medical Repository*. He remained enrolled for the next stage of his medical education until the spring of 1817. All the hard evidence indicates that Keats was seen by his teachers as an assiduous, dedicated and highly promising student of medicine. But in 1815 and onward he was writing poetry, and some realisation between his 'graduation' in mid-1816 and the spring of 1817 made him decide not to continue with medicine but instead to become a professional poet.

Despite later slighting dismissals of Keats's training by contemporary reviewers and by Byron, an 'apothecary' at that time was not just what we would call a chemist or pharmacist but a person fulfilling most of the tasks nowadays performed by a general practitioner, and besides, Keats was quali-fied in far more than the job of an apothecary. The tripartite qualification reflected a legal consolidation of what, up to the nineteenth century, had been three quite distinct professions, each with its own governing body and legal rights. The increasing legislation, and the later establishment of the Red Cross, came as public opinion hardened against appalling medical conditions of combatants in the Napoleonic War which ended in 1815. The Apothecaries' Act was passed in England on 11 July 1815, the year Keats entered Guy's, giving full accreditation to the licence issued by the Society of Apothecaries, entitling one who had served five years' apprentice-ship and six months at a hospital to practise one or more of the branches of medicine, as physician, surgeon or apothecary. (Ironically, the various func-tions have again diverged, this time creating a separation between general practitioner, dentist and a plethora of 'specialists'.) The tightened regula-tions were forced on the Royal College of Surgeons by public concern over medical practice in the military during the long wars with France which ended in 1815. It has been argued that by 1820 they had rapidly effected a transition to the modern assumptions about the localised 'authority' and prestige of the medical profession generally, and the establishment of a coherent and tight-knit medical community in which public hospitals ruled the hierarchy.[11]

The Hospital Pupil's Guide

There are in existence just three precious and yellowing copies of a *Guide* for students entering Guy's Hospital, written by somebody (or some bodies) under the pseudonym 'Aesculapius'.[12] The Preface to all three is dated 'this 20th day of Aug. 1816', when Keats was still in residence at Guy's. Since it includes timetables for students at Guy's and St Thomas's Hospitals, show-ing exactly when and where each lecture and demonstration took place each week during the academic term, we can presume that it had official status, and certainly was aimed at students. It is impossible finally to say whether, or in what form, Keats knew of it, but clearly the likelihood is high. It gives no more and no less than an unrivalled glimpse of the kind of life, ethos and ideas which Keats would certainly have encountered at Guy's. Its general and particular content complements Keats's later thinking in fascinating ways that have never been acknowledged. The full title of the guidebook by 'Aesculapius' in its 1816 edition is *Oracular Communications, addressed to Students of the Medical Profession*, that of the 1818 edition is *The Hospital Pupil's Guide, Being Oracular Communications, addressed to Students of the Medical Profession*. It is a 'prolegomena' to medical studies, offering inspiration, advice and some instruction, such as footnoted 'further reading' in each branch of medical studies, an invaluable guide to what Keats would most likely have read. There were contemporary precedents such as the anonymous *The Hospital pupil's guide through London* (1800), James Lucas's *A candid enquiry into the education, qualifications, and office, of a surgeon-apothecary* (Bath, 1800, second edition 1805), James Parkinson's *The hospital pupil: or, an essay intended to facilitate the study of medicine and surgery* (1800), the anonymous *An essay, addressed to medical students, on the importance ... of the profession* (1808), William Chamberlaine's *Tirocinium medicum: of a dissertation on the duties of youth apprenticed to the medical profession* (1812), and Robert Watt's *Catalogue of medical books, for the use of students ... with an address to medical students, on the best method of prosecuting their studies* (Glasgow, 1812). The form of the students' Guide to a medical career was almost a genre in its own right.

The work of 'Aesculapius', although slightingly reviewed at the time as a 'whimsical little performance ... not destitute of merit and utility',[13] tells us a huge amount about the prevailing paradigms of the medical profession, and about the ideas Keats would have encountered at Guy's, as well as specific evidence of what he studied. Almost certainly each section is written by the particular teachers in a field, but there is equally clearly a presiding spirit who, judging from occasional political statements, I take to be Sir Astley Cooper himself. At the heart of the major writer's message is a value system expressing liberal, even literary, rationalism and humanism which condemns superstition and high-handed authority:

> The science of Medicine has ceased to be an engine of priestcraft and slavery, and its professors are now ranked with the other *literati* of the age in which they live. Their minds are enlarged with a variety of useful knowledge. (p. 10)

The constant refrains of 'Aesculapius' are values that he wishes to instil in medical students and they are repeated watchwords in Keats's later letters: 'sensibility' or sympathy (with all its Romantic trappings of imaginative projection into states of suffering), complete open-mindedness ('negative capability') and 'useful knowledge' ('to do the world some good') rather than learning for its own sake or even for the narrow purpose of healing the sick. The emphasis on literature is surely significant for Keats. 'Aesculapius' insists that 'It is indeed true that the more extensive the *literary* acquirements of the student, the greater will be his professional advantages' (p. 20).

The last section of the book is an exhortation to read voluminously: 'books to the medical man are as necessary as his daily food, and ought to be a source of heavy expenditure. Reading can alone make the perfect man' (pp. 92–3).

> Become a literary character, a *Gourmand* if you will, but read authors for yourselves, and *digest them*. Nor let your reading be confined to a few favorites, but take an enlarged view; peruse the enemies, as well as the friends, of your darling system, and be open to conviction ... but I forbear [to argue further], believing that enough has been advanced, to induce you to prefer the pleasures of intellect to the gratification of the passions; and to lead you to substitute *literary pursuits* for the sports of the field, the pleasures of social conviviality, or the mystic delights of whist. (p. 94)

The writer quotes Wordsworth, Shakespeare and other poets, and his own prose aspires at times to poetic statements that mark him as a 'literary character'. I am not sure that first-year medical students are addressed in quite this way today.

The book is aimed at students before they came to London and covers priorities like finding accommodation. The writer is concerned that each student will avoid the 'loneliness of solitude' (p. 28), and advocates boarding 'in some respectable family'. In fact, Keats took a room sharing with two or three other students lodging close to the hospitals. This may not entirely have appealed to the former Enfield student who liked to read through meal-times, since reports suggest that medical students were unruly, swearing and noisy – like the patients and nurses[14] – and at least one of his flat-mates, Henry Stephens, seems to have harboured animosity since he was to fail the examinations (as did Keats's other, equally abrasive flatmate, George Mackereth) while Keats passed. Stephens was contemptuous of Keats's poetic dreaming as well as his allegedly pretentious mode of dressing 'à la Byron', open-necked and mustachio'd', both later denied by his much closer friend, Charles Brown. The first poem of Keats to be published in *The Examiner* even before he had met the editor Hunt was written here, significantly beginning ' O Solitude!', a title which may have been more a wish than a reality. Characteristic of his later poems, it moves from the real to the imagined:

> O Solitude! if I must with thee dwell,
> Let it not be among the jumbled heap
> Of murky buildings; climb with me the steep –
> Nature's observatory – whence the dell,
> Its flowery slopes, its river's crystal swell,
> May seem a span; ...

Much later in Keats's life Charles Brown was to comment on the poet's apparently lifelong 'incapability of living in solitude', but this poem shows him yearning for access to rural nature. The sonnet does not embrace the state but celebrates instead the liberating imagination able to project into nature, and also sociability, 'When to thy haunts *two* kindred spirits flee'. 'Aesculapius' sympathetically understands that 'Medical students are frequently not overflowing with cash', implying a mix of class backgrounds rather than the sons of homogeneously wealthy families, but also those from the petty bourgeoisie like Keats. 'Aesculapius' is also concerned to advise the student against distracting pursuits:

> The candidate for medical honours comes to London *to study* ... [He must relinquish] 'the amusements of the theatre' – leading into temptation and *billiards*: 'a fashionable pursuit with medical students'. This 'seductive game' leads into bad company and gaming.

Keats, no doubt alongside many of his student contemporaries, ignored this sage but unrealistic advice. He certainly attended the theatre, and he indicates that he was no stranger to a billiard table (*JKL*, 1, 147).

By description, 'Aesculapius' confirms the seriousness of Keats's choice to undertake a full year's training at Guy's rather than opting for the briefer, six-month qualification.

> There are two classes of students at the Hospitals, Dressers and Pupils. The advantages of the former are indeed very superior to those of the latter; inasmuch as they practise, while the others only contemplate: they obtain minute and sterling information, while the pupils gain only *general knowledge* ... Hence a dressership is desirable. (p. 29)

By choosing at the outset of his studies at Guy's the road of the dresser, Keats signalled that he had high ambitions in medicine, and therefore it is likely he made his decision to quit the profession because of his experiences on the hospital ward in his second six months. Since we know he was to become fastidious about surgery, it may have been a reading of 'Aesculapius's' stern words, encountered while he was a dresser in the first half of 1816, that eroded his confidence and finally convinced him that he should go no further with medicine:

> Allow me here, Gentlemen, to add one caution on the exercise of feeling and humanity in your profession. I have known surgeons who from excess of feeling could not operate; but this is not simple genuine sensibility. It is a spurious principle, occurring in a weak and sickly mind. Real feeling for the suffering of others, prompts a wish to relieve those sufferings as naturally as the needle points to the pole, and as necessarily

as the sun rises and sets, or the world revolves upon its axis; as exercise and fatigue, inanition and hunger, follow each other as cause and effect. They are entirely inseparable. Thus genuine sensibility, while it enters into the sufferings of others, is yet a principled feeling, and its first emotion is to relieve that suffering. In his prosecution of the line of conduct dictated by his judgment, the surgeon is deaf to the pains of his patient; he is inattentive to their expression, and forgets *his present anguish* in the pursuit of *his lasting good*. Real sensibility knows how to control the feelings, and consists in a principled self-denial of present ease, in exchange for the disinterested pursuit of the patient's welfare. Its possessor is not haunted, agitated, and disturbed during the performance of an operation by mental emotions: these are procrastinated, till he can 'feel to the rising bosom's inmost core,' the sufferings of *his friend* without injury to his patient. A man who has not obtained this self-control, is unfit for the practice of his profession, since in passing through life, he will frequently be placed in circumstances of danger, where this inattention to present emotions will be necessary, and where the continuance or preservation of life will depend on it.

There is, however, an incalculable difference between this condensed sensibility, and a *want of feeling* or indifference to suffering. There is an obvious distinction between subdued emotion, and an incapacity to feel.

...

Yet let it be remembered that humanity is a virtue; and he is guilty of an offence against this principle, who, by want of delicacy, inflicts more pain than is indispensable. This will go a great way in favour of a young practitioner, if in circumstances of distress, he sympathises with his patient, and inflicts as little pain as possible; – if when obliged to occasion suffering, he evinces that humanity and kindness which prove that he has a delicate mind, and a heart capable of the finer sensibilities of our nature. (pp. 88–90)

In this and other reported advice to students, we can detect the influence of the 'man of feeling' so popular in late eighteenth-century novels.[15] I have quoted this section at length because it seems profoundly important to the subject of Keats's decision to give up medicine in favour of poetry. If (as I believe) he read 'Aesculapius', he may have found influential on his own thinking the vocabulary of a 'disinterestedness' which is not 'indifference', 'sympathy' with suffering, and a 'condensed sensibility' that does not denote 'want of feeling'. But he may well have found himself in practice wanting, when judged against such a relentless standard.

It has always been acknowledged that one of the central facets of Keats's thought is what he himself described as the 'Negative capability' of being receptive, inquisitive ('speculation') and tolerant of ambivalences, as opposed to the 'egotistical sublime' of the closed and judgmental mind (*JKL*, esp. 1, 387). Although the literary prototypes he had in mind are Shakespeare and Milton/Wordsworth respectively, yet he would have found the basic principle of tolerating ambiguity and pluralism in 'Aesculapius'. Just as he was lucky in the liberal schooling he received at Clarke's School, so he was at least in some ways fortunate at Guy's, for the benign guide to the medical profession suggests, in fact, that to be unbiased is something of a bias:

> Above all things, let the student avoid becoming the slave of a system ... [avoid] bigotted and sectarian principles ... All knowledge will be of use to him. (pp. 22–3)

The key to avoiding 'bigotted' attitudes is human fellow-feeling and 'sympathy':

> What then is the great secret of this moral influence upon mankind? it is sympathy with their feelings and their sufferings, their joys and sorrows. Sympathy with suffering is a most powerful motive to action; and an eloquent expression of our real concern for the welfare of its subjects. It is likewise a powerful appeal to the affection of those who are its objects; and if there be any avenue to the heart of such, sympathy will reach it. This too is an active principle; for although there be a sensibility which weeps equally for fictitious woe, while it passes in silence the cottage of sorrow, and the bed of anguish, yet genuine sympathy ever seeks the relief of others' care. Humanity weeps, and Religion shudders at the sorrows and the miseries which may be crowded into the short space of human existence: the heart is softened, and irresistibly excited, to kindred action, in lightening the burden, and alleviating the wretchedness. This sympathy will be evinced as well by your attendance *on the poor*, as on the more wealthy. Native kindness of heart will prompt you to renewed exertions in alleviating human misery; and will give you a decided advantage in gaining the esteem of your patients. (pp. 87–8)

This passage exemplifies a unity of thought linking the creative imagination of Romanticism with the humanitarianism of enlightened medical practice during the period. The power of sympathy in lightening the burden is what poets and writers as different from each other as Wordsworth, Shelley and Hazlitt emphasised as a guiding light. We would call it empathy, the ability to project oneself into the feelings of others, and particularly the suffering and the poor. Keats speaks of a 'common tie of sympathy or suffering' (*JKL*, 2, 24), of 'sacred sympathy' in love, and he uses the word several times with a strong meaning.

The emphasis *'on the poor'* is important, since public, teaching hospitals were set up in this period specifically to cater for the indigent, a dawning of the public policy that led in 1948 to a formal welfare state in Britain. The rich would still have been treated at home and would not have dreamed of entering a hospital. They were initially charitable institutions, funded by philanthropists wishing to insure their immortal souls against damnation by doing good works. The rationale for public hospitals was at least threefold: to cure or at least alleviate the suffering of poor people unable to afford private medicine; to conduct medical research; and to train apprentice doctors, most of whom would return to practise in towns and villages throughout England. Altruism, sympathy for *'the poor'* and compassion were, at least in a formal sense, the very *raison d'être* of London hospitals in the early nineteenth century. Right from the outset, pupils were required not just to observe and learn, but also to labour in the role of servants to charity.[16] At the same time, the ambience of such places must have resembled the distressing health conditions nowadays associated with third world countries. They could not have been pleasant places in which to learn. Shelley, in his 'Essay on the Vegetable System of Diet' gives an eye-witness account: 'Hospitals are filled with a thousand screaming victims; the palaces of luxury and the hovels of indigence resound alike with the bitter wailings of disease, idiotism and madness grin and rave amongst us.' It was not until much later in the period 1842–50 that Edwin Chadwick, a socially responsible poet and lawyer, reported officially and critically on *Sanitary Conditions of the Labouring Population* which led to reforms such as sewers with running water. Not until 1848 did parliament legislate for clean water in London. Contaminated water caused dysentery, fever, pneumonia and typhoid, illnesses that accounted not only for a huge number of patients in hospitals but also could be contracted in the unclean wards.

'Aesculapius' holds in high esteem the notion of useful 'knowledge' mainly because it counteracts prejudice, dogma and bias. It can be the main instrument behind 'doing the world some good' in the pragmatic sense:

> *Knowledge is good; but it is only good as it is useful, only useful as it is retained and employed for the different and daily purposes of life.* (p. 54)

Even the phrases *'knowledge is good'* and the earlier 'All knowledge will be of use to him' (p. 23) are resonant in the light of Keats's own comments. One passage in his letters could even be a recollection of his reading 'Aesculapius', since the mentioning of knowledge invokes the whole context of his medical training and the *Guide's* cautioning against bias. He wrote to Reynolds on 3 May 1818 in this fashion:

> Were I to study physic or rather Medicine again, – I feel it would not make the least difference in my Poetry; when the Mind is in its infancy

a Bias [is] in reality a Bias, but when we have acquired more strength, a Bias becomes no Bias. Every department of knowledge we see excellent and calculated towards a great whole. I am so convinced of this, that I am glad at not having given away my medical Books, which I shall again look over to keep alive the little I know thitherwards; ... An extensive knowlege [sic] is needful to thinking people – it takes away the heat and fever; and helps, by widening speculation, to ease the Burden of the Mystery. (*JKL*, 1, 276–7)

He speaks of 'high Sensations' being stabilised by 'knowledge'; but then goes 'out of his depth' with what seems like a medical reflection: 'it is impossible to know how far knowlege [sic] will console [us] for the death of a friend and the ill "that flesh is heir to"' – we find that the word 'knowledge' and its variants are repeated time and again, especially in 1818, the year after he abandoned medicine.

The Hospital Pupil's Guide initiates the student into each of the branches of medicine that he will be expected to study at Guy's, each section following a common formula. A footnote entry indicates the specialist books which can be consulted – a basic 'reading list' for the student. This enables us to follow the likely course of Keats's reading during his medical training. An initial statement presents the subject in its most attractive and enticing light, then there is a brief sketch of the rudiments, and usually there follows a warning not to become solely preoccupied with the particular area, consistent with 'Aesculapius's' advice that medicine must be studied in breadth, without dogma or over-specialisation. At the same time, there is an implicit bias towards anatomy and surgery, the areas favoured by Cooper and the medical vanguard of the day.

Anatomy, physiology and surgery

It is much to be regretted that the prejudices of the ignorant still oppose so strong a barrier to the frequent examination of the dead: but do not be discouraged by the reiterated refusal of relatives to permit this investigation: pursue with ardour this delightful science, and in due time you will find prejudices subduing. (p. 37)

It is difficult to understand how the word 'delightful' could be attached to the study of anatomy in the early nineteenth century, except ironically (as it is here) or expressed by devotees of the science such as Sir Astley Cooper and his many followers, who described anatomy as 'our polar star'. The words may, indeed, be Cooper's own, since he helped to make Guy's one of the best anatomy schools in Europe, although the actual demonstrator in the subject when Keats attended was Joseph Henry Green, who was just as enthusiastic as Cooper. 'Aesculapius's' comments that anatomy is 'the basis of every other [branch of study]' and that dissection is 'certainly the most important way of learning anatomy' point to the importance of the subject when Keats was a student. None the less, it cannot have been 'delightful' in our sense of the word. Keats must not have been alone in feeling revulsion at the sight of 'chaps ... at work, carving limbs and bodies, in all stages of puterefaction, & of all colours'.[17] As the statement by 'Aesculapius' implies, examination of the dead, even those who died in the hospital itself, was illegal unless authorised by relatives, who were reluctant to give permission. To solve the problem, Cooper paid grave-robbers ('resurrection men'), such as 'hard-drinking Ben Crouch ... his brother Jack, Bill Butler, and Jack and Bill Harnett'[18] to supply him with corpses. In days before obligatory refrigeration, these must have been in a state of decay. A witness in 1834 described the anatomy theatre (whose stairs countless tourists like me still climb) in less than romantic terms: 'The dead-house (it was never called by any better name) was a miserable kind of shed, stonefloored, damp and dirty, where all stood around a table on which the examinations were made.'[19] Cowden Clarke reports that anatomy was the only part of the course Keats disliked:

> with that transparent candour which formed the mainspring of his rule of conduct, he at once made no secret of his inability to sympathize with the science of anatomy, as a main pursuit in life; for one of the expressions that he used, in describing his unfitness for its mastery, was perfectly characteristic. He said, in illustration of his argument, 'the other day, for instance, during the lecture, there came a sunbeam into the room, and with it a whole trop of creatures floating in the ray; and I was off with them to Oberon and fairyland.' (CCC, 132)

Despite Keats's words here, Clarke attests to Keats's expertise and 'technical precision' in describing medical conditions to him, which adds more evidence of his professional diligence and tempers the suggestion that his mind and imagination were elsewhere.

We have Keats's copy of his 'Anatomical and Physiological Note Book', a printed record of Cooper's lectures, interleaved with blank pages often filled with notes taken by Keats in the lectures. Generally speaking, their language is far from that we find later in his poetry:

> The Dens sapientiae would be quite in Contact with the Antrum were it not for a membrane – ... The foramen infra orbitarum is the Passage for the Nerve frequently affected with Tic douloureux –[20]

There are, however, touches of Cooper's famous witty asides: 'In diseases Medical Men guess, if they cannot ascertain a disease they call it nervous ...' (p. 57), which Keats may later parody in describing himself as *'narvus'*, but much of the prose is impenetrably technical. Words occur that must have arrested the budding poet: '[Aneurism is] a Pulsating swelling ...' (p. 12); 'The St[r]eam of Blood in a Vein near to an artery has a distinct Pulsation' (p. 13). The description of glands taken down by Keats in the lecture indicates the kind of illustrative digressions Cooper must have added verbally, and is full of suggestive images and ideas for a young poet:

> *The Use of Glands* The opinion now generally entertained is that the fluid produced depends upon the action of Arteries not of veins – Fluids when agitated in a particular Manner will change their nature and that the Gland performs an operation similar to Churning in which Cream is changed in Butter and Butter milk – ... The Passions of [the] Mind have great influence on the Secretions, Fear produces increase [of] Bile and Urine, Sorrow increases Tears ... (p. 64)

The presence of Sir Astley Cooper gave Guy's and St Thomas's Hospitals an international reputation. His main assets in surgery appear to have been simple *speed* and efficiency, vital in days before anaesthetics (which were not to be developed until the 1840s, and then in dentistry rather than surgery). His adeptness was clearly underpinned by intimate knowledge of anatomy, physiology and medicine in general, which would guide him as to what operations could and could not be done. The ghastly fate of poor Hippolyte in *Madame Bovary*, who lost his leg because of the ignorant attempt by Dr Bovary to correct a club foot by surgery, gives us a terrifying glimpse of the kind of surgery Cooper was correcting.[21] The individual surgeon to whom Keats was apprenticed as dresser at Guy's was the genial and well liked Dr 'Billy' Lucas, regarded by a contemporary student, John Flint, 'as no more than a butcher', 'a poor anatomist and not a very good diagnoser, which now and then got him into ugly scrapes', and 'neat-handed, but rash in the extreme, cutting amongst most important parts as though they were only skin, and making us all shudder from the apprehension of his opening arteries or committing some other error'.[22]

Keats attended Cooper's lectures. They were so famous that pirated copies of notes circulated amongst other medical teaching institutions for many years before their publication. Eventually in 1822 Cooper published his own lectures as a textbook, *Lectures on Surgery*, which was, like his anatomy lectures, issued interleaved with blank pages for students to take notes (a format described by 'Aesculapius'), though obviously it appeared too late for Keats to use as a textbook. Given his reputation as a silver-tongued lecturer and one who, like Keats himself from boyhood and later Charles Brown, was fond of puns and extempore word-play, Cooper's writing does not convey the entertaining verbal delivery in which he frequently digressed into anecdotes. His written prose is clear and professional. He acknowledges the great influence of John Hunter, his own teacher at Edinburgh, now known as the father of modern surgery, and he advises that 'Medicine and Surgery mutually assist each other' (p. 1). He defines surgery as intimately related to the 'constitutional' study of the body given by medicine as a discipline, 'the influence of local disease on the constitution; and the origin of local disease from constitutional derangement'. 'Aesculapius' echoes the sentiments: 'A good surgeon must be a good physician!' The surgeon should find out 'constitutional symptoms', examine 'constitutional derangement' which should then be 'relieved by *constitutional remedies*' (p. 55). 'Aesculapius' also writes, 'in the progress of surgical disease, symptoms of constitutional sympathy will be frequently excited'. The word 'constitution', referring to the whole body, mind and emotional habits of the unique patient, was to fall out of use in medical jargon, although, like much of eighteenth-century terminology, it has continued to the present day in use in homoeo-pathy which developed in Europe at exactly the same time and almost certainly as a reaction against the new 'school' of medicine based on sur-gery. However, despite his enthusiasm, Cooper clearly did not see surgery as the answer to all problems of ill-health, and he refers to other branches of medicine such as medicines and remedies in the *materia medica*, describing, for example, the use of arsenic as 'an excellent remedy in fever or bitter [?nausea]' to cure 'horrid pain in stomach, spasmodic contractions', and the symptoms of opium insensibility – 'dilated pupils, short exhilarating effects, slow pulse' – to be alleviated by administration of opium. The significance for Keats's poetry was to emerge much later in *The Fall of Hyperion*.

Cooper's lectures indicate other legacies of earlier medicine, for example his use of the doctrine of 'sympathy', which had a technical meaning which was centuries old in Western medicine. 'Irritation' can be local (a blow on the head, decayed tooth, etc.) but it can cause other problems: '*violent constitutional symptoms* are often caused by the most trivial circumstances'; a blow on the stomach can cause death because of the 'peculiar degree of sympathy between the stomach and the organs of respiration preventing the descent of the Diaphragm' (p. 2). Thereafter, Cooper continues to invoke sympathy in the technical sense, and he constantly refers problems like 'inflammation' back to the distinction between local and constitutional. Local treatment focuses on the particular inflammation; constitutional treatment for chronic conditions 'consists in a diminution of nervous excitement, and of the force of circulation' by various means. When Keats uses such words, as he sometimes does, they must carry some of the specific meanings of the learning he acquired at Guy's, rather than the vague modern meanings. The rest of Cooper's lectures systematically move through the various diseased conditions which should be ameliorated by surgery in the '*New mode* of operating, as suggested and practised by *Dr Hunter*' (p. 29).

Physic

Physic is described in the *Guide* as a general 'medical knowledge' of the many diseases that do not require surgery. However, notwithstanding Cooper's intention that the surgeon should also be a physician, a political gap between the two methods of practising medicine was opening up during the turn of the eighteenth century into the nineteenth, and Keats was to enter the medical profession just as it clarified. There was an emerging perception that surgery and anatomy were the pursuit of a new elite, and that this branch of medicine was the progressive 'cutting edge' (literally!) which involved investigative research, although it led to a detachment that could be dehumanising. Meanwhile, physicians were by contrast seen as reassuringly old-fashioned, traditional and humane:

> Physicians did chemistry, which had traditional connections to learned medicine, because it enhanced their mastery of the language and processes of internal constitutional disorders. Surgeons pursued questions in anatomy, morbid anatomy, and experimental physiology because these areas displayed their mastery of anatomical language and surgical skills.[23]

A transformation was occurring which was to lead in time to the modern hierarchy distinguishing hospital consultants and surgeons from general practitioners or 'family doctors'.

Keats encountered both branches of medicine while walking the wards at Guy's, and from the evidence we have it seems he was aware of the professional change and that his instincts inclined him away from the new and back to the old, from anatomy and surgery towards botany, the alleviation of pain, and people-centred physic with its awareness of individual 'constitutions'. Cooper seems to have been the last who could, with some genius, incorporate the two tendencies in his own practice. A double impulse of dispassionate laboratory experimentation and humane, personalised caring for the destitute and terminally ill would hit Keats in the face every day of his wardship. The conflict is inscribed in *Lamia*, in which the image of the snake may even relate to the traditional symbol for Aesculapius, the staff with entwined serpent, and in *Hyperion: The Fall*. By choosing to turn away from the modern profession of medicine towards poetry, he was in effect making his choice between two kinds of medicine, one physical and the other psycho-spiritual. There was a medical paradigm available which certainly influenced Shelley: 'vitalism' was a new science which proposed a non-materialistic basis for life which was simply and mysteriously 'held together' by the body which altered so dramatically after death.[24] Since this approach was pioneered by a local Edmonton figure, John Abernethy, it may have been known by Keats, but this would need further research to establish.

'Aesculapius' devotes a few pages to 'physic' or 'medical science', insisting on it as absolutely 'primary' to the practice of medicine, a study which the general practitioner 'will find useful ON EVERY DAY, as he passes through life' (p. 60), as well as being indispensable in forming a judgment as to when surgery is required. As elsewhere, we detect a change of writer in the *Guide* as presumably the teacher of physic takes over from Cooper's surgery. Surgery, he says, is the '*more simple*' branch of medicine, physic 'the *more abstruse study*', even though the former is given a higher status in hospital training. Surgery requires essentially knowledge of anatomy and some experience, while physic 'is conversant with a variety of theories, and contradictory opinions and doctrines, and moreover requires a knowledge of physiology, pharmacy, botany, and chemistry' (p. 61). 'Aesculapius' points out that however gratifying a successful surgical operation may be, for every one of these there will be ten cases where 'no scalpel can reach' (p. 62). There follows an admission of uncertainty and ambiguity that must have struck a chord in Keats, who was predisposed to accept the existence of 'contradictory opinions and doctrines':

the variety of medical disease is great, and the peculiarities induced by idiosyncracy in the patient, or by his local situation, atmospherical variations, mental emotions, and the different functions and sensibilities of the animal system, are almost interminable: in our ignorance, and total want of demonstrable truth, we are perplexed by a thousand hypotheses and conjectures, of which the last is always the best, till it is superseded by some bolder and more daring genius, with his dazzling chimera: – even the testimony of practical men is so frequently at variance with itself, and with each other, and the relation of facts is so distorted, that it is difficult to separate truth from error. (p. 62)

'We are in a mist' is a sentiment that the poet often repeats in different contexts. The writer of the *Guide* establishes himself as one who understands the alluring promise of surgery to solve all problems rapidly, but acknowledges the primacy of older medical knowledge and the mysteries of the spirit (if not a 'soul' in the religious sense which is conspicuously absent from the *Guide*), even as he admits its vagaries and mystique.

Chemistry

'Aesculapius' proclaims chemistry 'a pleasing science, indispensably necessary to the success of the medical practitioner ... an elegant accomplishment, and almost necessary to the character of the gentleman' (p. 68), which has the additional virtue to his student readers of contributing to 'the welfare of your patients' (p. 69). Again, the tone is that of a person trained in an older school where 'the bedside manner' and intuition are still important even as the dazzling successes of surgeons hold the limelight. Once again we find an appreciation of paradox, the fusing of opposites to form a new unity, which is a hallmark of Keats's own temperament:

> And when it is recollected, how great and indefinite is the reaction of different substances upon each other, and that their resulting compounds are frequently essentially different, from a simple combination of their constituent principles; when it is recollected, how easily a mistake on this head may be incurred, and that such a mistake may prove fatal even to the life of our patient; surely it is important!! The greatest and the best physicians have occasionally ordered those combinations of medicines, which, in consequence of their chemical affinities, have produced by their union a substance essentially differing in its properties from the views of the prescriber: how important, therefore, that you should be acquainted with the laws of chemical attraction. (p. 69)

Stuart Sperry has looked carefully at the processes of chemistry which Keats would have learned,[25] their distillations and crystallising into 'essences', but the statement by 'Aesculapius' of an observable, physical law of paradox, whereby two contradictory substances in combination create an essentially different compound, could have been the most 'alluring' aspect of the study of chemistry for the young poet predisposed to think experientially and through paradoxes. The conceptual basis of the science was more useful to him as a poet than colourful and detailed examples.

Botany

'Aesculapius' does not mention *materia medica*, but it was important for the study of medicine in the early nineteenth century, and was lectured on at Guy's. It was the fusion of chemistry and botany, the study of the effect on the human body of hundreds of chemical and organic substances that formed the doctor's repertoire of cure. The great forerunner of medical botanists was the Greek Dioscorides. He compiled a treatise describing the curative qualities of about five hundred plants in a book known as *De materia medica*, a term which is central to homoeopathy nowadays but otherwise not used. What Keats would have learned in his lectures from William Babington, James Curry and Henry Cholmeley was a fertile vocabulary taken from nature, invoking not only the intrinsic beauty of a range of flowers and metals, but also specific, medicinal properties known to characterise each. So far as can be judged, Keats, because of his medical learning, was the only professional poet of his time, apart from the older George Crabbe, trained systematically to recognise and draw upon such knowledge. As he was taught by William Salisbury while wandering through the Chelsea Physic Garden run by the Society of Apothecaries, we can imagine the power of such imagery and concepts on a mind predisposed to delight in paradoxes of organic growth and death.

Among Romantic 'nature poets', Keats is unique in using natural imagery not just for pictorial and sensuous effect, but also for precise medicinal signification.[26]

'Aesculapius' deliberately downplays botany since he assumes that students will need no enticement into a subject that seems peacefully distant from the more gruesome realities of anatomy and surgery, and the unpleasant symptoms of disease. 'The study is seductive; let it not enslave the heart, and preoccupy the intellect' (p. 72). It is likely that Keats needed to heed this advice. In the margins of his notes to the lectures by Astley Cooper on Anatomy and Physiology, he has sketched three bunches of flowers, one in a bottle. All who have commented on this, except for Donald Goellnicht,[27] interpret it as distracted doodling, evidence that Keats's attention wandered in his lectures. The doodling may not, however, have been so idle or so irrelevant. If his attention was wandering, it may have been in the direction of his lectures on botany, a subject which Keats must have preferred to anatomical and surgical matters, although unfortunately his own textbook or notes have not been preserved. Guy's Hospital had a botanical garden of curative herbs, which Keats would certainly have frequented. 'Aesculapius' was under no illusions about the seductive nature of botany to any student, let alone one who was a poet. The writer of this section (Salisbury?) must have had a soft spot for the study, since his original Greek namesake has been described as 'a root digger and a wandering quack'.[28] Agnes Arber points out that the Greek word for root diggers (or herb gatherers) comes from a word which signifies a medicinal plant in general.

Hermione de Almeida presents evidence to show that in England the period 1795–1820 (with the background of work by earlier botanists like Culpeper and Linnaeus, and contemporary Europeans) was the great age of categorising the effects on the human body of hundreds of poisons, and also the heyday of the medical application of material doses of poisons on the principle of 'like cures like', which was relatively standard practice by all doctors. Astley Cooper himself said 'there is no substance considered as poisonous which in very small doses is not capable of producing a beneficial effect'.[29] Some could act 'sympathetically', both destructively and benignly, on the mind and emotions, others on particular organs of the body. There would have been few better placed to appreciate the paradoxical logic of this pharmacology than the poet who wrote that 'The little sweet doth kill much bitterness' and 'there is richest juice in poison flowers' (*Isabella*, 97 and 104); to realise how philosophically suggestive was the phenomenon of sweet-smelling and evocatively named flowers – paeonia, deadly nightshade (belladonna), wolf's-bane (aconite), hemlock (conium), poison ivy (rhus toxicendron), opium, strychnos vine (nux vomica), Peruvian bark – all being deadly poisonous, signifying death and yet also miraculously curative and signifying renewed life.

'Aesculapius' lists the standard works on medical botany which are recommended to the students to consult. A glance at these books immediately confirms the 'seductive' nature of the study. The first listed is 'Smith's Introduction to Botany', more fully entitled *An Introduction to Physiological and Systematical Botany* 'By James Edward Smith, M.D. F.R.S. &c. &c. President of the Linnaean Society'.[30] The title page carries the biblical quotation, 'Consider the lilies of the field, how they grow'. Smith was not only President but founder of the Linnaean Society, and his book is intended as a student's guide based on the Linnaean system of classification of plants. His enthusiasm is manifest, as he describes his wider aims:

> To explain and apply to practice those beautiful principles of method, arrangement and discrimination, which render botany not merely an amusement, a motive for taking air and exercise, or an assistance to many other arts and sciences; but a school for the mental powers, an alluring incitement for the young mind to try its growing strength, and a confirmation of the most enlightened understanding in some of its sublimest most important truths. (p. ix)

He quotes poetry: 'I shall not labour to prove how delightful and instructive it is to "Look through nature up to Nature's God."' He refers to the words of Rousseau, and then says that the man who loves botany for its own sake 'would find himself neither solitary nor desolate, had he no other companion than a "modest daisy," that "modest crimson-tipped flower," so sweetly sung by one of Nature's own poets [Wordsworth?]' (p. xv). To such a man 'his thoughts will not dwell much upon riches or literary honours, things that "Play round the head, but come not near the heart"' (p. xvi). Smith himself waxes lyrical over the 'profuse flowery treasures of the summer':

> The yellow blossoms of the morning, that fold up their delicate leaves as the day advances; others that court and sustain the full blaze of noon; and the pale night-scented tribe, which expand, and diffuse their very sweet fragrance, towards evening, will all please in their turn. Though spring is the season of hope and novelty, to a naturalist more especially, yet the wise provisions and abundant resources of Nature, in the close of the year, will yield an observing mind no less pleasure, than the rich variety of her autumnal tints affords to the admirers of her external charms. (p. xviii)

So far as I know, no Keats scholar has looked at this book which was undoubtedly the first recommended botanical textbook by the most famous English botanist of the day. 'The pale night-scented tribe' gestures towards 'Ode to a Nightingale', and the rest leads to 'To Autumn'. And 'the yellow blossoms of the morning, that fold up their delicate leaves as the

day advances' has a poignant anticipation of the unbearably touching late
reference by Keats to his student memories of hothouses in the herbary:

> I muse with the greatest affection on every flower I have known from
> my infancy – their shapes and coulours as are new to me as if I had just
> created them with a superhuman fancy – It is because they are connected
> with the most thoughtless and happiest moments of our Lives – I have
> seen foreign flowers in hothouses of the most beautiful nature, but I do
> not care a straw for them. The simple flowers of our sp[r]ing are what
> I want to see again. (*JKL*, 2, 260)

After his enthusiastic Preface, Smith presents a sober and systematic account
of plants, their description and some medical properties, his prose often
shifting into a mode of prose poem. He describes the taste of fruit and perfume of flowers (quoting in full a love poem of Martial about the 'pale night-
scented flower, Sad emblem of passion forlorn' [p. 60]), 'the sweet smell of
new hay' (p. 61), and the 'richest tints and most elegant combinations of
colour ... reserved for the petals of flowers, the most transient of created
beings ...' (p. 63). He writes on the same page, 'We may be dazzled with the
brilliancy of a flower-garden, but we repose at leisure on the verdure of a
grove or meadow.' Smith describes in delicate detail the movement of flowers like daisies, sunflowers and marigolds, which turn to the 'radiant lumi-
nary' of the sun as it passes overhead (p. 159). At the back of his book, Smith
appends small etchings of the plants in black and white, perhaps prototypes
of the ones Keats sketched, understandably 'seduced' during his anatomy
lectures. The second and third books recommended by 'Aesculapius', *Milne's
Botanical Dictionary* and William Withering's four volumes of descriptive
botany, *A Systematic Arrangement of British Plants with an Easy Introduction
to the Study of Botany. Illustrated by copper plates*,[31] are more intimidating,
but if Keats needed more visual stimulation than Smith could provide he
would have found it amply in the other British book recommended by
'Aesculapius', William Woodville's *Medical Botany: Containing systematic and
general descriptions with Plates of all the Medicinal Plants, comprehended in the
catalogues of the materia medica as published by the Royal Colleges of Physicians
of London, Edinburgh, and Dublin ...*[32], which seeks to educate the practitioner
into distinguishing those plants that he may prescribe. The large format,
five-volume work is ravishingly illustrated with meticulously coloured, full-
page illustrations of each plant, individually painted under the 'immediate
Inspection' of G. Spratt from original specimens, accompanied by descriptions of each plant, and brief, sometimes arresting, indications of their
medical properties.

Keats did not forget his *materia medica* and herbals. His lines in 'Ode on
Melancholy', '... aching Pleasure nigh, Turning to poison while the bee-
mouth sips', contain, among other meanings and associations, a pithy

awareness of the basic principle of sympathies, that organic substances which are poisonous can also cure, if the symptoms of a disease match those produced by an overdose of the drug. Woodville need not be a specific source, but his descriptions of the poisonous but medically useful plants are examples of the kind of knowledge Keats's medical studies contributed to his poetry. There are clusters of such references at the beginnings of 'Ode to a Nightingale' and 'Ode on Melancholy' respectively:

> My heart aches, and a drowsy numbness pains
> My sense, as though of hemlock I had drunk,
> Or emptied some dull opiate to the drains
> One minute past, and Lethe-wards had sunk:
>
> ...
>
> No, no, go not to Lethe, neither twist
> Wolf's bane, tight-rooted, for its poisonous wine;
> Nor suffer thy pale forehead to be kiss'd
> By nightshade, ruby grape of Proserpine
>
> ...

Here are Woodville's descriptions of the plants Keats mentions:

> Conium Maculatum, Common Hemlock: 'Whether this species of hemlock was the poison usually administered at the Athenian executions, and which deprived Athens of those great characters, Socrates and Phocion, we are at a loss to determine; but that it is a deleterious poison there cannot be a doubt ...' [p. 106]. Recommended for tumours, ulcers, etc; causes giddiness among other things, and 'sopores'.

> Papaver Somniferum, White Poppy: juice collected from incisions is powerfully narcotic induces sleep, allays pain and restlessness: '... and although in many cases it fails of producing sleep, yet if taken in a full dose, it occasions a pleasant tranquillity of mind, and a drowsiness, which approaches to sleep, and which always refreshes the patient'. (p. 381)

> Aconitum Napellus, Common Wolf's-Bane or Monk's Hood: Strongly poisonous, affecting whole nervous system – anxiety, suffocation, convulsions, mania etc ...[33]

> Digitalis Purpuream, Common Fox-Glove: 'a dangerous remedy'; to cure dropsy; ... if the pulse be feeble, or intermitting, the countenance pale, the lips vivid, the skin cold, the swollen belly soft and fluctuating, the anasarcous limbs readily pitting under the pressure of the finger, we may expect the diuretic effects to follow in a kindly manner. (p. 220)

Keats's preferred fruits, from the evidence of the letters, include 'soft fruits' like apricots, nectarines and peaches (*JKL*, 2, 149), and these may not have

been as innocent in his mind as they seem to us, nor so humble. Woodville
writes,

> Amygdalus Persica, Common Peach Tree: 'The fruit, which is brought
> here from the East Indies, is said to be powerfully narcotic, and used for
> the purpose of intoxication.' (p. 512)

Another example of Keats's detailed knowledge of herbals is provided in a
brief and elegant article by Laura E. Campbell. In 'Ode to Psyche' the first
publishers print the phrase 'budded Tyrian' whereas Keats's manuscript
shows him using 'budded syrian'. Campbell persuasively argues that Keats
meant what he said: Syrian rue or *Peganum harmala*, and intense yellow (rather than the Tyrian blue) which has been used medicinally as an
anthelmintic and narcotic (to make a person 'gay and exultant'), in the
treatment of conditions like eye diseases, rheumatism and nervous ailments.
'It is a curative in small dosages and a poison in larger amounts', obeying
the law expounded by Astley Cooper: 'all poisonous substances in small
doses can be beneficial medicines'.[34] It is tempting to see Keats's references
to flora as evidence of a 'nature lover' like Wordsworth and Clare, but we
should keep in mind that he was the only poet of his age to study botany
professionally.

Other, shorter sections in 'Aesculapius' open up other areas for Keats the
future poet. One on midwifery stresses the sensitivity required of the male
doctor attending the mother, and it covers diseases of infants, while a section on Law introduces medical jurisprudence and forensic medicine. The
student is advised that in practice he may be asked by courts for opinions
in cases such as infanticide, poisoning and rape. These branches of study
suggest to me that Keats would have been more knowledgeable about social
and sexual realities at a young age than most poets of the time. It seems
almost too obvious to mention – which might be why other critics have
not done so – that as a medical student he would have learned much more
about female sexuality than most young, unmarried men of the time. The
subject was clearly taught, for in one of his textbooks he wrote the following
diagrammatic list:

> The Organs of Sense are 5 Feeling, Sight, Hearing, Smell, Taste.
> The Mind has 3 Functions
> 1 Memory, 2 Judgment 3 Imagination
> 3rdly Those of Generation,
>   In Man   Penis
>   Testicles &
>   Vesiculae Seminales

In Woman	Externally
	Mons Veneris
	Labia
	Perinaeum
	Clitoris &
Internally	Nymphae
	Vagina &
	Uterus

We notice already a habit of mind leading him to group things into three, but more pertinently a clinical study of the physiology of sex. Several of his early poems addressed to women are clearly and perhaps precociously sexually knowing, and we find him musing about whether the man or woman gains greater pleasure from the sexual act. Some biographers, and Gittings in particular, have been drawn to argue that Keats was sexually experienced himself, even that he had venereal disease (Gittings, 642–9), and Motion suggests he used prostitutes and contracted gonorrhoea[35] but these are not necessary conclusions. The evidence that he took mercury, crucial to this theory, does not inescapably suggest the conclusion, since mercury, although toxic (universal in felt hatmaking where it caused 'mad hatters'), was used for many medicinal purposes and in many forms (such as 'salts' and the compound 'calomel' – one of Keats's lecturers at Guy's was known as 'Calomel Curry' for his indiscriminate use), including as an antiseptic for cuts, an antidote to depression, as a laxative, and for toothache which everybody at the time suffered from – rather horrifyingly, it was administered to children suffering from teething pains. As an alternative suggestion concerning Keats's knowledge of sexuality, it is well documented that throughout the nineteenth century and indeed up to the 1920s, in the kind of practice in which Hammond apprenticed Keats, women presented themselves complaining of symptoms of 'hysteria' which clearly stemmed from sexual frustration and was regarded as a medical problem since 'self-pleasuring' was taboo. It was the doctor's task, either with 'medical' contraptions invented for the purpose, or by hand, to provide guilt-free 'treatment' to relieve these symptoms. One historian finds evidence that since this could be a tedious and lengthy procedure for the overworked physician he would delegate it to the apprentice or midwife.[36] One of Astley Cooper's own teachers, William Cullen, who wrote *First Lines of the Practice of Physic* (1777–84), still used in Keats's time, and who is still recognised as the inventor of the term 'neurosis' in the medical context, clearly approved, though he was aware of possible ethical problems involving 'propriety' for male doctors:

... turgescence of blood in the uterus, or in other parts of the genital system, may occasion the spasmodic and convulsive motions which appear in hysteria ... the exercise of venery certainly proves a stimulus to the vessels of the uterus; and therefore may be useful, when, with propriety, it can be employed.[37]

Obviously medical ethics have changed, but so has sex education, and in Keats's time a medical student would probably be the only category of male who would have anything like accurate physiological knowledge. Famously Keats did not become a doctor. Instead, even more to his guardian's horror, he declared himself a professional poet, and although he periodically considered the idea of returning to medicine, perhaps as ship's surgeon on an 'Indiaman', he never did.[38] In September 1819 he wrote to Charles Brown, 'In no period of my life have I acted with any self will, but in throwing up the apothecary-profession. That I do not repent of' (*JKL*, 2, 176). There were branches of medicine which he clearly enjoyed studying, particularly botany, but a central part of his decision to leave the profession may have been an antipathy to surgery itself, which was something of a specialism at Guy's Hospital. Brown, a reliable witness, reports Keats's words:

> He ascribes his inability [to operate] to an overwrought apprehension of every possible chance of doing evil in the wrong direction of the instrument. 'My last operation', he told me, was the opening of a man's temporal artery. I did it with the utmost nicety; but reflecting on what passed through my mind at the time, my dexterity seemed a miracle, and I never took up the lancet again. (Brown, 43)

With the stern warnings of 'Aesculapius' in mind – 'I have known surgeons who from excess of feeling could not operate; but this is not simple genuine sensibility. It is a spurious principle, occurring in a weak and sickly mind ...' – Keats must have felt in practice inadequate no matter how successful he may have been at his examinations. It was increasingly clear also to somebody like Charles Cowden Clarke, who had known him since the age of 7, as well as to his unsympathetic flatmates in London, that his imagination was held by poetry.

Whether he consciously thought about it or not is neither knowable nor relevant, but Keats entered the study of medicine during the decade in which the profession in England was undergoing what we would now call the revolution of a 'paradigm shift'. The underlying basis for medicine in England swung from one position to its opposite with astonishing speed, and the Apothecaries Act of 1815, coming mid-course for Keats, was the sign of a 'before' and an 'after'. It is inconceivable that his own decision to pursue poetry rather than medicine was not related to these changes, since his generation of students would have been directly caught in the crossfire of debate. At the very least his experiences at Guy's, although it was at the forefront of progressive medicine, would have shown him that the doctor of the future would be very different from his master Hammond, much more reliant on surgery and referral to 'specialists' trained in minute anatomy, than on herbal remedies and on local, constitutional knowledge of patients. It was the dawning of the great age of hospitals that were to flourish in Victorian England in which one can hardly imagine a man of Keats's sensitivity working for long. He could be forgiven for having entered the study of medicine with certain ideals, and leaving it when he discovered these expectations were rapidly being overturned in the very hospital in which he was placed. Keats's decision, which must have been made with some element of inner crisis and trauma, may have been precipitated by the fact that his own teachers were in the forefront of the radical revolution with which he found himself out of sympathy. He was obviously talented enough to master the new techniques, and intellectually to acknowledge their significance, but he also knew himself and his limitations well enough, even at what to most is a tender age, to realise that he could not with full integrity follow in the footsteps of his illustrious teachers. Instead, he sublimated the debates encountered in his medical training into poetry, and was for the rest of his life to dwell with focused attention on the primary aim of alleviating suffering in human beings by humanistic and literary means rather than medical. He seems to say good-bye to one healing vocation while welcoming the other in 'I stood tip-toe upon a little hill' in a hopeful vision that the poetry of mythology may cure the sick:

> The breezes were ethereal, and pure,
> And crept through half-closed lattices to cure
> The languid sick; it cooled their fevered sleep,
> And soothed them into slumbers full and deep.
> Soon they awoke clear-eyed: nor burnt with thirsting,
> Nor with hot fingers, nor with temples bursting:
> And springing up, they met the wondering sight
> Of their dear friends, nigh foolish with delight;
> Who feel their arms, and breasts, and kiss and stare,
> And on their placid foreheads part the hair.
> ...
> And so they stood, filled with a sweet surprise,
> Until their tongues were loosed in Poesy.

Not that his poetry abandoned medicine, for to a poet no experience is wasted. Recollections of the noisy and disturbing experience of walking the wards surely, as Goellnicht suggests, lie behind the words of 'Ode to a Nightingale':[39]

> Here, where men sit and hear each other groan;
> Where palsy shakes a few, sad, last gray hairs,
> Where youth grows pale, and spectre-thin, and dies;

> Where but to think is to be full of sorrow
> And leaden-eyed despairs,
> Where beauty cannot keep her lustrous eyes,
> Or new love pine at them beyond to-morrow.

He would have needed to dispense to dying patients the deadly narcotics that later appear in the 'Ode to a Nightingale' and 'Ode on Melancholy' and he must have seen many times the relief from pain that opium can bring:

> Ay, sleep; for when our love-sick queen did weep
> Over his waned corse, the tremulous shower
> Healed up the wound, and, with a balmy power,
> Medicined death to a lengthened drowsiness.[40]

Memories of specific human suffering can intrude at the most apparently inopportune moments in his poems, casting the shadow of mortality: the romantic escape into their future of Madeline and Porphyro in *The Eve of St Agnes* leaves behind 'Angela the old' who has 'Died palsy-twitched, with meagre face deform', and the equally ancient beadsman who sleeps (or lies dead) 'unsought for ... among his ashes cold'. Physical suffering and ugly death may be more distanced in poetry than on the hospital floor, more palatable perhaps. Even the Hippocratic Oath itself, which Keats would have taken on graduating, foregrounds the god Apollo, also god of poetry, who is to be the hero of his attempts to write *Hyperion*:

> I swear by Apollo the healer, by 'Aesculapius', by Health and all the pow-
> ers of healing, and call to witness all the gods and goddesses that I may
> keep this Oath and Promise to the best of my ability and judgement. (*The
> Hippocratic Oath*)

Keats seems genuine in feeling that in the final analysis poetry can play a 'healing' role in giving understanding and consolation even where medicine can offer no help.

3
'Was there a Poet born?'

Keats had registered as a student at Guy's Hospital on 1 October 1815, and passed his exams at the Apothecaries' Hall, Blackfriars, on 25 July 1816, thus achieving the primary medical qualification. Leaving his short-term options open he took advantage of the break from study to go to Margate on holiday with his brother Tom, while remaining enrolled for the higher level of surgeon. However, he had made up his mind to abandon medicine in the longer term and instead try his hand as a professional poet, a decision which I believe he made at Margate. His guardian Abbey was furious when he heard the news, and vowed never again to authorise such large payments from his wards' inheritances, beginning to regard the eldest John as particularly unreliable.

It was during his time at Guy's that Keats began to write poetry in earnest, no doubt partly to distract himself from the appalling conditions of his daytime activities in the hospital as much as a response to Clarke's encouragement. Charles Brown was later to write 'Though born to be a poet, he was ignorant of his birthright until he had completed his eighteenth year' (*KC*, 2, 55). While we need not be too pedantic about Brown's dating, Keats turned 18 in October 1813, and his first surviving poems were indeed written in 1814 during his apprenticeship to Hammond at Enfield, but the flow did not really start until mid-1815, his twentieth year. Surprisingly perhaps, this makes him a 'late starter' as a poet. Thomas Chatterton, whom Wordsworth dubbed 'The marvellous boy' and who was amongst Keats's own favourite poets, was dead before he had turned 18, leaving behind a body of verse which was controversial but substantial and which he had been writing since he was 7.[1] Keats, in his early sonnet 'To Chatterton' emphasised that the young poet had been 'a half-blown floweret' killed by 'the ingrate world and human fears', since Chatterton had died neglected and poverty-stricken. Later in the century, Rimbaud wrote the poems which were to be his most enduring while in his teenage years, and Victor Hugo described him as an *'enfant Shakespeare'*. Among Keats's contemporaries, Coleridge was recognised by his family as a budding poet in his childhood, and Wordsworth penned his earliest surviving poem, 'Lines Written at a School Exercise at Hawkshead' and first published poems when he was 17. Byron published a whole volume, *Fugitive Pieces* in his eighteenth year, another, *Hours of Idleness*, in his nineteenth, and by 22 had written Canto II of *Childe Harold*, while Shelley wrote poems which were later published in *The Esdaile Notebook* when he was 13. Tennyson wrote a whole verse play in imitation of the Elizabethans when he was 14, and published several poems written 'between 15 and 17' in a volume with his brother, *Poems by Two Brothers*. By the age Keats was writing his first recorded poems, which are not in themselves very distinguished, all these poets had a considerable corpus and were well and truly launched on poetic careers. For some reason poets, like musical geniuses, tend to be precocious, while novelists, at least up until the twentieth century, have generally found their craft later in life. Jane Austen and Thomas Hardy were in their thirties, Trollope in his fifties, before they started publishing novels, while Walter Scott single-handedly illustrated the general point by making his reputation with a great deal of poetry written before he was 40 and publishing his first novel when he was 43.

Keats's four verses named 'Imitation of Spenser' give few signs of a born poet, although they do have a verbal playfulness that marks them as more individual than would be expected from a poetic imitation. The lines reflect Keats's enthusiastic reading of Spenser which Cowden Clarke described 'as a young horse would through a spring meadow – "ramping!"' (CCC, 126). Partly an experiment in the Spenserian stanza form of nine lines ending with a couplet, the fragment shows also Keats's early delight in language and lush imagery. Written in the past tense, as a fairy 'reclined voluptuously', a swan 'oared himself along with majesty' and the fairy place described 'seemed an emerald in the silver sheen/Of the bright waters' glimpsed through 'clouds of fleecy white'.

Keats nailed his political beliefs to the mast in his earliest sonnets. 'On Peace' is a sonnet written in April 1814, celebrating the end of the war with France and echoing Leigh Hunt's published views on the political significance of the event. Keats greets England's peace as the harbinger of a European-wide movement against 'sceptred tyrants' destined to guarantee individual freedom and ensure that 'the great' are as subject to the law as others. Other sonnets written at roughly the same time were 'To Lord Byron' praising that increasingly popular poet's dark, sorrowful lining to the otherwise 'bright halo' of his work as 'the tale of pleasing woe' (the satirical poem *Don Juan* had not yet been published and Keats is alluding to the oriental verse tales). The poem of grief on the death of Alice Jennings with its quietly beautiful beginning, was the only time Keats in his poems uncritically implies a Christian afterlife, probably out of respect for his grandmother's faith rather than his own beliefs:

> As from the darkening gloom a silver dove
> Upsoars, and darts into the Eastern light,

On pinions that naught moves but pure delight,
So fled thy soul into the realms above,
Regions of peace and everlasting love.

Already we can see Keats's interest in the interplay between emotional states of darkness and light, gloom and joy, 'like fair veins in sable marble flow' ('To Lord Byron'). The more ambitious ode, 'To Hope', written in February 1815, is equally an exploration of contrary emotional states, 'Despondency' and 'Disappointment, parent of despair' on one side, 'cheerfulness' and 'bright-eyed Hope' on the other, though the weighting is on the former state when in solitude 'hateful thoughts enwrap my soul in gloom' and 'when dark thoughts my boding spirit shroud'. The 'Hope' of the title is presented as a political solution, freedom and 'Great Liberty – how great in plain attire!' as a bright light leading the poet out of despondency.

This conclusion seems to be connected with Keats's reception of the news that Leigh Hunt on 2 February was released from prison after his two-year sentence for libelling the Prince Regent in the pages of *The Examiner*. Keats greeted the event with a sonnet, 'Written on the Day that Mr Leigh Hunt left Prison', in which he claimed imaginative freedom for a poet who deserved to be in the company of Spenser and Milton. Keats, meeting Cowden Clarke on a walk, gave him the sonnet, perhaps hoping it would be passed on to Hunt by Clarke though the latter did not do so until two years had passed, by which time he had introduced Keats to Hunt in person. Hunt had lived famously well in prison, surrounding himself with his library, with flowers, and his friends' company, asserting his mental superiority of 'the sky-searching lark' over the prison walls and establishing for Keats a kind of political and poetical symbolism of freedom in both the physical and psychological senses. Perversely, the period in prison seems to have given Hunt a self-esteem which he was never to retrieve. In *The Examiner* he published an essay significantly titled 'Stone Walls No Prison'.[2] In the words of his first biographer, Nicholas Roe:

> From now on Hunt would try to recover the shelter and security that prison had given him. For the rest of his life, friends and acquaintances would be amazed at his spartan way of life, how he would sit wrapped in a dressing gown in a tiny study lined with books. It looked eccentric, unworldly, but what Hunt was forever trying to recreate was the infirmary in Surrey Gaol.[3]

In a six-line poem 'Written on 29 May The Anniversary of the Restoration of Charles the 2nd', Keats foregrounds again his political convictions, in dismissing the Restoration as a day of Britain's 'direst, foulest shame' and praising the Protestant resistance of Algernon Sidney, Lord William Russell and Sir Henry Vane, all of whom Keats had regarded as heroes since he had read at school Gilbert Burnett's *History of his Own Time*. He condemns his benighted contemporaries as 'Infatuate Britons'. The general political message which Keats in his earliest poetry was pursuing with candid explicitness was one that would not endear him to the Tory establishment in the world of literary reviewers. His condemnations of 'sceptred tyranny' applied as much to everyday life as to national politics, and when his friend Bailey in 1817 was passed over by the church authorities in his search for a curacy, Keats was full of righteous indignation on his behalf: 'That a mitre should cover a Man guilty of the most coxcombical, tyrannical and indolent impertinence!' (*JKL*, 1, 178). A more generally anti-authoritarian stance is implicit in such levelling attitudes, and in the modern phrase, to Keats politics are personal: 'Now the first political duty a Man ought to have Mind to is the happiness of his friends.' At the same time, his interest in fluctuating moods was emerging in more personal themes, not completely explained by comparison with conventional melancholy poems in the popular, eighteenth-century 'graveyard' genre popularised by Blair, Young and Gray since Keats's are not gloomy, religious and gothic.

In these early poems in 1815, Keats is clearly exploring the resources of shorter poetic forms, especially the sonnet and the ode. In November he wrote his first verse letter, addressed to George Felton Mathew (*JKL*, 1, 100) who was an exact contemporary with whom Keats was friendly for a time and even hoped for a collaborative relationship like that between Beaumont and Fletcher.[4] The real attraction may have been partly Mathew's cousins Caroline and Ann. Mathew had started the verse correspondence and Keats was responding in kind, in the spirit of coterie poetry between friends. The verse epistle as a form was first made famous by the Latin poet Horace who wrote verse letters to his patron, Maecenas, opening up philosophical discussions in an informal way which incorporates personal and social circumstances of the writer. In the Renaissance various writers had used the form, notably Sir Thomas Wyatt, John Donne, Ben Jonson and Katherine Philips, each of whom drew links between the subject of the letter and friendship itself. In the eighteenth century the verse epistle had a heyday since very diverse writers used it to discuss subjects in tones that range from the comic and satirical through to high seriousness.[5] The Romantic poet to become most accomplished in the medium was Coleridge, and his poems 'The Eolian Harp' (written to Sara Fricker), 'This Lime-Tree Bower My Prison' (to Charles Lamb) and 'Frost at Midnight' (to his baby son Hartley) are recognised as classic poems in their own right. Such 'Poems of Friendship' in the Romantic age, although singly composed on an occasion, were written not as ephemera but as studied compositions. In writing in this way to his friend Mathew, Keats was engaging in a serious poetic activity, adding to the form a distinctive Romantic celebration of 'a coterie life, a communal sense of poetry as a shared joy in life'.[6] At the same time there is an in-built spontaneity and playfulness about his verse letters, deriving partly from the context of personal friendship but also a technical result of his adoption of the very simple iambic pentameter in rhyming couplets so that rhythm and rhymes partly dictate content in a kind of whimsical association of thoughts and sounds. The artist Paul Klee described his drawings as 'taking a line for a walk', and Keats's conversation poems have something of a verbally equivalent quality. What the content of the verse letter 'To G. F. Mathew' tells us clearly is that Keats is saturating himself in Renaissance poetry and that he regards poetry itself as a collaborative activity rooted in a spirit of friendliness – 'a brotherhood of song' – conveying primarily 'loving heart, a feeling / Of all that's high, and great, and good, and healing', the last word perhaps a significant one since Keats was still a medical student. Quotations and allusions abound to Beaumont and Fletcher, the great Renaissance playwriting collaborators, to Milton's early poems like 'L'Allegro', to Spenser, 'that warm-hearted Shakespeare' of *A Midsummer Night's Dream* and *The Tempest*, and also the classical favourite of Renaissance writers, Ovid. The main contemporary reference is to Chatterton who, in turn, had made his name a generation earlier by writing pseudo-medieval verse. Already Keats is signalling that his primary poetic affinities are with Elizabethan poetry, unlike most of his contemporary poets who, like Byron, were developing directions initiated by eighteenth-century predecessors or, like Wordsworth and Coleridge, striving for originality by writing from direct observation, contemporary speech idiom, and from their imaginations alone. Even the concept of poetic imitation was central to Elizabethan poetics, and Keats's Spenserian fragment 'Calidore' with its prologue 'Specimen of an Induction to a Poem' (both of which Keats was to publish in his first volume so he did not regard them as simple exercises) look anachronistic in their age, not only for their subject matter of chivalric knights and ladies, but for their underlying intention of recreating Spenser's verse for his own age. The 'Induction' becomes a thinly veiled attempt at emulation:

> And tell thee that my prayer is very meek,
> That I will follow with due reverence,
> And start with awe at mine own strange pretence.

Overall, Keats will emerge as the most Elizabethan of the Romantic poets, a taste evident in his earliest attempts. Furthermore, if the term 'Renaissance' still has currency over the fashionable 'early modern' to describe the movement that rediscovered classical writers and myths, then in this sense Keats can even be claimed as the last of the Renaissance poets.

Poetry and politics, then, were among Keats's first choice of topics when he turned to writing verse in 1815 during his time at Guy's Hospital. The third preoccupation in a kind of trinity was women, and they too enter his poetry early: in lines beginning 'Fill for me a brimming bowl' which were later claimed by his publisher Woodhouse to have been written after

Keats glimpsed beside the Thames in August 1814 an unknown woman at Vauxhall Gardens, a suburb historically notorious for prostitutes but 'cleaned up' by the Regency period. Keats again focuses on mixed emotions like 'the joy of grief' (consciously quoted from Campbell's *The Pleasures of Hope*) to express his feelings about women. The poet seeks some narcotic to drown his soul 'to banish Woman from my mind', trying to avoid not only 'lewd desiring' but the more haunting attractions of 'melting softness' in a face of unforgettable beauty, 'bright eyes', breasts, and smile. The poet concludes with a premonition: 'for ever shall she be / The halo of my memory'. And so this mysterious woman did become for Keats, since over two years later he was to write other poems alluding to her ('When I have fears that I may cease to be' and 'To –' ['Time's Sea']). In the second of these he says to the woman in verse that he was 'tangled in thy beauty's web, And snared by the ungloving of thine hand' which have become unforgettable touchstones of beauty for him. T. S. Eliot a century later in his short poem 'La Figlia Che Piange' describes a similar moment of glimpsed epiphany:

> She turned away, but with the autumn weather
> Compelled my imagination many days,
> Many days, and many hours:
> ...
>
> I should have lost a gesture and a pose.
> Sometimes these cogitations still amaze
> The troubled midnight and the noon's repose.

Not yet able to bring himself to write of 'love', Keats is able to write of women in at least a spirit of flirtation. For example, a verse letter 'To Mary Frogley' written on Valentine's Day (14 February 1816) is playfully erotic and coy by turns, written to one whom he addresses as an 'enchantress'. On the same day, and probably to the same woman, he wrote a sonnet which presents himself as an inadequate chivalric lover ('Had I a man's fair form') but ends by coming very close to imagined sex ('steeped in dew rich to intoxication'). Biographer W. J. Bate says that Mary Frogley was introduced, like many of Keats's early friends including the Mathews, by his brother George who liked her himself, but she in turn seems to 'have had something of a crush on John'.[7] The former Valentine poem was later surmised by Woodhouse to have been written on George's behalf, but later poems show that John felt few inhibitions in addressing this 'dark-haired bright-eyed beauty'. He also wrote to and about the Mathew sisters, when they gave him as a 'keepsake' a 'curious shell' which they found on the seashore at Hastings in the summer of 1815. He describes them as akin to characters in the kind of novel written by Jane Austen (though Keats did not know of Austen's books), 'elegant, pure, and aërial minds' ('To Some Ladies'). One of the two (Ann and Caroline) may have been 'sensibility' to her sister's 'sense', since a much more physically suggestive poem is now (deriving from Woodhouse) sometimes called 'To Emma Mathew' or non-commitally known by its first line, 'O come, dearest Emma! The rose is full blown'. 'Emma' is clearly a poeticism rather than a true name, and the poet imagines himself pillowing her head on a bed of moss and roses, 'enraptured', telling her a story of love, breathing on her and pressing her 'fair knee' while studying her 'love-looking eyes'. The true addressee of this poem, which Keats never published, remains a mystery, however. Among three textual variants there is one that George transcribed as 'Stanzas to Miss Wylie', breaking the metre by substituting 'Georgiana' for Emma, and thus making the poem refer to the woman that George himself was to marry, Georgiana Wylie, even though John never expresses erotic sentiments about her. George at least, if not his aesthetically inclined older brother, knew the value of poetry as a seduction tool. Given the intimate tone and sexual suggestiveness of this poem, it is not inconceivable (though not to my knowledge suggested by editors) that Keats was again addressing Mary Frogley, who at her own instigation was given copies of most of these poems by George, including this one which ended up in her album, and whom Keats habitually addresses in a frankly intimate tone.

None of these sonnets is a 'love poem' in subject-matter, and they do not even deal with love. Rather, they are light-hearted and flirtatious messages to women, revealing already some of Keats's ambivalence. Three others, written in about March 1816 and perhaps companion pieces about the same woman, reveal the sides to women in the estimation of the young man. 'Woman! When I behold thee flippant, vain', as this first line suggests, is an unillusioned view of a woman who is presented as representative of the sex, described as 'Inconstant, childish, proud, and full of fancies'. When, however, the woman employs a 'downcast eye, repentant of the pain that its mild light creates to heal again –' and is 'meek and kind and tender', the poet is immediately aware of being entranced and his soul dances in 'exultation': 'Heavens, how desperately do I adore / Thy winning graces!'

The last lines take a typical turn into the self-consciously literary, as the poet likens himself to a Spenserian knight or a Leander in devotion. Keats was aware at the time of Byron's poetry so the sonnet may owe something to that poet's stance of cynicism and idealisation, but since the strain runs through these early sonnets it seems we are witnessing the emergence of an ambiguous attitude which will in time lead to *La Belle Dame sans Merci* and *Lamia*. The concentration is on the body – 'Light feet, dark violet eyes, and parted hair' ... 'soft dimpled hands, white neck and creamy breast' – while holding in reserve a sharper awareness of beauty as 'lures' and a self-awareness that allows the poet critically to distance his own feelings which are guided by an ear which is 'like a greedy shark' devouring beauty mingled with intelligence. He is fully aware of his voyeurism, and here is 'the male gaze' indeed, but it is presented disingenuously, critically aware of its own dubious constructions of womanhood. 'Ah, who can e'er forget so fair a being' dwells on the vulnerability of a woman, but ends up with the poet's self-consciousness of his own willing illusionment. The image of the flower is presumably an echo from *A Midsummer Night's Dream*, the play by Shakespeare which centrally focuses on the ambivalent states of young lovers:

> Had I e'er seen her from an arbour take
> A dewy flower, oft would that hand appear,
> And o'er my eyes the trembling moisture shake.

After Keats graduated as apothecary, he had two months to fill in before his twenty-first birthday, the date when he could either practise as a physician or continue his studies at Guy's to become a surgeon. To fill this gap, which may have been as short as a fortnight due to the need to return for two months of lectures and to fulfil his obligations as dresser at Guy's for which he had paid on top of his fees, in August John went to Margate with his brother Tom whose health was increasingly fragile.[8] The holiday, like his medical studies, was paid for out of his inheritance with an advance from Abbey. This was the first of Keats's sojourns as a tourist and it gave him the leisure to read Wordsworth and to embark on the first of his longer poems.

The brothers most likely stayed at the oldest hotel in the town, now known as the Northern Belle, named after an American ship which was wrecked at Thanet in 1858, but which in Keats's time was named the Waterman's Arms and rumoured to be a smugglers' pub. Margate is a seaside town in east Kent close to Dover and since the late eighteenth century has been a favourite resort for upper- and middle-class Londoners, one of the first such tourist destinations in England, and one of the first in the country to introduce bathing machines. John and Tom would have taken either a steamer down the Thames to Southend and then across the short stretch of open sea to Margate, or a coach the whole distance. Either way, the trip to Margate may have been the first opportunity Keats had of seeing the sea. Unlike Brighton, whose beach is famous for its pebbles, Margate is sandy. One of Keats's first poems when he arrived was a sonnet, 'To my Brother George', beginning 'Many the wonders I this day have seen' and going on to describe the time between the dewfall in the morning to the 'feathery gold of evening'. It is the sea which draws his attention:

> The ocean with its vastness, its blue green,
> Its ships, its rocks, its caves, its hopes, its fears –
> Its voice mysterious ...

As he writes, the moon 'is from her silken curtains peeping' and given the opportunity of writing to his brother in this way Keats ends by recalling,

'But what, without the social thought of thee, / Would be the wonders of the sky and sea?'

'The social thought of thee' is a particularly significant phrase because, as Jeffrey Cox has argued, 'We need to see that Keats's early poetry is social poetry, arising from a concrete social context and engaging debates over cultural, religious, and social issues',[9] even when the poetic vehicle is descriptive or imitative. 'Calidore', the Spenserian imitation, may have been written in Margate and it shows Keats's wish to write a long poem, but one can understand why he discarded it mid-flow since it is hard to see this meandering narrative leading very far in a conceptual way. Far more important to his poetic development, because they forced on him a more immediate tone and contemporary language, are two verse letters he wrote to important correspondents from Margate. As in the case of 'Calidore' and its 'Induction', Keats was to include these epistles in his first volume of poems, indicating that he regarded them as serious poems rather than occasional and personal ones. He abandoned the Spenserian verses in favour of almost their polar opposite in technical terms. In the verse letter he wrote to George, 'the social thought' is uppermost, again a function of the form of the verse letter which required the poet to write with some directness to a 'dear friend, and Brother!' It also incites him to develop with more urgency a train of thought which explores his own reasons for valuing poetry and revealing his personal ambitions in that direction. The verse letter follows both a controlled mood change and a consecutive argument.

The epistle 'To my Brother George' begins and ends in the present tense but there is a stark emotional difference between the start,

> Full many a dreary hour have I passed,
> My brain bewildered and my mind o'ercast
> With heaviness;

and the cheerfulness of the end:

> Why westward turn? 'Twas to say adieu!
> 'Twas but to kiss my hand, dear George, to you!

What comes between is a thought process which amounts to a conscious argument by the young medical student that poetry is an emotionally therapeutic vehicle for cheering people up, taking them out of dreary hours and overcast moods into sociability, healing and happiness. The work demonstrates while it argues, that poetry can be an active agency for positive change both in the inner world of emotions and the social world, a recurrent concern in Coleridge's conversation poems. There is an air of spontaneity and it is difficult to say whether the direction of thought is a serendipitous moment of self-discovery in the act of writing or follows a premeditated plan. In the melancholy mood of the opening, a poetic vision which creates beauty from nature is mentally out of reach, but in a transition Keats, directly addressing 'dear George' in a new jokey tone, reports that 'It has been said' poets can see visions of chivalric knights, 'enchanted portals' and can hear trumpets not accessible to others' ears. No mortal eye can reach the imaginary flowers only dimly discerned by the poet ('And 'tis right just, for well Apollo knows / 'Twould make the Poet quarrel with the rose'). One whose 'head is pregnant with poetic lore' sees 'wonders strange' even in familiar things like the moon and clouds, 'the living pleasures of the bard'. The verse letter now takes another turn, away from 'living pleasures' and towards the rewards of posterity. Keats speculates that as the poet leaves the world through death he comforts himself by bequeathing a remarkable legacy to the world. His words can inspire patriots to fight for freedom, allow politicians to 'thunder out' his verses in order to persuade and stir, while sages will create philosophies out of the 'thoughts sententious', carefree villagers will sing his songs to serenade the 'lovely lass' (who is evoked in detail), and the posthumous poet even prides himself that

> To sweet rest
> Shall the dear babe, upon its mother's breast,
> Be lulled with songs of mine.

Once again Keats draws his poem back to contact with his 'dear friend and brother' and he begins to reveal his own 'mad ambitions ... For tasting joys like these' and achieving such 'relief from pain' through poetry. He mentions his own sonnets which he routinely gave to George to transcribe and preserve, saying that the fact they are read by his brother gives him greater pleasure than finding 'hidden treasure'. He brings the poem to rest in the immediate present as he describes himself 'scribbling' these lines, outdoors at Margate:

> E'en now I'm pillowed on a bed of flowers
> That crowns a lofty clift, which proudly towers
> Above the ocean-waves.

Flanked by ripe stalks of 'drooping oats', 'through which the poppies show their scarlet coats' (likened to the 'scarlet coats' of soldiers 'that pester humankind'), and facing the wide ocean with a 'canvassed ship' in view, with larks and seagulls ceaselessly flying around, he brings himself to say 'adieu' to George. The movement of this poem is comparable to Coleridge's conversation poems, which are in practical terms the same as verse epistles – from dejection through poetic reverie to warm and sociable cheerfulness – but Keats in his lines declares at least obliquely his own emerging ambition to be a public poet. He is finding his poetic voice by writing informal verse letters.

Towards the end of his stay at Margate, Keats also wrote a verse letter to his old teacher and poetic mentor from his days at Enfield. 'To Charles Cowden Clarke' is dated 'September 1816' and it is significant that these epistles were written to the two men who were most aware of Keats's interest in poetry, and his earliest admirers. As his relationship with each was different, so are the poems. With George he is intimately confiding while to Clarke he is courteous and respectful, and while the former verse letter looks to the future, the latter is retrospective. Even the opening image of the swan, which Keats had described in several poems up to now, looks back to the large pond at the Enfield school where swans nested. Keats describes them drinking, the water drops falling like diamonds in the sun, 'as though they would be free, / And drop like hours into eternity'. Apologising for not writing poems for Clarke, Keats suggests that his own 'rude' lines from his 'dull, unlearned quill' will not be adequate for the learned tutor in poetry, who is addressed as being classically trained while also appreciating and introducing to the young Keats English poets like Spenser (whose vowels 'elope with ease'), 'Miltonian tenderness', and classical legends, as well as the music of Mozart, Arne and Handel which Clarke's father had played for them. At the end of the work Keats recalls the two men walking in rustic laneways and open plains, always talking of literature and absorbed in evening conversation over supper until they need to say goodnight, as the poem does: 'Again I shake your hand – friend Charles, good night'. This verse letter, offered in gratitude to Clarke for having enthused Keats in these poets, becomes also a celebration of the writers themselves, and implicitly a declaration of his own aspirations as a writer.

Sonnets written either in Margate or shortly after, and certainly before Christmas 1816, dwell on the same legacy. 'How many bards gild the lapses of time!' ponders the rich intertextuality of poetic history brought to bear on his own attempts 'to rhyme', influences that give 'no confusion, no disturbance rude' but instead interact with sounds of nature like birds' songs, whispering of leaves, 'the voice of waters', the village bell, to 'Make pleasing music, and not wild uproar'. 'On First Looking into Chapman's Homer', recalls the spellbinding wonder he had felt when introduced to Chapman's translation of Homer, akin to the feelings of a 'watcher of the skies' seeing a new planet, or Cortez seeing the Pacific Ocean for the first time (although in fact it was Balboa, a simple historical error by Keats):

> He stared at the Pacific – and all his men
> Looked at each other with a wild surmise –
> Silent, upon a peak in Darien.

Keats considers his first taste of poetic classics to be in the same category of monumental revelation as the discovery of the Pacific Ocean, which he had read about at school in Robertson's *History of America*.[10] The sonnet was credited by Hunt and later critics with being Keats's first poem to demonstrate aspects of his own distinctive greatness, and its subject is his own wonder of 'wild surmise' on recognising the arresting merits of literature by past 'bards in fealty to Apollo', the god he chose to follow himself.

The time at Margate had one cloud over its serenity. Unknown to John, Tom began receiving and hoarding love letters purporting to be from a French woman, 'Amena Bellafilla', all of which turned out to be a practical joke played by their mutual friend Charles Wells. When John found out much later, in fact when Tom was dying, he was furious at the 'cruel deception on a sanguine Temperament' and never forgave Wells whom he described in his strongest words including 'rat'. He felt the hoax came to intensify the sufferings of his brother, and his response reveals the rage at injustice said to have characterised him as a boy at school. At Margate, however, he was unaware of any of this.

After returning from Margate Keats took lodgings at 8 Dean Street in central London, now under London Bridge Station. The plan was to share with Tom but in the event Tom was to live with George while John lived alone. Having not yet finally decided on his future, he now began studying again to qualify himself for the Royal College of Surgeons, though with reluctance. He described in a letter to Clarke how to find his room, conveying something of the seedy locality and perhaps his mood:

> Although the Borough is a beastly place in dirt, turning and windings; yet No 8 Dean Street is not difficult to find; and if you would run the Gauntlet over London Bridge, take the first turning to the left and then the first to the right and moreover knock at my door which is nearly opposite a Meeting ... (*JKL*, 1, 114)

The 'Meeting [house]' was a Baptist chapel. He did not stay long, apparently, since by November he had moved to '76 Cheapside' (*JKL*, 1, 117, fn 4). Clarke later recalled visiting often, and Keats's gratitude to him for introducing him to poetry and music is fulsomely expressed in the verse letter:

> And can I e'er these benefits forget?
> And can I e'er repay the friendly debt?
> No, doubly no –

His letter in turn sparked an even greater 'benefit' from Clarke, and one which it is no exaggeration to say was the most significant turning point in Keats's poetic career. There are references in the verse letter and elsewhere to 'Libertas' who is Leigh Hunt. With his brothers Robert and John, Hunt edited *The Examiner* from its inception in 1808 almost until its demise in 1825, and this journal had been a favourite with the Clarkes at Enfield School, where Keats also read it regularly from 1810. Its object was unashamedly radical, 'to assist in producing Reform in Parliament, liberality of opinion in general (especially freedom from superstition), and a fusion of literary taste into all subjects whatsoever'.[11] Cowden Clarke, through his father, knew Hunt as editor of *The Examiner*, and at this stage he sent the letter and two other poems by Keats to him, and managed to arrange a meeting in October 1816 at Hunt's home in the poetically but rather inappropriately named Vale of Health in Hampstead. Though almost rural the area was low-lying and marshy and still remains a prey to mosquitoes. Keats was clearly excited – ''t will be an era in my existence' he wrote to Clarke. When the time came, Horace Smith was present, a wealthy businessman but one who happened also to be a poet, and he had read aloud with approval lines from some of Keats's poems when Clarke had sent them to Hunt. Keats was predisposed to idolise Hunt because of his accomplished poetry, his political radicalism and editorship of *The Examiner*, and from now on he was to imitate some of Hunt's style in his poems. In every way, the meeting with Hunt was momentous, an occasion which Clarke later recalled as 'a "red-letter day" in the young poet's life'. The older man warmed to the younger and saw promise in his poetry. With his literary connections and influence he adopted some of the roles of a patron, in particular publishing more poems in *The Examiner* and mentioning Keats in his review of 'Young Poets'. It has been argued that Keats was 'the house poet of *The Examiner* during late 1816 and early 1817', and suddenly he found himself accepted within the Hunt circle, meeting Horace Smith, Hazlitt, Haydon and Lamb: 'he entered a world of sonnet-writing contests, of debates on religion pitting Shelley and Hunt against Haydon, of musical evenings at the Novellos' or Lambs', of political discussions involving the Shelleys, Hunt and Hazlitt, of picnics on Hampstead Heath'.[12] His dreams of a life in poetry seemed to be coming rapidly true and the decision about his future career was finally sealed.

Hunt in his later book *Lord Byron and Some of His Contemporaries* (1828) recalled that he was equally impressed by Keats's poetry and presence: 'We became intimate on the spot, and I found the young poet's heart as warm as his imagination.' They talked excitedly and read poems, and Hunt loaned Keats some books. After the first meeting, Keats several times walked the five or six miles from his room in Cheapside north to Hunt's home near Hampstead Heath, and he was clearly a welcome guest. Keats's sonnet 'On Leaving some Friends at an Early Hour' records how inspiring such meetings were to him, as host and guests composed poetry to the sound of an Aeolian harp, after which ''Tis not content so soon to be alone'. 'Keen, fitful gusts are whispering here and there' is atmospherically compelling in the contrast between the starlit walk, 'many miles on foot' in the 'cool bleak air', surrounded by the dreary rustling of dead leaves, with the hospitality when he arrived: 'For I am brimful of the friendliness / That in a little cottage I have found', as he and Hunt speak headily of Milton and Petrarch.

On at least one occasion a bed was made up for Keats on the sofa to stay overnight with the Hunts rather than walk back, an event which had a direct poetic outcome. According to Clarke it was on this night that Keats composed the basis for the longest and most ambitious poem he had yet attempted, 'Sleep and Poetry'. This is an important work in his develop-ment, since in it he not only states 'presumptuously' his ambitions in poetry but he also begins to think systematically through one of his personal 'big questions' recurring in his thinking, the various connections between pas-sive absorption ('sleep') and original creativity ('poetry'). The distinction had been hovering in his verse letters, but now is posed more consciously. 'Sleep and Poetry' was written at the same time as the equally long 'I stood tip-toe upon a little hill', and they are similarly related to each other like 'book ends' as are Milton's 'L'Allegro' and 'Il Penseroso', poems which Keats obviously admired and quotes from in his early poetry. However, the distinction between Keats's two poems is not so sharp and clear as that between Milton's. Up to a point, 'I stood tip-toe' deals, like 'L'Allegro', with 'daytime' sights of nature described with exuberant optimism, while 'Sleep and Poetry' because of its subject revolves around sleeping and has some of Milton's 'pensive' reflectiveness but not the tendency to aesthetic melan-choly. Taken together, Keats's poems are complementary attempts to explain where poetry comes from – reverie and literary influence in 'Sleep and Poetry', more directly from observed nature in 'I stood tip-toe'. The latter poem is Keats's first attempt at describing nature, inspired, so Hunt tells us (reporting a time before he actually met Keats), by 'a delightful summer-day, as [Keats] stood beside the gate that leads from the Battery on Hampstead Heath into a field by Caen Wood'.[13] The two poems contain the kind of *florilegia* which was all too easy to identify with Hunt's nature poetry, as distinct from the more ruggedly realistic variety on offer from Wordsworth, and the poem has sometimes been read as an urban, Cockney salvo against the Lake poets, 'between a pagan celebration of life and a pietistic rejection of its social and sexual pleasures'.[14] In 'I stood tip-toe' there are 'May flowers, laburnum, violets, / A filbert hedge with wild briar overtwined, / And clumps of woodbine taking the soft wind', 'ardent marigolds', 'sweet peas, on tip-toe for a flight', and evening primroses. The sight of a stream leads to thoughts of classical myths, those of Psyche and of the flower of Narcissus wooing its own image, Diana or Cynthia as the reflected moon, and by association the moon-lover, Endymion. At this stage, Keats has reached the subject which initially he intended as the centre of the poem since in a letter and in his brother Tom's transcript the poem is entitled 'Endymion'. The 'Poet' takes pity on Diana/Cynthia and gives her the mortal lover Endymion. In the event Keats stops here because already a much longer piece on this subject may have been suggesting itself to his imagination. The poem ends rather abruptly: 'Was there a Poet born? – but now, no more, / My wandering spirit must no further soar. – '

Although the charge of being over-influenced by Hunt's poetry of flowers has been repeatedly levelled at Keats, it is worth pointing out that in 'Sleep and Poetry' at least some of the plants he mentions were considered medicinal and would have been encountered in his Botany lessons and in the Chelsea Physic Garden when he was a medical student. 'Intoxication by the breath / Of flowering bays, that [he] might die a death / Of luxury...' is enhanced by the sight of narcotic poppies ('Sleep, quiet with his poppy coronet'), willows which classically were associated with death, the laurel (bay) linked with poetic fame and also known as medicinal, 'almond blossoms and rich cinnamon' which were both also used as remedies, 'bitter weeds', vine leaves and others, all sensuously described and carrying a narcotic and healing significance. 'Sleep and Poetry' begins as a celebration of the passive state of sleep but quickly moves into its real subject, poetry, and this young poet's ambitions: 'O for ten years that I may overwhelm / Myself in poesy'. Acknowledging his youth and inexperience, Keats proposes a threefold chronology which will become a repeated pattern in his thinking. First he envisages a world of innocence in nature and classical mythology, enchantment and romance, the realm of Flora and Pan. Building transience into the vision ('life is but a day') he then farewells this kind of poetry for an epic realm, 'a nobler life, / Where I may find the agonies, the strife / Of human hearts', full of 'mystery and fear' but still an essentially imaginative and poetic realm, still 'visions' observed as from a chariot. Third,

> ... in their stead
> A sense of real things comes doubly strong,
> And, like a muddy stream, would bear along
> My soul to nothingness ...

Keats then parodies and dismisses his eighteenth-century predecessors like Pope and Boileau with a sideswipe at Byron to whom these couplet-writing poets were important sources, going back for inspiration to Shakespeare's contemporaries, and reviving 'the great end / Of poesy, that it should be a friend to sooth the cares, and lift the thoughts of man' in a healing and consoling function. Through this poem Keats is partially exploring the mysterious sources of poetic inspiration, contemplating

> ... many a verse from so strange influence
> That we must ever wonder how, and whence
> It came.

One answer offered about poetic origins is that it comes from reading earlier writers, another is from observation of nature, another from sociability with other poets, 'brotherhood, / And friendliness, the nurse of mutual good', and finally, bringing the poem full circle, from the 'indolence' of the mind at rest in sleep. It is here that the poem's material scene is introduced, in which Keats lies on Hunt's couch in a room haphazardly hung with portraits of bards and paintings based on mythological subjects. Sleep is 'quiet with his poppy coronet: For what there may be worthy in these rhymes I partly owe to him', but the poem ends in the morning light after a 'sleep*less*' night of poetic composition and the poet resolves 'to begin that very day / These lines' (my italics). We end on the threshold of the poem we have just read, having traced its inception while reading its execution as a kind of dynamic thought-journey.

Keats is indeed at this point on a personal threshold, since it was during the writing of 'I stood tip-toe upon a little hill' and 'Sleep and Poetry' in October through November 1816 that he came to a momentous decision, to publish in a slim volume all the poems he had written up to this point. If by the end of 1816 there was little evidence to anticipate the emergence of a great poet, just six months later, though still with only one short poem actually published in Leigh Hunt's *Examiner* ('O Solitude! If I must with thee dwell!', published 5 May 1816), Keats was being hailed by a small coterie as a bard of the future. The sonnets 'To a Young Lady who sent me a Laurel Crown', 'On Receiving a Laurel Crown from Leigh Hunt' and 'To the Ladies who Saw Me Crowned' were to be later written almost in a spirit of some embarrassment to celebrate his first published volume of poetry when to his admirers his promise was revealed to a world which unfortunately was less enthusiastic than them. Their memories may have been blurred by the wine Hunt opened in his garden, since he claimed they garlanded each other with ivy while Keats said it was laurel. It was a scene which Keats later wished to forget.

4
'Fraternal souls' and *Poems* (1817)

Keats had a gift for friendship, and by and large his choice of friends was fortunate. Not many poets have inspired such loyalty that several hoped to be remembered as 'friends of John Keats', sometimes even nominating that the fact be recorded on their gravestones. In their turn some benefited post-humously by having their letters published in handsome, edited volumes which would never have happened to them on their own merits, while others at the very least have items in the two-volume *The Keats Circle*, edited by Hyder Edward Rollins[1] by dint of their inclusion in the collection of Keatsiana at the Houghton Library at Harvard University. Of course famous people who have died young always attract moths who claim to have been intimates, but in the case of Keats's close circle of friends the attraction was mutual and based on personal affection and 'greeting of the Spirit' (*JKL*, 1, 243) on both sides, as is amply evidenced in the letters. Keats was also, of course, a remarkable correspondent, and his letters are an irresistible part of his creative *oeuvre* alongside his poetry. Friendship was an ethic to him, and one of life's 'chief intensities':

> But there are
> Richer entanglements, enthralments far
> More self-destroying, leading, by degrees,
> To the chief intensity: the crown of these
> Is made of love and friendship, and sits high
> Upon the forehead of humanity.
> All its more ponderous and bulky worth
> Is friendship, whence there ever issues forth
> A steady splendour ...

> (*Endymion*, I, 797–805)

His magnetic aura continued even into his afterlife, since it was a mutual interest in Keats's poetry that brought together others such as two of the main 'brothers' in the Pre-Raphaelite Brotherhood, William Holman Hunt

57

and John Everett Millais, at a time in the late 1840s when Keats's work was not famous and circumstances of his life were virtually unknown to the reading public.[2]

To give details of his friends and how Keats met each would double or treble the size of this book, and their lives can be traced elsewhere, but it is at least useful to note their various linkages to each other and to Keats. Recently, attention has been paid to Romantic 'circles' of poets and their friends, and the evolution of a circle around or including Keats is of more general interest.[3] Here is a very brief chart suggesting how Keats met each person in the little gallery and whose names pepper this book, and showing that his circle spread through certain key friendships.

JOHN, GEORGE, TOM, FANNY KEATS (siblings)

ENFIELD SCHOOL
EDWARD HOLMES (school friend, musician)
WILLIAM HASLAM (school friend, solicitor)
INTRODUCED KEATS TO
JOSEPH SEVERN (artist)

CHARLES COWDEN CLARKE (Keats's tutor at Enfield School)
INTRODUCED KEATS TO
BENJAMIN HAYDON (artist) (who introduced REYNOLDS – below)
LEIGH HUNT (writer and editor)
INTRODUCED KEATS TO
WILLIAM HAZLITT (editor, essayist and failed artist)
PERCY AND MARY SHELLEY (ALSO LAMB, WORDSWORTH, COLERIDGE)
JOHN HAMILTON REYNOLDS (poet, later lawyer) (AND SISTERS)
INTRODUCED KEATS TO
CHARLES ARMITAGE BROWN (literary and music critic)
JAMES RICE JR (lawyer with Reynolds)
BENJAMIN BAILEY (clergyman)
CHARLES DILKE (clerk, editor of Elizabethan drama) (AND FAMILY)
INTRODUCED KEATS TO
FANNY BRAWNE (and family)
JOHN TAYLOR AND JAMES HESSEY (publishers)
INTRODUCED KEATS TO
RICHARD WOODHOUSE (publishers' lawyer)

Some things that clearly link many of these friends of Keats include either a middle-class profession or a connection with poetry, music, art or publishing. Apart from the high-born Shelley, they were anchored in the middle class. Given the various introductions and interconnections, they also formed a loose network which was linked in ways independently of Keats himself, mainly around the figure of Leigh Hunt. What does not meet the eye is that compatible political beliefs and ideological sympathies provided links between people then as now, and in this case they were of a dissenting, liberal and radical kind. Religion itself was not centrally relevant since Haydon and Bailey were committed Christians while Hunt, Shelley and Keats himself were atheists, but a Nonconformist family background like Hazlitt's marks some of the people Keats befriended. Some, like Haslam, Brown and Severn, became more important to Keats as time went on, but others were intimately connected with his early decision to become a poet, to the extent, as Jeffrey N. Cox argues in detail, that he was a poet in a close coterie of like-minded 'Cockney' writers and artists[4] who self-consciously defined themselves against the Lake District poets around Wordsworth.[5]

At the centre of the somewhat bohemian coterie, and undoubtedly the person most useful to Keats's poetic career, was Leigh Hunt, a figure controversial in his own time and neglected ever since until recently, most comprehensively revalued by Nicholas Roe in *Fiery Heart: The First Life of Leigh Hunt*.[6] The connection was to become a mixed blessing for Keats because of Hunt's radical beliefs and also, at least arguably, because of his poetic style and taste which influenced the young Keats. In fact these two aspects of Hunt's makeup were at face value in some contradiction. His political stance was consistently anti-authoritarian as he was republican and pacifist (at a time when England was a monarchy and at war with France from 1803 until 1815) and liberal on virtually all issues, espousing anti-slavery, prison reform, abolition of child labour, liberty of the press, and many other such causes. But little of this can be discerned in most of his poetry which is focused on nature aesthetically idealised by an urban dweller, unlike the genuinely rustic farm labourer John Clare. Hunt may have deliberately avoided politics in his poetry, apart from some works like the allegorical, anti-war ballad *Captain Pen and Captain Sword*,[7] as part of a conscious aesthetic principle, since he viewed poetry as a vehicle for bettering mankind by turning attention away from social inequities and towards a love of the natural world,[8] an attitude that could easily be mistaken for escapism if one does not acknowledge Hunt's personal courage in the face of political hostility. It was a philosophical conviction that he pithily encapsulated when he quoted an excerpt from Keats's poetry, adding himself the title 'HAPPY POETRY PREFERRED'.[9] We can detect the same impulse at work when Hunt redecorated his prison cell to resemble his home in Hampstead, full of books, pictures and trellises of flowers. In some ways Hunt's aesthetic stance prefigures Oscar Wilde's, since it is as difficult to see in a single glance the latter writer's beleaguered life, the social wit of his plays and his epigrams, and *The Soul of Man under Socialism*. Keats, as a former medical student, could not forget or bring himself to ignore suffering and the healer's vocation and from his early poetry onwards builds in these perspectives, even when his choice of poetic vocabulary and imagery resembles Hunt's. However, Hunt could claim that he was the first to bring Keats's poetry to public attention, publishing in *The Examiner* the sonnet 'To Solitude' before he had met the poet, and later in his articles advancing claims to Keats's poetic abilities, confident of his future fame. He was thereafter to publish several of Keats's shorter poems, and to champion his cause consistently. Hunt was loyal to his protégés, even when they periodically became disenchanted with him.

Hunt linked three men as the major 'Young Poets' in 'a new school of poetry rising of late', 'its only object being to restore the same love of nature, and of *thinking* instead of mere *talking*', contrasting them to eighteenth-century 'versifying wits' whom he sees as mere 'bead-rollers of couplets'.[10] After praising the 'candour' of Byron in *Childe Harolde*, Hunt advocates the merits of Shelley, Keats and Reynolds. Shelley had published *Alastor, or the Spirit of Solitude* while Keats had published nothing except 'O solitude!' to be followed by 'On First Looking into Chapman's Homer'. Reynolds had recently published his second volume, whose central poem was *The Naiad*. It is difficult now to see how Hunt grouped Reynolds with Shelley and Keats, until we realise that he was looking for a certain kind of poetry delivered by this 'very true and amiable' young man. Reynolds did publish several volumes in his rather brief career as a poet, but most of his work was derivative and repetitious.[11] In 1817 and 1818 he was a close confidant and the recipient of some of Keats's most playful letters. He was a central presence in Keats's growing network of friends, having known since 1816 Hunt and Haydon, Bailey and Rice, Keats's future publishers Taylor and Hessey, and even Lamb and Hazlitt. Whereas Cowden Clarke, Hunt and the painter Haydon were all about ten years older than Keats, Reynolds was the same age (born 1794) and Keats could write to him more familiarly and without the hint of deference he reserved for the others. They became the closest of friends and Reynolds's four sisters were part of the circle that met and swapped letters and poems. The two men had much in common in their indebtedness to Hunt and in their poetry, and Reynolds was also a self-styled political radical and Unitarian. No doubt partly due to Hunt's praise, Reynolds rapidly became well known for his poetry, publishing several volumes of poetry between 1814 and 1825. Most were romances but he became instantly known for a satire, *Peter Bell: A Lyrical Ballad* which parodied Wordsworth even before that writer's poem of the same name had been published and led to others such as Shelley's *Peter Bell the Third*. However, Reynolds's career as a poet was truncated by the need to earn money after he had become engaged to a relative of James Rice, and he joined Rice as a lawyer. By 1825, having given up his job as a clerk to become a poet, and now without patronage or private income, he accepted his limitations and turned to law as a career (which also failed to give him a reliable income) and later became a disgruntled clerk on the Isle of Wight.[12] He described himself as suffering from 'melancholy imprudences' and he dwindled into obscurity in the years after Keats died, finally drinking himself to death. On his death in 1852 Reynolds's tombstone immortalised him as 'the friend of Keats'.

Interestingly, Keats always remained reserved about Hunt's third 'young poet', Shelley, partly one feels because of class differences between the two but also perhaps because Keats was conscious that his own poetic gifts could be inhibited by Shelley's presence. Shelley was only three years older than Keats but this can be a significant gap between people in their early twenties, and since he had begun writing and publishing at an earlier age, in particular *Alastor, Or the Spirit of Solitude*, he already had a mantle of professional seniority. His aristocratic background, privileged education at Eton and Oxford, and scandalous reputation after being expelled from Oxford for publishing a pamphlet espousing atheism, must have been somewhat intimidating to the more cautious and inexperienced Keats. Shelley, even at the age of 25, was already a man with a past: disinherited from a fortune and disgraced by his public atheism and political radicalism which attracted the surveillance of British government spies, married already twice – first to the 16-year-old Harriet Westbrook who committed suicide after he abandoned her to elope with Mary, in her turn daughter of the anarchist philosopher William Godwin, whom Keats met at least once and who somehow brooded in the background behind all the Romantic poets, and the equally formidable Mary Wollstonecraft, author of *A Vindication of the Rights of Women*. In early 1817 Keats dined several times with Percy and Mary Shelley, but he always showed signs of reticence in their company.

Another older and even more famous figure in the group was the musician Vincent Novello, whose daughter Mary Victoria was to marry Charles Cowden Clarke in 1826. She was only 8 at the time of Hunt's *soirées*, but many years later she was to reminisce about the musical evenings which included Keats, whom she unforgettably describes as 'with his picturesque head, leaning against the instrument [piano] one foot raised on his knee and smoothed beneath his hands'.[13] Charles Lamb was a member of the set and he was later to describe the musical parties too. Keats came to tire of their company later as he periodically retreated from Leigh Hunt, but undoubtedly these social gatherings of poets, artists and musicians, all linked in political sympathies around the figure of Hunt, were crucial in his intellectual and artistic development.

The friend apart from Hunt and Reynolds, who undoubtedly encouraged Keats to think of publishing his poems in a volume, was the artist Benjamin Haydon. However, two more different personalities than Hunt's and Haydon's could hardly be imagined, which points to another distinctive characteristic in Keats's friendships. He had a quality which increasingly came to intrigue even himself, the capacity to annul his own personal biases of identity and instead to appreciate people, books and experiences for their own sometimes contradictory sakes. In terms of writing he came to associate this quality with Shakespeare, dubbing it 'Negative Capability' in a much-discussed passage from a letter to his brothers Tom and George in December 1817:

> several things dovetailed in my mind, & at once it struck me, what qual-
> ity went to form a Man of Achievement especially in Literature & which
> Shakespeare possessed so enormously – I mean *Negative Capability*, that is
> when man is capable of being in uncertainties, Mysteries, doubts, with-
> out any irritable reaching after fact & reason – Coleridge, for instance,
> would let go by a fine isolated verisimilitude caught from the Penetralium
> of mystery, from being incapable of remaining content with half
> knowledge. (*JKL*, 1, 193–4)

He wrote in more detail about this to Richard Woodhouse, lawyer to Taylor and Hessey's publishing firm, one of Keats's most generous benefactors, and the one who recorded meticulously copies of his poems and recollections of conversations:

> As to the poetical Character itself, (I mean that sort of which, if I am any
> thing, I am a Member; that sort distinguished from the wordsworthian
> or egotistical sublime; which is a thing per se and stands alone) it is not
> itself – it has no self – it is every thing and nothing – It has no character –
> it enjoys light and shade; it lives in gusto, be it foul or fair, high or low,
> rich or poor, mean or elevated – It has as much delight in conceiving an
> Iago as an Imogen. What shocks the virtuous philosop[h]er, delights the
> camelion Poet. It does no harm from its relish of the dark side of things
> any more than from its taste for the bright one; because they both end
> in speculation. A poet is the most unpoetical of any thing in existence;
> because he has no Identity – he is continually in for – and filling some
> other Body – The Sun, the Moon, the Sea and Men and Women who
> are creatures of impulse are poetical and have about them an unchange-
> able attribute – the poet has none; no identity – he is certainly the most
> unpoetical of all God's Crertures. (*JKL*, 1, 387)

He speaks of how 'When in a room with People if I ever am free from specu-
lating on creations of my own brain, then not myself goes home to myself:
but the identity of every one in the room begins to press upon me that, I am
in a very little time annihilated', and Woodhouse recalls how Keats speaks of
being 'annihilated' even by a physical object like a billiard ball in motion,
'that it may have a sense of delight from its own roundness, smoothness
<& very> volubility. & the rapidity of its motion. –' (*JKL*, 1, 389). Whether
'Negative Capability' is primarily to be described 'negatively' as porous
impressionability, or positively as a non-judgmental magnanimity holding
in suspension a wide tolerance for differences, Keats feels it is congenital to
him and sometimes socially paralysing. He found the concept, if not the terminology, in Hazlitt's Shakespearian criticism as is evident from his linking

it with 'gusto' and with Shakespeare's morally paradoxical characters, but adapted it to his own unique perceptions. While it may have been a distinctive strength in writing creatively, it could also be a social handicap, and Keats was to lament his presumed inability to project a positive self-image and his high threshold for ambiguity, especially when in female company. However, we should qualify this by saying that in reality he could assert a strong personality when he felt confident, and that the quality he describes is not the whole story.

With an indomitable self-belief, Haydon was the temperamental opposite of Keats in this regard. A largely self-taught painter of monumental pictures on historical and religious subjects, he was dogmatically Christian, enormously egotistical, quarrelsome, and constantly alienating friends, including Keats himself later in the relationship, by asking them for money which he unashamedly would not be able to repay. It is a mark of his self-absorbed narcissism that his published works include a journal, a memoir, his autobiography, his own correspondence with Elizabeth Barrett Browning, and highly opinionated lectures on painting, all of which run to many volumes. His enthusiastic nature led Haydon by turns to hero-worship and denigrate the people who could, generally speaking, be described as his friends, tendencies reflected in many passages like this one:

> [Hazlitt] with his fine candour his consciousness of never shaving, & dirty linen, his frank avowal of his vices and follies, his anti-Bourbon thoroughbred noble hatred, his Napoleon adhesiveness, his paradoxical puttings forth at so much a sheet, his believing himself the fine metaphysical caustic philosopher, going about like Diogenes with a lantern, impaling all his acquaintances while he himself is the most impaled of the whole is worth ten thousand Wordsworths, and has more real virtue too at the bottom ... Wordsworth's face always puts me in mind when he laughs as if he was an old satyr who had suddenly been transformed into a Lake Poet – there is something so lecherous, animal & devouring lurking in those wrinkles & straggling decayed teeth – depend on it he is an old beast, cloked in piety and verse.[14]

It is not surprising that at the best of times Haydon was an unreliable friend to others in Keats's circle such as Hunt. Keats mostly kept on his good side since from the time he first met Haydon in late 1816 he realised that the volcanic painter invited and even required sycophancy. Keats was also genuinely elated at the man's indomitable energy and ambitiousness and found himself 'wrought ... up' enough to write and send to him the sonnet 'Great Spirits now on earth are sojourning'. This poem links together in fame Wordsworth, Hunt and Haydon himself as people about whom Keats advises the world, 'Listen awhile ye Nations and be dumb!' (copies sent 20 and 21 November 1816). Haydon was so impressed (and probably more pertinently,

flattered) that he offered to send it to Wordsworth. This he did after procras-
tinating a month, and Wordsworth loftily pronounced that the sonnet was
'assuredly vigorously conceived and well expressed'.[15] Their mutual friend
Reynolds, also inspired by Haydon's 'Genius', sent a sonnet beginning with
even more extravagant praise, 'Haydon! – Thour't born to Immortality! –'.[16]
Haydon in turn returned the compliments to both Reynolds and Keats,
and to the latter he wrote 'I have read your Sleep & Poetry – it is a flash
of light[e]ning that will sound men from their occupations, and keep the
trembling for the crash of thunder that *will* follow.' An enthusiastic amateur
phrenologist he paid the young poet the compliment of taking his life mask
in plaster as early as 1816, though even this would have been an ambiguous
experience since other models similarly honoured complained of the sheer
discomfort involved.

Keats and his circle were to use the tradition of the sonnet with a new
function, to celebrate sociability and friendship, and Keats seems to do so
consciously with an original insight into what he sees as the form's potential
raison d'être. He regards the sonnet not as a vehicle for personal expression
of praise or love as it had been in its Petrarchan heyday but as above all an
exercise in poetic form and control which can reflect the tight-knit structure of a circle of friends. He peels away the Renaissance layer of fictiveness
implicit in the structure of a sequence based on personae or characters, and
instead draws attention to the sonnet as a technical manipulation of rhymes
and organisational rules:

> I have been endeavouring to discover a better sonnet stanza than we
> have. The legitimate [Petrarchan] does not suit the language over-well
> from the pouncing rhymes – the other kind [Shakespearian] appears too
> elegiac – and the couplet at the end of it seldom has a pleasing effect –
> I do not pretend to have succeeded – it will explain itself. (*JKL*, 2, 108)

These comments come much later than the sonnets in the 1817 volume
(probably April 1819), but they extend the practice of the earlier sonnets.
The poem which 'will explain itself' is a sonnet about the sonnet, but its gist
leads us back to the idea of the form as one which is not only technical but
which intrinsically demands above all a facility in the linking qualities of
rhyme which, by analogy, stands in Keats's mind for social links in a friendly
world. We can see from the whole spirit of his letters that he 'rhymes' his
friends together, that he works hard at creating harmonious, sociable relationships, with as much care as he makes a sonnet, and in one example he
contemplates what he is doing:

> If by dull rhymes our English must be chained,
> And, like Andromeda, the Sonnet sweet
> Fettered, in spite of pained loveliness,

> Let us find out, if we must be constrained,
> Sandals more interwoven and complete
> To fit the naked foot of Poesy:
> Let us inspect the lyre, and weigh the stress
> Of every chord, and see what may be gained
> By ear industrious, and attention meet;
> Misers of sound and syllable, no less
> Than Midas of his coinage, let us be
> Jealous of dead leaves in the bay wreath crown;
> So, if we may not let the Muse be free,
> She will be bound with garlands of her own.

The rhyme scheme tended with 'ear industrious' adopted here by Keats (abcabd cab cdede with the final e a half rhyme) is certainly more elaborate and arguably more 'interwoven' than the earlier forms used by Sidney, Spenser, Shakespeare and Milton. By making its subject the very formalities of a rhyme scheme, Keats eliminates the emotional subjectivity which was, at least ostensibly, the main burden of Renaissance sonnets. He draws attention to the fact that such an impression of inwardness was always a façade behind which the technically accomplished and calculating poet was showing off to fellow practitioners his skill in manipulating sound and syllable. By making the problems in writing sonnets into the very subject, Keats frees himself to devote its undoubted strengths to the area where he considered it most appropriate – the expression of social unity. Even the convivial plural 'we' and 'us' replace the traditional 'I' of an impassioned persona.

Keats, Haydon, Hunt, Clarke and Reynolds were meeting regularly in early 1817 and writing often to each other. Haydon fostered Keats's interest in the pictorial arts, and walked him around galleries. They looked together at the Elgin Marbles which had been taken from the Parthenon by Lord Elgin, British ambassador to the Ottoman Empire when Athens was under Turkish administration. After he sold the fragmented reliefs to the British Museum, the British parliament voted in 1816 to buy them for the nation. To this day Greece has continued to demand back the frieze, and the dispute about the legality of their being owned by Britain has flared up again as I write. Haydon championed England's claim and Keats wrote a sonnet dedicated to him:

> My spirit is too weak; mortality
> Weighs heavily on me like unwilling sleep,
> And each imagined pinnacle and steep
> Of godlike hardship tells me I must die
> Like a sick eagle looking at the sky.
> Yet 'tis a gentle luxury to weep,
> That I have not the cloudy winds to keep

> Fresh for the opening of the morning's eye.
> Such dim-conceived glories of the brain
> Bring round the heart an indescribable feud;
> So do these wonders a most dizzy pain,
> That mingles Grecian grandeur with the rude
> Wasting of old Time – with a billowy main,
> A sun, a shadow of a magnitude.

A strong argument existed even then that they had been stolen from the Parthenon by Lord Elgin. Hunt for one argued this, disagreeing publicly with Haydon, and so did Hazlitt and Byron, all of which tested Keats's loyalties and perhaps accounts for a note of uneasiness in his phrase 'dizzy pain'.[17] Generally speaking, however, the main subject of the sonnet is not the work itself but Keats's own sense of being overwhelmed in the presence of such antique and awesome art and the feeling of inadequacy stirred in him.

Pictorial art provided a link through Keats between Haydon and Hazlitt. Keats and Haydon dined together in December 1817 to discuss the painting *Death on the Pale Horse* by Benjamin West who was an American and president of the Royal Academy with which Haydon had a typically adversarial involvement. Keats famously commented to his brothers:

> It is a wonderful picture, when West's age is considered; But there is nothing to be intense upon; no women one feels mad to kiss; no face swelling into reality. The excellence of every Art is its intensity, capable of making all disagreeables evaporate, from their being in close relationship with Beauty & Truth. (*JKL*, 1, 192)

Each of the terms in this quotation – 'intensity', 'disagreeables', 'Beauty & Truth' – is loaded with personal significance for Keats, but in origin they are not his own vocabulary as touchstones or 'provings' in literature and art. The criticism of West's picture, like much of Keats's aesthetic theory embedded in his letters, is influenced by an article in the *Edinburgh Magazine* by William Hazlitt, another man older than Keats (by seventeen years). He later became Keats's friend and mentor, although as an intellectual loner he was less easy to become intimate with than the gregarious and affable Hunt, and his saturnine presence had struck Coleridge as 'brow-hanging, shoe-contemplative, *strange*'. Hazlitt's ideas, bluntly expressed in his vigorous prose, particularly about a philosophy on which he had written at school concerning 'the natural disinterestedness of the human mind', about the politics of republicanism, poetic identity in general, and Shakespeare in particular, were to become increasingly influential in the poet's maturing thought.[18] Keats regularly attended Hazlitt's various series of lectures at the Surrey Institution and the two men were introduced by Hunt in the winter of 1816–17. Hazlitt was another republican and radical thinker, and a dissenter if not atheist, and his abrasively expressed and penetrating views became more important to Keats as the influence of Hunt waned. He was a painter *manqué* and the pictorial capacities of language, coloured by the imagination and passions and by a strong emphasis on contrast, are central to his notions of 'gusto' in art, 'power or passion defining any object ... some precise association with pleasure or pain'.[19] The importance of artists to Keats extended past his lifetime friends and into the future, since the Pre-Raphaelite painters were to be mainly responsible for initiating a true posthumous life for the poet.[20]

If Coleridge regarded Hazlitt as 'strange', so he himself appeared to Keats when he later met the by now venerable poet walking with Keats's 'Demonstrator at Guy's', Joseph Henry Green, in a laneway leading towards Highgate in April 1819. Keats's good-natured but slightly baffled description reveals his ambivalence about Coleridge who, though known as a brilliant conversationalist, could also be an insensitive listener and oblique in his association of ideas:

> I walked with him a[t] his alderman-after dinner pace for near two miles I suppose In those two Miles he broached a thousand things – let me see if I can give you a list – Nightingales, Poetry – on Poetical sensation – Metaphysics – Different genera and species of Dreams – Nightmare – a dream accompanied by a sense of touch – single and double touch – A dream related – first and second consciousness – the difference explained between will and Volition – so my metaphysicians from a want of smoking the second consciousness – Monsters – the Kraken – Mermaids – southey believes in them – southeys belief too much diluted – A Ghost story – Good morning – I heard his voice as he came towards me – I heard it as he moved away – I had heard it all the interval – if it may be called so. He was civil enough to ask me to call on him at Highgate Good Night! (*JKL*, 2, 88–9)

Keats's snapshot of the poet and his tumbling ideas comically captures much about Coleridge's self-centredness but also his generous and probably intuitive sense of what would in fact interest Keats, such as nightingales, dreams and 'a dream accompanied by a sense of touch' in particular, all of which occur in Keats's poetry.

It was undoubtedly the united encouragement of Clarke, Hunt, Haydon and Reynolds that helped to steer Keats's resolution towards his new vocation of poetry. Hunt even arranged for a friend, Charles Ollier, who was a musician and poet but had recently decided to join with his brother James in book publishing, to print a first collection of the poems Keats had written up to this point. Thus was born the project of publishing *Poems* (1817). The only one who advised against publishing too early in his career was

Shelley, in conversation during a walk on Hampstead Heath which Keats was to recall years later. In some ways his warning proved to be prophetic, although the volume when it appeared initially met not so much with hostility as deafening silence.

Poems by John Keats was published by C. and J. Ollier on or around 3 March 1817 (the day on which his appointment as surgeon at Guy's Hospital officially ended), or perhaps 7 March or 10 March. John Barnard has exhaustively analysed the evidence of the much-disputed date and circumstances of publication,[21] but the debates may be largely academic since, as any author knows, the actual 'publication date' often bears little resemblance to the day when a volume is made available in printed form to either the author or the public. The volume's title page shows the profile of a rather porcine and garlanded poet who may be either Spenser or Shakespeare (based on the famous image of the bust in Holy Trinity Church, Stratford),[22] bearing an epigraph from Spenser's *Muiopotmos* or 'Fate of the Butterfly': 'What more felicity can fall to creature, / Than to enjoy delight with liberty'. Ominously, Spenser's Elizabethan allegory had told the story of the butterfly, a high-flying Elizabethan courtier (Sir Walter Raleigh?) who is entrapped and destroyed by a sinister spider (perhaps Sir William Cecil?). A similar fate awaited the unsuspecting and ambitious Keats.

Keats's volume contained many of the poems which have been mentioned so far in this biography. Here are the contents:

Dedication. To Leigh Hunt
I stood tip-toe upon a little hill
Specimen of an Induction to a Poem
Calidore. A Fragment
To Some Ladies
On receiving a curious Shell, and a copy of Verses, from the same Ladies
To **** [Georgiana Augusta Wylie, afterwards Mrs George Keats]
To Hope
Imitation of Spenser
'Woman! When I behold thee flippant, vain'

Epistles
To George Felton Mathew
To my Brother George
To Charles Cowden Clarke

Sonnets
I.   To my Brother George
II.   To * * * * * * ['Had I a man's fair form']
III. Written on the day that Mr Leigh Hunt left Prison
IV.   'How many bards gild the lapses of time'

Sleep and Poetry

Before too roundly condemning a lack of taste in the general public of the day, we should reflect that even the most ardent lovers of Keats nowadays see most of these poems as promising things to come rather than marked by demonstrated poetic genius. Pressed to list the twenty or so poems on which Keats's reputation is built, probably few would include any of those published in *Poems*, except perhaps 'Chapman's Homer'. Despite his friends' high hopes of literary fame for him the little volume sank into almost complete obscurity, apart from an anonymous, rave review (in fact by Reynolds) in the *Champion* which placed Keats in the company of Shakespeare and Chaucer, and an anonymous, appreciative review in fact written by Leigh Hunt in *The Examiner*.[23] In *Eclectic Review* the editor (Joseph Conder, though the review is unsigned) damns with faint praise, hoping his stern criticism will be accepted as constructive by a young author 'capable of writing good poetry' (*Heritage*, 67). However, one review was especially ominous, an unsigned and unattributable piece in October 1817 in the *Edinburgh Magazine, and Literary Miscellany (Scots Magazine)*. The anonymous reviewer sees some merit in Keats's poems and is in fact quite complimentary, but menacingly confesses that he knows nothing of the 'very young man' except that he is 'a particular friend of the Messrs Hunt, the editors of *The Examiner*, and of Mr Hazlitt', which damns him for the company he keeps: 'If Mr Keats does not forthwith cast off the uncleanness of this school, he will never make his way to the truest strain of poetry in which, taking him by himself, it appears he might succeed.' The 'school', already dubbed Cockney, he says, is one of 'sickly refinement' whose subjects 'shew ingenuity, even though they be perverse, or common, or contemptuous'.[24] The reviewer in a coyly oblique way identifies the connection with Hunt as a liability, although at this stage Keats himself is seen to be not dangerous but young and corrigible. The impression created is that he may 'grow up' if he can shake off these dangerous influences. This journal should not be confused with the more influential *Edinburgh Review* whose inclinations to the Whig cause should have predisposed the editor, Francis Jeffrey, to the Hunt circle. Inexplicably, Jeffrey remained silent on all Keats's poems for several years until at last, in Keats's final twelve months and largely at Reynolds's prompting because the poet was clearly very ill by then,[25] he did write an appreciative piece. Given his status as a reviewer this would have helped Keats's reputation if it had come at the time of publication, but better late than never.

Beyond the minimal notices, for many years much of the stock remained unsold. Clarke, writing many years later, describes the book's lack of public reception:

> The first volume of Keats's minor muse was launched amid the cheers and fond anticipations of all his circle. Every one of us expected (and not unreasonably) that it would create a sensation in the literary world; for such a first production (and a considerable portion of it from a minor) has rarely occurred. The three Epistles and the seventeen sonnets (that upon 'first looking into Chapman's Homer' one of them) would have ensured a rousing welcome from our modern-day reviewers. Alas! The book might have emerged in Timbuctoo with far stronger chance of fame and approbation. It never passed to a second edition; the first was but a small one, and that was never sold off. The whole community, as if by compact, seemed determined to know nothing about it. (CCC, 140)

Clarke explained the failure on political grounds: 'the word had been passed that its author was a Radical'. The association with Leigh Hunt is brought into high relief by the first sonnet which is named a 'Dedication' to him ('Glory and loveliness have passed away'), and by inclusion of 'Written on the Day that Mr Leigh Hunt left Prison', while the general style of 'Sleep and Poetry' and 'I stood tip-toe upon a little hill' owes quite a lot to Hunt's 'flowery' language. However, direct statements on political events of the day do not loom large, and although Keats was to say later, 'I feel confident I should have been a rebel Angel had the opportunity been mine' (*JKL*, 1, 142), the poetry is cautious overall and only occasionally political in the sense that, say, much of Shelley's is. Keats himself was often to acknowledge his poetic double-sidedness as something of a literary conservative looking back to the Elizabethans and writing on classical myths, while also being a radical in terms of contemporary politics: 'Notwithstand my aristocratic temper ... I hope sincerely I shall be able to put a Mite of help to the Liberal side of the Question before I die' (*JKL*, 2, 180). For example, the sonnet 'To Kosciusko' is a paean to one of Hunt's (as well as Astley Cooper's) heroes, the Pole who represented for English liberals an ideal type of a revolutionary, since he fought in the American War of Independence and played a leading part in the Polish rising against Russia. However, the poem does not detail Kosciusko's revolutionary actions, but dwells on the man as hero-figure, inspiration and visionary, concerns that spoke from 'the aristocratic temper'. 'The loud hymn, that sounds far, far away' which is given 'tremendous birth' by his name must gesture towards freedom through revolution, although Keats does not openly say how. At this stage the lack of attention paid to his poems may have indicated simply critical indifference to a volume which, although judged with hindsight shows the seeds of what was to come, must have appeared slight and lightweight beside the established heavyweights among the older Romantics, Wordsworth, Coleridge and Southey, each of whom had retreated from their younger, radical views into conservatism, much to the disgust of Hazlitt in particular. More inexplicably to modern eyes, Keats's poems were eclipsed even by those of 'Barry Cornwall' (pseudonym for the lawyer Bryan Waller Procter) who was also in the 'Hunt stable' yet fashionably popular at the time.[26]

Meanwhile, the baleful opinion of Keats's disapproving guardian, Abbey, seemed to have been vindicated, that the young man who had already spent lavishly from his inheritance on a medical training which he seemed to be foolishly abandoning, was now wasting more money on living expenses in pursuing an ill-advised, youthful obsession with becoming a poet instead of even improving his qualifications as a surgeon let alone becoming a respectable tradesman like himself. Abbey denounced the young man as 'mad' and 'a Silly Boy', darkly prognosticating failure in the 'inconsiderate Enterprise'. John Barnard has argued that Keats had actually paid a sum up to £50 for the Olliers to publish the book 'on commission', which would have further eroded his inheritance and not returned anywhere near the expected profit. This mode of publishing a first volume was not unusual – Shelley, in fact, never managed to persuade publishers to risk their own money on his books – but it was another sign in Abbey's eyes of the young man's financial imprudence and recklessness. Barnard concludes: 'Keats was an altogether more driven man than previously realized, one prepared to borrow against his future expectations to gamble on a successful entry into the literary world.'[27]

This may be a little uncharitable because it looks certain that Keats, a naturally diffident character, was persuasively encouraged by the famous Hunt and Haydon and also by the published poet Reynolds. Naturally he was disappointed at the lack of success, lamenting that *Poems* 'was read by some dozen of my friends who lik'd it; and some dozen who I was unacquainted with who did not', and the former group must have included the recipients of seventeen presentation copies he gave away. Wordsworth, to whom Keats sent a copy inscribed 'in reverence', was to his dying day to leave most of the pages uncut. Even the publishers disowned *Poems* just a month later. James Ollier wrote to George Keats admitting, 'We regret that your brother ever requested us to publish his book' and 'declining any further connexion with it':

By far the greater number of persons who have purchased it from us have found fault with it in such plain terms, that we have in many cases offered to take the book back rather than be annoyed with the ridicule which has, time after time, been showered upon it.[28]

However, one auspicious sign came a month later, when Messrs Taylor and Hessey, publishers of Reynolds's well-received *The Naiad*, resolved to publish future works by Keats. The reasons are obscure but John Taylor in particular emerges as a good shepherd to writers who were misunderstood and 'high-risk low-profit' (in the words of Barry Symonds in the *Oxford Dictionary of National Biography*), since he was not only to prove an assiduous, if sometimes insensitive, editor to Keats but also to the equally controversial Hazlitt (who often ungratefully but characteristically argued with him) as well as a personal friend and saviour to John Clare whose *Poems Descriptive of Rural Life and Scenery* appeared a few months before Keats's third volume in 1820.[29] However the idea came about, on 15 April 1817, a month after the publication of *Poems*, Taylor wrote informing his father of a formal agreement with Keats to publish future volumes at the publishers' risk:

We have agreed for the Next Edit. of Keats's Poems, and are to have the Refusal of his future Works. I cannot think he will fail to become a great Poet, though I agree with you in finding much fault with his Dedication &c. These are not likely to appear in any other of his Productions. (*JKL*, 1, 127, fn)

The 'Dedication &c' refer to the overt links with Leigh Hunt. On 12 or 13 April 1817 Keats had written briefly on a 'scrap' of paper to Taylor and Hessey thanking them for their 'kindness' in inviting him to discuss the project. This, and his friends' staunch support, launched him on his next bold project, a resolution to leap 'headlong into the Sea' to write and publish, 'a huge attempt', a poem the length of an epic.

5

'That which is creative must create itself': 1817 and *Endymion*

Keats was living with his brothers, 'in apartments' as Cowden Clarke describes them, 'on the second floor of a house in the Poultry, over the passage leading to the Queen's Head Tavern, and opposite to one of the City Companies' halls – the Ironmongers', if I mistake not' (CCC, 137). In his letter to Taylor and Hessey, Keats says he will 'steal out of town in a day or two', and just three days later on 15 April we find him writing back to his brothers from Southampton. George and Tom had suggested he should travel ('anxious that I shod go by myself into the country' [*JKL*, 1, 125]), and we do not know whether this was to give him a rest and a change after the excitement of the book's publication or because he had become insufferable as a result, for which there is some evidence. He chose the Isle of Wight which was starting to become a holiday destination for writers with the visit of Jane Austen in June 1813. Dickens, Tennyson and Longfellow were to follow later. The trip is fortunate for us since it marks the time when Keats began writing regular long letters to friends and family or rather, this marks the time when they began to keep his letters so that we can still read them today.

The letters are not only biographically invaluable but also elevate his correspondence into an extraordinary contribution to the genre of letter-writing, placing him close to the top in this pantheon, valued for wisdom and wit, tumbling with perceptions that generate ideas, puns that turn into poetry, playfulness that suddenly turns serious and flies off again into digressions, concern for others mingled with indignant commentary on topical political issues, self-ridiculing modesty interspersed with claims to future greatness, obsessive myopia alternating with magnanimous curiosity. To save paper it was customary to 'cross' letters – to write on one sheet then turn it sideways and write over – and Keats turns this habit into a metaphor for the ensuing richness of the content:

> If I scribble long letters I must play my vagaries. I must be too heavy, or too light, for whole pages – I must be quaint and free of Tropes and

figures – I must play my draughts as I please ... This crossing a letter is not without its association – for chequer work leads us naturally to a Milkmaid, a Milkmaid to Hogarth Hogarth to Shakespeare Shakspear to Hazlitt – Hazlitt to Shakespeare and thus by merely pulling an apron string we set a pretty peal of Chimes at work – Let them chime on ... (*JKL*, 1, 279–80)

Infectious associations of words and thoughts drive the letters energetically forwards while often holding in tow an underlying, developed argument that sometimes can snap shut like a 'rat trap' in a conclusion, but more often fan outwards into yet more fertile possibilities. What every subsequent reader has noticed is the way Keats adapts his tone and substance to the personality of the recipient although the letters are also a vehicle for intimate self-representation, and even performance when he can dramatise or describe himself in a situation:[1]

the candles are burnt down and I am using the wax taper – which has a long snuff on it – the fire is at its last click – I am sitting with my back to it with one foot rather askew upon the rug and the other with the heel a little elevated from the carpet – I am writing this on the Maid's tragedy which I have read since tea with Great pleasure ... Could I see the same thing done of any great Man long since dead it would be a great delight: as to know in what position Shakspeare sat when he began 'To be or not to be' – such thing[s] become interesting from distance of time or place. (*JKL*, 2, 73)

This *bravura* passage written to his brother and sister-in-law in America continues equally characteristically in solicitude for them, imagining their own situation in the vein of a goodnight lullaby:

I hope you are both now in that sweet sleep which no two beings deserve more tha[n] you do – I must fancy you so – and please myself in the fancy of speaking a prayer and a blessing over you and your lives – God bless you – I whisper good night in your ears and you will dream of me –

An unselfconsciously irrepressible style is uppermost in the letter describing his holiday, breaking through in the breathless and cryptic snapshots from the overnight stage-coach journey from London to Southampton:

As the Lamplight crept along the following things were discovered – 'long heath broom furze' – Hurdles here and there half a Mile – Park palings when the Windows of a House were always discovered by reflection – One

Nymph of Fountain – *N.B.* – lopped Trees – Cow ruminating – ditto Donkey – Man and Woman going gingerly along – William seeing his Sisters over the Heath – John waiting with a Lanthen for his Mistress – Barber's Pole – Doctor's Shop – However after having had my fill of these I popped my Head out just as it began to Dawn ... (*JKL*, 1, 128)

The letter announces also his current saturation in Shakespeare's words since he quotes fleetingly from *The Tempest*, *The Two Gentlemen of Verona* and *A Midsummer Night's Dream* and describes feeling lonely at breakfast and 'unboxing' a volume of Shakespeare's works (the Johnson-Steevens multi-volume 'pocket-sized' series), exclaiming from *The Tempest* '"there's my Comfort"'. In Southampton he observes whimsically that 'the Men and Women do not materially differ from those I have been in the Habit of seeing' and that the tide-line was 'no better than a low Water ... it will have mended its Manners by 3'. On 17 April he had reached Carisbrooke on the Isle of Wight from where he wrote to Reynolds. At the guest house he found a portrait of Shakespeare which he thought auspicious and hung on the wall. He describes Shanklin where he had landed and debates whether he should stay there for its beauty and for the sea or inland at Carisbrooke because it is cheaper and has the ruins of Carisbrooke Castle whose ivy and jackdaws Keats describes. It has 'delightful' woodlands: '– As for Primroses – the Island ought to be called Primrose Island: that is, if the nation of Cowslips agree thereto ...' (*JKL*, 1, 131). The town is also central enough for Keats to explore the island in all directions, which he proceeds to do. He sees army barracks which disgust him 'extremely with Government for placing such a Nest of Debauchery in so beautiful a place', and finds scratched on a window in a room at Newport, '"O Isle spoilt by the Mil*a*tary"', reminding us of the recent war against France which had been the public backdrop of Keats's youthful years. When writing to Reynolds Keats regularly breaks into verse and here, haunted by Edgar's line to Gloucester in *King Lear*, 'Do you not hear the Sea?', he transcribes the sonnet he has just written (reproduced here as it appears in the letter rather than in its edited version):

> It keeps eternal Whisperings around
>   Desolate shores, and with its mighty swell
>   Of Hecate leaves them their old shadowy sound.
> Often 'tis in such gentle temper found
>   That scarcely will the very smallest shell
>   Be moved for days from whence it sometime fell
> When last the winds of Heaven were unbound.
> O ye who have your eyeballs vext and tir'd
>   Feast them upon the wideness of the Sea
> O ye whose Ears are dinned with uproar rude
>   Or fed too much with cloying melody –

> Sit ye near some old Cavern's Mouth and brood
> Until ye start as if the Sea Nymphs quired –

For a Londoner 'inland bred' who saw the sea only on his travels, Keats, like Shakespeare, is fascinated and haunted by its moods and music. The letter to Reynolds is again full of Shakespeare and 'On the Sea' shows the influence. Less than a month later, on 10 May, Keats writes to Leigh Hunt, this time back on the English coast staying with Tom at Margate in Kent, 'a treeless affair'. Signing himself with Hunt's nickname for him, 'Junkets', he explains that he returned from the Isle of Wight partly because for some reason he 'could not get wholesome food' but also because solitude and insomnia had made him 'not over capable in [his] upper Stories'. Even from the beginning of his stay he had hinted this to Reynolds, saying 'From want of regular rest, I have been rather *narvus*' and his words to Hunt show that he had been close to despair 'in continual burning of thought as an only resource'. His anxiety seemed to stem from solitude and a gathering sense of inadequacy in the pursuit of poetic fame '– that at last the Idea has grown so monstrously beyond my seeming Power of attainment ... – yet 't is a disgrace to fail even in a huge attempt ...' (*JKL*, 1, 139). On the same day he wrote to Haydon, again adverting to his 'forebodings' and again recollecting *King Lear*: '– truth is I have been in such a state of Mind as to read over my Lines and hate them. I am "one that gathers Samphire dreadful trade".' However, he takes heart 'notwithstanding occasional depressions' (*JKL*, 1, 141), hoping for the support of 'a High Power ... a good Genius' presiding over him: 'Is it too daring to Fancy Shakespeare this Presider?' He sees it as a good omen that the landlady on the Isle of Wight had given him the picture of Shakespeare to keep. He also finds reassurance in Haydon's words to him: 'I am very glad you say every Man of great Views is at times tormented as I am –.' In terms of the poetry he is writing, he feels positive that there are multiple levels of unity: 'for things which [I] do half at Random are afterwards confirmed by my judgment in a dozen features of Propriety –'.

The 'great attempt' which Keats has embarked upon is writing an epic, *Endymion*:

> – it will be a test, a trial of my Powers of Imagination and chiefly of my invention which is a rare thing indeed – by which I must make 4000 Lines of one bare circumstance and fill them with Poetry; and when I consider that this is a great task, and that when done it will take me but a dozen paces towards the Temple of Fame – it makes me say – God forbid that I should be without such a task! (*JKL*, 1, 170)

The methodical self-discipline and industriousness which marked his schooldays and his medical studies are now redirected to composing poetry, to the extent of making it seem like a rather unpoetical activity. He had broached the subject of the myth of Endymion in 'I stood tip-toe upon a little hill' and had started writing the new poem at Carisbrooke towards the end of April in a concentrated burst of labour that must have contributed to his exhaustion: 'I read and write about eight hours a day.' The task was to preoccupy him right through to the end of 1817 and in the light of his limited experience it was a massive project to set himself.

The process of composing *Endymion* can be traced through Keats's periodical references. The germ of the idea must have been set when he was at school, where he was reputed to have known almost by heart Lemprière's *A Classical Dictionary Containing a Copious Account of all the Proper Names Mentioned in the Ancient Authors* (first published in 1788 and regularly augmented in the nineteenth century). Unkind reviewers were to suggest that Keats's classical knowledge was all second hand from such a condensed source, though Cowden Clarke recalled him 'at his Latin and French translation', starting earlier than other students at school and working in school holidays and afternoons when others were at recreation (CCC, 122). Nonetheless, Lemprière provides a bare-bones summary which Keats would certainly have known:

> **Endymion**, a shepherd, son of Aethlius and Calyce. It is said that he required of Jupiter to grant to him to be always young, and to sleep as much as he would; whence came the proverb of *Endymion* is *somnum dormire*, to express a long sleep. Diana saw him naked as he slept on mount Latmos, and was so struck with his beauty that she came down from heaven every night to enjoy his company ... The fable of Endymion's amours with Diana, or the moon, arises from his knowledge of astronomy, and as he passed the night on some high mountain, to observe the heavenly bodies, it has been reported that he was courted by the moon ...

It was this 'one bare circumstance', more specifically the love between the shepherd and the moon goddess, that inspired Keats to write his epic, shifting the emphasis on to Endymion's love for the moon rather than the other way around. It is a fable of the mortal yearning for immortality, as Keats was doing through his poetry. Diana in Latin comes with slightly different roles and under different names such as Artemis (Greek), Cynthia (Greek), Luna (Latin) and Selene (Greek), opening up the possibility for Keats to split her identity into two personae, one immortal and the other mortal. In mythology Diana was also the goddess of chastity who never consummated her love for Endymion, but when Keats first dealt with the myth briefly in 'I stood tip-toe' and more allusively in 'Sleep and Poetry', he does not accept that the love was chaste, and suggests the union between sleep, mortal beauty and the moon (this time under her alternative name Cynthia) led to the birth of Poetry.

Endymion was begun on the Isle of Wight in about the last week of April 1817, and Keats coyly mentions his 'huge attempt' to Hunt on 10 May:

> I began my Poem about a Fortnight since and ... have done a good deal for the time but it appears such a Pin's Point to me that I will not coppy any out – When I consider that so many of these Pin points go to form a Bodkin point (God send I end not my Life with a bare Bodkin, in its modern sense) and that it requ[i]res a thousand bodkins to make a Spear bright enough to throw any light to posterity – I see that nothing but continual uphill Journeying? (*JKL*, 1, 139)

In the same batch of letters, he wrote to Haydon, 'I read and write about eight hours a day. There is an old saying "well begun is half done" – 't is a bad one. I would use instead – "Not begun at all till half done" so according to that I have not begun my Poem and consequently (a priori) can say nothing about it.' A week later on 16 May, now back at Margate where he had moved on about 25 April after becoming dissatisfied with the Isle of Wight, he wrote to Taylor and Hessey, again mentioning his mental state of morbidity and exhaustion:

> I went day by day at my Poem for a Month at the end of which time the other day I found my Brain so overwrought that I had neither Rhyme nor reason in it – so was obliged to give up for a few days – I hope soon to be able to resume my Work – I have endeavoured to do so once or twice but to no Purpose – instead of Poetry I have a swimming in my head – and feel all the effects of a Mental Debauch – lowness of Spirits – anxiety to go on without the Power to do so which does not at all tend to my ultimate Progression – However tomorrow I will begin my next Month – (*JKL*, 1, 146)

He was joined by Tom in Margate but restlessly moved again, this time to Bo Peep near Hastings, and back to Hampstead by 1 June. Through all the moves and bouts of depression and exhaustion, Keats stuck at the mammoth task of writing *Endymion* and by August could announce to Haydon that he had finished the second of four books. On 10 September he tells the story to his sister Fanny, concluding '– but I dare <yo> say have read this and all the other beautiful Tales which have come down from the ancient times of that beautiful Greece' (*JKL*, 1, 154), and continues:

> I have been writing very hard lately even till an utter incapacity came on, and I feel it now about my head: so you must not mind a little out of the way sayings – though bye the bye w[h]ere my brain as clear as a bell I think I should have a little propensity thereto. I shall stop here till I have finished the 3rd Book of my Story; which I hope will be accomplish'd in

at most three Weeks from to day – about which time you shall see me. (*JKL*, 1, 155)

By 14 September, now staying in Oxford with a new friend introduced through Reynolds, Benjamin Bailey, who was an earnest theology student at the university, Keats writes a comic account to the Reynolds sisters saying that he and Endymion are 'at the bottom of the sea' (Book III). On 28 September he tells Haydon that 'within these last three weeks I have written 1000 lines – which are the third Book of my Poem', though adding that his ideas about it are 'very low', that he is 'tired of it' and would prefer to be writing a new romance (*JKL*, 1, 168). He was beginning to see the writing of *Endymion* as an experience which will bear fruit in his 'next Poem'. By 8 October he was back in Hampstead lodging with his brothers in Well Walk and beginning to doubt the benefits of Leigh Hunt as an influence and editor of his own poetry (with 'his corrections and amputations' [*JKL*, 1, 170]), reporting to Bailey that Hunt, who had questioned Keats's decision to write a long poem in the first place, has claimed to Reynolds that he has prevented *Endymion* swelling from 4,000 lines to 7,000. Later critics have, however, tended to agree with Hunt, that the poem's lush profligacy of imagery could have been curbed even further. At the end of October Keats tells Bailey he is nearing completion: 'I am in a fair way now to come to a conclusion in at least three Weeks when I assure you [Bailey] I shall be glad to dismount for a Month or two' (*JKL*, 1, 172), and he quotes about thirty lines from Book 4. On 22 November he has travelled yet again – 'at present I am just arrived at Dorking to change the Scene – change the Air and give me a spur to wind up my Poem, of which there are wanting 500 lines ...' and a week later he has at last finished. During this whole period of seven months, full of restless travel, anxiety and sometimes near despair, Keats had never deviated from the crippling task he had set himself, not even to write short, 'spin-off' poems. It had not proved an unequivocal labour of love since he had always expressed dogged determination rather than great affection or enthusiasm for the enterprise. Nonetheless it was finished, and Keats had proved to himself that he could write a poem of the length and scope of an epic.

How should we read and evaluate *Endymion*? The structure follows many of the narrative conventions of epics like Virgil's *Aeneid*, showing the characteristic processes of heroic quest in, for example, Endymion's trip to the bottom of the sea. However, this pattern seems extrinsic to the poem's concerns. It also has elements of Spenserian allegory but cannot be read consistently in this way since the signifiers shift in symbolism. In Keats's treatment the goddess Diana is the female manifestation of the moon. Rivalling her for Endymion's attentions is a mortal Indian maid. The whole poem sees Endymion oscillating between the two females, and his confused situation has been taken to represent, among other things, the aspiring poet, first inspired and then brought literally back to earth, but it can also be read as a parable of love which to Keats here bears an immortal quality alongside a mortal existence. The various paradoxes generated by this theme are resolved – how successfully is debatable – when the moon, Diana and the Indian maid finally coalesce into one figure, so that Endymion, in the proverbial phrase from Keats's sonnet 'On Fame', can have his cake and eat it. The epic poem becomes a sustained meditation on the paradoxical nature of love, and at points on the nature of paradox itself. It is full of oxymorons such as 'tender madness' (I, 949), 'O what a wild and harmonized tune' (III, 170), 'gentler-mightiest' (III, 43) and 'pomp subservient' (III, 47). Its most inclusive comment on love is itself a paradox: 'O unconfined Restraint! Imprisoned liberty' (I, 455–6), phrases which could stand as a motto for each of Keats's poems about love, encapsulating his ambivalent and fluctuating attitudes.

In the final analysis, the way to read *Endymion* with most enjoyment, not too seriously and not too lightly, may be by following Keats's own advice in writing to his brother George words that he quoted later to Bailey:

> I have heard Hunt say and may be asked – why endeavour after a long Poem? To which I should answer – Do not the Lovers of Poetry like to have a little Region to wander in where they may pick and choose, and in which the images are so numerous that many are forgotten and found in a second Reading: which may be food for a Week's stroll in the Summer? Do not they like this better than what they can read through before Mrs Williams comes down stairs? a Morning work at most. Besides a long Poem is a test of Invention which I take to be the Polar Star of Poetry, as Fancy is the Sails, and Imagination the Rudder. Did our great Poets ever write short Pieces? (*JKL*, 1, 170)

Faux-naif as this sounds, by heeding it we can retrieve *Endymion* from its unread oblivion, for there are riches enough in its detail to allow us to 'wander' as readers and 'pick and choose' among lines and images. It is well within the poem's poetic theme to value intense and momentary effects – the 'touch ethereal' – while following the overall narrative and respecting the guiding ideas: 'Nor do we merely feel these essences / For one short hour ... They alway must be with us, or we die' (I, 25–6, 33). Local felicities abound in the poem as Keats visibly matures into his own signature poetic language and imagery:

> Rich with a sprinkling of fair musk-rose blooms (I, 19)
> The surgy murmurs of the lonely sea (I, 121)

Cryptic paradoxes are equally typical of all Keats's poetry: 'ardent listlessness' (I, 826), 'deathful glee', among many others. The sheer imaginative energy provides the onward pressure while the clusters of imagery allow readers 'a little Region to wander in where they may pick and choose' without being so coerced by a rigid plan as Keats manifestly had been during the process of composition. 'We hate poetry that has a palpable design upon us' wrote Keats to Reynolds (*JKL*, 1, 223–4).

At the same time, the suggestion made to 'lovers of poetry' holds lightly within it a more serious link with the poem's thematic centre. Keats was always modest and self-critical, but his comments here are not as gratuitous as they might seem, and in fact they are consistent with a substantial philosophical argument pursued in *Endymion*. 'A thing of beauty is a joy for ever', the bold first line declares, opening up the problem of reconciling transience with an apprehension of permanence. If the 'thing of beauty' were something material and permanent such as an art work like a Grecian urn or a painting, the statement would not hold logical problems. However, Keats immediately explains that he is speaking of more evanescent things like the nightingale's song, things which are either regularly changing, such as 'the sun, the moon, Trees old' (I, 13–14), or are as fleeting as dreams, flowers, clouds and streams, and pre-eminently, love. Keats seems to adopt a basically Platonic stance as did so many of his contemporaries, arising from 'the beautiful mythology of Greece' (Preface); a mode of thought where ideal forms remain the same and are only intuited, while observed natural phenomena are in a state of change and constantly varying manifestations. The ideal forms are a little more mystical in Keats than they were in Plato, and they turn on the word 'essences': 'Nor do we merely feel these essences / For one short hour ...' (I, 25–6). In many ways the whole poem turns on the definition of such essences, and in particular the maddening discrepancy experienced by Endymion in his quest, a gulf lying between essential experience and reality. Stuart Sperry traces the idea of 'essences' back to the chemical processes used in Keats's medical training, suggesting that the poet is speaking of the kind of distillation involved in making drugs. The word 'distil' is used many times, and it was admittedly a term of art used with a precise meaning in contemporary medicine. However, the primary allusion, I suggest, is to the literary influence of Shakespeare's Sonnets, where the word and concept repeatedly occur.

That Keats was connecting *Endymion* with the Sonnets is evident from the motto, 'The stretched metre of an antique song' (Sonnet 17). At least the first twenty-five Sonnets, and indeed all of them in more diverse ways, explore the very problems Keats is raising. Shakespeare's concern is with the capacity of time to destroy beauty, whether it is human in the form of the young man or natural in the passing of the seasons. In his version, a thing of beauty is *not* a thing for ever, unless it is made so by reproduction, by the poet's immortalising lines, through cyclical returns such as the seasons or by some feat of imaginative logic. In his argument against 'Time's scythe' Shakespeare proclaims the replicating imitation of 'copy' in either a child or a poem, both of which create some new form out of an existing template, and which will arrest time and capture the image of the young man at his most beautiful, guaranteeing his beauty's survival. In a mortal world where 'every thing that grows / Holds in perfection but a little moment' (Sonnet 15), the image must be captured at its height, like a snapshot in an age before cameras. The aim is not, however, the kind of pictorial realism of a modern photograph, but the idealism of beauty exemplified by the Elizabethan miniature portrait which also makes that form so annoyingly bland in its marmoreal perfection. We find out nothing specific or pictorial about what Shakespeare's young man looks like, or even his name, despite the sonneteer's determination to depict the lineaments forever. Like Spenser in his *Amoretti*, and in a very Elizabethan way, Shakespeare seeks to capture the *significance* of beauty rather than its appearance. For Keats, the crucial statement lies in Shakespeare's Sonnet 5:

> Then, were not summer's distillation left
> A liquid prisoner pent in walls of glass,
> Beauty's effect with beauty were bereft,
> Nor it, nor no remembrance what it was;
> But flowers distill'd, though they with winter meet,
> Leese but their show: their substance still lives sweet.

Curiously enough, Shakespeare's image does return us to the medical, for the words can mean the curative juice of flowers, or at least the preservation of their perfume, which enable an 'essence' to be kept long after summer has passed. Keats's intensifications are emotional rather than so literal:

> Nor do we feel these essences
> For one short hour; no, even as the trees
> That whisper round a temple become soon
> Dear as the temple's self, so does the moon,
> The passion poesy, glories infinite,
> Haunt us till they become a cheering light
> Unto our souls, and bound to us so fast,
> That, whether there be shine, or gloom o'ercast,
> They always must be with us, or we die.
>
> (I, 25–33)

Such a vision is both mystical and emotional, no trick of poetry but a mode of reality fusing the solidity of the temple and the insubstantiality of the breeze in trees. The movement of *Endymion* is premised on the unification of an 'uncertain path' (I, 61), moving between ever-changing nature and the 'marble altar' of permanence. His is a Romantic version of Shakespeare's preoccupation with time; the problems of reconciling the world of change, process and sequential time, with an apprehension of ecstatic timelessness and wholeness of experience. Although Keats is pursuing the same problem as Shakespeare, as a poet of his own later age he is, at least in this poem, not so interested in art as being nature's 'counterfeit', but in states of being such as visions, dreams, ecstasy which seem to collapse time and timelessness. It is these which legitimise a reading of *Endymion* as a series of intense moments, and they also seem consistent with the experience of love which is portrayed.

Peona, Endymion's sister, inhabits the mortal world of change. She feels anxiety, she cannot transcend knowledge of past and present to see into the future, she is associated with flowers, brooks, and is a 'midnight spirit nurse / Of happy changes' (I, 413–14). She is of, and at one with, the earth. Although able to play heavenly music on the lute, her more characteristic tone is 'self-possession' (I, 504) and earnest caution:

> ... Brother, 'tis vain to hide
> That thou dost know of things mysterious,
> Immortal, starry; such alone could thus
> Weigh down thy nature. Hast thou sinned in aught
> Offensive to the heavenly powers?

Endymion explains to her his dream-like experiences of being wooed by the goddess, and feeling a love envenomed by 'human neighbourhood' (I, 621), kissing 'at once to death – but 'twas to live' (I, 655). The bewildering cycle that happens to him time and again is one from enchanted transport to the 'disappointment' of returning to a life ruled by 'Time, that aged nurse' (I, 705). The dream becomes more powerfully real to him than reality, and he locates happiness in 'fellowship divine', 'A fellowship with essence / Full alchemized, and free of space' (I, 778–80). He does see a humanly possible route to such ecstasy since the 'chief intensity' is love with friendship, which in Neoplatonic fashion leads by degrees to the 'radiance' of interknitted souls, in a process which Keats suggestively described in a letter, again with a medical nuance, as a 'pleasure thermometer' to take the temperature of happiness. There is still, however, a dismaying gap between on the one hand the moment of 'love's elysium' of 'tender madness' (I, 951) and on the other 'ardent listlessness' (I, 825) and sober mundane existence.

In a shift of the narrative late in *Endymion* which marks other poems of love by Keats, Peona and the Indian maid are mortal agents for Endymion's temporary renunciation of immortal longings. He realises his dreams can be bought only at the expense of neglecting earthly beauties:

> ... I have clung
> To nothing, loved a nothing, nothing seen

> Or felt but a great dream! O I have been
> Presumptuous against love, against the sky,
> Against all elements, against the tie
> Of mortals each to each, against the blooms
> Of flowers, rush of rivers, and the tombs
> Of heroes gone! ...
> There never lived a mortal man, who bent
> His appetite beyond his natural sphere,
> But starved and died.
>
> (IV, 636–48)

He does not relinquish his love for Diana, but at least he recognises this love cannot be fulfilled on earth. He turns then wholeheartedly to the earthly lover:

> My Indian bliss!
> My river-lily bud! one human kiss!
> One sigh of real breath – one gentle squeeze,
> Warm as a dove's nest among the summer trees,
> And warm with dew at ooze from living blood!
>
> (IV, 663–7)

In love, however, there is always a price and at this moment of apparent reconciliation to the earth Endymion is reminded of death and separation in the mortal domain, by the Indian maid who promptly leaves him and goes into the forest. His grief-stricken sense of loss is desperate and he resigns himself to the life of a hermit votive to Diana the goddess, until one last encounter with Diana who, at the end of the poem, miraculously metamorphoses into the Indian maid, so that their marriage may form an eternal yet present union.

The resolution may be forced, but the attempt itself is symptomatic of his general attitude to love in poetry. Although it is clear that his *poetic* intention is realised, and that Endymion can have both immortal love and mortal existence simultaneously, yet nothing in the poem's oscillating rhythms and adversities makes this climax narratively convincing. The true 'essence' of love in *Endymion* lies not in some mystical resolution but in its very volatility, the fluctuating joys and disappointments. All the educative, Spenserian vignettes displayed to Endymion, such as the tales of Adonis and of Glaucus, are unhappy ones because of the insistent fact of mortality. The proper paradox is that a state of love can so powerfully touch extremes of emotion and become a source of knowledge in its own right, and that love would not be love without them. Just as in the later

'Ode on Melancholy', joy would not exist without its opposite, so that a constant interplay between contrasts is set up. By definition, stasis in love cannot be achieved without also losing love. This is the rather mournful burden of all Keats's poems on love in the mortal world, and never again does he falsify the unfathomable contradictions in its nature by applying such a schematic conclusion. His governing paradox is that love is both a constant emotion on the part of the lover, and yet that it inevitably pitches him into inconstancy and extremes of experience. In this 'state perplexing' (IV, 439) the lover is taken to the very height of ecstasy only to be cast down to despair: '... Is there naught for me, / Upon the bourne of bliss, but misery?' (IV, 461).

Another way in which we can revalue *Endymion* is by placing it alongside the contemporary poems that Keats was aware of as being similar. It may be regrettable that the poetic genre it belongs to, although one of the most prominent kinds in its day, did not survive in popularity and has never been revived: the extended poem based on a theme from classical mythology, partially a Romantic revival of the Elizabethan short epic like *Venus and Adonis* or *Hero and Leander*. It bears comparison with the heroic paintings on historical or mythological themes that were popular at the time, painted for example by James Barrie and Benjamin Haydon. What is surely significant is that the poets with whom Keats was grouped – his friends, in fact – published such poems in the year or two just before *Endymion* was written. Reynolds, for example, wrote *The Naiad* which was published anonymously with a selection of his other poems by Taylor and Hessey in 1816, with a dedication to Haydon, just six months before Reynolds met Keats. Although nowhere near as long or ambitious as Keats's poem and based on a Scottish ballad rather than on classical sources and written in a style recalling *Lyrical Ballads*, Reynolds's choice of subject bears some comparison in placing classical myth in landscape. The Naiads were nymphs who presided over gently flowing, fresh water in its various forms such as springs and fountains, but not rivers and the sea. If a water source dried up, its naiad died. Like most such myths, these figures invite allegorical interpretation while resisting fixed, one-to-one correspondences, so that the kind of poetry they inspired has loose and flexible aspects of allegory but is presented primarily as narrative. Reynolds's poem was greeted with reasonably favourable reviews, and since he himself was never a particularly original poet but rather one who imitated others like Byron and Wordsworth, his work is a good indication of what was popular at the time. So are Mary Tighe's *Psyche, or The Legend of Love* (1805, republished up to 1816), and *A Sicilian Story* (1820) by 'Barry Cornwall', the celebrity of whose 'amiable' verses bemused Keats (*JKL*, 2, 268). Leigh Hunt was probably working on his poem *The Nymphs* when he met Keats since it was published in *Foliage* (1818). Even more important, I would suggest, and the poem which may have been uppermost in Keats's mind, was Shelley's *Alastor; or, The Spirit of Solitude*, which was the titular centrepiece of the first work to be published under Shelley's name, appearing in 1816. The self-financed volume sold out, unlike Keats's, and it did not attract especially hostile reviews. It was this kind of poem, I suggest, that Keats was aiming to write, and the very thing which he had some reason to expect would make it sell is also the very thing which makes it unpopular nowadays – its genre. Alastor, like Endymion, was a classical character who appears in Homer's *Iliad* as well as in Aeschylus and Sophocles, and although his central associations were with outcast solitude and love, Shelley was to focus these aspects into a composite figure of the unnamed Poet, experiencing in much the same way as Endymion does the vicissitudes of life and love in sojourning through 'undiscovered lands' over seas and into valleys.[2] Just as an Indian maid provides Endymion with creature comforts, so an Arab maiden provides a 'daily portion' of food for Alastor and tends his footsteps, unobtrusively leaving him to his inturned solitude, watching him even as he sleeps. One section indicates the kind of narrative the poem presents, and suggests several similarities to themes and imagery in *Endymion*, while also illustrating differences between Shelley's skimming lightness of rhythm, contrasting to Keats's richly laden moments of enlarged psychic experience and full stasis:

> The Poet wandering on, through Arabie
> And Persia, and the wild Carmanian waste,
> And o'er the aërial mountains which pour down
> Indus and Oxus from their icy caves,
> In joy and exultation held his way;
> Till in the vale of Cashmire, far within
> Its loneliest dell, where odorous plants entwine
> Beneath the hollow rocks a natural bower,
> Beside a sparkling rivulet he stretched
> His languid limbs. A vision on his sleep
> There came, a dream of hopes that never yet
> Had flushed his cheek. He dreamed a veiled maid
> Sate near him, talking in low solemn tones,
> Her voice was like the voice of his own soul
> Heard in the calm of thought; its music long,
> Like woven sounds of streams and breezes, held
> His inmost sense suspended in its web
> Of many-coloured woof and shifting hues.
> Knowledge and truth and virtue were her theme,
> And lofty hopes of divine liberty,
> Thoughts the most dear to him, and poesy,
> Herself a poet. ...

> (*Alastor*, 140–61)

This is not the place to pursue a comparison of the two poems, but I hope it suggests a way in which to view *Endymion* that does justice to Keats's own intentions by drawing attention to contemporary exemplars.

Put very briefly, Keats's intention is to unite the ideal and the real, so that the poetry of the remote moon and the poetry in everyday beauty can be reconciled and found not to be contradictory but to be one and the same. Endymion's dream fuses with his waking state: 'The Imagination may be compared to Adam's dream – he awoke and found it truth' (*JKL*, 1, 185). These are parts of a kind of personal narrative which Keats was later to repeat in different ways in many of his poems and letters. It is a theme announced in the opening lines:

> A thing of beauty is a joy forever;
> Its loveliness increases; it will never
> Pass into nothingness; but still will keep
> A bower quiet for us, and a sleep
> Full of sweet dreams, and health, and quiet breathing.
> Therefore, on every morrow, are we wreathing
> A flowery band to bind us to the earth ...

Earthly beauty takes on an immortal quality that mediates between daily realities and the eternal. The opening sequence of *Endymion* shows the overall visionary plan of the poem, and it will be repeated again in different contexts. Abstract beauty, 'nothingness' and dreams are set against the real world of growing nature and of living people but the fable is designed to show the two realms not only as linked but the same. This is not the Platonism adopted by Shelley, where permanent forms are glimpsed through fleeting reality, but instead a personal concept adopted by Keats that the world of the senses *is* also and at the same time an eternal realm beyond the senses. It is his way of overcoming the static and separated quality of immortal forms, infusing them with movement and growth, while equally modifying the transience and evanescence of reality, giving it an exemplary quality that outlasts time. It is a profound and typically Keatsian idea, which he contemplates and develops throughout his life. The narrative supports the experiential inclusiveness. Endymion reproves himself for neglecting natural beauties and 'the tie / Of mortals each to each' (IV, 640): 'I have clung to nothing, loved a nothing, nothing seen / Or felt but a great dream!' (IV, 637–8). And yet it is only by dreaming and idealising that he can learn to see beauty and love in the world of reality. The recurrence and consistency of the idea throughout the poem and on its different levels provides, if not a systematic allegorical design, at least a guiding idea.

Keats was especially proud of the section in *Endymion* known as the Hymn to Pan (I, 232–306) in which critics have seen anticipations of the style of his great Odes. Writing in 1845, long after the event he is recalling, Haydon recorded the occasion when he introduced Keats to Wordsworth:

> When Wordsworth came to Town, I brought Keats to him, by his Wordsworths desire – Keats expressed to me as we walked to Queen Anne St East where Mr Monkhouse Lodged, the greatest, the purest, the most unalloyed pleasure at the prospect. Wordsworth received him kindly, & after a few minutes, Wordsworth asked him what he had been lately doing. *I* said he has just finished an exquisite ode to Pan – and as he had not a copy I begged Keats to repeat it – which he did in his usual half chant, (most touching) walking up & down the room – when he had done I felt really, as if I had heard a young Apollo – Wordsworth drily said
> 'a Very pretty piece of Paganism – '
> This was unfeeling, & unworthy of his high Genius to a young Worshipper like Keats – & Keats felt it *deeply* – so that if Keats has said any thing severe about our Friend; it was because he was wounded – and though he dined with Wordsworth after at my table – he never forgave him.
> It was nonsense of Wordsworth to take it as a bit of Paganism for the Time, the Poet ought to have been a Pagan for the time – and if Wordsworth's puling Christian feelings were annoyed – it was rather ill-bred to hurt a youth, at such a moment when he actually trembled, like the String of a Lyre, when it has been touched. (*KC*, 2, 143–4)

If Haydon's long memory is reasonably accurate, Wordsworth's comment was doubly hurtful in its judgmental condescension and because it misses the point of what Keats is doing in the passage and in the poem as a whole. Ironically, Keats almost certainly thought he was working within the spirit of Wordsworth's own attitude to pagan mythology which paid credit to its richness in ideas and its linking of imagination with nature in stories that 'signify [...] works / Of dim futurity, to Man revealed'.[3] It seems that in the conversation with Keats the older poet's deeply felt Christianity obscured his secular understanding, so that Keats became a minor victim of Wordsworth's contradictory stance which on the one hand gave him an honourable place within a history of Pantheism[4] while on the other led him to speak demeaningly of mythology as 'a pretty piece of paganism'. Keats's hymn to Pan in *Endymion* explicitly turns away from the kind of classical reference which is merely pictorial and engages with the poem's dominant idea that the mythology exists to explain and amplify our sense awareness of the world around us. The nature described in the passage is not Arcadian but English, 'our village leas their fairest-blossomed beans and poppied corn', with linnets, strawberries and 'pent up butterflies' with their 'freckled wings'. The fauns and satyrs are not decoratively antiquarian but mischievous and Puck-like, while the general direction of the passage, as in the design of the poem as a whole, is to affirm the immediacy of sense impressions with their 'touch ethereal' and their capacity to open 'the mysterious doors / Leading to universal knowledge'. That is, myth is used *not* as 'pretty' or decorative pagan imagery, but as a branch of knowledge acquired through experience. Keats was continually to deepen and reiterate this idea in other writings, but it is implicit here, and he could have hoped the revered Wordsworth of all people would notice it.

Even if Haydon overstated when he said that Keats never forgave Wordsworth, the young poet's attitude to the older was always to be profoundly ambiguous, split between a judgment of the intellectual man and of the poet: 'I am sorry that Wordsworth has left a bad impression wherever he visited in Town – by his egotism, Vanity and bigotry – yet he is a great Poet if not a Philosopher' (21 February 1818; *JKL*, 1, 237). Keats by this stage read Wordsworth through the prism of Hazlitt's unsympathetic eyes. Hunt was on good terms with Wordsworth though he did not like that poet's 'solitary morbidities', presumably because his poems did not fall in behind the credo 'HAPPY POETRY PREFERRED'. It cannot have endeared Keats when, if Clarke's report is to be trusted, at a social gathering he was about to disagree with Wordsworth on a point, when Mary Wordsworth put her hand on Keats's arm and warned him, 'Mr Wordsworth is never interrupted' (quoted in Gittings, 270).

Right to the end of writing *Endymion* Keats was dogged by misunderstandings. Even his friends, Keats wrote bitterly to Reynolds, were all agreed 'that the thing is bad' (*JKL*, 1, 266–7). He had written a Dedication to Chatterton as 'the most English of poets except Shakespeare' and he added a Preface written in an uneasy blend of self-deprecation and epistolary familiarity, excusing the poem's faults. He was persuaded by his friends to delete this, and although fulminating like a latter-day Coriolanus to Reynolds about how much he hates 'the public' – 'I have no feel of stooping, I hate the idea of humility to them' – he rapidly wrote an even more apologetic preface, virtually disowning *Endymion* as 'mawkishness' and as the work of somebody whose soul is in a ferment between childhood and adulthood. Other revisions advised by Taylor were grudgingly accepted by Keats as his responses to an editor whom he branded with some reservations as 'a consequitive Man' (*JKL*, 1, 218; see also 1, 184) perhaps too logical fully to appreciate Keats's 'regular stepping of the Imagination towards a Truth' in poetic language.

For a month after completing *Endymion* Keats relaxed to 'racket' by visiting friends and the theatre, then he started revising in January 1818. He supplied the publishers with manuscript copies in batches of the four Books and these were carefully and tactfully edited by Taylor after at least one meeting with the poet.[5] On 4 March, Keats went to Teignmouth in Devonshire to be with his brother Tom who was becoming more ill. The book was published sometime between 22 April and 19 May 1818, under the title *Endymion: A Poetic Romance*, bearing the epigraph 'the stretched metre of an antique song' and simply 'Inscribed to the memory of Thomas Chatterton'. The hastily revised preface stood as something like a hostage to the fortune of reviewers, and swoop they did, with a vengeance. Having ignored *Poems* (1817) with lordly disdain, reviewers seemed provoked by the young author's temerity in daring to publish another volume, and were determined this time, once and for all, to give his poem and his personality the malicious attention they thought it deserved. Keats's response to Hessey at that time, about six months after publication, has a kind of philosophical stoicism mingled with indignation and considerable pain:

> Praise or blame has but a momentary effect on the man whose love of beauty in the abstract makes him a severe critic on his own Works. My own domestic criticism has given me pain without comparison beyond what Blackwood or the <Edinburgh> Quarterly could possibly inflict. And also when I feel I am right, no external praise can give me such a glow as my own solitary reperception & ratification of what is fine. J.S. is perfectly right in regard to the slipshod Endymion. That it is so is no fault of mine. – No! – though it may sound a little paradoxical … It is as good as I had power to make it – by myself – Had I been nervous about its being a perfect piece, & with that view asked advice, & trembled over every page, it would not have been written; for it is not in my nature to fumble – I will write independantly. – I have written independently *without Judgment* – I may write independently & *with judgment* hereafter. – the Genius of Poetry must work out its own salvation in a man: It cannot be matured by law & precept, but by sensation & watchfulness in itself – That which is creative must create itself – In Endymion, I leaped headlong into the Sea, and thereby have become better acquainted with the Soundings, the quicksands, & the rocks, than if I had <stayed> stayed upon the green shore, and piped a silly pipe, and took tea & comfortable advice. – I was never afraid of failure; for I would sooner fail than not be among the greatest – But I am nigh getting into a rant. (8 October 1818, *JKL*, 1, 373–4)

Writing *Endymion* was partly intended as a learning experience, and Keats reflects that it gave him a deeper knowledge of the process of composition, of his own capabilities and limitations, and paradoxically it gave him the confidence born of self-criticism to begin thinking of another epic in verse.

It leapfrogs our chronology, but while *Endymion* is fresh in our minds it is timely to look briefly at the reviews which were to break like a thundercloud after publication. There were initially some favourable ones, not surprisingly since they were written by Keats's friends and supporters. One was more by way of an advertisement than a review, by Bailey, published in the form of two letters in issues of the *Oxford University and City Herald, and Midland County Chronicle*, 30 May 1818 and 6 June 1818.[6] The second was published anonymously in the *Champion* on 8 June 1818 and it may have been by Reynolds but is more likely by Woodhouse since it praises Keats's aptitude for empathy with what he is describing – a quality compared by the reviewer to Shakespeare's 'negative capability', the phrase which Keats had shared with Woodhouse in correspondence: 'Neither is it "the mere outwards signs of passions" that are given: there seems ever present some being that was equally conscious of its internal and most secret imaginings' (*Heritage*, 89). The writer contrasts this kind of poetry with that in which 'sympathy will be regulated by the disposition and bent of [an author's] mind' – what Keats called 'the wordsworthian or egotistical sublime' which he also associated with Milton. The distinction, which was to prove a kind of touchstone for Keats, can be attributed to the influence of Hazlitt who had found the two types exemplified, respectively, first in Shakespeare as the writer who ventriloquially effaces himself in his characters and narratives, and secondly Wordsworth who imposed his own view on the world with 'an intense intellectual egotism'. The third review or rather 'Critique' of Keats's poetry, was unsigned but is now proven to be by a 'Keatsian' poet who was himself beginning to enjoy celebrity at the time but now largely forgotten, 'Barry Cornwall' (Bryan Waller Procter). This was published in the *Edinburgh Magazine and Literary Miscellany* much later in 1820, late enough to include reference to all three of Keats's volumes published by then.[7]

Much less favourable than any of these was the unsigned review in *British Critic* in June 1818, which tended to damn *Endymion* with very faint praise as 'A monstrously droll poem'. The review gives a superficial account, parodying the plot and favourably quoting some lines but dismissing indignantly other 'immoral images' presented with 'impurity': 'we will not disgust our readers by retailing to them the artifices of vicious refinement, by which, under the semblance of "slippery blisses. Twinkling eyes, soft completion of faces, and smooth excess of hands" he would palm upon the unsuspicious and the innocent imaginations better adapted to the stews' (*Heritage*, 94). This was tepid compared to the onslaught by John Gibson Lockhart, signing himself 'Z' in *Blackwood's Edinburgh Magazine* dated August 1818. *Blackwood's* did not have a large circulation but its house style was biting and controversial, aimed at a younger readership that might today be compared to that of *Private Eye* in its heyday – a fashionable, satirical and quite mischievous publication. Lockhart is broadly writing on the 'Cockney School of Poetry', mainly as an attack on Leigh Hunt's political views: 'We had almost forgot to mention, that Keats belongs to the Cockney School of Politics, as well as the Cockney School of Poetry.' Politics is hardly central to *Endymion*, so Lockhart uses class grounds to ridicule instead Keats's pretensions to knowing classical mythology ('His Endymion is not a Greek shepherd, loved by a Grecian goddess; he is merely a young Cockney rhymester, dreaming a phantastic dream at the full of the moon'). His viciously personal attack has become notorious in Keats criticism:

> We venture to make one small prophecy, that his bookseller will not a second time venture £50 upon any thing he can write. It is a better and a wiser thing to be a starved apothecary than a starved poet; so back to the shop Mr John, back to 'plasters, pills, and ointment boxes,' &c. But, for Heaven's sake, young Sangrado, be a little more sparing of extenuatives and soporifics in your practice than you have been in your poetry.

Ironically, Lockhart had been given the ammunition unwittingly by a well-meaning Bailey, who, foreseeing trouble, had approached Lockhart and explained to him Keats's background as a medical student in order to establish his respectability, and had suggested Keats was young enough to outgrow the influence of Hunt. Lockhart promised not to use this knowledge, but broke his word to Bailey. It was this review which understandably wounded Keats most of all, because of its personal tone and its touching on his own insecurities.

The *Quarterly Review* had a much wider circulation (12,000) and was a more consistent bastion of conservatism. Its editor William Gifford was a public enemy of Hunt. The journal was to attack Shelley as harshly as Keats, in a review which Hunt branded 'Heavy and swelling, and soft with venom, it creeps through the middle of [the issue] like a skulking toad'.[8] The anonymous reviewer of Keats's volume was thought to be the editor, though in fact the review appearing in April 1818 was by John Wilson Croker, a secretary of the Admiralty and co-founder of the journal, and a man generally regarded as unpleasant. He pounces on Keats's self-deprecation in the Preface to *Endymion*, agreeing that the poem should never have been published, and proceeds to demolish it on the basis of having proudly read only the first of the four books. Keats is branded a 'neophyte' of Leigh Hunt and his 'insane criticism', and a writer of equally insane Cockney poetry – 'which may be defined to consist of the most incongruous ideas in the most uncouth language' (*Heritage*, 111) – even though Hunt himself had his own reservations about the poem. However, the critique tries to avoid the charge of direct political or personal bias by dwelling on perceived stylistic faults. The poetry is seen to be 'unintelligible', its subject obscure, and the verse is said to proceed arbitrarily not by connections of sense but of sound and rhyme-associations. Ironically, some of the language habits derided by Croker as 'imitation of Mr Leigh Hunt' can arguably be seen as Keats imitating Shakespeare – neologisms such as 'turtles *passion* their voices', 'an arbour was *nested*', 'the *honey-feel* of bliss', and making verbs out of adverbs ('out-sparkled', 'down-sunken') and adjectives out of adverbs ('*hushing* signs', '*spreaded* tail'). Croker may now be seen as simply parading his ignorance of poetry (which had been amply demonstrated in his own pathetic effort, *The Battle of Talavera*), but the dismissive and sneering tone is powerful. Various rebuttals came – from a John Scott in the *Morning Chronicle* and Reynolds, writing in the *Examiner*, though the latter makes the understandable mistake of criticising Byron's poetic egotism ('he is liked by most of his readers, because he is a Lord') since Byron from his position of popularity, perhaps provoked, was at least privately contemptuous of Keats's poetry: 'Here are Johnny Keats's *p-ss a bed* poetry ... There is such a trash of Keats and the like upon my tables, that I am ashamed to look at them ... No more Keats, I entreat: – flay him alive; if some of you don't, I must skin him myself: there is no bearing the drivelling idiotism of the Mankin'; and again 'such writing is a sort of mental masturbation – ******** his *Imagination* ... a Bedlam vision produced by raw pork and opium' (*Heritage*, 129). Only Byron's lordly disdain prevented him from dealing out the public 'flaying' that he threatened. As if to prove the class-related nature of the attacks, Byron himself condemns Keats as not coarse but 'shabby-genteel'. After Keats died Byron did to some extent recant, but more out of pity for Keats the young man than from a revaluation of his poetry. He did recollect that his own early poetry attracted equally scathing criticism which had hurt him more than he had admitted. The early attacks were so effective that even though they paradoxically helped to redeem Keats's reputation for posterity, yet we sometimes find modern critics such as Christopher Ricks and Marjorie Levinson recycling the criticisms in a manner only a little more sophisticated than the early reviewers, in the latter case pejoratively labelling Keats as culpably 'middle class', and in the former, distracted by Keats's own phrase 'O for a life of sensations rather than of thoughts', as a merely sensual poet, without the capacity to think.[9]

However, at the time when *Endymion* was actually published the critical nastiness was simply incubating and to return to our chronology, the fledgling poet could rest for the time being on a rare plateau of achievement and relief. For Keats and his circle, 1817 closed on a note of conviviality and even hilarity. On the last Sunday, 28 December, Haydon hosted at his new lodgings at 22 Lisson Grove North in London an event which came to be known as the 'immortal dinner'.[10] The evening was described several times by Haydon, once in his autobiography:

On December 28th the immortal dinner came off in my painting room, with *Jerusalem* towering up behind us as a background. Wordsworth was in fine cue, and we had a glorious set-to – on Homer, Shakespeare, Milton and Virgil. Lamb got exceedingly merry and exquisitely witty; and his fun in the midst of Wordsworth's solemn intonations of oratory was like the sarcasm and wit of the fool in the intervals of Lear's passion. He made a speech and voted me absent, and made them drink my health.[11]

There were others present, but not Hunt and Hazlitt who, although Haydon's friends, did not meet with his full approval because of their lack of religious faith, something Haydon seemed to forgive in Keats. '*Jerusalem*' was a stage towards the large painting Haydon was working on, which would take six years and not be completed until 1820, then titled *Christ's Entry into Jerusalem*. Its appropriateness as a 'background' for the literary gathering lay in the fact that Haydon had incorporated amongst the onlookers the faces of Wordsworth, Keats and William Bewick, as well as Voltaire. In order to paint these portraits, Haydon's technique was first to make a life mask of the subject from plaster, a process which was uncomfortable to the sitter and amusing to spectators, as seen in Haydon's description of unsuccessfully taking a life mask of Francis Jeffrey.[12] His plaster cast of Keats, which still exists, was taken in December 1816. The evening proceeded amicably and later degenerated into hilarity with the arrival of a man who had invited himself, John Kingston. Unbeknownst to Wordsworth, Kingston was Comptroller of Stamps and the immediate superior of Wordsworth in the poet's menial part-time appointment in the civil service. Kingston was (in Haydon's words) 'frilled, dressed, and official' and, presuming on his professional link, was delighted to converse with the famous poet Wordsworth, plying him garrulously with rhetorical questions such as 'Don't you think, sir, Milton was a great genius?' Lamb, who was drunk and dozing, and later confessing that he had taken an instant dislike to Kingston as representing the officiousness and even 'tyranny' of the petty administrator, woke and proceeded to ridicule and goad him, between hiccups calling him 'a silly fellow', taking a candle to examine his cranium in the interests of the then popular 'science' of phrenology, and constantly chanting, 'Diddle diddle dumkins, my son John / Went to bed with his breeches on.' Wordsworth was discomfited and tried to restrain Lamb, Haydon was embarrassed at the poet's unease, while the deaf painter Landseer tried vainly to lip-read what was being said. Keats, who had met and disliked Kingston a week earlier at a more solemn gathering at Horace Smith's, tried to suppress his laughter by pretending to bury his head in books. His part in the evening was mainly to quote Shakespeare whenever he had the opportunity, and also mildly to ridicule the hapless Kingston. He described the scene to his brothers in a letter written on 5 January:

– I forget whether I had written my last before my Sunday Evening at Haydon's – no I did n{o}t or I should have told you Tom of a y{oung} Man you met at Paris at Scott's of the n{ame of} Richer I think – he is going to Fezan in Africa there to proceed if possible like Mungo Park – he was very polite to me and enquired very particularly after you – then there was Wordsworth, Lamb, Monkhouse, Landseer, Kingston and your humble Sarvant. Lamb got tipsey and blew up Kingston – proceeding so far as to take the Candle across the Room hold it to his face and show us wh-a-at-sor-fello he-waas I astonished Kingston at supper with a pertinacity in favour of drinking – keeping my two glasses at work in a knowing way ... (*JKL*, 1, 197–8)

It was clear that Keats had been fully accepted now in a network of writers and artists, consolidating a year in which he had published his first volume of poems and had written his second which already had a publisher's agreement. As a professional poet, he was on his way, and he no longer considered medicine a serious option except in panicky moments of financial difficulty. The last morning of 1817, 31 December, Keats spent walking on Hampstead Heath and there he met Wordsworth, mentioning this fact casually, even tantalisingly, without elaboration in a brief letter to Haydon written that afternoon.

6
'Dark passages': 1818, January to June

A new year and the completion of the draft of *Endymion* unlocked a more relaxed part of Keats's mind, judging from the tumbling letters he wrote in January alone. He wrote to Bailey at Oxford 'perhaps more goes through the human intelligence in 12 days than was ever written' (*JKL*, 1, 209), and it is the sheer diversity of his activities, ideas and pithy descriptions that challenge any biographer who seeks to reflect the complexity of a life as it is lived day by day, without becoming overwhelmed with detail. He wrote three times to his brothers who were still in Teignmouth, Devonshire, chatting about attending and reviewing for the *Champion* a pantomime at Drury Lane, a 'Covent Garden New Tragedy' and watching Kean playing Richard III; drinking wine and attending dances; observing 'the Perplexity' of quarrels between Reynolds and Haydon, Haydon and Hunt, and pondering the nature of tolerance: 'Men should bear with each other ... the best of Men have but a portion of good in them – a kind of spiritual yeast in their frames which creates the ferment of existence – by which a Man is propell'd to act and strive and buffet with Circumstance' (*JKL*, 1, 210). He was reading novels by Scott and Smollett, and conceiving his next major poem, *Hyperion*, once again on a classical theme but this time not of 'deep and sentimental cast' like *Endymion* but treated 'in a more naked and grecian Manner'; and after the long ardours of *Endymion* he was at last writing new short pieces like the 'On Seeing a Lock of Milton's Hair. Ode' for Hunt's collection and the sonnet 'On Sitting Down to Read *King Lear* Once Again' (as named in his letter to George and Tom Keats on 24 January).

He was able to see his sister Fanny, aged 14 at the time, a rare event since she had gone to live in Walthamstow with the Abbeys who seemed actively to prevent her seeing much of her brothers. She was just as sharply observant and pert as John, judging from his cameo: 'she has been unwell but is improving – I think she will be quick – Mrs Abbey was saying that the Keatses were ever indolent – that they would ever be so and that it was born in them – Well whispered fanny to me "If it is born with us how can we help it" ...' (*JKL*, 1, 198). Emphasising their rudeness in passing such judgment on an unwell Fanny, Keats also sardonically mentions to his brothers that 'Mr Abbey does not overstock you with Money – you must insist' (*JKL*, 1, 200), a constant refrain about their guardian's tight-fistedeness with their inheritance. However, more ominous linings emerge amongst his preoccupations. An objectionable article by Lockhart, the editor of *Blackwood's Edinburgh Magazine* on 'The Cockney School of Poetry' had appeared, aiming its barbs mainly at Hunt but also by implication his protégés as well. More worrying is Tom's 'spitting of Blood ... the Palpitation and the spitting and the Cough', and a related, more philosophical brooding on pain, illness and death in response to Bailey's question '"*Why should Woman suffer?*"' to which Keats replies to the theology student in a secular fashion, 'these things are ... to heal this bruised fairness is like a sensitive leaf on the hot hand of thought' (*JKL*, 1, 209), that is, a distressing impossibility. Despite Keats's sprightly and cheerful tone in the letters to his brothers, it is clear he is concerned about his brother Tom, then only 18, in a situation which would only get steadily worse as 1818 wore on.

Rather than lingering at this stage over his worries and the poems Keats was writing in early 1818, it is revealing to follow the flow of his correspondence into the spring, at a time when he was effervescently developing his ideas about poetry. He was revising *Endymion* with Taylor whom he thanks for his 'admonitions', attending Hazlitt's lectures (sometimes arriving late), talking a lot to Dilke and Charles Brown (but not Hunt), exchanging poems – 'dishes of filberts' – with his 'Coscribbler' Reynolds and writing to George and Tom on a weekly basis, apologising if it were longer. This combination, occurring at a time when he was not putting himself under the strain of writing a long poem, encourages Keats to follow his thoughts in a rapidly developing way, several times commenting to Reynolds how the leisure of each day reading 'a certain Page of full Poesy or distilled Prose' allows him to 'wander with it, and muse upon it, and dream upon it – until it becomes stale – but when will it do so? Never ... How happy is such a "voyage of conception," what delicious diligent Indolence! A doze upon a Sofa does not hinder it, and a nap upon Clover engenders ethereal finger-pointings ...' (*JKL*, 1, 231). He declares that he is drawn to Elizabethan poets and especially Shakespeare rather than contemporaries like 'Wordsworth &c' who, 'but for the sake of a few imaginative or domestic passages' are calculated to bully readers 'into a certain Philosophy engendered in the whims of an Egotist – Every man has his speculations, but every man does not brood and peacock over them till he makes a false coinage and deceives himself –' (*JKL*, 1, 223). Elizabethan poets by contrast are like beautiful 'retired flowers', not 'throng[ing] into the highway crying out, "admire me I am a violet! Dote upon me I am a primrose"'. 'Poetry', he writes to Reynolds, 'should be great & unobtrusive, a thing which enters into one's soul, and does not startle it or amaze it with itself but with its subject' (*JKL*, 1, 224). 'Let us have the old Poets, & robin Hood.' Writing to Reynolds still in praise of idleness, Keats thinks of the distinction between the 'giving' bee and the 'receiving' flower: '... let us open our leaves like a flower and be passive and receptive – budding patiently under the eye of Apollo and taking hints from every noble insect that favors us with a visit – sap will be given for Meat and dew for drink' (*JKL*, 1, 232). He notices the underlying sexuality of his metaphor: 'The f[l]ower I doubt not receives a fair guerdon from the Bee – its leaves blush deeper in the next spring – and who shall say between Man and Woman which is the most delighted?'

In praising passive receptivity, Keats sees it not as inactive laziness but as an activity in itself, and he is lightly developing his own theory of the creative process: that it should proceed not from a sense of self or a set of fixed beliefs but from an other-centredness and openness to experience. This is the state which he had described to his brothers on 27 December 1817 as the capacity which Shakespeare 'possessed so enormously' '– I mean *Negative Capability*, that is when man is capable of being in uncertainties, Mysteries, doubts, without any irritable reaching after fact & reason ... This pursued through Volumes would perhaps take us no further than this, that with a great poet the sense of Beauty overcomes every other consideration, or rather obliterates all consideration' (*JKL*, 1, 194). Such a psychology of creativity gives priority to drama as the mode in which there is no mediating narrator or visible poet but juxtaposed states of mind, and writing to Taylor on 30 January 1818 Keats confirmed that his own larger aim is to write drama, '– the playing of different Natures with Joy and Sorrow' (*JKL*, 1, 218–19). Developing his ideas in a different direction, Keats declared to Taylor, on 27 February, that poetry should above all be 'natural':

> In Poetry I have a few Axioms, and you will see how far I am from their Centre. 1st I think Poetry should surprise by a fine excess and not by Singularity – it should strike the Reader as a wording of his own highest thoughts, and appear almost a Remembrance – 2nd Its touches of Beauty should never be half way therby making the reader breathless instead of content: the rise, the progress, the setting of imagery should like the Sun come natural too him – shine over him and set soberly although in magnificence leaving him in the Luxury of twilight – but it is easier to think what Poetry should be than to write it – and this leads me to another axiom. That if Poetry comes not as naturally as the Leaves to a tree it had better not come at all. (*JKL*, 1, 238)

It is significant that Keats use the word 'naturally', not 'easily', since he knew from writing *Endymion* the often agonising labours of composition, however compulsive the task was. The imagery of these passages show that by 'naturally' he means 'like nature' operating in its organic processes of time as it passes, and of inevitable growth. Keats may even be distantly recalling a passage in Aesculapius's *Hospital Guide* which seems to have especially influenced him: 'Real feeling for the suffering of others, prompts a wish to relieve those sufferings as naturally as the needle points to the pole, and as necessarily as the sun rises and sets' (pp. 88–90).

His brothers were still staying in Teignmouth, and Keats, worried about Tom's illness and their shortage of cash – a constant refrain while they remained under the guardianship of Abbey, though Keats himself had spent part of his inheritance on his medical training and most likely on publishing *Poems* – planned to visit them. This became necessary for Tom's welfare in his illness when George decided to return to London at the end of February. Keats left Hampstead on the night of 6 March sitting '*outside*' the coach in a dreadful storm, and arriving three days later to the 'abominable Devonshire weather' where it rained continuously. There, because of Tom's condition, he had to stay through the time of final revisions and publication of *Endymion* in early May. The trip back to Hampstead was even longer and more difficult, taking a full week. Tom lost blood on the way and felt by turns manically merry and in low spirits, to the extent that John wrote that he 'could not have stood it many more days'. The reasons they returned were first because Tom wished to be back in London and secondly in response to the rather tumultuous events in George's life, since he was to marry Georgiana Wylie on 28 May. Continually short of money, George had also decided to emigrate to America and become a farmer, booking to leave England in early June. He cashed in his portion of the inheritance, leaving £500 with Abbey to cover debts and also to help John and Tom. Although Keats was to live on this money for some time, the whole financial sequence was bitterly disputed after his own death by his friend Charles Brown, who no doubt perceived George's actions during the time of Tom's illness as thoughtless. Since Brown was himself to spend the next few months in the company of John, his later perception of the situation cannot be ignored. However, despite the inconvenience of George's plan, his wanderlust may have infected John and he too resolved to travel. Writing to James Rice on 24 March he weighed up the comparative merits of staying within comfortable familiar surroundings and seeing other places:

What a happy thing it would be if we could settle our thoughts, make our minds up on any matter in five Minutes and remain content – that is to build a sort of mental Cottage of feelings quiet and pleasant – to have a sort of Philosophical Back Garden, and cheerful holiday-keeping front one – but Alas! This never can be: <the> for as the material Cottager knows there are such places as france and Italy and the Andes and the Burning Mountains – so the spiritual Cottager has knowledge of the terra semi incognita of things unearthly; and cannot for his Life, keep in the check rein – Or I should stop here quiet and comfortable in my theory of Nettles. You will see however I am obliged to run wild, being attracted by the Loadstone Concatenation. (*JKL*, 1, 254–5)

In the event, he aimed not immediately for France and Italy, though he harboured longer plans for these destinations, but for the north of England and for Scotland. The desire for knowledge and experience outweighed domestic comfort.

In terms of his poetic output after being freed from his single-minded travails through *Endymion*, Keats returned to his earlier practice of writing short, occasional poems on whatever struck his attention – the colour blue, for example, in 'Blue! 'Tis the life of heaven'. Amongst what Charles Brown called Keats's 'fugitive poems', we find the 'light-hearted eroticism'[1] of more lyrics sent to women for their 'albums' such as 'Think not of it, sweet one, so', 'Apollo to the Graces', 'Oh, blush not so, oh, blush not so', 'In drear-nighted December', snatches of sexually charged ballads such as 'Where be ye going, you Devon maid', 'Over the hill and over the dale', and 'To – ['Time's Sea']' beginning 'Since I was tangled in thy beauty's web, / And snared by the ungloving of thine hand', written for the mysterious woman he had glimpsed at Vauxhall four years before and who was still haunting his memory. 'On the Grasshopper and the Cricket' and 'To the Nile' were products of the sonnet competitions held between Keats, Hunt and the circle of poets which included Shelley, where they gave each other fifteen minutes to compose on a nominated subject. We find political satire in 'Nebuchadnezzar's Dream', which seems allegorically to allude to the acquittal of William Hone the radical journalist and reminds us of Keats's consistent political convictions, and comic pieces like 'To Mrs Reynolds's Cat', 'Hence burgundy, claret and port', 'Robin Hood', 'For there's Bishop's Teign' written from Teignmouth, 'Lines on the Mermaid Tavern', a drinking song for those Elizabethan 'Souls of Poets dead and gone', showing once again Keats's special affinity with Renaissance poets over his contemporaries, and the droll 'Lines Rhymed in a Letter from Oxford', written when Keats was visiting Bailey, noticing 'The black tasselled trencher and common hat':

> The chantry boy sings,
> The steeple-bell rings,
> And as for the Chancellor – *dominat*.

There are also more profound short works that signal a new poetic maturity as Keats turns away from the romance of *Endymion* and the light strains of Hunt towards more bracing mentors, Milton and Shakespeare. 'On Seeing a Lock of Milton's Hair' is a serious imitation of Milton's own ode, 'On the Morning of Christ's Nativity' as well as personal tribute:

> Hymning and harmony
> Of thee, and of thy works, and of thy life
> But vain is now the burning and the strife,
> Pangs are in vain, until I grow high-rife

> With old philosophy,
> And mad with glimpses of futurity!

'On Sitting Down to Read *King Lear* Once Again' traces in sonnet form Keats's personal farewell to the poetry of Spenser, Reynolds, Hunt and his own *Endymion* – 'golden-tongued Romance, with serene lute' – to embrace a more realistic, painful and 'bitter-sweet' kind of poetry:

> Leave melodizing on this wintry day,
> Shut up thine olden pages, and be mute.
> Adieu! For, once again, the fierce dispute
> Betwixt damnation and impassioned clay
> Must I burn through, once more humbly assay
> The bitter-sweet of this Shakespearian fruit.

The very title provides an example of Keats's emerging theory of creativity, showing how he has passively experienced and submitted to Shakespeare's *King Lear* in a reading, before finding his own voice in a 'prologue' to his reading of the play. The sonnet is often read as confirming Keats's wish to break the poetic connection with Leigh Hunt, though Roe has suggested (not entirely convincingly) that it was written in fact to regain the attention of Hunt at a time when Keats felt jealous of the increasing favouritism Hunt was showing to Shelley. A companion piece is the earlier, wonderfully atmospheric sonnet, 'On the Sea', written on the Isle of Wight in April 1817 and inspired by Edgar's phrase in *King Lear* slightly misremembered by Keats: 'Do you not hear the Sea'.

Keats's correspondence also gives examples of the continuum between reading and original composition that he explores in the sonnet on re-reading *King Lear*, linking a starting-point in sympathetic absorption followed by active assertion of personal ideas and finally the creation of original poetry. He writes to Bailey on 27 February 1818: '– As Tradesmen say every thing is worth what it will fetch, so probably every mental pursuit takes its reality and worth from the ardour of the pursuer – being in itself a nothing –':

Ethereal thing[s] may at least be thus real, divided under three heads – Things real – things semireal – and no things – Things real – such as existences of Sun Moon & Stars and passages of Shakespeare – things semireal such as Love, the Clouds &c which require a greeting of the Spirit to make them wholly exist – and Nothings which are made Great and dignified by an ardent pursuit – Which by the by stamps the burgundy mark on the bottles of our Minds, insomuch as they are able to '*consec[r]ate whate'er they look upon*' I have written a Sonnet here of a somewhat collateral nature – so don't imagine it an a propos des bottes. (*JKL*, 1, 242–3)

Here he transcribes his sonnet 'Four seasons fill the measure of the year' whose somewhat opaque 'collateral' connection to the idea in the letter seems to be that the progression of seasons in nature are 'things semireal' which require personal, imaginative realisation or 'a greeting of the Spirit to make them wholly exist' as analogies for phases in a person's life. They are simply neutral until they are given meaning in a human, creative act of signifying value.

Examples of unselfconscious empathy and Negative Capability leading to a personal 'egotistic' statement come most often in Keats's letters to his fellow poet Reynolds. After justifying inactivity and 'a sense of Idleness' on a beautiful winter morning in February ('I have not read any Books – the Morning said I was right – I had no Idea but of the Morning and the Thrush said I was right – seeming to say –' [*JKL*, 1, 232–3]) he transcribes the sonnet 'O thou whose face hath felt the winter's wind' which argues that after the winter's wind and nocturnal darkness the spring will come as a 'harvest-time' bringing new ideas and warmth, just as idleness or dreaming are preludes to wakeful activity. The idea comes not from the persona of the poet, but is the thrush's song of reassurance as it returns from its annual migration in warmer climes:

> Oh, fret not after knowledge – I have none,
> And yet my song comes native with the warmth.
> O fret not after knowledge – I have none,
> And yet the evening listens. He who saddens
> At thought of idleness cannot be idle,
> And he's awake who thinks himself asleep.

The playful whimsicality of relative experience – knowledge comes from not seeking knowledge, a wakeful consciousness operates in the subconsciously alive state of sleep – is typical of Keats in his letters, and emerges with full poetic force in his later Odes. However arduous and against the grain had been the task of writing *Endymion*, it had, as he partly hoped, led to a remarkable maturation of his ideas and poetic range.

The verse letter 'To J. H. Reynolds, Esq' written from Teignmouth on 25 March, distils into its 'unconnected subject, and careless verse' (*JKL*, 1, 263) many of Keats's preoccupations and characteristic intellectual patterns at the time. Given that at least three of his friends and acquaintances were trained artists – Haydon, Severn and Hazlitt – it is clear that he has thought deeply about the relationships between visual art and poetry, and this is the most sustained contemplation on the nexus that he has written up to now. Unfurling in free-wheeling associativeness the letter keeps coming back to the idea that a visual image can coax the imagination into what Keats had called 'speculations', taking art out of its static element and providing it with a temporal context, a before and after, and this opens up the realm of poetry: 'A Question is the best beacon towards a little Speculation' (*JKL*, 1, 175). The letter begins with images as Keats lies in bed at night seeing 'shapes, and shadows, and remembrances', at first eccentric and miscellaneous domestic details but 'all disjointed' as in a dream which looks like becoming a nightmare. This touches off a connection with pictures that become more specific in reference – 'Titian colours touched into real life' followed by Claude Lorraine's 'Landscape with the Father of Psyche sacrificing at the Milesian Temple of Apollo' showing the ritual slaughter of a 'milk-white heifer' surrounded by humans celebrating, while beyond a white sail is visible on the sea, from whose ship mariners have come to join the sacrifice. Keats then evokes another Claude painting, which has come to be known as 'The Enchanted Castle' but which was named by the artist 'Psyche seated outside Cupid's Palace'. Keats would have seen both as engravings and the latter had been given a literary abode by Mrs Radcliffe whose novels with their gothic castles Keats had read.[2] Keats proposes 'To show this castle in fair dreaming wise / Unto my friend, while sick and ill he lies'. Illness is a quiet subtext of the letter-poem since not only is Keats trying to distract and cheer up his sick friend but he is also at the time witnessing his brother's ominous haemorrhaging. This is a clue to the work's deeper meaning since it exists on an interface between art and life, where the former can at least temporarily hold at bay the distresses of the latter but only in a fragile and unstable way. The knife of the sacrificer 'Gleams in the sun' and although providing an aesthetic image it also presages death of the creature. The castle itself is marked by mystery, 'a Merlin's hall, a dream', set beside mountains which seem to be invisibly lifted by 'some giant, pulsing underground', another hint that the beauty of what is seen emanates from something more disturbing which is unseen. The description of the castle proceeds in a way which has impressed an art critic with its imaginative insight into the jumble of architectural styles in Claude's imagined 'palace of art' with the 'heterogeneous nature of its architecture in style and period', 'existing in a dimension that is truly magical'.[3] As Keats evokes the scenery of the painting, so he vivifies it, turning it into poetry by suggesting the sound of 'An echo of sweet music', and movement in time with windows opening and mariners rowing. But the vision of the poem still teeters on something darker as Keats wishes that 'our dreamings' could all be so colourful, dreams instead of nightmares, 'Rather than shadow our own soul's daytime / In the dark void of night'. He abruptly and conspicuously tries to break off this train of thought but it insistently reasserts itself in 'the lore of good and ill' in ideas that 'tease us out of thought' leading the imagination into 'a sort of Purgatory blind'. At this stage the poet's vision inescapably is submerged in a more uncomfortable dimension of reality, which 'forces us in summer skies to mourn' and 'spoils the singing of the nightingale'. Here the poet at last decides to contemplate steadily and directly in a 'mysterious tale'

the shadow line separating the domains of art and life, and the poem itself
finds its darker destination:

> 'Twas a quiet eve;
> The rocks were silent; the wide sea did weave
> An untumultuous fringe of silver foam
> Along the flat brown sand. I was at home,
> And should have been most happy, but I saw
> Too far into the sea – where every maw
> The greater on the less feeds evermore.
>   ...
> But I saw too distinct into the core
> Of an eternal fierce destruction,
> And so from happiness I far was gone.
> Still am I sick of it; and though today
> I've gathered young spring-leaves and flowers gay
> Of periwinkle and wild strawberry,
> Still do I that most fierce destruction see;
> The shark at savage prey, the hawk at pounce,
> The gentle robin, like a pard or ounce,
> Ravening a worm ... Away ye horrid
> Moods of one's mind ...

Possibly recalling the lessons of his anatomy classes as a medical student,
and Albany's line in *King Lear*, 'humanity must perforce prey upon itself, /
Like monsters of the deep', as well as bringing to the surface a line of
thought hovering in the verse letter as a whole, it is in this spellbinding
passage that, I suggest, Keats is marking out the territory of the next phase
of his poetry and his life. Art, whether pictorial, poetic or sonorous, comes
directly from experience in a distressing world of circumstances, while at
the same time the very function of its separate realm is to keep at bay those
circumstances by taking them out of temporal flux.

In the same month that he wrote the verse letter to Reynolds, March 1818,
Keats began a poem which reflects some of the 'horrid / Moods of one's mind'
through a romantic narrative, *Isabella; or, The Pot of Basil*. He completed it in
April. The idea of writing verse tales based on stories by Boccaccio was suggested as a somewhat abstract exercise by Hazlitt in a lecture later published
in *Lectures on the English Poets* (1818), and Keats and Reynolds decided to
collaborate on such a collection. Another who, either with or without the
knowledge of Keats and Reynolds, also followed up Hazlitt's idea was Bryan
Wallace Proctor whose pen-name was 'Barry Cornwall', a poet who moved
in and out of the Hunt circle and met Keats several times. His offering was
A Sicilian Story (1820) which was based on the same story as Isabella. Keats's poem
was one outcome, but rather than reflecting Boccaccio's straightforward form

of story-telling, its narrative presents a macabre incident as an occasion for exploring mental or emotional illness caused by grief-in-love and images of death, which are in turn transmuted into art, all in tune with Keats's current preoccupations as reflected in the verse letter. Love is the subject, but it is presented as 'malady' rather than melody.[4] Over a year after writing the poem, Keats himself, in a phrase often used by critics to denigrate *Isabella*, came to say he thought it 'too smokeable' (easily mocked): 'There is too much inexperience of live [life], and simplicity of knowlege [sic] in it – ...' (*JKL*, 2, 174). Although the word was popularly current, it is possible, since Keats knew Congreve's play *The Way of the World*, that he found it in Witwoud's encouragement to mock Sir Wilfull, 'To him, to him, Petulant, smoke him ... Smoke the boots, the boots, Petulant, the boots: ha, ha, ha!' Keats's self-critical comment has often been taken to mean that *Isabella* is naïve and sentimental, especially since Keats also calls it 'A weak-sided Poem' and implies that it can be laughed at. But this is not the only possible meaning of his pithy words. He adds 'There are very few would look to the reality. I intend to use more finesse with the Public', and in its favour he says it has 'an amusing sober-sadness about it'. '– If I may say so, in my dramatic capacity I enter fully into the feeling: but in Propria Persona I should be apt to quiz it myself ...'. What is the 'reality' that most will overlook? What would more 'finesse' do to the poem? Why is the sober-sadness 'amusing'? It is at least a sustainable reading to suggest that the answers lie in Keats's distinction between the poet's 'dramatic capacity' and 'in Propria Persona'. It may be 'weak-sided' because the balance is not quite right between the two, the tale being told with more 'feeling' than is supported by the kind of inbuilt irony which would provide a running 'quizzing' or sceptical questioning of the sentiments, supplied by the narrator's 'experience' of the world. On the other hand, there is enough conscious, narratorial doubleness to say that the 'reality' of the design is discernible. There are signs, as Jeffrey N. Cox suggests, that it was more experimental than meets the eye, and rather than being like the conventional gothic romances of the time, it develops instead a vein of 'patently urban, chic and cheeky' poetry of the 'Cockney' school.[5] We should also take into account that Keats's comment came some eighteen months after his writing of the poem, and given his remarkably fast development between early 1818 and late 1819, his hindsight view may be harshly critical of the earlier work because he had moved on creatively. We should also recall that the poem is a retelling of a tale by Boccaccio, and Keats may have faced a technical problem in adjusting his perspective on such a simple source. He virtually says as much in canto XX, when he mentions the difficulties of turning 'old prose' into 'modern rhyme more sweet': 'The tale / Shall move on soberly, as it is meet'. The narrative itself is straightforward. Isabella and Lorenzo fall in love, are separated by her evil brothers who kill Lorenzo, and Isabella finds the mouldering head and grows basil on it in a pot. The fable itself is somewhat unpromising in its closeness to absurdity. Keats deepens the 'sober-sadness' with the Romantic ambience to be valued by the Pre-Raphaelites and particularly Holman Hunt whose painting is the most famous. The overlay of 'roses amorous of the moon', 'sunrise, o'er the balustrade / Of the garden-terrace', the 'palsied Druid's harp unstrung' in 'weird music', 'Red whortle-berries' and a host of pictorial touches create an ambience close to rich sickliness. But what the commentary offers is something more hard-edged and even cynical, as 'poor simple Isabel' has her youth and her very life itself wasted away through grief for lost love. The narrator balefully remarks, on the period of early love, before the catstrophe,

> Were they unhappy then? – It cannot be –
>   Too many tears for lovers have been shed,
> Too many sighs give we to them in fee,
>   Too much of pity after they are dead,
> Too many doleful stories do we see,
>   Whose matter in bright gold were best be read;
> Except in such a page where Theseus' spouse
> Over the pathless waves towards him bows.
>
> (XII)

Consciously detaching himself from the poet's 'dramatic capacity' of empathy, the narrator tells us not to be sentimental about this stage of their love, and he contrasts the more serious grief caused effectively by marital desertion of Dido by Theseus.

After the death, Isabella's feelings are presented in a critical light. She is said to have 'brooded o'er the luxury alone', to have initially succumbed to 'Selfishness, Love's cousin', and then to have fallen prey to 'tragic-passion not to be subdued' (XXXI). From here on the sheer waste of this young woman's life through grief is emphasised, as she 'By gradual decay from beauty fell'. She comes close to death herself. After she finds the corpse, the tone implicates Isabella in the macabre events of 'wormy circumstance'.

> Why linger at the yawning tomb so long?
> O for the gentleness of old Romance,
>   The simple plaining of a minstrel's song!
>
> (XLIV)

This, the narrator says, is now no simple romance but a 'vision pale' with more than a touch of disease in it. 'Love never dies, but lives, immortal Lord', and it becomes a recipe for losing touch with living things:

> And she forgot the stars, the moon, and sun,
>   And she forgot the blue above the trees,

> And she forgot the dells where waters run,
>   And she forgot the chilly breeze;
>   ...
>
> (LII)

And so on with more of the same as Isabella feeds the basil and the moulder-ing head with her thin tears in an increasingly obsessive and anorexic way recalling Keats's medical notes on 'hypochondriasis'. She never recovers, but pines. When the brothers steal the pot and discover 'The thing ...vile with green and livid spot' they repent and flee the country 'With blood upon their heads, to banishment' (LX), and Isabella dies. The whole presentation recalls nothing so strongly as Olivia's exaggerated grief for her dead brother in *Twelfth Night*, and the emotional paralysis felt in this play by Viola, Orsino and Olivia alike.

> She never told her love,
> But let concealment, like a worm i' the bud,
> Feed on her damask cheek: she pined in thought,
> And with a green and yellow melancholy
> She sat like patience on a monument,
> Smiling at grief.

The part of the brothers as murderers becomes less significant in the telling of the story than the consequences of blighted love. If romantic love leads to such appalling waste and death-consciousness, then what is the value of love? As we have seen in our analysis of *Endymion*, such a sardonic moral was by no means uncharacteristic for Keats, especially because in that poem the denouement turns away from the unattainable moon and towards the human woman. The hint that no love is worth dying in life for, or worth forgetting the world of the living and of natural beauties, accords also with his own determined, temperamental need to appreciate life before death comes, and even *because* mortals are conscious that death is inevitable. Only the emblem of Dido abandoned by her husband stands as the token of real grief, when set beside the young lovers' separation. With such a complex and dark attitude to romantic love running beside a rendering of the heart-felt feelings, it is no wonder that Keats felt he had not quite brought mastery to the tone, and that the 'reality' may be obscured for many readers.

The poem contains a startling digression which is one of Keats's rare insertions of directly contemporary, radical politics into a poem. We find an outraged condemnation of the world of slavery and commercial exploita-tion of people:

> XIV
> With her two brothers, this fair lady dwelt,
> Enrichèd from ancestral merchandise,

And for them many a weary hand did swelt
    In torchèd mines and noisy factories,
And many once-proud-quivered loins did melt
    In blood from stinging whip – with hollow eyes
Many all day in dazzling river stood,
To take the rich-ored driftings of the flood.

XV

For them the Ceylon diver held his breath,
    And went all naked to the hungry shark;
For them his ears gushed blood; for them in death
    The seal on the cold ice with piteous bark
Lay full of darts; for them alone did seethe
    A thousand men in troubles wide and dark;
Half-ignorant, they turned an easy wheel,
That set sharp racks at work, to pinch and peel.

XVI

Why were they proud? Because their marble founts
    Gushed with more pride than do a wretch's tears? –
Why were they proud? Because fair orange-mounts
    Were of more soft ascent than lazar stairs? –
Why were they proud? Because red-lined accounts
    Were richer than the songs of Grecian years? –
Why were they proud? again we ask aloud,
Why in the name of Glory were they proud?

The angry attack on forced labour and the slave trade here is as fully felt as anything in Byron's invective against war in *Don Juan*, or D. H. Lawrence's condemnations of the exploitation of Nottingham miners, but the most apt reference is to Goldsmith's *The Traveller*.[6]

Laws grind the poor and rich men rule the law;
The wealth of climes, where savage nations roam,
Pillaged from slaves to purchase slaves at home;
Fear, pity, justice, indignation start,
Tear off reserve and bare my swelling heart;
Till half a patriot, half a coward grown,
I fly from petty tyrants to the throne.
                    ...
Have we not seen, round Britain's peopled shore,
Her useful sons exchanged for useless ore?

(*The Traveller*, lines 385–92, 398–9)

The links traced by Goldsmith between wealth and exploitation, commerce, empire and human slavery, are equally powerfully expressed in the angry lines from Keats, but it might be objected that such sentiments are less surprising in the context of Goldsmith's poem on foreign travel than in a romance. We should remember that in his letters Keats often shows himself to be passionately indignant when he sees injustice, even on the domestic front and in his siblings' constantly frustrating economic dependence on Abbey, let alone in national and international politics. But what are we to make of the passage in *Isabella* in its unexpected context of a poem primarily about love? It could be seen as a digressive flurry of personal feeling on a specific matter but not accommodated within the material. Keats's clear and strong message is a digression from the apparently more important enterprise of retelling the old story, and its status is that of an incidental, opportunistic statement which risks losing effectiveness because it is detached from the context, an intervention in the anti-slavery campaign which had been waged in parliament for twenty years. The passage was found to be aesthetically offensive even to more moderate, contemporary critics:

> There are some stanzas introduced into his delicious tale of 'Isabel – poor simple Isabel,' in this volume, which, we think, dreadfully mar the musical tenderness of its general strain. They are no better than extravagant school-boy vituperation of trade and traders; just as if lovers did not trade, – and that, often in stolen goods – or had in general any higher object than a barter of enjoyment! These stanzas in Mr. Keats's poem, when contrasted with the larger philosophy of Boccaccio, and his more genial spirit, as exemplified with reference to the very circumstances in question, are additionally offensive ... (*Heritage*, 222)

Modern critics would not be so explicit about what disturbs them in this passage, but generally speaking they argue that it is not organically a part of the whole.[7]

However, it would be possible to assert the integrated centrality of the passage, especially since thematically related digressions from a narrative were seen as part of the conventions for Elizabethan short, erotic epics which Keats was following. The link with the rest is the statement that Isabella herself is, like her brothers, 'Enrichèd from ancestral merchandise', and living off the proceeds of exploitation and financial extortion. However innocent and beautiful, she is trapped by her situation, and one could explain her imprisonment ultimately by reference to the alienating and corrupting nature of the accumulation of wealth. Shakespeare's Timon of Athens may respond in a different way, but the conditions he faces in others are those faced by Isabella and Lorenzo who, significantly, is not considered a suitable marriage-partner for her because of his lack of wealth, 'When 'twas their plan to coax her by degrees / To some high noble and his olive-trees'

(Stanza XXI). Both Isabella and her lover are the victims (like the 'hunted hare' in Stanza XVIII, borrowed from Shakespeare's epyllion *Venus and Adonis*) of 'money-bags' and the commercial world of merchants who are accustomed to treat people as commodities. Such an approach to the poem might explain the problems of tone created by the strange co-presence of beauty and ugliness, the heroine's self-destructive grief, the omnipresent atmosphere of corruption and decadence in a story of essentially innocent love.

An ambitious poem written later in 1818 (between September and December) which more integrally presents a political message was Keats's first attempt of several to write on the classical myth of the overthrow of the Titans. *Hyperion. A Fragment* has to some extent been analysed in the light of his political views. Kenneth Muir writes:

> I am not suggesting that Keats's political views found direct expression in *Hyperion*, and still less that it is an allegory of the French Revolution. But it is not fanciful to suggest that the revolutionary climate of the time contributed to, if it did not suggest, the subject of the poem. It is, on one level, a poem on Progress. Keats's desire for an England in which the progress interrupted by the Tory reaction after the revolution is reflected in the poem ...[8]

The passage in *Hyperion. A Fragment* which most closely parallels the political interests and preferences expressed by Keats in his letters comes in Oceanus's advice to Saturn and the Titans, amounting to a call for revolution to overthrow an *ancien régime*:

> We fall, by course of Nature's law, not force
> Of thunder, or of Jove. Great Saturn, thou
> Hast sifted well the atom-universe;
> But for this reason, that thou art the King,
> And only blind from sheer supremacy,
> One avenue was shaded from thine eyes,
> Through which I wandered to eternal truth.
> And first, as thou wast not the first of powers,
> So art thou not the last; it cannot be:
> Thou art not the beginning nor the end.
> From Chaos and parental Darkness came
> Light, the first intense fruits of that intestine broil,
> That sullen ferment, which for wondrous ends
> Was ripening in itself. The ripe hour came,
> And with it Light, and Light, engendering
> Upon its own producer, forthwith touch'd
> The whole enormous matter into life.

Upon that very hour, our parentage,
The Heavens and the Earth, were manifest:
Then thou first-born, and we the giant-race,
Found ourselves ruling new and beauteous realms.
Now comes the pain of truth, to whom 'tis pain –
O folly! for to bear all naked truths,
And to envisage circumstance, all calm,
That is the top of sovereignty ...

(Book II, 181–205)

Oceanus goes on to warn the Titans that now there exists another race,

who do tower
Above us in their beauty, and must reign
In right thereof; for 'tis the eternal law
That first in beauty should be first in might.

(Book II, 226–9)

Here we find Keats's interest in the 'ripe hour' for revolutionary change, his sceptical recognition of the limitations upon the wisdom of rulers and kings, and his notion of the existence of a power-struggle which goes on ceaselessly in the interests of progress, 'Nature's law'. The use of the word 'circumstance' betrays a specific contemporary reference which was in Keats's mind when he was planning the poem:

... the march of passion and endeavour will be undeviating – and one great contrast between them will be – that the Hero of [*Endymion*], being mortal, is led on, like Buonaparte, by circumstance; whereas the Apollo in Hyperion being a fore-seeing God will shape his actions like one. (*JKL*, 1, 207)

An implication for the poem is that Hyperion, who never achieves 'the top of sovereignty' by being above circumstance, is an image of Buonaparte, overcome by the next 'fore-seeing' regime which has yet to reveal itself. Keats tended to follow Hazlitt, who eventually wrote an admiring biography of Napoleon in four volumes, in recognising the historical necessity of that figure, but he also saw more clearly than Hazlitt that Buonaparte must eventually in turn be replaced by a newer order.

The weakness of the unfinished poem, as many readers including Keats himself have found, lies in the insubstantiality of the forces which Apollo represents, at least in so far as the fragment reaches. Apollo may be beautiful and poetic, but Keats in the fragment does not yet come to the point of giving body to Apollo's moral right to succeed to power. It seems that his mind was still on the process of change itself, the movement 'of great import' which he detected in England, rather than focusing directly upon the proposed result of change, or what particular qualities are represented by the new, superior order. *Hyperion. A Fragment* is a poem as much about revolution as Shelley's *Prometheus Unbound*, but (again, as far as it goes) it lacks Shelley's clarity about the fundamental political issues involved. As a poem focused on change through both revolution and historical evolution, it confirms Keats's equivocation on certain problems and his own attempt to move forward as a poet. The poem lacks a 'future tense' since we do not know how Keats intended to proceed, and when he came to revise it later, he abandoned the fragment and started again from a different place in the myth. The style, however, marks an important stage in his development since he is consciously absorbing the influence of the massive epic paragraphs and vocabulary of Milton's *Paradise Lost*. He came to tire of this model which partly explains why he discarded the first *Hyperion* at an early stage, but the concentration adds a powerful capacity to his Spenserian and Shakespearean repertoire of styles.

Keats may have given up the poem also because he realised that his preferred poetic theme was inner change rather than outer, psychological rather than political. Reynolds was the recipient of another letter from Teignmouth, written this time on 3 May 1818, in which Keats presents one of several figurative ways of describing experience in terms of a maturing sequence from a state of innocence to experience, a subject dealt with at length in Milton's *Paradise Lost* and by Keats's Romantic contemporaries, in particular Wordsworth and Blake.[9] Keats obviously knew of Milton's and Wordsworth's versions and he explicitly acknowledges both (but not Blake's, whose works were not well known). However, his own account is entirely personal and 'Keatsian' and is signalled by the statement, 'Well – I compare human life to a large Mansion of Many Apartments ...' (*JKL*, 1, 280). This theory, like his other famous 'set-piece' passages of philosophy, can be seen to have a pervasive application throughout Keats's poetry from *Endymion* to *The Fall of Hyperion* and beyond, although it would be misleading to suggest one-to-one correspondences between the prose thoughts and specific poems and passages. The relationship between his letters and poems is always oblique and complementary rather than direct. Keats himself gives one of the reasons in this letter:

... for axioms in philosophy are not axioms until they are proved upon our pulses: We read – fine things but never feel them to the<e> full until we have gone the same steps as the Author. – I know this is not plain; you will know exactly my meaning when I say, that now I shall relish Hamlet more than I ever have done – ... Until we are sick, we understand not; – (*JKL*, 1, 279)

In saying this, Keats is reflecting the human context of the letter he is writing, and its train of thought. He is conscious that Reynolds is not only ill but also seriously grappling with a reluctant decision to change his profession. Moreover, because he himself has been caring for Tom he has 'been in so an uneasy a state of Mind as not to be fit to write to an invalid' in a way which may inadvertently 'have loaded' his correspond-ent 'with an addition of gloom'. However, Tom, after a sleepless night with fever has had a 'refreshing day sleep and is better than he has been for a long time', looking forward to walking on Hampstead Heath with his brother and Reynolds once again. In his new-found cheerfulness, Keats comments optimistically on Reynolds's plan to give up poetry and move into the law, which draws him into considering his own reverse choice of occupation:

> Were I to study physic or rather Medicine again, – I feel it would not make the least difference in my Poetry; when the Mind is in its infancy a Bias [is] in reality a Bias, but when we have acquired more strength, a Bias becomes no Bias. Every department of knowledge we see excel-lent and calculated towards a great whole. I am so convinced of this, that I am glad at not having given away my medical Books, which I shall again look over to keep alive the little I know thitherwards; ...
> (JKL, 1, 276–7)

He is reassuring Reynolds that pursuing law will not radically change him but will add 'knowledge' to his poetic soul, just as medicine has enlarged Keats's mental reach and is not wasted or lost in his poetic profession. The idea of ever-widening knowledge he sees, quoting from *King Lear*, as 'needful to thinking people – it takes away the heat and fever; and helps, by widening speculation, to ease the Burden of the Mystery: a thing I begin to understand a little ...' He illustrates this by saying that 'high sensations' *without* knowledge causes helpless alternations of mood and affections like an unfeathered bird in the wind, but *with* knowledge 'our shoulders are fledge<d>, and we go thro' the same [air] and space without fear' – 'This is running one's rigs on the score of abstracted benefit'. At this stage in his thinking he addresses the various emphases upon illness and knowledge: '– it is impossible to know how far knowlege [sic] will console [us] for the death of a friend and the ill "that flesh is heir to<o>" –' (JKL, 1, 278).

Hamlet's 'ill that flesh is heir to' which is on Keats's mind is undoubtedly the increasingly serious medical condition of his brother Tom. As always, however, the tangle of his thoughts has profound connections with his meditation on the kind of art and literature which will lead him beyond the fictive realms of *Endymion* into addressing serious problems of suffer-ing. He tries one more allegorical model to explain to himself the cluster of thoughts gathering around knowledge, sorrow and poetry, and once again he chooses the characteristic tripartite process of creativity to explore:

> ... in fine, as Byron says, 'Knowledge is sorrow,' and I go on to say that 'Sorrow is Wisdom' – and further for aught we can know for certainty! 'Wisdom is folly'... Well – I compare human life to a large mansion of Many Apartments, two of which I can only describe, the doors of the rest being as yet shut upon me – The first we step into we call the infant or thoughtless Chamber, in which we remain as long as we do not think – We remain there a long while, and notwithstanding the doors of the second Chamber remain wide open, showing a bright appearance, we care not to hasten to it; but are at length imperceptibly impelled by the awakening of the thinking principle – within us – we no sooner get into the second Chamber, which I shall call the Chamber of Maiden-Thought, than we become intoxicated with the light and the atmosphere, we see nothing but pleasant wonders, and think of delaying there for ever in delight: However among the effects this breathing is father of is that tremendous one of sharpening one's vision into the <head> heart and nature of Man – of convincing ones nerves that the World is full of Misery and Heartbreak, Pain, Sickness and oppression – whereby This Chamber of Maiden Thought becomes gradually darken'd and at the same time on all sides of it many doors are set open – but all dark – all leading to dark passages – We see not the ballance of good and evil. We are in a Mist – We are now in that state – We feel the 'burden of the Mystery,' To this point was Wordsworth come, as far as I can conceive when he wrote 'Tintern Abbey' and it seems to me that his Genius is explorative of those dark Passages. Now if we live, and go on thinking, we too shall explore them. (*JKL*, 1, 277–81, *passim*)

As always, context is important in contemplating the implications of this wonderfully rich and suggestive passage about the relationship between experience and poetic creativity, since Keats's 'we' includes himself and Reynolds in terms of Hunt's hopes for their future greatness. The letter becomes a meditation running alongside and complementing his writing of *Isabella* and the first *Hyperion*. However 'smokeable' the former and fragmentary the latter, both represent strenuous attempts to leave the 'Chamber of maiden-thought' and enter the 'dark passages' with new kinds of poetry focused respectively on grief and revolutionary political change. Keats's sudden shift in consciousness towards a new poetic maturity is so startling that we need to remind ourselves that the poet was still only 22 when he wrote it. In a conscious process of self-creation, he is leaving his palace of art for the dark passages of his mind, his poetry, and the glimpsed distresses to come soon enough in his life.

7
Walking North and the Death of Tom: 1818, July to December

Charles Armitage Brown was a friend who came later into Keats's life, introduced by Dilke, untainted by any association with Leigh Hunt and posing to the young poet no distracting tinge of professional rivalry. He was eight years older and his involvement with the world of culture was through drama and theatre, having written a comic opera, *Narensky*, which was reasonably successful in a run at Drury Lane in 1814. He had inherited £10,000 from his brother, a merchant dealing disastrously in 'bristles' among other things, although the amount shrank to £3,000 by the time the assets were finalized. Nevertheless he could afford to buy land and in association with Dilke built a house and lived comfortably for some years leading a 'literary' life without a pressing need to earn a living. Brown was 'a convivial, corpulent, bearded, balding gentleman of property and leisure, an epicure, and something of a ladies' man'.[1] He was to become an utterly loyal and devoted friend, the one who fully deserved the epithet which he asked to be inscribed on his grave, 'friend of Keats', in fact his closest friend of all. Brown, always a stocky, rubicund and fit man who was full of schemes, suggested the idea to Keats that they should travel together, and the plan that evolved was for them to begin on 22 June 1818 accompanying by coach up to Liverpool Keats's brother George and his new wife who were to sail from there to either Baltimore or Philadelphia. Keats and Brown would then continue northwards, first by coach to Lancaster and then on foot for four months through the Lake District and Scotland, during what they hoped after the solid rain of Teignmouth would be warm days of summer and autumn. That Tom was left in Hampstead might seem neglectful, but the Keats brothers were so mutually loyal that it seems likely Tom had reassured them his health had improved sufficiently to fend for himself: 'he has been getting much better' wrote Keats to Marian and Sarah Jeffrey just before leaving (*JKL*, 1, 290).

In the event Brown and Keats left Liverpool before George and Georgiana had left England, and almost a month later on 14 July Keats wrote to ask

Tom if he had heard details of them: 'I want very much to know the name of the Ship George is g{one} in – also what port he will land in – I <k>now nothing about it' (*JKL*, 1, 333) – in fact the boat was the *Telegraph* and its destination Philadelphia. They took with them, according to the official record, 'Beds Bedding & five packages',[2] and eventually, after two months' overland travelling in America, reached Shawneetown in Illinois and much later moved to Louisville, Kentucky. Meanwhile, we can trace the travels of the two friends through Brown's Journal, parts of which were published much later in 1840 and Keats's letters mainly to Fanny, George, and especially Tom, to whom he began writing, 'Here beginneth my journal, this Thursday, the 25th day of June, Anno Domino 1818' (*JKL*, 1, 298ff.). 'This morning we arose at 4, and set off in a Scotch mist; put up once under a tree, and in fine, have walked wet and dry to this place, called in the vulgar tongue Endmoor, 17 miles; we have not been incommoded by our knapsacks; they serve capitally, and we shall go on very well.' He describes the walk from Lancaster to Kendal and Bowness, then Winandermere (the old name for Windermere) and Ambleside. He notes many social 'disfigurements' introduced by 'fashionable visitors' from 'the miasma of London', 'contaminated with buck and soldiers, and women of fashion – and hat-band ignorance': 'The border inhabitants are quite out of keeping with the romance about them, from a continual intercourse with London rank and fashion', many of them having travelled up to see 'Lord Wordsworth'.

Hoping himself to see Wordsworth at Rydal on the morrow, Keats is mildly shocked to hear the news ('Sad – sad – sad') that the venerable poet is actively campaigning for the conservative Lord Lowther against the more democratic Henry Brougham in the local election. What specifically would have dismayed Keats was that Brougham had been the lawyer who defended the Hunts in court and therefore would have been considered a natural ally by Keats. Partly due to some dirty electoral tricks, Lowther won, to the chagrin of Keats who satirised the political situation in 'All gentle folks who owe a grudge / To any living thing':

> Is there a man in Parliament
> Dumbfounded in his speech?
> O let his neighbour make a rent
> And put one in his breech.
>
> O Lowther, how much better thou
> Hadst figured t'other day,
> When to the folks thou mad'st a bow
> And hadst no more to say,
>
> If lucky gad-fly had but ta'en
> His seat upon thy arse,

> And put thee to a little pain
> To save thee from a worse.

A meeting with Wordsworth was a high priority but was deferred into non-existence. With high hopes Keats slept overnight at Ambleside, two miles from Wordsworth's home at Rydal, looking forward to the next day:

> We ate a Monstrous Breakfast on our return (which by the way I do every morning) and after it proceeded to Wordsworths He was not at home nor was any Member of his family – I was much disappointed. I wrote a note for him and stuck it over what I knew must be Miss Wordsworth's Portrait and set forth again & we visited two Waterfalls in the neighbourhood, and then went along by Rydal Water and Grasmere through its beautiful Vale – ... (*JKL*, 1, 302–3)

Keats perceives the landscape through literary allusions to Wordsworth and Milton, the latter perhaps stimulating his choice of 'vale' since Keats annotated his copy of *Paradise Lost* with praise of the word's 'cool pleasure' – 'the english word is of the happiest chance'. Keats was also sharply observant himself of 'the tone, the coloring, the intellect, the countenance' of the place, hoping all the time to 'learn poetry here' and 'add a mite to that mass of beauty which is harvested from these grand materials, by the finest spirits, and put into etherial existence for the relish of one's fellows'. 'I live in the eye', he declares, 'and my imagination, surpassed, is at rest'. His letters are intended to be read by more than Tom and he adds coyly that he is 'Content that probably three or four pair of eyes whose owners I am rather partial to will run over these lines'.

The differences in style and choice of incidents and sights between Brown's Journal and Keats's letters are significant, and raise the general topic of travel literature of the time. Brown's descriptions are much more typical of the genre than Keats's. Carol Kyros Walker in the introduction to her handsome photographic retracing of the journey provides a valuable account of this genre, an example of which Keats and Brown used as their guidebook. It has been surmised that the book they used was the constantly reprinted *The Traveller's Guide through Scotland and its Islands* (no author named), though this is frustratingly impossible to confirm since writers of travel guides, then and now, constantly repeat their predecessors.[3] Like today, such books ranged from the practical guidebook to lavish works of reminiscence, and could also include powerful rough diamonds like John Clare's *Journey from Essex*[4] and picaresque quasi-novels of ruminative reflection on society, literature and politics. Such was *The Peripatetic* (1793) by the radical social reformer and writer John Thelwall whom we recall was coincidentally in the 1790s a close friend of Sir Astley Cooper and other surgeons at Guy's and St Thomas's who had taught Keats. This fictionalised record of wanderings around London and its environs by 'Theophrastus', which Thelwall claimed had influenced Wordsworth's *The Excursion*, was a repository of his opinions about society, history and literature and included 'ejaculations against the various systems of despotism under which it is the misfortune of the race of man to be oppressed'. Thelwall adopted the conventions of the travel record or 'tourist companion' to advance his political views.[5] Ever since the journey by Johnson and Boswell in 1773, a tradition of such travel writing, often written by and for lovers of literature, had grown up particularly concerning the journey through the Lakes and Scotland. As Keats himself noted, the Lakes had been discovered and populated by the fashionable but less than aristocratic set from London, characterised by what Brown calls 'the London sharper' of the dandyish middle class. The true aristocracy went to Europe. These two men were, at least in their own eyes, more like our modern 'backpackers' than those pretentious and socially aspiring tourists, and their interests were as much social and literary as picturesque. However, even between these two there are some differences of perspective and style in their respective accounts of their journeys.

Robin Jarvis in *Romantic Writing and Pedestrian Travel*[6] has briefly summarised some of the differences between Brown's and Keats's accounts, and has compared also Hazlitt's 'On going a Journey' which was published later in *Table Talk* (1821), but there is more to be said since they reveal the two men's attitudes. Brown wrote up his observations in what he describes as his 'pains-taking journal' and some of this was published some twenty-three years later in 1840 in four issues of *The Plymouth and Devonport Weekly Journal* (1, 8, 15, 22 October), more in the spirit of honouring Keats's memory than for their own sake. These have been reprinted in Rollins's edition of Keats's *Letters*, from which I quote. Keats playfully mocked Brown's orderly routine:

> Brown keeps on writing volumes of adventures to Dilke – when we get in of an evening and I have perhaps taken my rest on a couple of Chairs he affronts my indolence and Luxury by pulling out of his knapsack 1st his paper – 2ndy his pens and last his ink – Now I would not care if he would change about a little – I say now, why not Bailey take out his pens first sometimes – But I might as well tell a hen to hold up her head before she drinks instead of afterwards (*JKL*, 1, 344)

Keats may have written a journal that has not survived, but this seems unlikely and instead it is his letters which he seems to regard as his primary record. Given the epistolary spontaneity, they are not like Brown's rather conventional travelogue, but more characteristically a repository for all thoughts and associations that strike Keats as being of interest to his immediate correspondent. For example, in the letter to Bailey from which the quotation comes, less than half describes the mountains he has seen in

Scotland, the oatcakes he has eaten, a visit to Burns's cottage, and walking in the 'missling rain and splashy way', while the rest flits from Milton to Dante (he had in his knapsack a three-volume 'pocket' edition of Cary's translation of *The Divine Comedy* published by Taylor and Hessey just days before he left), veiled romantic allusions to the Reynolds sisters, and his doubts about having 'a right feeling towards Women'. Perhaps with an element of playful provocativeness, Keats frequently chose to share sexual innuendo with the staid clergyman Bailey. He closes the letter with verses, 'There is a joy in footing slow across a silent plain ...' which poetically attempts to capture a historical recreation of the Scottish landscape as it would have been visible to a 'forgotten eye' in earlier centuries.

Brown's account is written more like a conventional guidebook's: 'On the next morning, after reaching Kendal, we had our first really joyous walk of nine miles towards the lake of Windermere. The country was wild and romantic, the weather fine, though not sunny, while the fresh mountain air, and many larks abut us, gave unbounded delight' (*JKL*, 1, 425). Brown captures Keats at his most innocently enthusiastic, exclaiming at the sight of the lake at Bowness, 'How can I believe in that? – surely it cannot be!' and 'He warmly asserted that no view in the world could equal this – that it must beat all Italy' (*JKL*, 1, 426), whereas Keats himself in his letters maintains a guard of self-deprecating irony and satirical detachment, rarely expressing himself with such wide-eyed wonder. For one who saw himself as 'negatively capable' Keats's observations on the journey are often self-referential and self-conscious, usefully reminding us of two sides of his character, the one genuinely empathetic and the other hedged in by detached irony, often side by side. The differences go deeper. Brown's prose is not only more conventionally literary – 'there were a thousand enchanting peeps through the branches of the trees as we journied on' (*JKL*, 1, 427) – but also more infused with the vocabulary of art critics: 'Here are the beautiful and the sublime in unison...', 'the setting sun shot broad and defined rays of gold through the purple hue of the cloud...', 'the finest landscape we enjoyed in this stage ...', 'Perhaps [the waterfall at Ambleside] was better for a picture ...', 'we beheld our mountain scenery in miniature, and were made fully aware of the reason, why the best artist's representation must necessarily be inefficient', and so on. Likewise, *The Traveller's Guide*, in the main impressively factual and statistical, breaks into passages as purple as Brown's, using the vocabulary of art criticism:

> Nothing can appear more awful, or more interesting to a stranger, than the general scenery of the Highlands. The dusky mountains towering above each other in rival majesty, and veiling their heads in the clouds; their sides either broken into abrupt and dreadful precipices, or embrowned with heath, fill the mind of the spectator with a kind of pleasing horror, heightened in no small degree by the thundering roar of the torrents,

which pour down them with inconceivable impetuosity. The vales and glens below, narrow, deep, and so overshaded as to be impenetrable to the rays of the sun, add much to the sublimity of the scene. (2)

Such framing of descriptions in the perspective of formal landscape is a part of the genre of 'quality' travel guides of the time, clearly intended for a relatively literary and cultivated readership. There is some of this kind of 'framed' description in Keats's account, but more often he dispenses with the frame and takes us 'inside' what he is seeing, which becomes more than a picture with 'tone' and 'colouring' and more an immediate, sensory experience. The waterfall at Ambleside awakens all his senses:

> At the same time the different falls have as different characters; the first darting down the slate-rock like an arrow; the second spreading out like a fan – the third dashed into a mist – ... What astonishes me more than any thing is the tone, the colouring, the slate, the stone, the moss, the rock-weed ... (*JKL*, 1, 300–1)

Brown often rejects detouring to see sights and ruins declaring them 'scarcely worth the while', but Keats alights on the surprising and the human detail rather than landscape for its own sake. One of the most graphic and revealing contrasts comes in their respective descriptions of a dancing school in the inn they stayed in at Ireby. Brown talks of 'the skill of these rustic boys and girls – fine, healthy, clean-dressed, and withal perfectly orderly, as well as serious in their endeavours ... the feet moved, and graceful, with complete conformity to the notes; and they wove the figure, sometimes extremely complicated to my inexperienced eyes, without an error, or the slightest pause'. Keats, on the other hand, spontaneously flings himself into capturing the rhythms of the dance and the vernacular Scottish language:

> No they kickit & jumpit with mettle extraordinary, & whiskit, & fleckit, & toe'd it, & go'd it, & twirld it, & wheel'd it, & stampt it, & sweated it, tattooing the floor like mad; the differenc[e] between our country dances & these scotch figures, is about the same as leisurely stirring a cup o' Tea & heating [*for* beating] up a batter pudding. (*JKL*, 1, 307)

Alongside evocative descriptions of the colours of lochs ('fine Blue silverd'), mountains ('a dark purple'), the sun, Ben Lomond 'covered with a rich Pink Cloud', there are wry notes of self-ridicule:

> We were up at 4 this morning and have walked to breakfast 15 Miles through two t[r]emendous Glens – at the end of the first there is a place called rest and be thankful which we took for an Inn – it was nothing but a Stone and so we were cheated into 5 more Miles to Breakfast. (*JKL*, 1, 334)

If in fact they used the *Traveller's Guide* they may not have paid close attention since it describes '*Rest and be thankful*' as simply a 'summit' where 'a seat is formed, and a stone placed with the above inscription, which accords with the feelings of every traveller' (533). Sometimes Keats replaces prose description with a poem like the sonnet 'To Ailsa Rock' which describes a 'mighty Power', seen to the accompaniment of the sound of 'Sea fowls screams'. His prose descriptions are kinetic, lively and imitative of local dialects, and they include senses of sound and touch rather than routinely prioritising the visual. Keats could be equally disturbed by sights of poverty bordering on squalor, women walking barefoot and 'plenty of wretched Cottages, where smoke has no outlet but by the door' (*JKL*, 1, 309), the travellers dining on 'dirty bacon dirtier eggs and dirtiest Potatoes with a slice of Salmon' (*JKL*, 1, 319), whilst Brown was at the same time noting the people's cleanliness and neatness.

At Dumfries Keats visited Burns's tomb and cottage and wrote 'in a strange mood, half asleep', a sonnet – 'On visiting the Tomb of Burns' – which includes the lines 'Though beautiful, Cold – strange – as in a dream' and 'All is cold Beauty; pain is never done', as though the attractiveness of Burns's poems and of this region, like breaks in its inclement weather, is hard won from grinding adversity and from the Scottish poet's ambiguous life, his 'Fickly [perhaps for Sickly] imagination & sick pride' (*JKL*, 1, 308). Keats clearly found the juxtaposition of beauty and seaminess very disturbing and depressing, both in the environment and in Burns's poetry and his chequered life:

> One song of Burns's is of more worth to you than all I could think for a whole year in his native country – His Misery is a dead weight upon the nimbleness of one's quill – I tried to forget it – to drink Toddy without any Care – to write a merry Sonnet – it wont do – he talked with Bitches – he drank with Blackguards, he was miserable – we can see horribly clear in the works of such a man his whole life, as if we were God's spies ... (*JKL*, 1, 325)

Keats becomes palpably aware of Burns's 'melancholy' in his cottage while he is being bored by an old man drinking whisky (as Brown and Keats did, diluted, all around Scotland) and composing rough lines beginning 'This mortal body of a thousand days'. This repelled Brown who saw it as transforming any historical charm Burns's cottage may have had into 'a whiskey-shop, together with its drunken landlord', a poem which in Brown's eyes, 'went far towards the annihilation of [Keats's] poetic power' (*JKL*, 1, 332, fn 3). Keats addresses Burns as 'Happy and thoughtless of thy day of doom!' and continues:

> My pulse is warm with thine own barley-bree,
> My head is light with pledging a great soul,

> My eyes are wandering, and I cannot see,
> Fancy is dead and drunken at its goal:
> Yet can I stamp my foot upon thy floor,
> Yet can I ope thy window-sash to find
> Thy meadow thou hast tramped o'er and o'er,
> Yet can I think of thee till thought is blind,
> Yet can I gulp a bumper to thy name –
> O smile among the shades, for this is fame!

Brown's fastidious disapproval may stem from a perception that Keats has forgiven and even romanticised squalid circumstances for a poetic afterlife of 'fame', which does indeed seem to be the intention behind the sonnet.

Such intuitive and emotional responses are far from Brown's tourist's vision, and they accompany Keats's descent into a gathering depression as he appears to become aware of his own declining health and fitness. Keats also gives glimpses of grotesque and far from conventional sights like 'an old woman in a dog-kennel Sedan with a pipe in her Mouth' (*JKL*, 1, 326) in Belfast. In another description, he dubs her 'the Duchess of Dunghill', and amplifies:

> It is no laughing matter tho – Imagine the worst dog kennel you ever saw placed upon two poles from a mouldy fencing – In such a wretched thing sat a squalid old Woman squat like an ape half starved from a scarcity of Buscuit in its passage from Madagascar to the cape, – with a pipe in her mouth and looking out with a round-eyed skinny lidded inanity – with a sort of horizontal movement of her head – squab and lean she sat and puff'd out the smoke while two ragged tattered Girls carried her along – What a thing would be a history of her Life and sensations. (*JKL*, 1, 321–2)

The reflectiveness of the last phrase comes unexpectedly after a description suggesting that one of Keats's primary 'sensations' was to be repulsed by the sight of such material deprivation. As he remarks himself at times, an eye of Negative Capability does not flinch or look away, no matter what the arresting experience. Gillian Russell suggests that the sight is comparable to Wordsworth's agricultural vagrants[7] and the last sentence may suggest the kind of moral story Wordsworth would have made of it, but Keats's description inescapably suggests his own urban sense of being affronted by provincial grotesquerie and beggardom. The comparison highlights the contrast between two poetic temperaments. For Keats himself, coexistences of beauty and ugliness, good and evil, and the necessity of light and shade for a full understanding of people, are inevitable and cannot be rationalised away. Burns is an exemplary figure embodying the incorporation of dark and light. In both Ireland and Scotland, he notices the resilience of the people but also their degraded circumstances, and rather than glamorising or mystifying their existence he draws more political conclusions: 'On our walk in Ireland we had too much opportunity to see the worse than nakedness, the rags, the dirt and misery of the poor common Irish ... here and there were poor dirty creatures and a few strong men cutting or carting peat ... – What a tremendous difficulty is the improvement of the condition of such people – I cannot conceive how a mind "with child" of Philantrophy could gra[s]p at possibility – with me it is absolute despair' (*JKL*, 1, 321).

There was one indomitable, fictional character who rose above the degrading effects of poverty. While walking from Kirkcudbright through Auchencairn on 3 July, Brown spoke of the gipsy Meg Merrilies in Scott's *Guy Mannering*. Keats had not read the novel, but as Claire Lamont has suggested, not only was the figure already famous through the text but also outside it since a widely reviewed dramatised version had been staged at Covent Garden in 1816, at the time when Keats was reviewing theatrical performances and therefore no doubt reading them. Meg was played by Mrs Sarah Egerton and was praised in *The Examiner*. The actress had even been painted in this role and hung at the Royal Academy and the British Institution.[8] Brown reports Keats saying 'there ... in that very spot, without a shadow of a doubt, has old Meg Merrilies often boiled her "kettle!"'. Brown goes on to describe the spot: 'It was among pieces of rock, and brambles, and broom, ornamented with a profusion of honeysuckle, wild roses, and foxglove, all in the very blush and fullness of blossom.' Keats wrote the poem for his sister, Fanny, which may partly explain its form and tone which make it close to a rhyme for children:

> Old Meg she was a Gipsy,
>   And liv'd upon the Moors:
> Her bed it was the brown heath turf,
>   And her house was out of doors.
>
> Her apples were swart blackberries,
>   Her currants pods o' broom;
> Her wine was dew of the wild white rose,
>   Her book a churchyard tomb.
>
> Her Brothers were the craggy hills,
>   Her Sisters larchen trees –
> Alone with her great family
>   She liv'd as she did please.
>
> No breakfast had she many a morn,
>   No dinner many a noon,

And 'stead of supper she would stare
Full hard against the Moon.

But every morn of woodbine fresh
She made her garlanding,
And every night the dark glen Yew
She wove, and she would sing.

And with her fingers old and brown
She plaited Mats o' Rushes,
And gave them to the Cottagers
She met among the Bushes.

Old Meg was brave as Margaret Queen
And tall as Amazon:
An old red blanket cloak she wore;
A chip hat had she on.
God rest her aged bones somewhere –
She died full long agone!

Although some details are indebted to Scott's novel, yet Meg emerges as more of a Wordsworthian solitary character, independent and proud. The genre Keats adopts is ballad, with its rhythms, its neutral descriptions and its relinquishing final two lines which mirror the last stanza of *The Eve of St Agnes*. Keats's Meg becomes a complement to Scott's character rather than a duplication, both works heralding what Lamont calls 'the birth of that enigmatic figure, the Romantic Gipsy'.

As they approached the north of Scotland the walk had become gruelling. Brown is observed by Keats 'with his feet blistered and scarcely able to walk'. Their diet had been largely eggs, 'cursed' oatcakes and whisky with only occasional variation due to their limited budget. They were as often as not walking 'in a soaking rain' (*JKL*, 1, 339) and 'in a missling rain and splashy way' (*JKL*, 1, 343), and staying in Spartan accommodation often fugged with smoke from fireplaces without ventilation. An unobtrusive but ominous note is struck when Keats reports to Tom that he has 'a slight sore throat' (*JKL*, 1, 351) and realising that he must slow down and rest more, he begins to visualise being 'home'.

Still, however, Keats and Brown remained determined to see all the 'curiosities' they could, visiting islands such as Kerrara, Mull, Staffa (Fingal's Cave), a 'magic' place with its 'hollowing out of Basalt Pillars', on which Keats began but left unfinished the 'magian' narrative 'On Visiting Staffa', Icolmkill (now named Iona), visiting Ireland, climbing Ben Nevis. The 'fag and tug' of the last of these Keats describes at length in a letter to Tom dated 3, 6 August. A deep chasm near the top he calls 'a shattered heart or Core in itself' to Nevis and he finds the misty clouds 'finer' than the views – these cloud-veils opening with a dissolving motion and showing us the mountainous region beneath as through a loop hole – these Mouldy [probably misspelling for Cloudy] loop holes ever varrying and discovering fresh prospect east, west north and South – Then it was misty again and again it was fair – then puff came a cold breeze of wind and bared a craggy chap we had not yet seen though in close neighbourhood – Every now and then we had over head blue Sky clear and the sun pretty wa[r]m...'

> It was not so <clo> cold as I expected – yet cold enough for a glass of Wiskey now and then – There is not a more fickle thing than the top of a Mountain – what would a Lady give to change her head-dress as often and with as little trouble! (*JKL*, 1, 354)

The 'head-dress' of swirling mist persisted to the top. Stanley Plumly suggests that the whole description is so intense that 'Keats realizes that Nevis, perhaps even more than Fingal's Cave, is the surpassing presence, the natural greatness that he has been in search of this whole journey', an experience perhaps in the same category for Keats as crossing the Alps was for Wordsworth.[9] Keats appends to Tom an imagined, comic dialogue in poetry between the mountain and a fat old lady who climbs it ('She ought to have hired Sysiphus – "Up the high hill he heaves a huge round – Mrs Cameron"'). He closes the letter 'My sore throat is not quite well and I intend stopping here a few days' (*JKL*, 1, 357), followed by a sonnet which encapsulates his prose imagery:

> Read me a Lesson muse, and speak it loud
> Upon the top of Nevis blind in Mist!
> I look into the Chasms and a Shroud
> Vaprous doth hide them; just so much I wist
> Mankind do know of Hell ...

Since Milton's *Paradise Lost* was in his knapsack and on his mind, the first three lines may reveal its influence. On the same day, 6 August, he writes to his sister-in-law's mother, Mrs Wylie, lightly summing up the journey:

> But I must leave joking & seriously aver, that I have been *werry* romantic indeed, among these Mountains & Lakes. I have got wet through day after day, eaten oat cake, & drank whiskey, walked up to my knees in Bog, got a sore throat, gone to see Icolmkill & Staffa, met with wholesome food, just here & there as it happened: went up Ben Nevis, & N.B. came down again; Sometimes when I am rather tired, I, lean languishingly on a Rock, & long for some famous Beauty to get down from her Palfrey in passing; approach me with – her saddle bags – & give me – a dozen or two

capital roast beef sandwiches – When I come into a large town, you know there is no putting ones Knapsack into ones fob; so the people stare – We have been taken for Spectacle venders, Razor sellers, Jewellers, travelling linnen drapers, Spies, Excisemen, & many other things else, I have no idea of – When I asked for letters at the Post Office, Port Patrick; the man asked what Regiment? I have had a peep also at little Ireland. Tell Henry I have not Camped quite on the bare Earth yet; but nearly as bad, in walking through Mull – for the Shepherds huts you can scarcely breathe in, for the smoke which they seem to endeavour to preserve for smoking on a large scale. Beside riding about 400, we have walked above 600 Miles, & may therefore reckon ourselves as set out. (*JKL*, 1, 359–60)

Sadly, however, the journey was over for Keats. On 7 August Brown wrote from Inverness to Dilke: 'Mr Keats however is too unwell for fatigue and privation. I am waiting here to see him off in the Smack for London. He caught a violent cold in the Island of Mull, which far from leaving him, has become worse, and the Physician here thinks him too thin and fevered to proceed on our journey. It is a cruel disappointment. We have been as happy as possible together' (*JKL*, 1, 362). The next day Keats boarded a ship at Cromarty on a nine-day voyage back to London Bridge, while Brown 'trudged' on through the highlands.

The months from the time he arrived back at Well Walk in Hampstead until the end of 1818 were ones Keats would dearly have wished to forget. The devastating reviews of *Endymion* were published and friends testified to his paralysed dismay although he claimed his own 'domestic criticism' (*JKL*, 1, 374) inflicted more pain than *Blackwood's* or the *Quarterly Review* could ever do. Keats was also dogged by financial problems after spending on the northern journey his allowance and money left by George, and his sore throat persisted along with a painful toothache. He treated the latter with mercury, a choice of remedy which has raised some speculation that he feared his ill-health might be caused by venereal disease,[10] although there is no confirming evidence for this. As I have mentioned earlier, it was more likely to be one of several possible medicinal compounds containing mercury rather than the metal alone. Most seriously of all, he returned to find Tom approaching the terminal stages of tuberculosis. The day after arriving home he wrote to his sister Fanny that 'Tom has not been getting better since I left London and for the last fortnight has been worse than ever – he has been getting a little better for these two or three days …' (*JKL*, 1, 364). For the remaining months of 1818, Keats's letters echo and re-echo with news of 'poor' Tom's worsening health, and although he protects his sister from knowing his own state, he confides in Dilke his state of pessimistic depression:

His identity presses upon me so all day that I am obliged to go out – and although I intended to have given some time to study alone I am obliged

to write, and plunge into abstract images to ease myself of his countenance his voice and feebleness – so that I live now in a continual fever –
it must be poisonous to life although I feel well. Imagine 'the hateful
siege of contraries' [*Paradise Lost*] – if I think of fame of poetry it seems a
crime to me, and yet I must do so or suffer – I am sorry to give you pain –
I am almost resolv'd to burn this – but I really have not self possession
and magninimity enough to manage the thing othe[r]wise – after all it
may be a nervousness proceeding from the Mercury – (*JKL*, 1, 369)

To Reynolds he writes that he is haunted by 'the voice and shape of woman',
who appears to be Jane Cox, but he finds relief in poetry – 'There is an awful
warmth about my heart like a load of immortality. / Poor Tom – that woman –
and Poetry were ringing changes in my senses ...' (*JKL*, 1, 370).

Tom was clearly suffering from pulmonary tuberculosis, known then
as consumption or by the Greek word phthisis, which had killed their
mother some eight years earlier. It had been for thousands of years a deadly
disease, and still accounts for millions of deaths around the world. It was
the nineteenth century's equivalent of the Elizabethan plague, and in 1815
it killed one in four people in England, especially among the poor in cities
because of overcrowded living conditions. Historians have estimated that life
expectancy rose from thirty-five years to forty years between 1781 and 1851
due to some advances in medicine, and the rise would have been far greater
if tuberculosis had not been so prevalent.[11] To make this point, it is enough
to consider that those in the Keats circle alone who escaped the fate did in
fact live into ripe old age. Fanny Keats reached 86, Hessey 85, Fanny Brawne
65, Cowden Clarke 90, Dilke 75, Leigh Hunt 75, Proctor ('Barry Cornwall')
87, Severn 86, Taylor 83 and Georgiana Wylie (George Keats's wife) 82. This
in itself emphasises the harsh fate dealt to the Keats family as a whole (and
also to Woodhouse, the only other in the circle to die of tuberculosis outside
the actual family). Tuberculosis is highly contagious and spread by airborne
droplets through a sneeze, cough or saliva, thus accounting for its prevalence
in families. Some of this was known in the early nineteenth century though
it was not until 1882 that Koch discovered tuberculosis was caused and
transmitted by a bacillus, *Mycobacterium tuberculosis*. It is apparently not
genetic in cause although the experience of the Keats family suggests at least
a possible predisposition. Keats's teachers at Guy's, Babington and Curry,
had not only described in detail in their classes the symptoms and danger
signals but had suggested that such signs were alarming 'where hereditary
tendency [is] traceable'.[12] It is now known that the bacillus can lie dormant
in an individual for many years, or it can erupt suddenly when resistance
is low. The main symptoms are a bloody cough, fever and bodily wasting.
John, having nursed his mother and studied medicine, must have been
only too familiar with the fatal disease picture, and also aware of his own
vulnerability which no doubt added to his concern while with Tom and

suffering from a sore throat and cough himself. He expressed anxiety that George would some day die of the disease, which in fact he did, though not until twenty years later. This fact in itself suggests the possibility of a family predisposition since it is unlikely George would have carried the actual bacillus latently for that length of time. It could explain also why Brown, Severn and Fanny Brawne were unaffected, despite their close, daily association with sufferers. Consumption was at the time popularly associated with male creativity and female beauty, and taken as an example of the adage from Herodotus that 'those whom the gods love die young'. There may still be a vestigial belief that it causes heightened sexuality, if the rather incongruous British comic film *Twice Around the Daffodils* (1962), also known as *What a Carry On*, one of the more gentle *Carry On* films and set in a TB clinic, can be credited as having such a serious theme.

With his usual solicitude for others, Keats downplayed his worries to his sister Fanny, and regularly assured her that Tom is 'a little better', though to Dilke he was more anxiously frank. Back in London he could expect to see more of Fanny but Abbey kept his iron grip over their freedom of access. Keats had to ask him to let her come from Walthamstow to see him in Hampstead, and the guardian clamped down 'when he seemed averse to letting [her] come again from having heard that [she] had been to other places besides Well Walk' (*JKL*, 1, 385). Keats advises her to exercise 'prudence' in not telling Abbey of her 'little pleasures'. She was now 15 going on 16 and, even by the standards of the day, Abbey's interference in her liberty to see her own brothers, one dying and the other then 23, lest she should also see other company, seems excessively restrictive and suspicious. Keats emotionally draws his family closer when he resumes with George and Georgiana a correspondence which had been truncated by unfortunately misleading advice from Haslam. Writing a long letter spread over the second half of October, he does not bring false comfort concerning Tom's health: 'I could not bring myself to say the truth, that he is no better, but much worse – However it must be told, and you must my dear Brother and Sister take example from me and bear up against any Calamity for my sake as I do for your's.' Since mail to and from America was obviously slow, Keats was well aware that the worst may have happened by the time his letter arrived.

> Our's are ties which independent of their own Sentiment are sent us by providence to prevent the deleterious effects of one great, solitary grief. I have Fanny and I have you – three people whose Happiness to me is sacred – and it does annul that selfish sorrow which I should otherwise fall into, living as I do with poor Tom who looks upon me as his only comfort – the tears will come into your Eyes – let them – and embrace each other – thank heaven for what happiness you have and after thinking a moment or two that you suffer in common with all Mankind hold it not a sin to regain your cheerfulness. (*JKL*, 1, 391–2)

He hastens to reassure them that his own 'bad sore throat which came of bog trotting in the Island of Mull' has now cleared up – a little white lie in the face of the more alarming truth about Tom's present condition – and he downplays the shocking review in the *Quarterly*, almost casually adding 'This is a mere matter of the moment – I think I shall be among the English Poets after my death' (*JKL*, 1, 394). Keats was clearly aware that the letter to America would take some time to arrive, and he left it until around his birthday on 31 October to send off, perhaps hoping to give better or at least more definite news of Tom.

The 'one great, solitary grief' came all too soon. By 30 November he wrote to tell Fanny, who was still, incredibly in the circumstances, forbidden by Abbey to visit, that Tom 'is in a very dangerous state' (*JKL*, 1, 408). Tom had just turned 19 on 18 November. He died at 8 a.m. on 1 December, 'quietly & without pain' in the words of Brown who wrote at Keats's request to Woodhouse. Keats had walked to Brown's house to wake and tell him the news that morning, and he asked Haslam to write to tell George in America. Sensing Keats's desolation, Brown that morning offered him accommodation in the room next to his in Wentworth Place, Hampstead, adjoining the Dilkes' home:

> Early one morning I was awakened in my bed by a pressure on my hand. It was Keats, who came to tell me his brother was no more. I said nothing, and we both remained silent for awhile, my hand fast locked in his. At length, my thoughts returning from the dead to the living, I said – 'Have nothing more to do with those lodgings, – and alone too. Had you not better live with me?' He paused, pressed my hand warmly, and replied, – 'I think it would be better.' From that moment he was my inmate.

Since Brown's side of the house was soon vacated to make way for a family by the name of Brawne, the change in itself was to turn out to be a doubly significant event in Keats's life, on one of his saddest days. He moved almost immediately and spent the rest of 1818 'confined at Hampstead with a sore throat', commenting to Haydon, 'my general life in Society is silence' and 'great solitude', adding with a note of bitter misanthropy, 'I admire Human Nature but I do not like *Men* – I should like to compose things honourable to Man – but not fingerable over by *Men*' (*JKL*, 1, 414–15).

During the dark months at the end of 1818, Keats was working on what he intended to be his next long, narrative poem. From September until December he was writing the unfinished poem later to be published under the title *Hyperion. A Fragment*, a project which he had forecast in his letter to Haydon way back in January of the same year. Its altogether more austerely epic scope signalled a final retreat from Hunt's influence and his 'set'. Haydon was irritating Keats with requests for money at a time when he was facing financial difficulties himself. Keats gives vent to his irritation with

Hunt in a long 'journal' letter written to George and his family over several weeks in December:

> The night we went to Novello's there was a complete set to<o> of Mozart and punning – I was so completely tired of it that if I were to follow my inclinations I should never meet any one of that set again, not even Hunt – who is certainly a pleasant fellow in the main when you are with him – but in reallity he is vain, egotistical and disgusting in matters of taste and in morals – He understands many a beautiful thing; but then, instead of giving other minds credit for the same degree of perception as he himself possesses – he begins an explanation in such a curious manner that our taste and self-love is offended continually. Hunt does one harm by making fine things petty and beautiful things hateful – Through him I am indifferent to Mozart, I care not for white Busts – and many a glorious thing when associated with him becomes a nothing – This distorts one's mind – make[s] one's thoughts bizarre – perplexes one in the standard of Beauty – ... (*JKL*, 2, 11)

Tom's death, his own illness and the negative reviews had all taken their toll on Keats's patience, and his mood had become altogether less tolerant of Hunt and his circle. He could now see more clearly that Hunt had a 'vain' and 'egotistical' streak, though this was a probably understandable emotional shield for the beleaguered editor of *The Examiner*,[13] and that Haydon could be arrogant and financially parasitic. It is significant that in the same letter Keats mentions with approval Hazlitt's lectures. Hazlitt, just as politically radical as Hunt and a self-styled 'good hater' in his essays and theatre criticism, is an altogether more bracing and serious influence for Keats at this time, and from now on he replaced Hunt as intellectual mentor for the poet who found himself in his own 'dark passages'.

8
'A gordian complication of feelings': Love, Women and Romance

As I put the finishing touches to this book, Jane Campion's film *Bright Star* (2009) was playing at cinemas around the world. The biographical fact which has become so well known amongst even the most casual of Keats's readers today was in his lifetime kept the most secret. Even some of his closest friends and his remaining brother and sister did not know how deep was the 'understanding' between John and his next-door neighbour at Wentworth Place, Miss Fanny Brawne. By mutual consent they kept from public knowledge their love and engagement, and it was not until 1878, sixty-seven years after his death, that his letters to her were published by Buxton Forman, against the wishes of many including a descendant of the Dilkes and the advice of some who wished to honour his living wish for privacy. Oscar Wilde wrote an indignant poem on the occasion, 'On the Sale by Auction of Keats's Love Letters':

> These are the letters which Endymion wrote
> To one he loved in secret, and apart,
> And now the brawlers of the auction mart
> Bargain and bid for each poor blotted note.
> Ay! For each separate pulse of passion quote
> The latest price. – I think they love not art
> Who break the crystal of a poet's heart
> That small and sickly eyes may glare and gloat.

In such circumstances, some facts take on significance only in retrospect, and here the history is intimately connected with the history of the building which is now called Keats House in Keats Grove, Hampstead, then named Wentworth Place after its first owner and builder, Charles Wentworth Dilke, in John Street. The single building held semi-detached properties, one owned by the Dilkes and the other by Charles Brown. The Keats brothers had known Wentworth Place well, due to their friendship from 1817 with the Dilke family and then with Brown. During the summer of 1818 while

Brown was in Scotland, his half of Wentworth House was rented by a widow, Mrs Frances Brawne, with her three children, Fanny (Frances), Samuel and Margaret. When Brown returned they moved elsewhere in Hampstead, but returned to rent the Dilkes' dwelling when that family moved in April 1819 to inner London since their son was attending Westminster School. Keats was invited to share Brown's house on the day of Tom's death, 1 December 1818.

Fanny was born on 9 August 1800, thus turning 18 ten days before the Brawnes moved into the house. Living in the house of Keats's closest friend while he was travelling with Keats, it is likely that they met, as Dilke himself was to recall, at his house, at the latest in August on returning from the north. Others set the date either earlier or later in the year, but certainly Christmas Day 1818 was later recalled by Fanny Brawne writing to Fanny Keats after her brother's death as the happiest day she 'ever then spent' (*FB*, 41), and although the reason is shrouded in mystery it is usually taken to suggest an understanding of some sort with the young poet. Whatever disputes remain about the dates, Keats certainly declared in a letter to her close to the end of his life, 'the very first week I knew you I wrote myself your vassal'. They again became next-door neighbours in October 1819, around about the time in which they became formally engaged, and remained so until May 1820. During August–September 1820 Keats moved into their home and was nursed by the Brawnes, until he left for Italy on 13 September. These are a few of the only facts we can be confident of, and the particulars of what passed between Fanny and John were, not unusually between lovers, kept from public knowledge.

Despite his later declaration to Fanny that he had been her 'vassal' in the first week of meeting her, this may not have been quite the case. Like Romeo at the beginning of Shakespeare's play he gave signs of being ready for love, but there were other contenders for his affections. He had admirers, such as Marian Jeffrey at Teignmouth, the Reynolds sisters, Ann and Caroline Mathew, and Mary Frogley, and others he regarded as potential lovers. For one, there was a beautiful 'enigma' (Keats's word), Mrs Isabella Jones, who ran a boarding school and who regularly gave Keats grouse for Tom and himself. Her room had 'a bronze statue of Buonaparte' which certainly at that time meant her politics were radical, and she held *soirées* to which she invited at least Keats's publisher John Taylor, to drink whisky, and no doubt Keats too.[1] We know nothing of a 'Mr Jones' and her behaviour suggests the freedom of a widow or separated person rather than a wife. Robert Gittings may be a little heavy-handed with scant evidence in suggesting she made love with Keats on 20 January 1819 and inspired him to write the short erotic poem 'Hush hush ...' and the 'Bright Star' sonnet,[2] but at the least, after a rather strange meeting when she invited him under mysterious circumstances into her lodgings, they remained close friends from 1817. True to her sphinx-like behaviour, she had asked him to keep their acquaintanceship secret even from their mutual friends. Isabella is reputed to have stimulated Keats's interest in the Mrs Radcliffe-like neo-medievalism apparent in *The Eve of St Agnes* and the unfinished *The Eve of St Mark*, where she herself is certainly captured in the poet's artist-like gaze, reading with absorption amongst her paraphernalia of furniture:

> All was silent, all was gloom,
> Abroad and in the homely room;
> Down she sat, poor cheated soul!
> And struck a lamp from the dismal coal,
> Leaned forward, with bright drooping hair,
> And slant book full against the glare.
> Her shadow, in uneasy guize,
> Hovered about, a giant size,
> On ceiling beam and old oak chair,
> The parrot's cage, and panel square;
> And the warm angled winter screen,
> On which were many monsters seen,

One wonders if the puzzling phrase 'poor cheated soul' applies only to the fictional heroine of the poem or also is a tacit explanation of Mrs Jones's problematical marital state.

Another woman entered Keats's life and imagination in September 1818 when he met the Reynolds sisters' cousin, an 'east indian' named Jane Cox. Judging from his comments to George and Georgiana in America, he appears to have been instantly entranced:

At the time I called Mrs R[eynolds] was in conference with her up stairs and the young Ladies were warm in her praises down stairs calling her genteel, interesting and a thousand pretty things to which I gave no heed, not being partial to 9 days wonders – Now all is completely changed – they hate her; and from what I hear she is not without faults – of a real kind: but she has othe[r]s which are more apt to make women of inferior charms hate her. She is not a Cleopatra; but she is at least a Charmian. She has a rich eastern look; she has fine eyes and fine manner. When she comes into a room she makes an impression the same as the Beauty of a Leopardess. She is too fine and too conscious of her Self to repulse any Man who may address her – from habit she thinks that nothing *particular*. I always find myself more at ease with such a woman; the picture before me always gives me a life and animation which I cannot possibly feel with any thing inferiour – I am at such times too much occupied in admiring to be awkward or on a tremble. I forget myself entirely because I live in her. You [the George Keatses] will by this time think I am in love with her; so before I go any further I will tell you I am not – she kept me awake one Night as a tune of Mozart's might do ... (*JKL*, 1, 394–5)

Methinks he doth protest too much. Despite his claim of indifference, he goes on for another half page on Jane Cox's presence as 'a fine thing speaking in a worldly way', chiding the Reynolds sisters for their jealousy and pettiness. Elsewhere to Reynolds he reveals of the encounter that 'I never was in love – Yet the voice and the shape of a woman has haunted me these two days' (*JKL*, 1, 370).

The stunned description of Jane Cox and the mysteries surrounding Isabella Jones (as well as the haunting woman glimpsed at Vauxhall whom we encountered earlier) all contrast with Keats's initially matter-of-fact and casually unillusioned description of Fanny Brawne, written once again to his brother and sister-in-law on 16 December 1818 just nine days before Fanny's 'happiest day':

> Mrs Brawne who took Brown's house for the Summer, still resides in Hampstead – she is <her> a very nice woman – and her daughter senior [Fanny] is {I t}hink beautiful and elegant, graceful, silly, fashionable and strange we {h}ave a l{ittle} tiff now and then – and she behaves a little better, or I mus{t} have sheered off ... (*JKL*, 2, 8)

He returns to the subject two days later on 18 December in the same letter, which in its entirety covers a period from 16 December 1818 to 4 January 1819:

> Shall I give you Miss Brawn? She is about my height – with a fine style of countenance of the lengthen'd sort – she wants sentiment in every feature – she manages to make her hair look well – her nostrills are fine – though a little painful – he[r] mouth is bad and good – he[r] Profil is better than her full-face which indeed is not full [b]ut pale and thin without showing any bone – Her shape is very graceful and so are her movements – her Arms are good her hands badish – her feet tolerable – she is not seventeen – but she is ignorant – monstrous in her behaviour flying out in all directions, calling people such names – that I was forced lately to make use of the term *Minx* – this is I think no[t] from any innate vice but from a penchant she has for acting stylishly. I am however tired of such a style and shall decline any more of it ... (*JKL*, 2, 13)

After describing less flatteringly one of Fanny's friends, he concludes, 'Miss B – thinks her a Paragon of fashion, and says she is the only woman she would change person with – What a Stupe – She is superio[r] as a Rose to a Dandelion.' Keats has her age wrong – she was in her nineteenth year – but despite the facetious and mock-critical tone, we can divine his absorption in describing Fanny's face and body and theatrical manner, and the intimacy of their teasing tone with each other. By 14 February he says '– Miss Brawne and I have every now and then a chat and a tiff – ...' (*JKL*, 2, 59). She was just as interested in the theatre as he was, and he nicknamed her Millamant after the witty and materialistic heroine of Congreve's *The Way of the World* (1700) who was independent and spirited enough to demand equality in her 'pre-nuptial agreement' struck with Mirabell.

Perhaps the main aspect of the relationship lies in the fact that Keats seems able from the start to speak to Fanny without the kind of crippling self-consciousness or tongue-tied self-annulment he felt in the presence of other women. Perhaps unexpectedly he chooses Bailey the clergyman as the person to write to about this problem, acknowledging that Bailey 'appeard to wish to avoid any words on this subject ... don't think it a bore dear fellow – it shall be my Amen':

> I am certain I have not a right feeling towards Women – at this moment I am striving to be just to them but I cannot – Is it because they fall so far beneath my Boyish imagination? When I was a Schoolboy I though[t] a fair Woman a pure Goddess, my mind was a soft nest in which some of them slept though she knew it not – I have no right to expect more than their reality. I thought them etherial above Men – I find the[m] perhaps equal – great by comparison is very small ... When among Men I have not evil thoughts, no malice, no spleen – I feel free to speak or to be silent – I can listen and from every one I can learn – my hands in my pockets I am free from all suspicion and comfortable. When I am among Women I have evil thoughts, malice, spleen – I cannot speak or be silent – I am full of Suspicions and therefore listen to no thing – I am in a hurry to be gone – You [Bailey] must be charitable and put all this perversity to my being disappointed since Boyhood – Yet with such feelings I am happier alone among Crowds of men, by myself or with a friend or two ... an obstinate Prejudice can seldom be produced but from a gordian complication of feelings, which must take time to unravell<ed> and care to keep unravelled ... I am wronging no one, for after all I do think better of Womankind than to suppose they care whether Mister John Keats five feet hight likes them or not. (*JKL*, 1, 341–2)

Tantalising questions about his mother's behaviour when his father died play about his mentioning 'being disappointed since Boyhood', and certainly his height was always an insecurity. Elsewhere Keats patronisingly scorns 'the generality of women – who appear to me as children to whom I would rather give a Sugar Plum than my time ...' (*JKL*, 1, 404), although in context his primary point here is a rejection of marriage in favour of a solitary life. His sister-in-law Georgiana was the one woman he feels completely at ease with, and he says to her even of his sister Fanny, 'her character is not formed; her identity does not press upon me as yours does' (*JKL*, 1, 392). With Fanny Brawne he seems able to communicate in an intellectually equal way involving a mix of tones including flirtatiousness, mutual teasing and genuine companionship.

Fanny Brawne obviously became an integral part of Keats's life as his confidante and lover. Posterity has constructed her character in diverse ways, as fickle temptress or soul companion and muse for Keats. There are three pictorial likenesses of her which have survived, all dating from after Keats's death. A silhouette cut by Augustin Edouart in 1829 shows her full body profile and she is certainly dressed 'fashionably' with hair up in *bouffant* style, a bustle on her back, gown reaching to the floor and holding a fan. The second is a miniature painting (unknown artist, 1833) which shows her as a young woman with a slender face looking upwards, with arched eyebrows above large, laughing eyes and slightly lopsided lips, apparently wryly smiling. She wears on her straight, dark hair which is parted in the middle, a headband colourfully adorned in white, green and blue, fixed under her chin with a white ribbon bow, her neck open above a rich, dark purple gown fringed with white embroidery. The third is an ambrotype (1850s), a photographic plate, showing her in her fifties (though looking much younger) in pensive mood with the long fingers of her right hand resting under her chin. The hair is still dark, straight and parted, but let down and much longer, the eyes expressive but now serious and looking downwards, the mouth decidedly downturned as if in sadness. Her gown again has the air of being fashionable but it reaches to her neck and is somewhat matronly in its complex folds. She is upright and elegant in the silhouette, attractive and perhaps mischievous in the painting, darkly beautiful and soulful in the photograph. Her correspondence with Fanny Keats begun just before the poet's death tends to reinforce his own evaluation of her as educated, well-read and a keen theatregoer, intelligently opinionated and by turns humorous, commonsensical, fashion-conscious, lively and loyal.

However we assess and interpret Keats's feelings of love and attitudes to women in his personal life, it was undoubtedly under their influence that he wrote his first unequivocally great poem, *The Eve of St Agnes*. It stands out for its sustained, structural completeness amongst the many short poems, 'fragments' and the unwieldy and sprawling *Endymion*, which constituted his output up until then. It is written in Spenserian stanzas which are unobtrusively accommodated to Keats's own poetic voice, rather than being self-consciously antiquarian and intrusive as in his early imitations. Keats borrows from Spenser not only the stanza form but the neo-medievalism of 'faery land' though without the didactic purpose and moral quest.[3] There are also signs of the influence of Chatterton and of Mary Tighe's *Psyche, or the Legend of Love* (which also fed into his 'Ode to Psyche'), although by this time Keats claims to have rejected her poetry (*JKL*, 2, 18). But the most potent poetic presence is, I will suggest, Shakespeare. The signs are that the poem was written fluently and over a very short period for its comparative length, between 18 January and 2 February 1819, to be revised in September in ways that, as we shall see, irritated his publishers.[4]

Although the chronology of composition is not entirely clear, Keats claims to have written *The Eve* during an uneventful fortnight staying with Brown at the home of Dilke senior at Chichester (Sussex) and then Mr John Snook, an in-law of the Dilkes, at Bedhampton (Hampshire), before retiring to Wentworth Place to nurse his sore throat: '– Nothing worth speaking of happened at either place – I took down some of the thin paper and wrote on it a little Poem call'd "St Agnes Eve"' (*JKL*, 2, 58). It does seem that in this case, unlike that of *Endymion*, the poem came as 'naturally as the leaves to the tree', and although he calls it 'a little Poem' yet it is 42 stanzas and almost 400 lines long, about the same length as *Isabella* and 'Sleep and Poetry', both of which had been written with some labour. However, it is more tightly structured and evenly paced than either, richer in concentrated imagery, and economical in its presentation of a narrative. Later alterations proposed by Keats, adding erotic explicitness to stanza 36, were rejected by Taylor and Woodhouse for fear of giving offence to readers, and arguably Keats's first instincts were more fortunate. There are various literary and artistic influences behind *The Eve*, but its central idea, obviously suggested by the date, comes from English medieval folklore, that if a maiden fasts on 20 January – the Eve of St Agnes who was patron saint of young girls – then after following some domestic rituals she will dream of her future husband. In the telescoped plot of the poem, not only does Madeline's lover appear in her dream but he becomes all too corporeal, having come 'heart on fire' for her, 'Upon the honeyed middle of the night', and they consummate their love and flee into the stormy night and their unknown destiny.

The great literary and dramatic prototype of fictional love, *Romeo and Juliet*, is a pervasive influence, as the intense privacy of love is contrasted to a hostile social environment, the gothic, cobwebbed household's menacing inmates who are Madeline's possessive relatives:

> ... barbarian hordes,
> Hyena foemen, and hot-blooded lords,
> Whose very dogs would execrations howl
> Against his lineage.

Keats was saturating himself in Shakespeare at the time:

> ... I shall read a passage of Shakespeare every Sunday at ten o Clock – you [the George Keatses] read one {a}t the same time and we shall be as near each other as blind bodies can be in the same room ... (*JKL*, 2, 5)

All Shakespeare's plays about love express ambiguity surrounding this emotional state. The complementary vision encapsulated in a line from *All's Well That Ends Well* which Keats was fond of quoting, 'Life is a mingled yarn, good and ill together', was one that struck a chord. *Romeo and Juliet* contains not only the lyrical celebration of love through the poetry of its young characters, but also the more circumspect attitude of the Friar, and the Nurse's bawdy physicality, mirrored respectively in Keats's poem by a benign older order, the ancient beadsman and the aged Angela, who worries when she meets Porphyro that 'men will murder upon holy days'. *Antony and Cleopatra*, which had occurred to Keats in his meeting with Jane Cox, demonstrates that ageing lovers themselves might be gloriously poetic figures but also ridiculous and ineffectual in worldly eyes. The narrative poem *Venus and Adonis* is mostly comic in tone but ends on a note revealing the tragic aspect of love, while *As You Like It*, another of the plays which Keats quotes from more than once, points out through the words of its central character Rosalind that love may be more words than deeds, that famous lovers died, 'and worms have eaten them, but not for love'. In each of Keats's poems about love, he presents a similarly ambiguous vision of love as simultaneously alluring and fatal, incorporating darkness and light, good and ill, and it is in *The Eve of St Agnes* that he achieves the most convincing and unified poise between conflicting points of view. Even descriptions of objects in the building and the architecture itself, which Gittings argues is based on a medieval building and on Stansted Chapel, both of which Keats and Brown visited during their stay at Chichester,[5] intensify a set of contrasts ranging from the bleak wintry weather outside, the emotionally cold, gothic building reminiscent of descriptions in Mrs Radcliffe's popular novels published in the 1790s, the colours cast by moonlight through stained glass in Madeline's room, to the 'poppied warmth' of the sleeping woman herself, her discarded bodice still carrying her body heat. Synaesthesia creates the air of spiced richness in the golden dishes of fruit which Porphyro assembles, 'Filling the chilly room with perfumed light'. The ending, with its sudden, temporal shift from the narrative present to an eternal past of balladic history, is optimistic for the lovers, but the world they leave is unchanging except for an apparent sacrifice of the only two benignant figures:

> And they are gone – ay, ages long ago
> These lovers fled away into the storm.
> That night the Baron dreamt of many a woe,
> And all his warrior-guests, with shade and form
> Of witch, and demon, and large coffin-worm,
> Were long be-nightmared. Angela the old
> Died palsy-twitched, with meagre face deform;
> The Beadsman, after thousand aves told,
> For aye unsought for slept among his ashes cold.

By maintaining a narrative stance which, although neither aloof nor simple storytelling, builds into itself an even-handed, questioning and binary point of view, allowing both identification with and critical distancing from the lovers, Keats avoids the uncertainties of attitude that he regretted in *Isabella* and which open that poem up to misunderstandings. As in *Romeo and Juliet*, *Antony and Cleopatra* and *As You Like It*, there are at least two points of view equally available in *The Eve of St Agnes*, and while Keats notes the possibility that readers may attach themselves to one or the other, he really means to hold both in suspension, the one equally weighed against the other. Taken together they form a unitary, complex truth, an experiential paradox about the nature of love. Fortuitously, two actual readings of *The Eve* are available and they neatly illustrate the poem's duality. The first emerged even before the poem was published, and Keats was forced to address it. When he came to revise *The Eve* in September, those responsible for publication, Woodhouse and Taylor, vehemently objected to aspects of the manuscript and the revision. Woodhouse wrote to Taylor on 19 September (*JKL*, 2, 162ff.) describing the changes. He objected to two in particular. The first was the insertion at the end of the deaths of old Angela, 'dead stiff & ugly' and the beadsman, which he thought left the reader 'with a sense of pettish disgust'. Woodhouse reported Keats's indignant reaction:

> He says he likes that the poem should leave off with this Change of Sentiment – it was what he aimed at, & was glad to find from my objections to it that he had succeeded. (*JKL*, 2, 163)

Keats at least changed the words, and also allowed the beadsman to sleep rather than die (though it seems a metaphor for death), but kept Angela's death. Woodhouse regrets this desire 'to leave on the reader a sense of pettish disgust' and blames the influence of Byron's *Don Juan* which Keats had just read, with its 'style of mingling up sentiment & sneering'. Their second objection drove Woodhouse and later Taylor to distraction. It concerns the poem's consummation, in both narrative and sexual senses, which Keats wanted to revise in this way:

> See, while she speaks his arms encroaching slow,
> Have zoned her, heart to heart – loud, loud the dark winds blow!
>
> XXXVI
> For on the midnight came a tempest fell;
> More sooth, for that his quick rejoinder flows
> Into her burning ear: and still the spell
> Unbroken guards her in serene repose.
> With her wild dream he mingled, as a rose

Marrieth its odour to a violet.
Still, still she dreams, louder the frost wind blows.

Woodhouse says that in the original version readers (that is '*we* innocent ones (ladies & myself)'), could assume that the lovers merely get up and flee 'to be married, in right honest chaste & sober wise'. Taylor was even more dismissive of what he saw as 'the most stupid piece of Folly I can conceive'. Woodhouse reported the author's equally furious reaction:

> But, as it is now altered, as soon as M. has confessed her love, P. <instead> winds by degrees his arm round her, presses breast to breast, and acts all the acts of a bona fide husband, while she fancies she is only playing the part of a Wife in a dream ... and tho' there are no<t> improper expressions but all is left to inference, and tho' profanely speaking, the Interest on the reader's imagination is greatly heightened, yet I do apprehend it will render the poem unfit for ladies, & indeed scarcely to be mentioned to them among the 'things that are.' – He says he does not want ladies to read his poetry: that he writes for men – & that if in the former poem there was an opening for doubt what took place, it was his fault for not writing clearly & comprehensibly – that he shd despise a man who would be such an eunuch in sentiment as to leave a <Girl> maid, with that Character about her ... &c &c &c – and all this sort of Keats-like rhodomontade ... (*JKL*, 2, 163)

Keats was clearly defiant, but finally gave in and reluctantly allowed the original reading to stand so that it allows but veils the sexual explicitness in metaphors, and the final version reverts to:

> XXXVI
> Beyond a mortal man impassioned far
> At these voluptuous accents, he arose,
> Ethereal, flushed, and like a throbbing star
> Seen mid the sapphire heaven's deep repose
> Into her dream he melted, as the rose
> Blendeth its odour with the violet –
> Solution sweet: meantime the frost-wind blows
> Like Love's alarum pattering the sharp sleet
> Against the window-panes; St. Agnes' moon hath set.

It is not entirely clear why Keats's revision should be seen as more prurient than the original, and indeed it is arguable that the revision was not so poetically effective. Zachary Leader in a detailed study of Romantic authorship and revisions[6] suggests that at some level Woodhouse and Taylor inadvertently touched a raw nerve in Keats. Because of his height and his emotional paralysis with women, he always had some insecurities about his masculinity, a fact which cruel reviewers and Byron had exploited. At the same time, the publishers' attitude was largely commercial, since the genre of romance in which *The Eve* was written was angled overwhelmingly at a female readership and to alienate or offend this readership would diminish the market disastrously. The two interesting points about Woodhouse's attitude (and Taylor's, since he agreed) are that they come immediately after Woodhouse has praised the 'tenderness & excessive simplicity' of *Isabella* while Keats in conversation had distanced himself from that poem's 'mawkishness', and secondly that the influence of *Don Juan* had intervened. The latter's *louche* and satirical tone had surely suggested to Keats that his own poetry could be read as over-sentimental, which he tried to remedy. Some have interpreted his sensitivity in the light of the fact that Fanny Brawne as a schoolgirl was 'half wild' for Byron's poetry, an attitude guaranteed to stir Keats's jealousy which could be easily aroused even at the best of times. After an early enthusiasm he was himself becoming predisposed against Byron. Fanny Brawne almost certainly reports Keats's distaste when alive, when she wrote after his death, 'I have been credibly informed that Lord B. is not *really* a great poet, I have taken a sort of dislike to him when serious and only adore him for his wit and humour' (*FB*, 63). Woodhouse and Taylor, perhaps unsympathetic to these sensitivities in Keats's makeup, clearly prefer the veiled tone they assumed would be likely to appeal to female readers. But Keats went back and added the two unpalatable incidents specifically in order to pre-empt the Byronic attack (which he failed to do since Byron himself in 1820 was to accuse Keats on the very point of sentimentality). He injected at the end a greater realism by being more explicit about sex and including the death of Angela. In both cases he is, as he says, trying to make the poem less vulnerable to attacks on his 'innocence' and making the poem less 'smokeable'. This fits with his comments on *Isabella*, as he is trying to strengthen a sardonic, narrative perspective which frames the romantic story. In this context, Woodhouse's comments are not just guilty of the very naïvety Keats was trying to expunge in himself, but also an incitement to his sensitive irritation. Our first 'reading' of *The Eve*, then, is that by Woodhouse and Taylor, and it emphasises, to the extent of seeking to censor recalcitrant elements, the idea that the nocturnal encounter of Porphyro and Madeline was an innocent and ethereally romantic ploy to rescue the virgin from her unsympathetic household and to insert her into a conventional marriage. Although such a simplistic and sentimental reading cannot fully be sustained since Keats had most of his way in the final version of the poem, it was and is still possible (as, indeed, Byron's own reaction indicated) to highlight these aspects of the poem and see the hints of harshness as being simply an atmospheric contrast. The sexual explicitness, on this reading, is no more than an extension of the sentiment and an anticipation of wedded bliss. In an odd sort of way, even a reading by a contemporary feminist objecting to Keats's gender stereotypes[7] presupposes a variant on this reading which was emphatically not Keats's own, by arguing that here we see revealed Keats's perception of women as asexual dreamers while men are active agents. The evidence suggests, on the contrary, that despite his insistence on writing for men, Keats intended the complicity of Madeline in the elopement, and that with 'her burning ear' she is an active and willing agent undergoing her own sexual awakening.

Another reading that has been advanced, although more modern than Woodhouse's, may be equally perverse, this time ironically by overstating the poem's countervailing refusal of sentimentality. Jack Stillinger, in an essay which has become widely influential among students and teachers,[8] argues that the whole fable is one depicting Porphyro's predatory deceitfulness, his forcible rape of the 'hoodwinked' Madeline, and her dismayed awakening from a safe dream of innocence into a world of adult sexuality. According to this view, the passages showing a harsh reality simply provide further confirmation that the poem is the opposite of sentimental, and is an attempt at realism that is taken as far as the sensibilities of the Romantic age's readership would allow. Admittedly, apart from Byron (and Blake, the great exception to all rules and something of an outsider figure at the time), one is hard pressed to find other poems of the period which turn so decisively and graphically on sex itself, for even Shelley contents himself more with pleas for frankness rather than exemplifications of it in his poetry. Again, however, such a single-minded reading as Stillinger's simultaneously gains persuasiveness and loses credibility by highlighting ambiguities of language in *The Eve* while tacitly ignoring the clear line of the myth as a whole. It is undoubted – as Keats himself uneasily felt – that the 'colouring' of innocent sentiment which Woodhouse responded to is genuinely present in the poem as a whole, but at the same time the more realistic elements were intended by Keats to add a bracing element rather than to skew the poem in a completely different direction. Given the framing, unsympathetic context of the Baron's drunken household with its 'sleeping dragons' ('What is clear is that the castle and its inhabitants are inimical to their love', John Barnard[9] sensibly points out) and the resistant subjectivity of Madeline's dream, Porphyro's 'ardent pursuit' is a function of the plot, designed to rescue rather than violate. To apply standards of narrow causation and social realism to the climax of what is clearly intended as a romance myth based on quest and wish-fulfilment would surely be as pointless as asking whether the lovers ate the feast prepared by Porphyro, when he managed to secrete the food in a cupboard or to purchase the unseasonal fruits from such distant countries, and whether it provided a balanced meal:

> While he from forth the closet brought a heap
> Of candied apple, quince, and plum, and gourd,
> With jellies soother than the creamy curd,
> And lucent syrups, tinct with cinnamon;

Manna and dates, in argosy transferr'd
From Fez; and spicèd dainties, every one,
From silken Samarkand to cedared Lebanon.

However, the very existence of these two apparently incompatible readings proves Keats right in anticipating criticism of the poem. The description
is surely romantically evocative and not intended to be read literally. Like
Shakespeare, he is consistent throughout his career on maintaining a double vision where he expects both perspectives to remain equally available
in the reader's mind. *The Eve of St Agnes* is his most unified yet ambivalent
treatment of love, and he himself correctly places it between *Isabella*, which
tends towards the sentimental, and *Lamia*, which gives a perhaps not fully
intended emphasis to the rationalistic enemies of love. In *The Eve* he walks
the tightrope between, on the one hand, a world of drunken, feudal corruption, potentially invasive and violent male sexuality and also the ugly facts
of physical death, and on the other the timeless universe of young lovers'
aspirations for an unknown future of private intimacy, and the inviolable
dream of mutually uncorrupted but sexually awakened innocence. The
poem's great influence, *Romeo and Juliet*, walks a similar tightrope, finally
creating a single, paradoxical truth about the nature of dawning sexuality
and adult love. The poem itself, like its lovers, escapes the time-bound lit-
eralness of a dilemma, and entices rather than coerces the reader away into
a world where the joys and responsibilities of love may be reconciled. That
such a unifying vision, consistent with the ending of *Endymion*, lies just
beyond the poem's narrative closure, is Keats's wholly characteristic acceptance that perfection is not possible, except in the most transitory way, in
the world of time and place, that an idealised realm of romance, art and
dreams may not be simultaneously compatible with the 'real world'. Taken
as a whole, *The Eve of St Agnes* adds to the store of poetry a magnificently
inclusive fable, incorporating love's urgency and all-consuming emotional
amplitude, its transgressive opposition to a world of conflict, corruption and
restrictiveness, its simultaneous hopes and fears, realism and escapism, all
encapsulated in a detailed atmospheric ambience of rich colours, mysterious
shadows, and breaths of air that lift the carpets eerily.[10]

Porphyro in *The Eve of St Agnes* plays on Madeline's lute 'an ancient ditty,
long since mute, / In Provence call'd, "La belle dame sans mercy"', perhaps a
fleeting reference to the fact that Fanny Brawne was fluent in French as well
as a reference to Alain Chartier's medieval poem, but also a prompt for Keats
later to write his own version in poetry. Burton's descriptions of love-melan-
choly in *Anatomy of Melancholy* were also in Keats's mind, since he constantly
echoes this book. *La Belle Dame sans Merci, A Ballad* briefly encapsulates Keats's
ambiguous attitudes to women and sexual love in general. As McGann demonstrates in *The Beauty of Inflections*, the material circumstances of the transmis-
sion of this brief but strange text have implications for the critics.[11] There are

four relevant versions. The first was transcribed by Keats himself on 21 April 1819, abruptly introduced in a letter to his brother George and sister-in-law Georgiana in America. In the letter this is dated a few days after Keats on 16 April had described a dream, as prelude to a sonnet. He had been reading Dante and contemplating the meeting of Paulo and Francesco in 'the circle of the lustful' in Canto 5 of the *Inferno* section of *The Divine Comedy*:

> I had passed many days in rather a low state of mind and in the midst of them I dreamt of being in that region of Hell. The dream was one of the most delightful enjoyments I ever had in my life – I floated about the whirling atmosphere as is described with a beautiful figure to whose lips mine were joined a[s] it seem'd for an age – and in the midst of all this cold and darkness I was warm – even flowery tree tops sprung up and we rested on them sometimes with the lightness of a cloud till the wind blew us away again – I tried a Sonnet upon it – there are fourteen lines but nothing of what I felt in it – o that I could dream it every night – (*JKL*, 2, 91)

The sonnet does not convey a scene which is 'beautiful' but rather one that is disturbing and 'melancholy'. After beginning with a glimpse from classical mythology it turns,

> ... to that second circle of sad hell,
> Where in the gust, the whirlwind and the flaw
> Of rain and hailstones lovers need not tell
> Their sorrows – Pale were the sweet lips I saw
> Pale were the lips I kiss'd and fair the fo[r]m
> I floated with about that melancholy storm –

Commentators have not paid much attention to the links, but the context of this dream seems the one that Keats, five days later on 21 April, turned into his haunting ballad. In the letter it begins:

> La belle dame sans merci –
> O what can ail thee knight at a[r]ms
> Alone and palely loitering?
> ...

> (*JKL*, 2, 94–6)

Keats's only comment in the letter is a facetious one on the lines 'And there I shut her wild wild eyes / With kisses four' (rhyming with 'sore'):

> Why four kisses – you will say – why four because I wish to restrain the headlong impetuosity of my Muse – she would have fain said 'score'

without hurting the rhyme – but we must temper the Imagination as the Critics say with Judgment. I was obliged to choose an even number that both eyes might have fair play: and to speak truly I think two a piece quite sufficient – Suppose I had said seven; there would have been a three and a half a piece – a very awkward affair – and well got out of on my side – (*JKL*, 2, 97)

The satirical tone of this recalls most strongly that of Byron's *Don Juan* (Books One and Two of which appeared in the same year), a comic distancing from the narrator's rapt solemnity by a poet, self-consciously aware of his craft:

> A long, long kiss, a kiss of Youth, and Love
>
> ...
>
> Each kiss a heart-quake, - for a kiss's strength,
> I think, it must be reckoned by its length.
>
> (Byron, *Don Juan*, Canto the Second, CLXXXVI)

The second context for Keats's poem is the version printed under the name 'Caviare' in the *Indicator* on 10 May 1820:

> La Belle Dame Sans Merci, A Ballad
> Ah! what can ail thee, wretched wight,
> Alone and palely loitering
>
> ...

It is easy to argue that the changes here make the tone even more ironic than Keats's comment, since 'wretched wight' is a more critical and judgmental phrase than 'knight at arms', and the reference to the poem as 'A Ballad' (albeit a fragmentary one) shifts the poetic mode away from the subjectivity of lyric. John Barnard in the notes to his edition points out that most critics feel the revisions make the printed poem inferior to the letter version. This is by no means self-evident, as McGann argues. The *Indicator* was edited by the liberal Leigh Hunt, and the pseudonym 'Caviare' would seem to provide an ironic, French-tinged frame and recalls Hamlet's phrase, 'caviare to the general', that encourages us not to read the poem as subjective or personal. Bate's argument that 'One can only suppose that Hunt – possibly Woodhouse – thought, with myopic good-will, that the magic, dreamlike quality of the poem would be considered "sentimental"'[12] can easily be upturned to suggest that Keats himself intended to eliminate any 'sentimental' reading that critics or readers 'with myopic good-will' might construct – that he meant it to be an ironic and even harsh view of the man in love. The third printing of the poem sealed the letter version as authoritative, since Milnes returned to this, which I take as the fourth version, in his edition of Keats's poems in 1848 (the poem was not included in either of Keats's collections of short poems).

The differences between the versions are not of mere pedantic interest, as McGann points out, but rather their existence makes impossible a single, conflated or 'authoritative' text. Stillinger in his monumental edition explains the textual intricacies. There can be said to be two poems, differing from each other at a tonal level. They can be summarised briefly. The first is that of the 'sentimentalist', constructing a sincere poet thinly disguised as narrator, forsaken in love by a merciless *femme fatale* with wild eyes who had cosseted him, looked at him 'as she did love, / And made sweet moan' and who had confessed seductively 'in language strange', ' "I love thee true" '. She then lulls the hapless man to sleep, where he dreams ('Ah! woe betide! –') that she had enthralled and deceived many 'pale kings and princes too', leaving them starved on the cold hill's side. A variant on this reading has been proposed though not especially convincingly, that the poem is Keats's comment on the cruel joke played by Charles Wells who had written fake love letters to Tom from 'Amena Bellafilla'. Given Keats's later anger this would make the lyric deadly serious in its tone, suggesting that the fictional female seductress has literally helped to kill his brother. When the knight awakens, we presume that he too has been forsaken, and he sojourns forever, 'Alone and palely loitering' in a world that is withered, barren, birdless and futile. It is extraordinary, however, that so little needs to be changed to make a virtually opposite reading. If we accept that the poem is a distanced ballad rather than a lyric, that the man is an 'everyman' in love, a generalised 'wretched wight', rather than a noble knight at arms, and that, moreover, it is not the poet at all but one whom the poet in mood of superiority and irony ('Caviare') is not pitying but scorning, then the whole adds up to a condemnation of male fantasy. The woman's own view is not directly given, but rather it is constructed through the man's consciousness, and his responses are guided more by his own dream and lovesick state than by anything we definitely know the woman has done. She is the woman in courtly poetry, aloof and not seductive. Does the poem reveal Keats's masculinist and misogynistic distaste for powerful women who seduce and then betray innocent men? Or is it a wry and harsh judgment passed on the tendency of men to create such self-justifying and self-pitying fantasies that the actions and feelings of real women become irrelevant? Sarah Wootton, pointing out that interest in the poem was not really sparked until the *fin de siècle* replaced conventional Victorian gender norms with more open debates about gender ambiguities, suggests that Keats's *femme fatale* in this poem is a truly indeterminate being whose 'enigmatic qualities invite feminist readings of the text'.[13] Elizabeth Fay has summarised briefly one among many possible gendered interpretations:

> The poem's subtext, regardless of version, is a serious critique of romance. Despite the characters' gendering, the poem depicts the very real

enthralment in which romance holds women. The effeminated knight stands in for the woman reader, while the belle dame is romance itself. Yet the knight is also the male reader, he who is taken in by romance's promises, its fantastic time. Situated in false (or fictive) time, unreliable genderings and enthralment, the poem calls into question the problem of true love, fantasy and escape and the workings of the imagination, the very conditions of romance.[14]

Aware of the danger of his poems about love being 'smokeable', Keats builds in a radical ambivalence that makes the poem itself a paradox in both senses of that word, insoluble riddle and experiential complexity, as enigmatic as its lady. The ambiguity turns on a pattern which is very characteristic in Keats's poems and especially visible in 'Ode to a Nightingale'. A dream of undoubted ecstasy, full of 'relish sweet / And honey wild and manna dew' as well as 'strange' language, turns into a vision which is disillusioned and detached, as the poet sees 'pale' figures 'in thrall', their 'starv'd lips' gaping 'With horrid warning', to be followed by the moment of waking up 'On the cold hill's side':

> And this is [why] I <wither> sojourn here
> Alone and palely loitering;
> Though the sedge is wither'd from<e> the Lak[e]
> And no birds sing – ...

Enough has been said in the earlier chapter on *Endymion* to mount a similar argument about the poem's indeterminacy of point of view, although we might suspect that in *Endymion* the shifts are the result of genuine emotional uncertainty on Keats's part rather than of artistic distance. There is plenty of evidence in the letters that he was capable of swinging between extremes of self-absorption and ironic self-awareness of the man in love.

> Nothing strikes me so forcibly with a sense of the rediculous [sic] as love – A Man in love I do think cuts the sorryest figure in the world – Even when I know a poor fool to be really in pain about it, I could burst out laughing in his face – His pathetic visage becomes irrisistable [sic] ... (*JKL*, 2, 187–8)

Significantly, this passage is followed by an openly comic, 'nonsense' verse about 'a party of Lovers' whom Keats contrasts with 'Knights of old': 'Pensive they sit, and roll their languid eyes ...' Even the misprint 'rediculous' is symptomatic of Keats's attitude of the embarrassing conduct of the blushing man in love (not necessarily, as Christopher Ricks argues, Keats's own embarrassment). Even when he could perhaps be forgiven some distress on his own account, Keats does not always abandon this critique of men.

In a letter to Fanny Brawne he contrasts his night-time moods ('when the lonely day has closed, and the lonely, silent, unmusical Chamber is waiting to receive me as into a Sepulchre') and the 'more reasonable' morning mood when he recognises that his distress is one 'which I have often laughed at in another', even 'a little mad' (*JKL*, 2, 122). Keats's true subject is the ambiguous effect of love on human beings, and poems such as *Endymion*, *Isabella* and *Lamia* present love as a comparably paradoxical state. In each he is trying different ways to distance his thoughts from his feelings on this subject, to contemplate love critically rather than to praise or re-experience it.

Lamia lies in the same territory, though it was written two or three months after *La Belle Dame*, between 28 June and 11 July 1819 when Keats was staying on the Isle of Wight, and completed in Winchester between 12 August and 5 September. The germ of the poem's leading idea once again came from Lemprière's classical dictionary, where lamias are described as 'certain monsters of Africa, who had the face and breast of a woman, and the rest of the body like that of a serpent. They allured strangers to them, that they might devour them ...' In pinpointing the problems about *Isabella; or, the Pot of Basil*, Keats had added 'There is no objection of this kind to Lamia – A good deal to St Agnes Eve – only not so glaring –' (*JKL*, 2, 174), and if the analysis above is accepted then it becomes clearer what he means about the other two poems. It is hard to say why *Lamia* has had such a muted response from critics, since it seems one of Keats's most successful poetic deployments of myth. Usually his own harshest critic, he described the poem as giving what readers want, 'sensation':

> I have been reading over a part of a short poem I have composed lately call'd 'Lamia' – and I am certain there is that sort of fire in it which must take hold of people in some way – give them either pleasant or unpleasant sensation. What they want is a sensation of some sort. (*JKL*, 2, 189)

Just as there are two simultaneous points of view, the romantic and the rational, the Lamian and Apollonian respectively, so there are two styles. Perhaps recalling Shakespeare's snake in *As You Like It*, 'green and gilded' which 'wreathed' itself around Orlando's brother and then 'with indented glides did slip away', Keats can pull out the organ stops of a Shakespearian richness of imagery when dealing with the dazzling impression of the 'palpitating snake, / Bright, and cirque-couchant in a dusky brake' (*Lamia*, I, 46–7); 'the words she spake / Came, as through bubbling honey' (I, 64–5);

> Ravished, she lifted her Circean head,
> Blushed a live damask, and swift-lisping said,
> 'I was a woman ...'

> (I, 115–17)

He can equally move into the calm, Grecian style of Milton's 'L'Allegro' and 'Il Penseroso': 'Now on the moth-time of that evening dim ...' (I, 220); 'His silent sandals swept the mossy green' (I, 239):

> Men, women, rich and poor, in the cool hours,
> Shuffled their sandals o'er the pavement white,
> Companioned or alone ...

(I, 355–7)

Lamia avoids the danger posed by the narrative technique in *Isabella*. Here, Keats does not try to balance a narratorial voice against dramatic involvement with the characters' feelings, but rather maintains a tone which is neutral while inviting us to give equal weight to the two opposing points of view which are presented both allegorically and dramatically. We can then by turns 'empathise' with each, allowing the contrast to be registered, but at the same time both are contained within an overall perspective of impartial narration. This time Keats comes close to realising his simultaneously double view of love which he had balanced in *La Belle Dame*: when in love a man is full of unselfconscious passion, but viewed from the outside he may be 'rediculous', and both are true.

The fact that Keats is able to do this is a result of his choice of myth. Unlike the Boccaccio story of the pot of basil, the very fable of the snake-woman and the philosopher, taken from Burton's *Anatomy of Melancholy*, builds into itself a dialectic. Fascinating beauty, deception, self-deception and love are carried by the Lamia thread, while cool rationality and piercing clarity characterise Apollonius. There is a sense in which, thematically, the latter must 'win' the debate for, in Shakespeare's words in *As You Like It*, 'men are April when they woo, December when they wed; maids are May when they are maids, but the sky changes when they are wives', and dream cannot survive too much reality:

> Love in a hut, with water and a crust,
> Is – Love, forgive us! – cinders, ashes, dust.

(*Lamia*, II, 1–2)

However, where Keats goes further and turns simple contradiction into paradox, is in building into the presentation of each separate point of view a further ambiguity. Looking towards his preferred vocation as dramatist, Keats presents both Lamia and Apollonius as sympathetic and unsympathetic in equal measures. Both are seen from objective and subjective perspectives. Keats makes it emotionally impossible not to respond to Lamia's position, trapped as her 'human' feelings are within a snake's body. Her loneliness, 'loveliness invisible', and grief invite 'compassion' (I, 106). Even though she is 'yet free / To wander as she loves, in liberty', she lacks the fundamental freedom of her former 'woman's shape' (I, 108–9, 118). On the other hand, the reason she was metamorphosed into a snake was as punishment for deceptive charm, and when she is changed back into a woman by Hermes, deception takes over again. Masquerading as 'A virgin purest lipped', yet she is 'in the lore / Of love deep learned to the red heart's core', able to

> Intrigue with the specious chaos, and dispart
> Its most ambiguous atoms with sure art;
> As though in Cupid's college she had spent
> Sweet days a lovely graduate ...

> (I, 195–8)

The 'ambiguous atoms' are those of love itself in Keats's view, for on this level Lamia is just as unillusioned and even cynical as Apollonius, and she becomes more unsympathetic as she exploits her love-lore in seducing Lycius. It is probably impossible to deny the charge convincingly. However, she is not only deceptive but also has human desires and vulnerabilities that lead her love into deception. If this is a stereotype of female wiles, it is not being brought forward for its own sake as a comment on women but is being used in a broader myth of love itself – it is love that is deceptive, a moral that might apply equally to men as women. Like Shakespeare's Venus, although Lamia is immortal yet she has human feelings and frailties, and love itself contains such contradictions.

Apollonius is just as much a stereotype of male reason, but again Keats complicates the issue by presenting him in a dual light in relation to the world of feelings, beauty and love. In his positive light, Apollonius is a scholar and teacher, dignified, 'Slow-stepped, and robed in philosophic gown', a 'trusty guide / And good instructor' who may even recall Astley Cooper, and his role, for all its ruthlessness, has an inherent stability lacking in the volatile lovers. It comes as no surprise when, at the wedding banquet,

> The bald-head philosopher
> Had fixed his eye, without a twinkle or stir
> Full on the alarmèd beauty of the bride

> (II, 244–6)

His pitiless gaze not only disrupts the joyful occasion, causing the music to stop, but also turns Lamia back into a snake with his words, 'Begone, foul dream!', his cool reason dispersing the mists and shimmering colours of night-time's dreams. He is one who makes the world safe for gullible youth, disrobing the fantasies of besotted lovers and bringing them back to their senses. It may even be Hazlitt that Keats has partly in mind, that is, the Hazlitt of the essays and not of *Liber Amoris: The Book of Love* in which even his often corrosive rationalism is shown to be not immune to the 'rediculous' sentiments of those smitten with love.

However, the narrator does not shirk the negative aspects of this forbidding character, and he might even weight them over the positive. While love, however chimerical, is warm-blooded, exciting and life-embracing, the philosopher is cold and cruel in his tendency to rob life itself of its colourfulness, although correct in his judgment of the duplicitousness of Lamia. Keats makes a comment on modern, rationalistic science,[15] echoing his agreement with Lamb that Newton had 'destroyed all the Poetry of the rainbow, by reducing it to a prism':[16]

> Do not all charms fly
> At the mere touch of cold philosophy?
> There was an awful rainbow once in heaven:
> We know her woof, her texture; she is given
> In the dull catalogue of common things.
> Philosophy will clip an Angel's wings,
> Conquer all mysteries by rule and line,
> Empty the haunted air, and gnomèd mine –
> Unweave a rainbow, as it erewhile made
> The tender-personed Lamia melt into a shade.
>
> (II, 229–38)

The 'sage, old Apollonius' is decorated with 'spear-grass and the spiteful thistle' which 'wage War on his temples' (II, 228–9), his clarity scarred by malice, and it is he who condemns the young lovers to wear the plants of grief and forgetfulness, willow, adder's tongue and thyrsus, all a recollection from Keats's classes in botany. He is, after all, a gatecrasher to the party, 'an unbidden presence [amongst] the bright throng / Of younger friends' (II, 167–8). His capacity to destroy mirth and love simply because he has, in his elderly scepticism, seen through the veil of beauty as though he has solved 'some knotty problem', can be seen as a blow to all youthful idealism and an unpleasant intrusion.

There is an overarching conflict in the fable itself which makes the blighted ending inevitable and points to another characteristic Keatsian theme which turns on a paradoxical context. Like Shakespeare in *Venus and Adonis*, and like himself in *Endymion* for that matter, Keats throws together the incompatible mortal and immortal in impossible fashion. Whether they like it or not, Venus and Lamia, Cynthia and Endymion, Adonis and Lycius, inhabit worlds that are absolutely different. Venus and Lamia are immortals while Adonis and Lycius are mortals, and whatever love they contract is bound to be terminated by death. The immortal must always live on in grief and loss, unless, as in *Endymion*, a convenient transformation can be effected, a poetic manipulation that seems unsatisfactory in avoiding the fact of death for a mortal or even the loss of love. The poem takes its place in Keats's continuing debate with himself about the limits of art standing outside time and its relation to reality which is bound by time. *Lamia* does not fudge the issue, but Keats can be said to have enriched the problem by allowing us to reserve sympathy for Lamia and anger against Apollonius. The paradox works in this poem by acknowledging the brevity of human life and suggesting, at least tacitly if not explicitly, that it is only a conscious cruelty that would interrupt and destroy the immediate fulfilment and joy of lovers. Even if life is transitory and will inevitably be ended, so, the poem suggests, is love, no matter how boundless it may feel, and if the one can be the element in which the other exists, then at least they may overlap temporarily. If love is long while life is short, will the agony not be averted if love is not ended before life is, if we are left to live within illusions for as long as possible, even until the end at least of the mortal span?

> It was no dream; or say a dream it was,
> Real are the dreams of Gods, and smoothly pass
> Their pleasures in a long immortal dream.

> (I, 126–8)

However, the paradox is rounded into the vicious circle of a contradiction, since it is not only mortality but consciousness also which is an element of human beings, and 'but a moment's *thought* is passion's passing-bell' (II, 39, my italics). Whichever way we turn, love, like poetry, is both precious, natural and beautiful, while simultaneously built on deception, wilful avoidance and ulterior motives. If we were ever given in summary fashion Keats's conclusion about love, it may be a statement like this. One critic who did acknowledge the tensions in *Lamia* was his constant supporter, Leigh Hunt, who positively reviewed the volume in which it appeared in the *Indicator* in August, 1820.[17] Hunt knew from conversation about Keats's distaste for 'consequitive' thinkers like Apollonius, and he regrets that the power of the philosopher, 'an ill-natured and disturbing thing' should triumph:

> Lamia though liable to be turned into painful shapes had a soul of humanity; and the poet does not see why she should not have her pleasures accordingly, merely because a philosopher saw that she was not a mathematical truth. This is fine and good. It is vindicating the greater philosophy of poetry. At the same time we wish for the purpose of his story he had not appeared to give into the common-place of supposing

that Appolonius's sophistry must always prevail, and that modern experiment has done a deadly thing to poetry by discovering the nature of the rainbow, the air, etc: that is to say, that the knowledge of natural history and physics, by shewing us the nature of things, does away the imaginations that once adorned them ... (147)

Hunt was aware of Lamb's criticism of Newton for demystifying the rainbow but at the same time *Lamia* may reveal the poet's greater ambivalence, as the boy at school who had been led by his headmaster into a genuine fascination with astronomy and who had chosen to become a medical student, while also feeling the contrary pull of poetry, beauty and the imagination. It was a conflict which he had internalised through his unique personal experiences as an apprentice surgeon.

It was inevitable that Keats, like other writers, should be exposed to the full rigours of a feminist critic, and Margaret Homans in 'Keats Reading Women, Women Reading Keats' obliges.[18] Undoubtedly, in his poems and letters, Keats is more comfortable with the idea of woman as an 'abstract Idea ... of Beauty' rather than with the domestic proximity of marriage with 'an amiable wife and sweet Children' (*JKL*, 1, 403) which on several occasions he rejected as part of his own future. He can at times regard women 'as children to whom I would rather give a Sugar Plum than my time', and at the other extreme make women the emotional target for all his ardent insecurities, as if a sexual relationship will be the ultimate fulfilment not only for his male, poetic questers but for himself. He can uncritically reinforce stereotypes of the woman as passive and flower-like, receptively enjoying sex more than the mercurial male who is 'hurrying about and collecting honey-bee like, buzzing here and there impatiently from a knowledge of what is to be arrived at' (*JKL*, 1, 232), and yet at the same time equate his own creative process with this kind of 'feminine' receptivity, as Anne Mellor analyses it:

A self that is permeable, continually overflowing its boundaries, melting into another, and being filled by another has historically been associated with the female, and especially with the pregnant woman who experiences herself and her fetus as one.[19]

He can claim angrily when challenged on the score of prurience that he writes for men, not for squeamish women, and express the wish to shock the literary 'bluestockings' whom he intemperately loathed as 'Devils' 'who having taken a snack or Luncheon of Literary scraps, set themselves up for towers of Babel in Languages, Sapphos in Poetry, Euclids in Geometry – and everything in nothing' (*JKL*, 1, 163), while at the same time expecting and even relying on a female readership. To invoke the eastern paradox of *yin* and *yang*, the feminine and the masculine are seen as different principles or 'ideas' which may be in creative tension with each other or which may merge in the 'solution sweet' of the climax to *The Eve of St Agnes*. Throughout his adult life Keats was concerned to prove his 'masculinity' and he gives signs of being at times 'deeply threatened by an idea of feminine otherness' while simultaneously reaching out to female company and women readers.[20] He uses the word 'effeminacy' with equivocation, sometimes identifying it with a creatively 'ardent listlessness' (*Endymion*, I, 825)[21] and at other times as a weakness. Keats can speak in a loftily condescending way about women as flirts or as Cleopatra-like, powerful beauties, and can reprimand petty jealousies of other women, and yet at the same time be fascinated by them and 'enthralled'. All in all, he betrays an abiding and quite extreme vacillation in his attitude to women, but it is equally clear that he adores their intimate company and appreciates their mystery. The later letters to Fanny Brawne which earlier biographers like Richard Monckton Milnes (Lord Houghton) and Sidney Colvin sought to suppress for their tendency to diminish the poet and show him as jealous and paranoid, might now be condemned rather for their tendency to demean the woman, degrading her in typically male fashion, as the angel and the whore, and thus made exclusively for male possession and jealousy. However, we can charitably also see a more humanly mixed, and sometimes confused young man who was still only 23, seeking to contain and control his own sexual feelings, trying as in all other spheres to resolve the contradictory feelings he has about sexual passion in poetic paradox. Simple, biographical points can quietly be made, that to judge every young man or woman on the basis of their intimate or public statements on gender while they are inexperienced, in late adolescence and entering adulthood, living moreover in an unremittingly sexist society, and in Keats's case engaged to be married but estranged from the beloved by a disease which will prove fatal, is surely unfair. Judge us all on this basis and, in Hamlet's words, 'who shall 'scape whipping?' Secondly, the fact that Keats never in his lifetime attracted the vast female readership of Byron is not necessarily a function of his resentment of their power over him, as Homans tends to suggest, but conversely a result of the very overtness and even complacency of Byron's confidence about female stereotypes, contrasting with Keats's honest vacillation and uncertainties, his very failure to adopt the 'strong' male position of his rival poet. Adrienne Rich, a feminist and poet, suggests that Keats's 'weak ego boundaries', his 'Negative Capability', make him more intuitively sympathetic with women than with men, a conclusion that seems borne out by his readership.

9
'Tease us out of thought': May 1819, Odes

The long journal letter quoted in the last chapter which Keats wrote to his brother George and sister-in-law Georgiana between 14 February and 3 May 1819 shows a rapid and startling process of intellectual development in the wake of his brother Tom's death. It is punctuated by descriptions of sociability with friends like Brown, Rice, Reynolds and the Dilkes, dining with them and attending the theatre, but also recounts self-imposed solitude as he tries to cure his sore throat by staying at home and reading 'two very different books', William Robertson's four-volume *The History of America* (1777) and even more ambitiously, Voltaire's *Le Siècle de Louis XIV* in five volumes, perhaps to impress the French-speaking Fanny. The period is one of concentrated writing as well: *The Eve of St Agnes*, the unfinished *The Eve of St Mark* and *La Belle Dame*, alongside a retrieval of polished sonnets like 'On Fame', 'Another on Fame', and 'To Sleep', and finally the transcription of the first of the great odes, 'Ode to Psyche'. In a portion dated 21 April, lies a remarkable meditation in which Keats attempts to formulate a kind of personal philosophy of existence amounting to a theology (*JKL*, 1, 101–4). At its heart lies a need to find an explanation for the question which had troubled him from the time of his mother's death when he was 14, through the ghastly sights he must have seen on the wards at Guy's Hospital, to the recent lingering death of Tom – how can human suffering be justified in a way that does not rely on Christian faith, notions of immortality or belief in an afterlife?[1] The period April/June 1819 marks the climax of a significant change in Keats, away from a poet who had exclaimed in 1817, 'O for a Life of Sensations rather than of Thoughts!' (*JKL*, 1, 185) towards one who in early June 1819 was aspiring to be valued as a thinker: 'I hope I am a little more of a Philosopher than I was, consequently a little less of a versifying Pet-lamb' (*JKL*, 2, 116).

> The common cognomen of this world among the misguided and superstitious is 'a vale of tears' from which we are to be redeemed by a certain arbit[r]ary interposition of God and taken to Heaven – What a little circumscribe[d] straightened notion! (*JKL*, 2, 102)

Keats seeks 'a grander system of salvation than the chryst<e>an religion', a 'system of Salvation which does not affront our reason and humanity'. The section, like the letter as a whole, proceeds in fits and starts – 'I can scarcely express what I but dimly perceive – and yet I think I perceive it' – and asks a lot of his correspondents' understanding, but the train of thought shows the depth of Keats's intellectual questing, and lies behind his maturing poetry in 1819. His opening point derives from his reading of Robertson's *The History of America*. Robertson's book in particular infuses his thought, since it contributes to the current debate about the 'noble savage' initiated by Rousseau in *Émile* (1762). Robertson studies two civilisations living more or less side by side, the 'primitive' Indians and the 'civilised' Mexicans and Peruvians.[2] Keats reflects Robertson's analysis that both groups faced different problems and neither can be idealised.[3] 'Men might seem to inherit quiet of Mind from unsophisticated senses; from uncontamination of civilisation; and especially from their being as it were estranged from the mutual helps of Society and its mutual injuries – and thereby more immediately under the Protection of Providence', since death (or probably more accurately awareness of death) still occurs – 'even there they had mortal pains to bear as bad; or even worse than Baliffs, Debts and Poverties of civilised Life'. He is positing a form of original innocence rather than original sin (which Christians hold to be the reason for death). However, quoting *King Lear*, Keats says we must accept mortality rather than explain it away: 'The whole appears to resolve into this – that Man is originally "a poor forked creature" subject to the same mischances as the beasts of the forest, destined to hardships and disquietudes of some kind or other.' Even with material improvements in comforts, yet there are still 'a fresh set of annoyances – he is mortal and there is still a heaven with its Stars abov[e] his head'. The words of wise, 'disinterested' men like Socrates may create happiness, even 'happiness carried to an extreme', 'but what must it end in? Death – and who could in such a case bear with death', since its approach can 'fritter away' a lifetime's satisfactions in a final period of torment. He cannot accept the 'perfectibility' of any notion that death allows us to leave the world for a better place – the world is the only place we have:

> the inhabitants of the world will correspond to itself – Let the fish philosophise the ice away from the Rivers in winter time and they shall be at continual play in the tepid delight of summer … For instance suppose a rose to have sensation, it blooms on a beautiful morning it enjoys itself – but there comes a cold wind, a hot sun – it cannot escape it, it cannot destroy its annoyances – they are as native to the world as itself: no more can man be happy in spite, the world[l]y elements will prey upon his nature.

He scorns the Christian idea that such a life is ' "a vale of tears" ' from which we are liberated by God into heaven.

Having stated his intention to find a humanist way to rationalise human suffering without resorting to ideas of life as a 'vale of tears' burdened by original sin and leading to death and liberation through eternal life, Keats turns his attention to his own solution. He accepts some notion that 'human nature' can be 'immortal' but looks only at what we know from experience of life rather than conjecturing what happens afterwards. His model is of life as 'The Vale of Soul-making' rather than of tears. We are born, he says, as 'Intelligences', 'atoms of perception' or 'sparks' – but without identities or souls. Asking how each comes in time 'to possess a bliss peculiar to each ones individual existence', he answers 'How, but by the medium of a world like this?' He claims his description is a 'grander form of salvation' than the one offered by Christianity, and 'rather it is a system of Spirit-creation', with the cornerstone being the inescapability of time and the necessity to confront adversity in creating an individual identity:

> This is effected by three grand materials acting the one upon the other for a series of years – these three Materials are the *Intelligence* – the *human heart* (as distinguished from intelligence or Mind) and the *World* or *Elemental space* suited for the proper action of *Mind and Heart* on each other for the purpose of forming the *Soul* or *Intelligence destined to possess the sense of Identity*.

In terms of the history of ideas, Keats is modifying Locke's idea that we are born as *tabulae rasae* or empty slates, suggesting rather that we are born with a *potential* and a comprehending mind. He is drawing also on natural law thinking, once again modifying it to argue that not only does the species have a unique set of imperatives stemming from the fact of being human, but also that each individual in the species has an innate and specific potential stemming from the fact of being that particular individual. Concerned that his description is becoming too abstract for comprehension, he changes the model in order to 'put it in the most homely form possible' and in his characteristic way thinks in a threesome:

> – I will call the *world* a School instituted for the purpose of teaching little children to read – I will call the *human heart* the *horn Book* used in that School – and I will call the *Child able to read, the Soul* made from that *school* and its *hornbook*. Do you not see how necessary a World of Pains and troubles is to school an Intelligence and make it a soul? A Place where the heart must feel and suffer in a thousand diverse ways! Not merely is the Heart a Hornbook. It is the Minds Bible, it is the Minds experience, it is the teat from which the Mind or intelligence sucks its identity – As various as the Lives of Men are – so various become their souls, and thus does God make individual beings, Souls, Identical Souls of the sparks of his own essence – This appears to me a

faint sketch of a system of Salvation which does not affront our reason and humanity.

Keats makes references to 'God' but he goes on to explain that this is not exclusively the Christian deity. The 'System of Soul-making' he has 'sketched' is, in Keats's estimation, a prototype which he suggests is a 'Parent of all the more palpable and personal Schemes of Redemption, among the Zoroastrians the Christians and the Hindoos', since all such religions are merely variations using different gods, 'Mediators and Personages' such as Christ and Vishnu, deriving from before Greek times and conveyed in myths from the ancient Greeks onwards. Finally, for the sake of his brother and sister-in-law, he provides another summation:

> If what I have said should not be plain enough, as I fear it may not be, I will [p]ut you in the place where I began in this series of thoughts – I mean, I began by seeing how man was formed by circumstances – and what are circumstances? – but touchstones of his heart –? And what are touchstones? – but proovings of his heart? – and what are proovings of his heart but fortifiers or alterers of his nature? And what is his altered nature but his soul? – and what was his soul before it came into the world and had These provings and alterations and perfectionings? – An intelligence<s> – without Identity – and how is this Identity to be made? Through the medium of the Heart? And how is the heart to become this Medium but in a world of Circumstances?

The effort of logical argument brings out in Keats his more scientific mind evidenced in the vocabulary. 'Proovings', or 'provings' does not have its modern meaning of 'giving proof' but seems more likely to be a technical, homoeopathic term recalled from Keats's medical training: 'A test in which a drug is given to healthy people (or animals) in order to ascertain its effect' (*OED*), with an implication also of 'improving' as well, 'fortifiers and alterations and perfectionings', with its homely reference to bread-making. 'Touchstone' may also have the specific scientific meaning, 'A very smooth, fine-grained, black or dark-coloured variety of quartz or jasper (also called BASANITE), used for testing the quality of gold and silver alloys by the colour of the streak produced by rubbing them upon it; a piece of such stone used for this purpose' (*OED*), although Keats would have found its more general sense of a criterion in Hazlitt's *Table Talk*: 'Well-digested schemes will stand the touchstone of experience'. Keats leaves his argument with a lighthearted concession to his readers' patience:

> – There now I think what with Poetry and Theology you may thank your Stars that my pen is not very long winded ...

And with some relief and lightheartedness he turns away from intense reasoning to domestic thoughts and his own 'old sins', namely his sonnets. What is philosophically impressive about Keats's 'scheme' (and partly what has impressed some philosophers about it[4]) is that he seeks to reason only from known elements rather than from conjectures: humans are born more or less alike, they live through and endure personal circumstances, and through the act of living each acquires uniqueness and individuality, so that encountering experiences has a function in creating the personal identity and soul which finally meets death – life is the vale of soul-making, the medium through which individuation is achieved while death inscribes a final meaning upon the furthest point reached by that soul.

As though this deeply reasoned and somewhat opaque witness to his thoughts at an abstract level has provided a kind of seed-bed for his creativity, Keats over the following month wrote a series of Odes which are recognised as amongst the greatest poems ever written. They seem to have come to him more or less spontaneously (which does not in each case mean easily), 'as naturally as the leaves to the tree', and they must have been in some sense products of his metaphysical musings when his 'consequitive' mind was at full stretch, 'sublimations' into art of his thought in both the scientific and psychological senses of that word. By turning from philosophical and theological language to images and poetry, he can sidestep into poetry as a more congenial, instinctive mode, producing short works that have their origin in an imagined world-view which exists in a metaphorical and yet fully visualised context. In essence, Keats has been contemplating the function of 'time passing' in relation to human growth through its experiences of happiness and suffering towards individuation. He now uses the form of the ode to explore a dimension which excludes or redefines time, contemplating the thin but all-important line that separates what is possible and impossible in life and what is possible and impossible in art. Whereas in life diversity and unity are contingent on the medium of time, art can control time so that the two states of 'the all and the one' can paradoxically coexist and be simultaneously analysed. This is one of the driving perceptions behind the Odes which he was about to write, and an answer they provisionally offer is that in *art*, unlike life, time can be arrested, repeated or evaded – 'a thing of beauty is a joy forever' in the words which had begun *Endymion*. Whereas outside art something may be beautiful only because it *cannot* exist 'forever', art may offer the one example of something that *can* last forever. Keats to the very end of his life affirmed the sentiment 'I have lov'd the principle of beauty in all things' (*JKL*, 2, 323) as though there is some quintessence of irreducible beauty whose 'principle' is a protection from the ravages of time, a solution which Shakespeare and Spenser, his beloved Elizabethan poets, had pursued: 'For short time an endlesse moniment' in the words of Spenser's *Epithalamion*. The existence of art might be some consolation to humans living in the time-bound confines of their individual lives, but as such it is all the more tantalising since it proves that art has a different status of existence from life, and that no matter how much it can illuminate life and even offer consolation for pain, it can never be a substitute for that life. The rules that life imposes of 'soul-making' through time operate differently in art, which is embalmed in time, inhabiting a realm which can be glimpsed and re-experienced but not permanently inhabited. We can learn from art but never live in its aloof mode of existence. Keats's challenging ideas expressed in his letter can be interpreted in different ways and extended into different contexts, but the aspect which I will follow here is his way of talking about life as though it is a work of art, as something which happens in between birth and death, or beginning and end, with no reality before and after; what the philosopher R. G. Collingwood in *The Principles of Art* (1938) referred to in the context of art as a 'monad', whose relevant meaning in the *Oxford English Dictionary* is 'An indivisible unit of being; an absolutely simple entity' which has no relation to other things.

At the very end of the radiant letter to the George Keatses, the entry dated 30 April which would have ushered in spring of 1819, Keats transcribes his first draft of 'Ode to Psyche', prefacing it with some explanation of its composition and origins:

> The following Poem – the last I have written is the first and the only one with which I have taken even moderate pains – I have for the most part dash'd of my lines in a hurry – This I have done leisurely – I think it reads the more richly for it and will I hope encourage me to write other thing[s] in even a more peacable and healthy spirit. You must recollect that Psyche was not embodied as a goddess before the time of Apulieus the Platonist who lived afteir the Augustan age, and consequently the Goddess was never worshipped or sacrificed to with any of the ancient fervour – and perhaps never thought of in the old religion – I am more orthodox tha[n] to let a hethen Goddess be so neglected – (*JKL*, 2, 105–6)

Since the passage inserts phrases from Lemprière's dictionary entry on Psyche, this seems again to be his source for the story, reading in part, 'The word signifies *the soul* ... Psyche is generally represented with the wings of a butterfly, to intimate the lightness of the soul, of which the butterfly is the symbol, and on that account, among the ancients, when a man had just expired, a butterfly appeared fluttering above, as if rising from the mouth of the deceased.'[5] The image suggests that the soul is inseparable from the breath of life, that which defines both an origin and a closure, and therefore existing with the principle of creation itself whether through love or artistic composition. Another influence must have been the long, narrative poem, *Psyche or, The Legend of Love* (1805 and 1811) by Mary Tighe, a poet who 'once delighted' Keats though he later saw through her and found only 'weakness' in her poetry (*JKL*, 2, 18). The unusual part of the story Keats chooses to depict, and some of the imagery, are reminiscent of Tighe's:

> Her cheek with that of borrowed roses blooms:
> Used to receive from all rich offerings,
> She quaffs with conscious right the fragrant fumes
> Which her attendant from a censer flings,
> Who graceful feeds the flame with incense while she sings.[6]

However, Keats's real subject is not the actual narrative of Psyche and Eros, but the process of myth-making behind their story, and the inner processes of the imagination in the act of creating such a story. Although the poem is very different in tone from the philosophical section of his letter, it has analogical connections in dwelling on the soul and, as Keats's semi-facetious words indicate, in lifting a neglected mythical figure into a quasi-religious framework. While Venus and Cupid as aspects of Love and Mars as War have always been pagan deities inspiring poetry, by contrast Psyche as Soul, Thought or even Mind seems unpoetic and requires a new 'priest' to celebrate her and raise her into the pantheon of poetic subjects. Keats's own investment in this idea is that his philosophical meditations on 'soul-making' locate this unsung goddess at the source of the process of self-creation.

The ode takes the story at the point when Psyche and Cupid (or Eros) are observed by the poet in a typically Keatsian moment of pictorial stasis at a point just before or just after kissing – 'their lips touched not, but had not bade adieu' – as they lie 'calm-breathing' on grass in a natural bower. The observing poet praises the 'latest born and loveliest vision far / Of all Olympus' faded hierarchy' and regrets that she has no temple to her name,

> Nor alter heaped with flowers;
> Nor virgin-choir to make delicious moan
> Upon the midnight hours;
> No voice, no lute, no pipe, no incense sweet
> From chain-swung censer teeming;
> No shrine, no grove, no oracle, no heat
> Of pale-mouthed prophet dreaming.

These lines are repeated affirmatively rather than negatively as the poet himself vows to rectify the neglect: 'I see, and sing, by my own eyes inspired. So let me be thy choir ...' The chanted obeisance is religious in nature but the significance the poet is giving to the rites offered to Psyche is that of celebrating an originating, unexplored part of the mind, perhaps the 'spark' or 'intelligence' from which the identity and a soul are formed:

> Yes, I will be thy priest, and build a fane
> In some untrodden region of my mind,

> Where branchèd thoughts, new grown with pleasant pain,
>   Instead of pines shall murmur in the wind:
>   ...

Psyche is placed in a region of the mind where creativity begins. She is seen as the handmaiden of 'the gardener Fancy' working on 'the wreathed trellis of a working brain', 'breeding' endless cascades of flowers which are all uniquely individual and never the same – just as Keats's philosophy of the vale of soul-making envisioned diversity evolving from a unitary origin in childhood, or as poems sprout from some 'natural' source in the mind. In the poetic version, at the centre of such imaginative creativity is the union between Psyche and Cupid in a mind open to love:

> And here there shall be for thee all soft delight
>   That shadowy thought can win,
> A bright torch, and a casement ope at night,
>   To let the warm love in!

The ode is the lightest possible analogy to Keats's abstract conceptualising but it has an intrinsic connection none the less, and in its 'peacable' yet 'rich' leisureliness it rehearses a poetic equivalent of the model of the mind in which 'pleasant pain' is the process by which 'branchèd thoughts' of a soul's identity come into being, grow and diversify into branches. Death is not an issue in this vision, since it is a myth of beginnings where endings are not yet in sight. The basic purpose of life, it is assumed, is not to suffer and die but to live and grow, and such growth comes from the union of love and the soul.

There is an air of a teasing joke or logical conundrum about 'Ode on a Grecian Urn', and its enigmatic riddling lies in the same territory as paradoxes like infinity or Zeno's arrow. Its effect is to 'tease us out of thought as doth eternity'. If the ode's intellectual playfulness is respected, it must also be conceded that the urn has had the last laugh, since it has generated immense amounts of solemn critical commentary and speculation over some of its puzzles. When was it written? Though its composition is always dated in May 1819 on little evidence, the first we know of it is its publication in January 1820 in the *Annals of Fine Arts*, a journal in which Haydon published essays on art. Which particular Greek urn is represented? The answer shown by Ian Jack is that details are taken from many sources rather than just one.[7] Is the ode literally inscribed 'on' the urn as its 'motto' or is the urn merely the subject of the poem? And what exactly do the words (possibly) attributed to the urn in the last two lines, mean? Even points of punctuation change with mysterious significance between the published texts, often making a profound difference to the meaning.

Just as its subject raises questions, the poem begins by interrogating its own object of contemplation, the figures shown in relief around the urn:

> What men or gods are these? What maidens loth?
> What mad pursuit? What struggle to escape?
> What pipes and timbrels? What wild ecstasy?

And yet for all its defiant logical twists, it is at the same time one of the most beautifully simple poems one could imagine. At the heart of the enigma, I will suggest, is again a link with the philosophy of the vale of soul-making. Art exists in a tantalising realm which is outside and beyond the only life we can know, giving its gnomic utterances a status which appears weightily true and yet can never be tested. At the same time, the ode is a thought-experiment concerning the nature of pictorial art as a medium of expression existing in a non-temporal zone, since any picture is an example of arrested time, a moment that is not actually a moment since it is not *in* time though it can imply a narrative depending on an inferred passage of time from past to future:

> Fair youth, beneath the trees, thou canst not leave
> Thy song, nor ever can those trees be bare;
> Bold Lover, never, never canst thou kiss,
> Though winning near the goal – yet, do not grieve;
> She cannot fade, though thou hast not thy bliss,
> For ever wilt thou love, and she be fair!
>
> Ah, happy, happy boughs! That cannot shed
> Your leaves, nor ever bid the Spring adieu;
> And happy melodist, unwearied,
> For ever piping songs for ever new;
> ...

The unanswered questions accumulate: 'Who are these coming to the sacrifice?'; 'What little town ... Is emptied of this folk, this pious morn?', a town whose streets 'for evermore / Will silent be'. In all these senses the opening line which ostensibly hails the Grecian urn as a 'still unravished bride of quietness' also pays homage to the impenetrable contradictions and paradoxes of the subject and the poem itself, which is just as much an 'unravished bride of quietness' as the art-work which is its subject. Where 'Psyche' is warm, open-ended and full of a sense of exponential growth, 'Ode on a Grecian Urn' depicts the passionate gestures of lovers whose very moment of 'wild ecstasy' is paradoxically finished and 'cold', permanently immobilised and textualised. The stasis between Cupid and Psyche had been a pause between kisses, whereas here the kisses are maddeningly never to be delivered, or else the lips are always and forever fixed together. The ode is coolly rational in its progression of thought, static in its imagery, and almost locked shut in a tight, logical closure that forbids the reader to enter an emotional world where lovers are 'All breathing human passion far above'. They represent passion, but are themselves 'cold'. 'Ode on a Grecian Urn' is Keats's *Mona Lisa*, in more ways than one.

However, regarded as an enigma in itself, 'Ode on a Grecian Urn' can become a central comment on its own nature, a paradox which deals with paradox. For surely this is the word that encapsulates the subject of the poem and the varying effects it has had on readers. Turning it around and around we cannot enter its world, and yet this is precisely what the urn tempts us to do. It is an encapsulation of the very *raison d'être* of art itself, teasing us out of thought by its strange blending of the familiar and the remote, 'living' feelings represented on a centuries-old artefact. Continually in his letters and other poems Keats worries about the interrelationship of beauty and truth and *Endymion*, *Lamia* and *The Fall of Hyperion* are comments on the debate. In its very nature the urn, like any work of pictorial art, is problematical in its inference yet exclusion of time. It appears to be 'true' in all sorts of ways, from the lifelikeness of its images to its marmoreal permanence as the one thing that is not ravaged by time. And yet it is the one thing that is untrue, merely representational, non-living, and outside the element we live in, time. Its world is 'For ever' whereas its representation is of a world in which this phrase cannot operate. Its lovers will always appear to be passionate and yet they can never touch; a village will always be empty because its people are all 'here' and will never be 'there' – but equally because the village does not exist anyway. Just as the ode is packed with oxymorons like 'unravished bride', 'unheard melodies', 'ditties of no tone',[8] and with contradictions such as sociability and solitude, passion and coldness, lovers who will always love and yet cannot love, so it becomes a sustained meditation on the paradoxes it raises which all stem from the nature of art, and in particular the arts that exist outside time such as painting and sculpture. At the same time, and in common with other poems like *Lamia* and 'Ode to a Nightingale', there is a strongly self-reflexive note in 'Grecian Urn' which makes the reasoning about art's imperviousness equally applicable to poetry, if the poem is seen as a self-sufficient monad, standing complete and independent. The same paradoxes operate in relation to Shakespeare's dramatic characters such as Falstaff and Cleopatra, 'trapped' within the unchanging monad of a play and yet always tempting us to provide them with a real-life identity, an imagined past and future.

As I have suggested earlier, Keats is the most Renaissance of all the Romantic poets, in his verse forms, paradoxical thought, his reverence for classical sources, and in the subjects he chooses. In dwelling on the problematic relationships between beauty and truth, he is, of course, quoting indirectly his own Letters – 'What the Imagination seizes as Beauty must be truth – whether it existed before or not' (*JKL*, 1, 184), 'the excellence of every Art is its intensity, capable of making all disagreeables evaporate, from their being in close relationship with Beauty & Truth' (*JKL*, 1, 192). However, he seems also to have taken his cue from Shakespeare's Sonnets, and in his paradoxical enterprise more generally, from Renaissance writing. He would have found the collocation of beauty and truth in Shakespeare's Sonnet 54 which is about appearance and reality, while the Sonnets that flank it, 53 and 55, are about the very kind of visual art represented by Keats's Urn. Shakespeare seems also to be thinking about the same classical period as Keats, and he may even have been writing on mythology in *Venus and Adonis* at the time he was writing the Sonnets:

> Describe Adonis, and the counterfeit
> Is poorly imitated after you;
> On Helen's cheek all art of beauty set,
> And you in Grecian tires are painted new.

> (Sonnet 53)

These Shakespearian sonnets develop typical Elizabethan conceits concerning 'art of beauty' and imitation. Sonnet 53 plays on the discrepancy between the painted 'counterfeit' of fabled beauties such as Adonis and Helen, and the beauty of an androgynous youth to whom the Sonnet is addressed, perhaps a boy actor who 'counterfeits' Shakespeare's female characters. To beauty, this person adds the 'constant heart' which is not present in the pictures. The distinction lies between 'all *art* of beauty set' (my italics) and the reality of a person with not only 'external grace' but also a more durable, 'constant' quality which is one meaning of 'truth'. That kind of truth is immediately supplied in Sonnet 54:

> O, how much more doth beauty beauteous seem
> By that sweet ornament which truth doth give!

The conceit in this Sonnet turns on different kinds of natural beauty: canker-blooms and sweet roses may each have 'as deep a dye', but the latter have a perfume which lingers in the mind after their death:

> And so of you, beauteous and lovely youth,
> When that shall vade [or 'fade'], by verse distills your truth.

The third Sonnet in this sequence again picks up the closing couplet of its predecessor and relates the thought back to the kind of static art which is like the Grecian urn, asking why,

> Not marble, nor the gilded monuments
> Of princes, shall outlive this powerful rhyme?

> (Sonnet 55)

The narrator of the Sonnet argues that while statues can be overturned, masonry can be rooted out, marble can be 'besmear'd with sluttish time', yet still the poem itself will preserve the youth's beauty for posterity till the day of judgment:

> So, till the judgement that yourself arise,
> You live in this, and dwell in lovers' eyes.

In each of these Sonnets, Shakespeare is constructing a paradox which draws upon the same raw materials as Keats's Ode. Beauty is evanescent and in flux and yet it can be made into a permanent truth at the cost of losing the very mobility which gives it human beauty. The youth can be made more permanently 'true' than even the work of art which is by definition permanent.[9] Reading 'Ode on a Grecian Urn' alongside Shakespeare's Sonnets can add another 'feature of propriety' to it. The veiled point which the artful writing conceals, is that in the final analysis, behind the Urn which makes beauty and truth coalesce, is the poet writing the Ode as a representation of a representation (of a representation). Only a poet, the subtext says, can ventriloquially make a dead object 'speak', or can create an art that can freeze reality into an image of unchanging perfection, or, as in the case of Shakespeare's plays, create characters who will last forever through unending stage representations. But if this is so, then the poet can surreptitiously tell us other things and in particular that we need not believe what the Urn says. Its motto that beauty is truth, truth beauty, is certainly not 'all we know on earth' – if anything we know the opposite, that beautiful things 'on earth' do not last as the Urn does and are thus not truthful. It is, however, all the Urn wishes us to know *about it*. Nor is it 'all we need to know', because, for example, in order even to understand the Urn's point we must 'know' that lovers wish to kiss rather than to be left frustratingly in unfulfilled suspension. But again invoking the words and characters of Shakespeare, in *art* this is all we can, or need to know, since there is nothing outside the play, which is not referential but self-sufficient. Keats in his Ode does not say the same things as Shakespeare in his Sonnets, but both writers are playing with the same concepts, dealing equally wittily with similar paradoxes, and they finally baffle the rational mind in comparable ways. And Shakespeare, of course, is not the only precursor since he himself had poetic antecedents. Spenser in his *Mutabilitie Cantos* as Book 7 of *The Faerie Queene*, turns on the same set of crossovers between the ideal and the real, mythological and actual, while the whole allegorical design of *The Faerie Queene* works from the assumption that art can indeed be more consistent and truthful than life, as well as more beautiful. Sidney's sonnet sequence, 'Astrophil to Stella' and his theory of imitation in *The Defence of Poetry* allow art to mock life for its deficiencies and frustrations, but life to mock art for its static qualities: 'Fool', said my muse to me; 'look in thy heart, and write'.[10]

'Ode on a Grecian Urn', then, can meaningfully be interpreted in a historical context. As a reflection of an essentially Renaissance way of thinking rather than a Romantic, it reveals itself as an exercise in defending the indefensible statement, the activity so beloved of the generation that produced John Donne's *Problems and Paradoxes*, revelling as these poets did in witty conceits.[11] The reported words of the Urn[12] are both paradoxical and a description of how paradox exists and defines works in art:

> When old age shall this generation waste,
>   Thou shalt remain, in midst of other woe
> Than ours, a friend to man, to whom thou say'st,
>   'Beauty is truth, truth beauty,' – that is all
> Ye know on earth, and all ye need to know.[13]

Things which are contradictions in one context can be resolved into unified thought if the context is changed. 'Living is dying' is an absurd proposition to one person, consolation to another, depending on the circumstances and temperament of each pursuing an individual 'vale of Soul-making'. I would argue that this is a part of what the Urn as dramatic voice 'says', and what the poem as a whole is enacting. On earth, within the element of time that exists this side of death, beauty is *not* truth: beautiful things die and are not true in the alchemist's sense of immutability, and beautiful things can be misleading and untruthful, as Keats had shown in *Lamia*. But change the context, see the world of static art as separate, self-sufficient and autonomous, with its own structure based on the self-consistent nature of fiction and on its independence from time, then this is precisely what it would say if it could talk – *does* say by its still existence within our time-dominated world: 'Beauty is truth'. Simultaneously, beauty is not truth and beauty is truth – the overarching paradox of a poem which brings to fulfilment an important part of Keats's thinking, and a poem which, while tantalising post-Romantic readers, would have made any Renaissance poet in the great age of paradox proud to have written. Indeed, one of its many contexts of reading could make it into Keats's homage to literary paradox in the Renaissance, an age which seems to have been in some ways more 'real' to Keats than his own. At that same time, the full weight of his own age's understanding of poetic imagination lies behind Keats's celebration of 'the authenticity of the Imagination': 'the holiness of the Heart's affections and the truth of Imagination – What the imagination seizes as Beauty must be truth' (*JKL*, 1, 184).

'Ode to a Nightingale' was also published first in *Annals of the Fine Arts* (July 1819), a hint that it too is a meditation upon art. In this case, the art is the one that exists *only* within time, namely music, the medium that lacks referential content or explicit subject-matter.[14] Before the age of sound recordings, the fleeting nature of music was even more acutely intrinsic to its nature, literally leaving no material trace when it had stopped. In this sense Keats's ode is once again not about its apparent subject, an urn or a bird, but about an art – music – and its relationship to time and by analogy to poetry itself as word music. Helen Vendler says that in 'Nightingale' the poet is 'pure ear, pure audience'[15] and it would be just as apt to describe 'Grecian Urn' as based on pure eye, pure viewer. The two poems are like bookends, holding up each end of a wider exploration into some philosophical problems of art and its problematical relationship to life. So far as we can tell, both were written in May 1819, but we do know a little more about the context of 'Nightingale' than 'Grecian Urn' as we have little reason to doubt the general authenticity of Charles Brown's account since, although writing some twenty years after Keats's death, he had been living with the poet at the time.

> In the spring of 1819 a nightingale had built her nest in my house. Keats felt a tranquil and continual joy in her song; and one morning he took a chair from the breakfast-table to the grass-plot under a plum-tree, where he sat for two or three hours. When he came into the house, I perceived he had some scraps of paper in his hand, and these he was quietly thrusting behind the books. On inquiry, I found those scraps, four or five in number, containing his poetic feeling on the song of our nightingale. The writing was not well legible; and it was difficult to arrange the stanzas on so many scraps. With his assistance I succeeded, and this was his 'Ode to a Nightingale', a poem which has been the delight of every one. (*KC*, 2, 65; Brown, 53–4)

The draft of the poem still exists and in fact it is on only two sheets of paper so Brown's detailed memory was playing tricks, and probably, as Gittings suggests, confusing it with 'Ode on Indolence'. A succession of plum trees has been planted on the spot assumed to be where the original one was (though the same mulberry, perhaps dating from the seventeenth century, still stands in place). Keats read the poem to an admiring Haydon while they walked in Kilburn Meadows. But the occasion and setting when it was composed or written have little obvious influence on the Ode. It may even, as Joseph Severn pictured it in his painting much later (1851), have been conceived by moonlight on Hampstead Heath, and as the Ode itself stresses, the nightingale had been a poetic motif since classical Greek and Latin literature,[16] biblical times, the medieval period (by Lydgate and the anonymous *The Owl and the Nightingale*), in Shakespeare and Milton, down to Keats's time in poems by many writers including Coleridge and Wordsworth, and beyond to Elizabeth Barrett Browning and T. S. Eliot. It has always been a distinctly literary bird. Robert Gittings shows that the provenance of the poem was more literary than literal, citing Keats's reading at the time of Dryden's translation of the anonymous poem *The Flower and the Leaf* and also sections of Burton's *Anatomy of Melancholy*.[17] It may also carry a memory of the little 'chamber concerts' of music hosted first by Cowden Clarke senior for his students and then by Hunt and Novello in Keats's earlier, coterie days when his 'heart / Was warmed luxuriously by divine Mozart; / By Arne delighted, or by Handel madden'd' ('To Charles Cowden Clarke'). We can if we wish also see enacted in miniature a process of 'soul-making', as 'disagreeables' are forged into the 'identity' of a unified poem. But all these contexts miss the point that 'Ode to a Nightingale' is set nowhere, at no time, and recounts an imaginative rather than actual experience. Despite the verbal richness and density, it is simple in the same way that 'Ode on a Grecian Urn' is simple, once we understand that the poem is 'about' the nature of music as an art form. Keats is recalling the ancient analysis of Pliny who 'declares that [the nightingale] sings with a perfect knowledge of musical art and that it can produce an astonishing variety of musical effects: a great range of pitch and volume, very long and very short notes, staccato and legato, in short everything that man's ingenuity can achieve with wind instruments'.[18]

In this poem there is a kind of narrative, a movement from one point of time to another, and a very definite sequence of beginning, middle and end, and this is significant since, unlike pictorial art, music has duration and exists between a 'before' and 'after'. The Ode begins in a mood of self-conscious depression, heart-ache and 'drowsy numbness' as if in a state drugged by herbs such as hemlock (conium, which causes paralysis) or opium, as the poet first hears the nightingale singing. Nightingales are heard, but rarely seen, and they sing only at night. Keats builds his poem on the idea that the moods and images evoked by music are the listener's imaginative construction, a trick of the 'fancy' rather than something that has external existence. The poet now longs to be transported away from a depressive here-and-now to a summery place of wine, 'Dance, and Provençal song, and sunburnt mirth!' evoked by the music. Stanza 3 shows the poet still land-locked in a state of hypersensitivity to pain, sickness and suffering in the world around him, but stanza 4 signals in its opening – 'Away! Away!' – a releasing and relinquishing movement 'on the viewless wings of Poesy' into the music which engenders a state where time either 'stands still' or expands to infinity. Time becomes non-existent in the experience of ecstasy and as the poet surrenders to the music he enters a state of mental synaesthesia where all senses become absorbed into the sense of sound. Although he 'cannot see' the flowers around his feet yet he can 'in embalmed darkness, guess each sweet', he can smell summer's aromas even if they are not truly apparent, and can hear 'The murmurous haunt of flies on summer eves' even if they may not literally be around him. 'Darkling I listen' (borrowing a word from *King Lear*) is central to the poem's movement. At this stage the poet is doing nothing *but* listening in the dark, but this one sense when heightened creates a whole, imagined environment that includes impressions from all the senses, like phantom limbs or like sounds to a blind person. The feeling of expanded consciousness in the presence of beautiful music comes close to an 'ecstasy' likened to a swooning death-wish: 'Now more than ever seems it rich to die' in order to avert a transition back to the reality prefigured in 'To thy high requiem become a sod'. The bird itself, the poet believes, can never die, if it is conceived not as a single bird but as a repeated song, a disembodied and beautiful sound which was heard as much in ancient times and still has the capacity to charm magic casements, 'opening on the foam / Of perilous seas, in faery lands forlorn'. At this stage of the poem, consistent with the subject of the essence of music as an affective art, it is a sound that creates a dismaying transition, in the word itself, 'Forlorn!' which 'tolls' the poet back from the experience of the music to his 'sole self', locked once again in time and space. The music fades as the nightingale flies away, and the poet finds himself alone and left dazed, tricked by the 'deceiving elf' of imagination, and barely able to categorise the emotional state created by music, now that it has stopped:

> Was it a vision, or a waking dream?
> Fled is that music: – Do I wake or sleep?

The final words call into question the reality status of the experience as a whole, asking whether the dream-like suspension of time is in fact more real as a richly all-inclusive state than the desolate isolation of the 'sole self' mentally imprisoned in time.

These two odes, along with 'To Autumn', are the best known of all Keats's poems, and probably among the best-known poems in the English language. To read them as 'playfully' as I have done might seem to demean their profundity, and I readily admit there are more complex readings such as those by Vendler, Wasserman and Plumly. But there are reasons to believe Keats may not have foreseen their celebrity, since his generic preferences for fully 'serious' poetry were epic, romance and poetic drama. Brown's anecdote of Keats with 'some scraps of paper in his hand, and these he was quietly thrusting behind the books', contains a suggestion that at least 'Nightingale' and perhaps all his odes were among his 'fugitive poems' not destined to be valued as highly as even *Endymion* or *Otho the Great*. The spirit driving them may have been akin to a mental 'holiday' from the preoccupations that were weighing him down – continued grief at Tom's death, anxiety over his own sore throat, constantly troubling money problems, his emotionally volatile love for Fanny Brawne, and his weighty philosophical ponderings on the purposes of suffering in human experience. Amongst these thickets, the odes seem to have something quite cerebral and even intellectually lighthearted in their riddling analysis of pictorial art and music. In some senses they are attempts to escape pressing adversities by entering a world of art, while in other ways they sublimate the very problems into forms that may provide solutions. It is a semi-conscious part of their composition that they contemplate in different ways the complex processes that connect and separate art and the 'vale of Soul-making'. At the same time their relative spontaneity drew from Keats's imagination an instinctive and almost unprecedented perfection of language in each ode as vehicle for its meanings. Alongside sections from other poems like *The Eve of St Agnes*, *Lamia* and the second version of *Hyperion*, the rich word-music of these three odes, with their complex employment of internal rhyme and half-rhyming, assonance, subtle alliteration and onomatopoeia, employed with subtle differences in each poem, invites the epithet 'Shakespearian'. His own insight about the composition of the first *Hyperion* applies even more aptly to these poems: '... for things which [I] do half at Random are afterwards confirmed by my judgment in a dozen features of Propriety – Is it too daring to Fancy Shakespeare this Presider?' (*JKL*, 1, 142).

Two other odes are usually assumed to have been written at the same time. Once again, with the exception of 'Psyche', the poems are impossible to date with accuracy, though the fact that they all seem to 'fit together' thematically and that two of them mention May, has encouraged critics to place them in May 1819. 'Ode on Indolence', indeed, seems to be a spin-off from 'Ode on a Grecian Urn' and although not published until 1848 it was written in May 1819, which suggests that it too focuses on an aspect of the nature of art. Indolence was the state which Abbey had unkindly associated with the whole Keats family, when Fanny was ill, and which Keats had celebrated in his letters to Reynolds. The poet is in a state which we can assume to be a reverie induced by semi-sleep in 'the drowsy hour' of 'summer-indolence', the product of the kind of daytime nap which Keats several times in his letters mentions as a particularly creative experience. He sees three white-robed figures with joined hands, rather like Botticelli's three graces, who pass three times 'like figures on a marble urn, / When shifted round to see the other side'. As each appears and disappears the poet is left with an aching impulse to follow, only to see the next come into view. They are given allegorical significance. The first is 'a fair maid, and Love her name', the poet recognises the second as 'my demon Poesy', and the third is 'poor Ambition' springing from 'a man's little heart's short fever-fit'. The final verse brings three concepts together in a comment on his own poetic aspirations:

> So, ye three ghosts, adieu! Ye cannot raise
>   My head cool-bedded in the flowery grass;
> For I would not be dieted with praise,
>   A pet-lamb in a sentimental farce!

> Fade softly from my eyes, and be once more
> In masque-like figures on the dreamy urn;
>   Farewell! I yet have visions for the night,
> And for the day faint visions there is store;
>   Vanish, ye phantoms, from my idle spright,
> Into the clouds, and never more return!

One implication is that creativity can be an unexpected outcome of the kind of 'wise passivity' that Keats extols in early letters, though it is enriched by the suggestion that poetry also requires love, a 'demon' impulse, and burning ambition. However, these three feelings, no matter how powerful and overwhelming, are so active as to be not only antithetical to a mood of simple 'indolence' but also antithetical to each other. The figures cannot all be seen at once as the urn needs to be turned around so that as one disappears the next appears, which suggests that although mutually linked, they are also mutually exclusive in the process of poetic composition. From other comments Keats makes in his two sonnets on Fame and in his letters, he seems to be wrestling here with two sides of his own personality of which he was fully aware, an almost arrogant belief that he can be 'among the English poets', and a crippling self-doubt, modesty and self-deprecation of a man just over five feet high, aware that in aiming so high he can become a figure of ridicule, 'A pet-lamb in a sentimental farce'. Something of the context of the poem is suggested in Keats's letter to Sarah Jeffrey on 9 June, which again points to what I have called a playful tone in the odes:

> I have been very idle lately, very averse to writing; both from the overpowering idea of our dead poets and from the abatement of my own love of fame. I hope I am a little more of a Philosopher than I was, consequently a little less of a versifying Pet-lamb ... You will judge of my 1819 temper when I tell you that the thing I have most enjoyed this year has been writing an ode to Indolence.

However, no matter how much he 'enjoyed' writing it, Keats did not persuade himself to include it amongst his published poems.

If 'Ode on Indolence' is as much about a mood as the nature of art, so is 'Ode on Melancholy', which for once seems to proceed from a 'real world' reference beyond its own artifice, a feeling of deep depression. However, we find once again a contemplation of the nature of art which is characteristic of Keats in the odes. The thought seems to be another spin-off, this time from 'Ode to a Nightingale', at least in its point of departure, as is recognisable from the imagery of the first verse:

> No, no, go not to Lethe, neither twist
>   Wolf's-bane, tight-rooted, for its poisonous wine;

> Nor suffer thy pale forehead to be kiss'd
>> By nightshade, ruby grape of Proserpine;
> Make not your rosary of yew-berries,
>> Nor let the beetle, nor the death-moth be
>> Your mournful Psyche, nor the downy owl
> A partner in your sorrow's mysteries;
>> For shade to shade will come too drowsily,
>> And drown the wakeful anguish of the soul.

His tendency to swing between moods of despairing depression and something close to ecstasy was known to Keats himself – 'truth is I have a horrid Morbidity of Temperament which has shown itself at intervals' (*JKL*, 1, 142) – and it worried his friends to the extent that he would afterwards feel the need to reassure them. He was clearly conscious of this cycle of his 'human heart' and, for example, it drives the sonnet which he had written just a couple months earlier in March, 'Why did I laugh tonight? No voice will tell' in which, out of a state of being 'sad and alone' in 'mortal pain' he inexplicably laughs and contemplates the intensity of death as 'life's high meed'. Given the imagery linking intense sensuous experience, love and death in 'Nightingale' and 'Melancholy' we might not see this as more than a poetic conceit, but Keats realised it could send alarm bells about his mental and emotional state to those who loved him.

> Yet would I on this very midnight cease,
> And the world's gaudy ensigns see in shreds.
> Verse, Fame, and Beauty are intense indeed,
> But death intenser – Death is Life's high meed.

He immediately reassured his brother that it was not a suicide note. 'Ode on Melancholy' likewise seems partly a kind of self-therapy or at least self-analysis, as it advocates neither denying the mood of melancholy nor following it either to drugged oblivion or suicide. Instead, the Ode advocates accepting the 'melancholy fit' of depression as a valid response to the passing of transient beauty: 'Then glut thy sorrow on a morning rose ...' when the rain falls in April, killing the petals, or 'feed deep, deep' upon the animated eyes of a lover in anger. The mistress 'dwells with Beauty – Beauty that must die' and joyful pleasure is always beckoning and yet always retreating, 'Turning to poison while the bee-mouth sips'. Once again, Keats is taking his theme of beauty destroyed by time from Shakespeare's Sonnets, but he is adding his own tone of 'wakeful anguish' linking pain and pleasure more energetically and closely than Shakespeare had done:

> Ay, in the very temple of Delight
> Veil'd Melancholy has her Sovran shrine.

Allott detects a post-coital sexuality in the conclusion which advocates using the 'strenuous tongue' 'to burst Joy's grape against his palate fine' [19] after which the 'soul shall taste the sadness of [Joy's] might ...' In this poem beauty is not truth but a principle of impermanence, and all that can be done is to merge with the moment rather than resist it. By the last lines the 'she' of the poem seems not to be the unattainable and beautiful courtly lady but an equally tantalising work of art, as the poet becomes a sacrificial victim to art, one of its 'cloudy trophies': 'His soul shall taste the sadness of her might, / And be among her cloudy trophies hung'. Even here as he rationalises cheering himself up from depression, Keats must have had in mind a specific work of literature, Burton's *Anatomy of Melancholy* whose writer was certainly among the 'cloudy trophies' of the emotional affliction, having in his own words 'lived and died by melancholy'. The ode may have been in part Keats's homage to one of his favourite Renaissance books. In all the odes the poet and readers become as much victims as the hapless 'wight' or 'knight' in *La Belle Dame*, in this case baffled by the curtain that divides lightly but firmly art from the 'soul-making' element of lived experience.

10
Playwright

The summer of 1819 was a confusing time for Keats. He wrote prolifically, including some of his best poems like *Lamia* which has already been discussed in an earlier chapter, the great odes, and the second *Hyperion*, to come in the next chapter, but money was shorter than ever. This problem had dogged him ever since he had left Guy's Hospital, and even entered comic lines from *Robin Hood*, a poem about the passing of the golden age: 'strange! That honey / Can't be got without hard money!' set in a time when 'men knew nor rent nor leases'. Much to Keats's irritation Haydon was repeatedly asking for money but not repaying the loans, and Abbey was unable to release money from the legacy, reporting instead that the estate was now being sued by the Keatses' aunt, an in-law to the Jennings family. George was finding his fortunes in America not as auspicious as he had expected and was also asking for financial help, apparently unaware of John's own straitened circumstances.

Meanwhile, the sore throat which had stalked him for almost a year since the Scottish journey persisted. It seems likely that the sensory indulgences he records, so deplored for their apparent epicureanism and sexual connotations by later Victorian taste, were comforting to ease the pain – drinking claret 'For really 't is so fine – it fills the mouth with a gushing freshness – then goes down cool and feverless – ...' (*JKL*, 2, 64), drinking wine with spicy cayenne pepper on his tongue (perhaps an apocryphal story, spread by Haydon) and, as he himself rhapsodises, 'holding to my Mouth a Nectarine – good god how fine – It went down soft pulpy, slushy, oozy – all its delicious embonpoint melted down my throat like a large beatified Strawberry. I shall certainly breed' (*JKL*, 2, 179). At the end of May Keats did some stock-taking, returning borrowed books to people like Taylor and Hessey, trying to deliver to Fanny a letter which had just arrived from George, though he had lent it to Haslam who unaccountably 'returned it torn into a thousand pieces' (*JKL*, 2, 111), and making a bonfire of old letters, sparing those from Sarah Jeffrey and her sister Marian (or Marianne) in Teignmouth, Devon. He asks them on 31 May if there is 'any Lodging commodious for its cheapness' in Teignmouth, hinting at his money problems:

> I have the choice as it were of two Poisons (yet I ought not to call this a Poison) the one is voyaging to and from India for a few years; the other is leading a fevrous life alone with Poetry – This latter will suit me best – for I cannot resolve to give up my Studies ... Yes, I would rather conquer my indolence and strain my n[e]rves at some grand Poem – than be in a dunderheaded Indiaman ... I have been always till now almost as careless of the world as a fly – my troubles were all of the Imagination – My brother George always stood between me and any dealings with the world – Now I find I must buffet it – I must take my stand upon some vantage ground and begin to fight – I must choose between despair & Energy – I choose the latter – though the world has taken on a quakerish look with me, which I once thought was impossible –
> 'Nothing can bring back the hour
> Of splendour in the grass and glory in the flower'
> I once thought this a Melancholist's dream – (*JKL*, 2, 113)

In the event, as he told Sarah on 9 June, he decided neither to reside in Teignmouth nor to become a ship's doctor on an 'indiaman', despite the latter's appealing opportunity for a writer to make 'speculations of the differences of human character and to class them with the calmness of a Botanist. An Indiaman is a little world' (*JKL*, 2, 115). Instead he accepted an invitation to accompany his friend James Rice back to the Isle of Wight, and write. There Rice and Keats went, after a cold and wet coach journey, to be joined by Brown and his friend John Martin who was a publisher. Given that Keats was determined to write, it was merciful that Rice and Martin left after only a few days, since the four men would stay up overnight playing cards, leaving Keats exhausted and unable to find time to himself. Brown remained during July until mid-August at Shanklin this time for cheapness, after which the two men went straight to Winchester and stayed until early October. Keats's travels may have helped to stimulate his writing but the enforced separation from Fanny Brawne, judging from his letters to her, was clearly beginning to cause him distress and jealousy. He felt himself to be 'a little mad' and certainly melancholy: 'I have never known an unalloy'd Happiness for many days together: the death or sickness of some one has always spoilt my hours' (*JKL*, 2, 123). In this case Rice was suffering from a congenital illness and rapidly became tiresome company; the cheerful Brown had been a welcome arrival. The publication of Keats's letters to Fanny from Shanklin and afterwards were regretted by the later Victorian readers such as Matthew Arnold and others who wished them to be suppressed, but to modern readers, unhampered by fastidious sensibilities, they are irresistible in their expressions of passion and take their place beside his fictional love poetry:

> The morning is the only proper time for me to write to a beautiful Girl whom I love so much: for at night, when the lonely day has closed, and the lonely, silent, unmusical Chamber is waiting to receive me as into a Sepulchre, then believe me my passion gets entirely the sway, then I would not have you see those Rapsodies which I once thought it impossible I should ever give way to, and which I have often laughed at in another, for fear you should [think me] either too unhappy or perhaps a little mad ... Ask yourself my love whether you are not very cruel to have so entrammelled me, so destroyed my freedom. Will you confess this in the Letter you must write immediately and do all you can to console me in it – make it rich as a draught of poppies to intoxicate me – write the softest words and kiss them that I may at least touch my lips where yours have been ... I almost wish we were butterflies and liv'd but three summer days – three such days with you I could fill with more delight than fifty common years could contain ... (*JKL*, 2, 122–3)

The ambitious and demanding projects pursued from his 'little coffin of a room at Shanklin' and then at Winchester were rewriting the *Hyperion* fragment, composing *Lamia*, and writing a full five-act play. The third was at Brown's suggestion and was motivated mainly by the pressing need to earn money, though also by Keats's longstanding and repeated ambition to write drama:

> My having written that [Passage] ... is my first Step towards the chief Attempt in the Drama – the playing of different Natures with Joy and Sorrow. (*JKL*, 1, 219)

In 1818 Keats had composed various short poems intended as songs towards an opera, and Brown had already written *Narensky*, a comic opera which was produced at the Drury Lane theatre in 1814. Though it received no critical acclaim, it had earned Brown £300 and a 'silver pass' with life membership of the theatre, allowing him free entry which he had enjoyed many times in Keats's company. The two men now resolved to write a play which, they hoped, would be chosen by Edmund Kean as his star-vehicle in a London West End theatre. It had to be Kean and they wrote with him specifically in mind.

'Aesculapius' had strongly disapproved of the young medical students at Guy's Hospital attending London theatres which were seductively close by, but Keats, no doubt like most fellow students, did not heed the advice and instead acquired a lifelong enthusiasm for the theatre.[1] From his student days he was a frequenter of all kinds of performances, even in a small and undistinguished theatre in Teignmouth where he was inexplicably 'insulted' by a member of the audience. In January 1818 he reviewed for the *Champion* a pantomime *Harlequin's Vision* and a 'Don Giovanni' tragedy *Retribution*. He even attended and mercilessly parodied a performance by strolling players in a 'Barn' in Scotland, notable mainly for the eruptions of bagpipes:

> On ente[r]ing Inverary we saw a Play Bill – Brown was knock'd up from new shoes – so I went to the Barn alone where I saw the Stranger accompanied by a Bag pipe – there they went on about 'interesting creaters' and 'human nater' – till the Curtain fell and then Came the Bag pipe – When Mrs Haller fainted down went the Curtain and out came the Bagpipe – at the heartrending, shoemending reconciliation the Piper blew amain – I never read or saw this play before; not the Bag pipe, nor the wretched players themselves were little in comparison with it – thank heaven it has been scoffed at lately almost to a fashion. (*JKL*, 1, 336–7)

It is slightly surprising that he had never seen Kotzebue's *The Stranger* since revivals of it were quite popular in London after its first performance at Drury Lane in 1798. London's theatrical life was vibrant but heavily regulated and subject to monopoly. Only Covent Garden, Drury Lane and (in summer) the Haymarket were licensed to stage 'legitimate' drama along the lines of five-act traditional plays, while the King's Theatre produced opera. Pantomimes, melodramas, burlesques and visual spectacles erupted in other performance spaces, but if there were words they could be heavily censored. 'Illegitimate' non-verbal performances flourished around London and interacted with the 'legitimate' in various ways.[2] Such entertainment competed with many forms of spectator sports such as cricket, football, foot racing, cudgelling contests and prize-fighting on the more innocent end of the spectrum, while on the other were cockfighting, bear baiting, 'riding for geese' (don't ask!) and – most dramatic of all – the gruesome ritual of public executions.[3] In an anecdote which biographers might prefer to overlook, Cowden Clarke described Keats's imitation of a baited bear which he had seen, interpreted by Clarke at least as amusing though we cannot know the source of Keats's feelings in this 'minor scene of low life' (CCC, 145). Such spectacles were coming under increasing criticism for their cruelty to animals.[4]

Predictably, Keats's true taste in drama was for Shakespeare's plays, especially when performed by Edmund Kean, whom he had ample opportunity to see at Drury Lane and Covent Garden between which theatres Kean oscillated during his career.[5] Keats's first foray into theatre reviewing was when he published on 21 December 1817 a passionately complimentary review simply called 'Mr Kean', in which he expressed gratitude that in tame days 'Habeas Corpus'd' as we are out of all wonder, uncertainty and fear' in 'these cold and enfeebling times!' when 'romance lives but in books', there was Kean to bring 'some excitement by his old passion in one of the old plays. He is a relict of romance; – a Posthumous ray of chivalry, and always seems just arrived from the camp of Charlemagne.'[6] Keats's impressionistic reviewing style is in conscious emulation of his admired Hazlitt who had first announced to the world the brilliance of Kean, and he reuses that critic's word 'gusto' to describe Kean's voice changes, 'by which we feel that the utterer is thinking of the past and the future, while speaking of the instant'. In a review in *The Examiner* on 26 May 1816, Hazlitt had announced that 'Gusto in art is power or passion defining any object ... it is in giving this truth of character from the truth of feeling, whether in the highest or the lowest degree, but always in the highest degree of which the subject is capable, that gusto consists.'[7] In Keats's usage, it has something of the force of our use of the term 'method acting' developed by Stanislavsky, as he describes Kean's ability to speak Shakespeare's language as though he really is the character, expressing turbulent storminess, impatience or lyricism. In contrasting 'Wordsworth, or any other of our intellectual monopolists' Keats shows that he finds 'negative capability' in Kean's acting, the capacity to feel the quality of the moment without intellectual reserve or distance. Above all he admires Kean's interpretive risk-taking and refusal to be conventional and 'correct' as the other great actor of the day, Philip Kemble, was perceived to be. In the twentieth century similar comparisons were made between Olivier ('the Body') and Gielgud ('the Voice'). Kean was Keats's model for speaking and acting Shakespearian verse, just as Hazlitt was his model for writing about it:

A melodious passage in poetry is full of pleasures both sensual and spiritual. The spiritual is felt when the very letters and prints of characterized language show like the hieroglyphics of beauty; – the mysterious signs of an immortal freemasonry! 'A thing to dream of, not to tell!' The sensual life of verse springs warm from the lips of Kean, and to one learned in Shakespearian hieroglyphics.

The metaphor of hieroglyphics, also used by Hazlitt[8] and Coleridge,[9] was no doubt prompted by news of the Rosetta Stone which had been brought to France in 1798, its inscription not finally deciphered until 1824. The word is used by Keats to suggest that Shakespeare's language is densely 'coded' and needs mediation through an actor who has almost the status of a high priest. Kean, who was as short as Keats in stature, was a fiery actor, often described as 'electric' in charisma, although often, one suspects, his unpredictable acting was the result of intoxication. He played many characters from many plays, but his most famous roles were those of complex Shakespearian villains like Richard III, Iago and Shylock, another way in which his performances influenced Keats by making him aware of the alternating light and shade, good and evil, in Shakespeare's plays and in the kind of poetry he wanted to write himself. Keats wrote of his dramatic ambitions to Bailey:

> It was the opinion of most of my friends that I should never be able to {write} a {s}cene – I will endeavour to wipe awa{y the prejudice – } I sincerely hope you will be pleased when my Labours since we last saw each other shall reach you – One of my Ambitions is to make as great a revolution in modern dramatic writing as Kean has done in acting – another to upset the drawling of the blue stocking literary world – if in the course of a few years I do these two things I ought to die content – and my friends should drink a dozen of Claret on my Tomb – (*JKL*, 2, 139)

Even Brown himself admitted that the process of collaborating on their play, *Otho the Great*, was 'curious':

> I engaged to furnish him with the fable, characters, and dramatic conduct of a tragedy, and he was to embody it into poetry. The progress of this work was curious: for, while I sat opposite to him, he caught my description of each scene, entered into the characters to be brought forward, the events, and every thing connected with it. Thus he went on, scene after scene, never knowing nor inquiring into the scene which was to follow until four acts were completed. It was then he required to know, at once, all the events which were to occupy the fifth act. I explained them to him; but, after a patient hearing, and some thought, he insisted on it that my incidents were too numerous, and, as he termed them, too melodramatic. He wrote the fifth act in accordance with his own view. (Brown, 54–5)

There is some suggestion that Keats's intention was ultimately to use his share of the anticipated theatrical proceeds to pay back money that Brown had lent him. Whether it was due to the circumstances of collaboration or to Keats's own limitations, his usually reliable and self-critical judgment about his own aptitudes may have let him down in his belief that drama was a natural *forte* for him. His genuine and astute appraisal of his temperament as one marked by the 'negative capability' and empathy shown by Shakespeare in his plays and by Kean in his acting, did not inevitably mean Keats would be especially good as a playwright. He certainly had an eye for theatrical situations and characters, as we see continually in his letters, especially in those written from Scotland and from Winchester. However, this kind of prose talent perhaps stemmed more from an auditor's interest in the theatre (and perhaps even a potential novelist's instinct) than from the specific skills needed to create plausible and consistent characters within a firm dramatic and narrative structure, which are essential to the playwright's craft. He seems to have finally conceded as much, when he confessed to Taylor, 'The little dramatic skill I may as yet have however badly it might show in a Drama would I think be sufficient for a Poem', mentioning *The Eve of St Agnes*. He did not relinquish his long-term hope, believing that two or three such poems would 'nerve' him: 'up to the writing of a few fine Plays – my greatest ambition – when I do feel ambitious' (*JKL*, 2, 234). We should remind ourselves also that most of the Romantic poets had the same ambition and that drama was seen as a privileged genre mainly because of Shakespeare's precedent and because successfully staged plays could be financially lucrative and give prestige to a writer. Coleridge's *Remorse* (1813) was quite successful on the stage, as was Cornwall's *Mirandola* (1821), but others did not reach performance. Shelley's *The Cenci* is the most impressive as a stageworthy script, though its theme of incest would certainly have fallen foul of censors and many of the works self-financed by Shelley and published by Ollier remained unsold, while Wordsworth's *The Borderers*, Shelley's *Prometheus Unbound* and Byron's *Manfred* may never have been intended for staging. They were successful as closet dramatic poems rather than as poetic dramas on the stage, or at least their authors would have been well aware that the state's Examiner of Plays in the Lord Chamberlain's office would have refrained from issuing a licence: 'politics is the forbidden fruit, lest the people's eyes should be opened and they become as gods knowing good and evil' as a contemporary wrote.[10] Although there has been a recent revaluation of Romantic drama, showing it to have been more lively than has been believed, yet the canonical Romantic poets seem all to have had arguably non-dramatic skills despite their aspirations.

Otho the Great is set during the Hungarian wars in the tenth century and depicts the unsuccessful rebellion against Otho I by his son Ludolph and the Red Duke Conrad of Lorraine.[11] Although the general tone is typical of Romantic stage melodrama, many motifs remind us strongly of Beaumont and Fletcher, writers whom Keats read and admired. Given the collaborative nature of the enterprise, as Brown fed him the story and he supplied the poetry, Keats must have felt something like a Fletcher to his companion's Beaumont. We find similarities of construction. Beaumont and Fletcher concentrated on dramatic situation and scenic effectiveness rather than on depth of characterisation, a mark of *Otho* which has been held up as a fault but, with the possible exception of Shakespeare, this was typical of plays in the early seventeenth century. They were also adept at constructing their plots around a series of relationships which are intense and intricate, involving duplicity and often a measure of sexual blackmail (as in *A King and No King* and *The Maid's Tragedy*), rather than employing the Shakespearian method of concentrating upon one tragic protagonist. Again, then, it may be quite a conscious decision that, as Beaudry puts it, 'there is no particularly outstanding character in the play as a whole', but that 'each major personage is able to hold the reader's interest at some stage of the action'. Finally, there are two character types which are reminiscent of Beaumont and Fletcher's. Ludolph, the role intended for Kean, is very like their rather ineffectual heroes who are acted upon rather than asserting themselves (for example, Philaster), while Erminia, like Evadne, is the even more passive, suffering figure of virtue. Conrad and Auranthe are effective embodiments of evil, but little sentiment can be spared over their deaths which are in accordance with the rules of poetic justice. One suspects that Keats was temperamentally incapable of understanding evil with any subtlety. His only poetic attempt to depict it is in creating the profoundly ambiguous snake-woman Lamia, who is herself partially redeemed emotionally by the strength of her love. It is Ludolph, and to a lesser extent Albert and Erminia, who emerge as the ones involved in tragic predicaments. Ludolph goes mad as a consequence of the situation that has confronted him. All the time, although he is introduced as a warrior and a man of pride and righteous anger, Ludolph is given very little choice over what happens to him. He is reconciled with his father by accident when Otho recognises his son through the disguise of an Arab soldier, he is married off to Auranthe (not against his wishes, certainly, but not of his own volition), he is completely tricked by his wife and her evil brother, but he clings to his trust in her honesty. Albert, the man of truth 'Whose words once utter'd pass like current gold' (III.ii.210) is faced with a conflict of loyalties, between supporting the truth which Erminia speaks and telling a lie to protect Ludolph's marriage and his feelings. The lie which he tells cannot go unchanged in such a pillar of truth-telling, and in attempting to rectify it he loses his life. His death is represented with tragic intensity (V.ii), for he dies full of grief and guilt which have not yet been atoned for. His motives can ultimately be traced back to a praiseworthy loyalty to Ludolph and to Otho. Finally, although Erminia does not die, the eventual revelation of her honesty and virtue, coming after she has been publicly calumniated during the action of the play, appears too late to help the situation or her immediate reputation. She witnesses the events of the ending in possession of a total understanding denied to anybody else, and she speaks words of pity recalling Cordelia's: 'Alas! Alas!' (V.v.167). The figures whose fates represent the tragic spirit in the play, then, are all people who suffer for their sympathy or their honesty, and they are helplessly caught in a web of circumstances that are none of their making. Evil lies outside them, in the characters of Conrad and Auranthe. They are, in fact, people who live and die by their 'negative capability'.

There is a consistency here with what Keats was thinking about in the two or three months before he began writing *Otho the Great*. The long letter to his brother and sister-in-law of April 1819, in which he sees life as 'the vale of soul-making' emphasises the helplessness of the sensitive individual in controlling his circumstances. There is more than a hint of tragic consciousness in the description of such a fate:

> For instance suppose a rose to have sensation, it blooms on a beautiful
> morning it enjoys itself – but there comes a cold wind, a hot sun – it

cannot escape it, it cannot destroy its annoyances – they are as native to the world as itself: no more can man be happy in spite, the world[l]y elements will prey upon his nature ...

The parable of life as 'soul-making' which Keats had formulated as a stoical answer to the 'vale of tears' emphasises the creative, self-instructive potential in the act of enduring. However, he also repeatedly contrasted as character types those heroes like Endymion who are 'led on, like Buonaparte, by circumstance' with Apollo, the 'fore-seeing God' who in *Hyperion* 'will shape his actions like one' (*JKL*, 1, 207), just as he detects inside himself the warring impulses towards 'despair' or 'energy', resolving to choose the latter.

In respect to *Otho the Great* Keats saw himself only as 'midwife' to Brown's 'child'. At one stage Brown suggested bringing an elephant onto the stage for its spectacle, and although this seems laughable, in fact a mechanical elephant was included in Colman's *Blue-Beard; or, Female Curiosity!* at Drury Lane in 1798. At least on this point, Keats disagreed. Even his own contribution, the poetry, although functional and competent, is dictated to some extent by the narrative and generally lacks Keats's rich amplitude. In the last Act he wrote more independently, refusing Brown's direction, and there is some lift in the dramatic or poetic temperature, although this is not unusual at the climax even of a play which otherwise is undistinguished. He must have been mouthing to himself the words of the dying Ludolph in full flight as he imagined Kean speaking them:

> Must I stop here? Here solitary die?
> Stifled beneath the thick oppressive shade
> Of these dull boughs, – this oven of dark thickets, –
> Silent, – without revenge, – pshaw! – bitter end, –
> A bitter death, – a suffocating death, –
> A gnawing – silent – deadly, quiet death!
>
> (V.i.18–23)

We find poetry which signals that Keats was returning to rewriting *Hyperion* at the time:

> I would have, as a mortal I may not,
> Hangings of heaven's clouds, purple and gold,
> Slung from the spheres; gauzes of silver mist,
> Loop'd up with cords of twisted wreathed light,
> And tassell'd round with weeping meteors!
>
> (V.v.35–9)

Robert Gittings suggests that the description of the unfaithful Auranthe was provoked by Keats's own strong jealousy on hearing that Fanny Brawne had enjoyed herself at a ball amongst soldiers:

> *Sigifred.* Bid the musicians soothe him tenderly.
>   [A soft strain of music.]
> *Ludolph.* Ye have none better? No, I am content;
> 'Tis a rich sobbing melody, with reliefs
> Full and majestic; it is well enough,
> And will be sweeter, when ye see her pace
> Sweeping into this presence, glisten'd o'er
> With emptied caskets, and her train upheld
> By ladies, habited in robes of lawn
> Sprinkled with golden crescents, others bright
> In silks with spangles shower'd, and bow'd to
> By duchesses and pearled margravines!
> Sad, that the fairest creature of the earth –
> I pray you mind me not – 'tis sad, I say,
> That the extreme beauty of the world
> Should so entrench herself away from me,
> Behind a barrier of engender'd guilt!
>
>   (V.v.80–95)

Despite Brown feeling 'sanguine' about the play being performed, in the event Keats's own pessimistic forecasts prevailed since both Drury Lane and Covent Garden turned it down, and Kean, though Brown says he 'desired to play the principal character', had decided to go to America. The news disheartened Keats:

> That was the worst news I could have had. There is no actor can do the principal character besides Kean. At Covent Garden there is a great chance of its being damn'd. Were it to succeed even there it would lift me out of the mire. I mean the mire of a bad reputation which is continually rising against me. My name with the literary fashionables is vulgar – I am a weaver boy to them – a Tragedy would lift me out of this mess ...
> (*JKL*, 2, 186)

The reference to the 'weaver boy' shows not only his insecurity about class but also his age and perhaps even his height. Socially, Keats could identify himelf with Kean as he could to some extent with Burns, pouring scorn on 'fashionables' with 'mannerisms ... in their mere handling a Decanter – They talked of Kean and his low company – Would I were with that company instead of yours said I to myself! ...' But it had to be Kean and nobody else, and he revealed to his sister more of his general thoughts on actors in the West End theatres:

> I had hoped to give Kean another opportunity to shine. What can we do now? There is not another actor of Tragedy in all London or Europe – the Covent Garden Company <are> is execrable – Young is the best among them and he is a ranting, coxcombical tasteless Actor – A Disgust A Nausea – and yet the very best after Kean – What a set of barren asses are actors! (*JKL*, 2, 149)

The play eventually had a belated world première in London in 1950, to some critical acclaim.

After finishing *Otho*, Keats tried again, again on Brown's suggestion but this time without 'leading-strings': 'I will do all this myself' (*KC*, 2, 67), he said, beginning a historical tragedy to be called *King Stephen*. Again, Kean was the target actor, though forthwith he left for the American tour and Keats abandoned the play. In the first and only four scenes he wrote, the dramatic speech does show a greater vigour and a conscious modelling on the iambics and concentrated language of Shakespeare:

> STEPHEN
> If shame can on a soldier's vein-swollen front
> Spread deeper crimson than the battle's toil,
> Blush in your casing helmets! For see, see!
> Yonder my chivalry, my pride of war,
> Wrenched with an iron hand from firm array,
> Are routed loose about the plashy meads,
> Of honour forfeit ...

Shakespeare's influence may explain another puzzle. One very disconcerting and chilling fragment of poetry by Keats, which has sometimes been read autobiographically as an address to Fanny Brawne, is more generally assumed to be intended as dramatic monologue for a play:

> This living hand, now warm and capable
> Of earnest grasping, would, if it were cold
> And in the icy silence of the tomb,
> So haunt thy days and chill thy dreaming nights
> That thou would wish thine own heart dry of blood
> So in my veins red life might stream again,
> And thou be conscience-calmed – see here it is –
> I hold it towards you.

A suggestion I have not seen elsewhere is that this fragment is an imitation of Shakespeare's Sonnet 71 whose tone of misanthropic defiance it resembles:

> No longer mourn for me when I am dead
> Then you shall hear the surly sullen bell
> Give warning to the world that I am fled
> From this vile world, with vilest worms to dwell:
> Nay, if you read this line, remember not
> The hand that writ it; for I love you so
> That I in your sweet thoughts would be forgot
> If thinking on me then should make you woe.
> O, if, I say, you look upon this verse
> When I perhaps compounded am with clay,
> Do not so much as my poor name rehearse.
> But let your love even with my life decay,
> Lest the wise world should look into your moan
> And mock you with me after I am gone.

It has sometimes been claimed that another scene from a play known as *Gripus* was also written by Keats. Evidently intended as a comedy of manners, it depicts a nobleman contemplating marrying his longstanding housekeeper in order to beget an heir, and has been plausibly suggested as a private exchange between Keats and Brown, since the latter did (or at least may have) married Abigail O'Donoghue under similar circumstances, to Keats's disapproval. In 1818, indicating yet another theatrical direction he had flirted with, Keats had even written some verses that he seems to have intended as libretti to an opera.

Having not succeeded as a dramatist, Keats decided to try 'prosing' in periodicals in order to maintain himself 'decently' (Brown's words). Some critics have regretted the 'grievous expenditure of Keatsian time and effort' spent on the apparently abortive exercise of writing plays[12] in the midst of 1819, his 'living year'. However, such a judgment is made with a hindsight denied to the poet, and if indeed Kean had been able to play Ludolph in *Otho* as Keats and Brown intended, it is not inconceivable we would have had a rare, staged success by a canonical Romantic poet, which might have achieved the aim of stimulating public reappraisal of his reputation and earned him money. *Otho* is no worse, and probably much better than many of the original plays performed in the West End of London during the period. Given time, Keats may, as he intended, have returned to drama, but as it is, he did have at least one completed work to show in the genre which was at the top of his own hierarchy of literature.

11
Autumn in Winchester

Keats and Brown arrived in Winchester on 12 August 1819. Brown left in the first week of September, and Keats, by this time on his own, left on 8 October. Although he felt 'mired' not only in his poetic reputation and through financial difficulties, but also in his helpless emotional dependency on his love for Fanny Brawne, he was at the same time proud of his recent output, which he summarises for Bailey:

> Within these two Months I have written 1500 Lines, most of which besides many more of prior composition you will probably see by next Winter. I have written two Tales, one from Boccaccio call'd the Pot of Basil; and another call'd St Agnes' Eve on a popular superstition; and a third call'd Lamia – (half finished – I {hav}e a{l}so been writing parts of my Hyperion and {c}completed 4 Acts of a Tragedy ... (*JKL*, 2, 139)

It is interesting that Keats does not include in this impressive list the Odes, the poems on which nowadays his reputation is most strongly based, helping to confirm my suggestion that he wrote these poems in an intellectually playful way as a distillation of many of the preoccupations in his letters at the time. He continues in his commitment to poetry, despite bouts of being disheartened. He was facing serious money problems and spent the first few days at Winchester writing uncomfortably to the staunchly supportive Woodhouse and Taylor asking them for loans to repay his own. Both responded positively which eased the pressure a little, but both also, like Abbey, reprimanded Keats for his own tendency to lend money so willingly (especially, one guesses, to Haydon and others of his ilk). Despite his financially straitened circumstances, the failing health which increasingly prevented him exerting himself, and fraught communication by letters with Fanny Brawne whom he had ignored on his brief 'business' trip to London following a lover's tiff caused by his over-intensity and jealousy, this period was to be amongst, if not the happiest, at least the most creative and even settled times of his life. At least he was able to write and his days took on a comforting routine. By now he had steeled himself to 'get a livelihood' from his writing, and to develop his 'Pride and egotism' as a defence against the 'literary world' which he regarded with 'hate and contempt', though he perhaps faced a contradiction in spurning yet courting a sympathetic reading public:

> I am convinced more and more day by day that fine writing is next to fine doing the top thing in the world; the Paradise Lost becomes a greater wonder – The more I know what my diligence may in time probably effect; the more does my heart distend with Pride and Obstinacy – I feel it in my power to become a popular writer – I feel it in my strength to refuse the poisonous suffrage of a public – My own being which I know to be becomes of more consequence to me than the crowds of Shadows in the Shape of Man and women that inhabit a kingdom. The Soul is a world of itself and has enough to do in its own home – ... (*JKL*, 2, 146)

His confidence as a poet was high:

> I am convinced more and more every day that (excepting the human friend Philosopher) a fine writer is the most genuine Being in the World – Shakespeare and the paradise Lost every day become greater wonders to me – I look upon fine Phrases like a Lover ... (*JKL*, 2, 139)

He wishes only for 'a free and healthy and lasting organization of heart and Lungs – as strong as an ox<e>'s – so as to be able unhurt [to bear?] the shock of extreme thought and sensation without weariness'. He writes, 'I could pass my Life very nearly alone though it should last eighty years. But I feel my Body too weak to support me to the height; I am obliged continually to check myself and strive to be nothing' (*JKL*, 2, 146–7).

Winchester in late summer and early autumn suited Keats, although he frequently mocked its sleepiness, the 'excessively maiden-like' gentility of its respectable and elderly inhabitants: 'a modest lifting up of the knocker by a set of little wee old fingers that peep through the grey mittens, and a dying fall thereof – The great beauty of Poetry is, that it makes every thing every place interesting' (*JKL*, 2, 201). He savoured especially the day when they elected their mayor (*JKL*, 2, 200–1), which reminds him of his own imagined town described in the fragment *The Eve of St Mark*. The details he observes in this market town which had known grander and busier times feed his theatrical eye. Even though he had sought a place with the convenience of a 'tolerable Library, which after all is not to be found in this place' (*JKL*, 2, 147), there was at least a bookshop called Robbins (now Wells) on the street on College Street, and to the literary-minded bookshops have always been among the most comforting places in the world. Jane Austen had spent her final days (in 1817) along the road at 8 College Street, though Keats does not seem to have known even of her novels. We do not know exactly where he stayed himself and the only clues are that it was 'in tolerably good and cheap Lodgings' very close to the cathedral and unpromisingly looking out on 'a beautiful blank side of a house'. The best guess, based on maps of the time and local knowledge today, is that the house is now destroyed but most likely was 'in the western part of Colebrook Street, which then ran parallel to Paternoster Row'.[1] He developed the daily routine of taking an hour's walk from Winchester's 'fine' and ubiquitous cathedral with its avenue of lime trees, past the College, alongside the river and out across the meadows to the Hospital of St Cross with its Norman church, up St Catherine's Hill and back again. Parts of his route he described to his sister and then to the George Keatses in more detail. Now known as 'the Keats Walk' it can be followed today.

> It is the pleasantest Town I ever was in, and has the most reccommendations of any. There is a fine Cathedrall which to me is always a sourse of amusement ... The whole town is beautifully wooded – From the Hill at the eastern extremity you see a prospect of Streets, and old Buildings mixed up with Trees – Then There are the most beautiful streams about I ever saw – full of Trout – There is the Foundation of St Croix about half a mile in the fields – a charity greatly abused – We have a Collegiate School, a roman catholic School; a chapel ditto and a Nunnery! ... The delightful Weather we have had for two Months is the highest gratification I could receive – no chill'd red noses – no shivering – but fair Atmosphere to think in – a clean towel mark'd with the mangle and a basin of clear Water to drench one's face with ten times a day: no need of much exercise – a Mile a day being quite sufficient – My greatest regret is that I have not been well enough to bathe though I have been two Months by the sea side [at Shanklin] and live now close to delicious bathing [the River Inch] – Still I enjoy the Weather I adore fine Weather as the greatest blessing I can have. Give me Books, fruit, french wine and fine whether and a little music out of doors, played by somebody I do not know – not pay the price of one's time for a gig – but a little chance music: and I can pass a summer very quietly without caring much about Fat Louis, fat Regent or the Duke of Wellington. (*JKL*, 2, 147–9)

The reference to the Prince Regent comes as Keats had on his way to Winchester seen that portly figure's royal yacht at anchor with a flotilla of boats approaching it, while the Duke of Wellington, after defeating Napoleon at Waterloo in 1815 had recently in 1819 entered politics as Major General of the Ordnance to Liverpool's Tory government. Given Keats's political views, he was relieved to have both distant from him. The feeling of living in a quiet, social backwater gave him some sense of diurnal stability, and when Brown went to Bedhampton for a fortnight Keats took some pleasure in his solitude, 'like a Hermit', enjoying the air which on the 'chalky down' outside the city he considered 'worth 6d a pint'.

Once again a very long journal letter to George, Georgiana, and now their daughter, dated from 17 to 27 September, gives a colourful narrative of the time Keats spent at Winchester. It begins, as usual, with news of the family's financial situation. George was just as perilously placed as John, since a businessman in America, John James Audubon, had inveigled him into parting with his money to invest in a boat business on the Ohio and Mississippi rivers, but had been ruined, drowning with his fortunes the entire inheritance of George Keats who understandably felt defrauded. 'I cannot help thinking Mr Audubon a dishonest man –' comments John indignantly: 'Why did he make you believe that he was a Man of Property? How is it his circumstances have altered so suddenly? In truth I do not believe you fit to deal with the world; or at least the American worrld' (*JKL*, 2, 185), the spelling of the last word probably being Keats's joking attempt to reproduce in orthography the American accent. John reports his visit to Abbey in London, who was at least working on the brothers' behalf in trying 'to get rid of Mrs Jennings's claim' to the contested will but unable to do anything helpful in the short run for the Keats brothers beyond promising to forward money to George as soon as he was able. 'We are certainly in a very low estate', writes John, revealing his own situation frankly but equally expressing optimism about his prospects as a writer, mainly, one senses, to allay George's anxieties. With his characteristic solicitude for protecting the feelings of others, he keeps returning with reassurance to George's situation and family circumstances: 'You have done your best – Take matters as coolly as you can and confidently expecting help from England, act as if no help was nigh' (a version of 'hope for the best, expect the worst'). He is distracting and informative by turns, transcribing a comic poem, 'writing' as he says 'as boys do at school' a few nonsense verses ('Pensive they sit, and roll their languid eyes...'), writing an acrostic for his sister-in-law, using each letter of her name – Georgiana Augusta Keats – to begin each line ('Give me your patience Sister while I frame ...'), describing *Lamia* as having 'that kind of fire in it which must take hold of people in some way ... What they want is a sensation of some sort ...', copying a whole page from Burton's *Anatomy of Melancholy* which satirically recounts how lovers are absurdly blind to their beloveds' physical imperfections, and giving news and amusing anecdotes of their mutual friends such as the Dilkes, Reynolds and Brown. He describes his visit to London on the money business and to see their sister as an alienating experience since all his friends were away – 'I was out and every body was out' – apart from Rice whom he now values as 'the most sensible, and even wise Man I know – he has a few John Bull prejudices; but they improve him. His illness is at times alarming ...' (*JKL*, 2, 187). He imagines fondly his new niece in America:

> I admire the exact admeasurement of my niece in your Mother's letter – O the little span long elf – I am not in the least judge of the proper weight and size of an infant. Never trouble yourselves about that: she is sure to be a fine woman – Let her have only delicate nails both on hands and feet and teeth as small as a May-fly's. [sic] who will live you his life on a square inch of oak-leaf. And nails she must have quite different from the market women here who plough into the butter and make a quatter pound taste of it. I intend to w[r]ite a letter to your Wifie and there I may say more on this little plump subject – I hope she's plump – 'Still harping on my daughter' – (*JKL*, 2, 189)

The letter amplifies some of Keats's political views as he gives his own version of European history as a constant class-struggle contesting 'The obligation of kings to the Multitude' and pitting noblemen who are agents for monarchical tyranny against 'the people as creatures continually endeavoring to check them':

> Then in every kingdom therre was a long struggle of kings to destroy all popular privileges. The english were the only people in europe who made a grand kick at this ... the example of England, and the liberal writers of france and england sowed the seed of opposition to this Tyranny – and it was swelling in the ground till it burst out in the french revolution – That has had an unlucky termination. It put a stop to the rapid progress of free sentiments in England; and gave our Court hopes of turning back to the despotism of the 16 century. They have made a handle of this event in every way to undermine our freedom. They spread a horrid superstition against all inovation and improvement ... (*JKL*, 2, 193)

In the section dated 18 September Keats gives a long account of his attitudes to these events in this letter to his brother and sister-in-law in America. Opening with 'I will give you a little politics', he presents briefly his own reading of political history, leading up to contemporary events. Showing a Godwinite bent, his stress is upon progress and enlightenment as being inevitable historical processes, and it is significant that each example he gives turns upon the curbing of 'official' power of nobles, kings and standing armies by the resistance and occasional rebellion of 'the people'. His allegiances are firmly with 'popular privileges' and 'the common people'. Keats sees the events of his own day fitting into a process of gradual change effected in three stages, 'First for the better, next for the worse, and a third time for the better once more'. While much of the thought and many of the words come from Hazlitt writing in *The Examiner*, Keats's analysis is so vividly expressive (his mounting excitement signalled by the degeneration of spelling), that full quotation alone can do justice:

> The present struggle in England of the people is to destroy this superstition. What has rous'd them to do it is their distresses – Perpaps on this account the pres'ent distresses of this nation are a fortunate thing – tho so horrid in their experience. You will see I mean that the french Revolution put a temporry stop to this third change, the change for the better – Now it is in progress again and I thing [sic] in an effectual one. This is no contest beetween whig and tory – but between right and wrong. There is scarcely a grain of party spirit now in England – Right and Wrong considered by each man abstractedly is the fashion. I know very little of these things. I am convinced however that apparently small causes make great alterations. There are little signs wherby we may know how matters are going on – This makes the business about Carlisle the Bookseller of great moment in my mind. He has been selling deistical pamphlets, republished Tom Payne and many other works held in superstitious horror. He even has been selling for some time immense numbers of a work call 'The Deist' which comes out in weekly numbers – For this Conduct he I think has had above a dozen [Prosecutions] inditements issued against him; for which he has found Bail to the amount of many thousand Pounds – After all they are affraid to prosecute: they are affraid of his defence: it [would] be published in all the papers all over the Empire: they shudder at this: the Trials would light a flame they could not extinguish. Do you not think this of great import? (*JKL*, 2, 193–4)

Keats reaffirms a radical position that hopes for a repeat of the French Revolution in England – 'This is no contest between whig and tory – but between right and wrong' – and he praises the courage of the bookseller Carlisle who republished radical political works such as Tom Paine's *Rights of Man* and the journal *The Deist* and went to jail for his beliefs. During his whirlwind visit to London he had witnessed from an upper window overlooking the Strand a vast crowd which he reports as numbering 30,000 gathered to hear Henry 'Orator' (or 'Bristol') Hunt, the man who had addressed the crowd at the Peterloo meeting in Manchester rallying for universal suffrage and repeal of the Corn Laws which had caused so much hardship among working people.[2] At Peterloo the militia had taken bloody steps to disrupt the meeting by riding horses into the crowd, trampling them so that many died and hundreds were injured. No doubt Keats took his information and views from acquaintances like Leigh Hunt and Hazlitt and from *The Examiner* which he was still reading regularly and now bundling up to send to George, but the argument is put in his own way and his own words as a matter of personal conviction. However, he brings himself down from abstract theorising to the specific task: 'Now the first political duty a Man ought to have a Mind to is the happiness of his friends' (*JKL*, 2, 213). Following this prompt, the letter meanders on through 'Pun-making' and anecdotes, inconsequential vignettes brought to life by Keats's acute eye, and interspersing whimsically self-revealing thoughts:

> From the time you left me, our friends say I have altered completely – am not the same person – perhaps in this letter I am for in a letter one takes up one's existence from the time we last met – I dare say you have altered also – every man does – Our bodies every seven years are completely fresh-materiald ... this is the reason why men who had been bosom friends, on being separated for any number of years, afterwards meet coldly, neither of them knowing why – The fact is they are both altered – Men who live together have a silent <p> moulding and influencing power over each other – They interassimulate. (*JKL*, 2, 208)

He speaks of reading Ariosto and Dante in order to learn Italian and praises Milton, Chatterton and Chaucer. The rambling but associative progress of the letter becomes a proof of its aphorism:

> That Dilke was a Man who cannot feel he has a personal identity unless he has made up his Mind about every thing. The only means of strengthening one's intellect is to make up ones mind about nothing – to let the mind be a thoroughfare for all thoughts. Not a select party. (*JKL*, 2, 213)

The implied distinction between 'negative capability' and 'the egotistical sublime' of some others is still an active part of his thinking and his preference as ever is for accepting contradictions as paradoxes and the mind as a non-judgmental 'thoroughfare'. Keats's feelings towards Dilke had cooled since the latter's family disapproved of his engagement to Fanny, for reasons probably relating to his own parlous financial situation.

In July 1819 on the Isle of Wight Keats had taken up again the abandoned idea of writing an epic on the myth of Hyperion. In Winchester he resolved to start over again from the beginning. However, once again he gave up midstream around 21 September after completing only the First Canto and 61 lines of the Second. This fragment was not published in his lifetime, and the fact that he did not include it in his next published volume, *Poems* (1820), need not primarily be because he was dissatisfied with what he had written, as is often assumed, but because he intended to come back yet again to the project and produce it in a finished state that could be published as a single volume like *Endymion*. There is not enough of it to tell us where he wished to take the narrative this time, but there are dominant centres of concentration and questioning which reflect some of his current preoccupations, and the emotional states depicted are strong and clear. However, even allowing for the fact that the details of Graeco-Roman mythology were then more familiar than nowadays, Keats made things difficult by such things as beginning *in medias res*, changing the order of events of the story, and by switching between alternative names of the characters, perhaps intending later to impose more consistency and clarity. Reduced to its essentials it is, as its subtitle declares, a 'dream' or as Brown described it a 'vision', in which the poet-narrator in an 'antechamber of this dream' is guided by Moneta (Mnemosyne, Greek goddess of memory and mother of the nine Muses, though the word also means 'money' or 'mint') as Dante was by Virgil, to observe the aftermath of one sequence of the wars amongst Titans. It shows the demoralised Saturn, overthrown by his sons, being comforted by Thea who Moneta describes as 'softest natured of our brood'. While the rest of the Titans are 'self-hid or prison-bound' and listening for Saturn, one is wakeful but 'unsecure' – 'Bright Hyperion' – who under his alternative name Apollo in *The Fall* had been destined for future rule.

In rewriting *Hyperion. A Fragment* as the equally fragmentary poem now known as *The Fall of Hyperion. A Dream*, Keats shows that his medical allusion to not being 'the same person' as he was applies as much to poetic composition as to friendships. He changes the point of view in a way which radically alters the central issues, turning the new poem, in Vincent Newey's words, into 'a fragment, baffled and baffling ... a monumental, and deeply honest, failure'.[3] The last word is surely unfair in its judgment of a work which, apart from being unfinished through no true fault of Keats and not intended for publication in this form, also contains some of Keats's most mature and powerful poetry, but the other epithets are apt. This time it is the poet himself, or at least a narrator who is a poet, speaking at the very inception of his mission, and the concentration is not upon the process of political rebellion but on personal change, nor upon worldly power but upon the moral duty to alleviate the suffering of the overthrown Titans. In its concentration on the distress of political 'losers' rather than the triumph of 'winners', the poem is comparable to Charlotte Smith's earlier and very moving poem *The Emigrants* (1793) with its account of political refugees from revolutionary France, whose political cause the radical Smith did not share but whose human misery stirred her compassion. Making the poet figure so central allows Keats to write more urgently and even autobiographically about his own concerns than he does in his other narrative poems where we find personal material sublimated into narrative stances from either classical or romance literary forms. He is ambitiously using the persona of the Odes to drive a longer, epic poem. One question in particular lies at the heart of the innovative portions of *The Fall of Hyperion*, and it anticipates the character who is to be the true hero of the projected work, Apollo as god of both poetry and of healing. Of what use to the world are poets as healers of psychic wounds? Potentially, Keats announces, in a way that suggests he is still thinking of Robertson's *History of America*, even the 'savage' could be a poet, if he could write down his dreams with 'melodious utterance',

> For Poesy alone can tell her dreams,
> With the fine spell of words alone can save
> Imagination from the sable charm
> And dumb enchantment. Who alive can say
> 'Thou art no poet; may'st not tell thy dreams?'

(Canto, I, lines 8–12)

Robertson had given credit to native South Americans and their ancient civilisations as having intellectual capabilities but lacking the developed forms of expression available to European civilisation to write them down. Keats goes on to discriminate between different kinds of poetry. In seeking to discover its utility, the narrator finds that some followers of Apollo 'are useless' (I, 189), for example, the pure 'dreamer' who muddies human experience by not discriminating joy and pain, and '… all mock lyrists, large self worshippers, / And careless hectorers in proud bad verse' (I, 207–8).

The best the dreamer can do is superficially cheer people up, 'that happiness be somewhat shared' (I, 177). Many critics believe the 'large self worshippers' barb is aimed at Byron, provoked by Abbey's snipe at Keats's poetry by offering admiration of Byron's, no doubt because it earned money. However, *The Fall of Hyperion*, consistent with its more personal approach, does seem in part to be recapitulating in a self-critical spirit Keats's own earlier works and experiences. For example, the way the landscape is observed echoes early poems like 'I stood tip-toe upon a little hill' and 'Sleep and Poetry'. The distinction between dream and realism had been central to *Endymion*, and Moneta's emphatic advice to 'think of the earth' formed a theme of that poem as it did also *Isabella; or the Pot of Basil*; the exotic meal, here partly consumed, was a centrepiece in the same poem and in *The Eve of St Agnes* and *Endymion*, narcotics and poisons were motifs in 'Ode to a Nightingale' and 'Ode on Melancholy', while the classical concentration on antiquity recalls 'Ode to Psyche' and 'Ode on a Grecian Urn'. The sacrifice of white heifers and the image of 'Silenus on an antique vase' echo the latter. A memory of the vivid dream that had led to the sonnet on Dante's *Inferno* and *La Belle Dame* must still have been fresh in his mind. On a more direct physical level it is hard not to read phrases like 'bright-blanched by an immortal sickness' and 'the dying man forgets his shroud' without thinking of Keats's observations on the wards of the hospital and of his dying brother, or to read the 'palsied chill' which is 'ascending quick to put the cold grasp / Upon those streams that pulse beside the throat' without thinking of his own sore throat which had been worrying Keats for a year since he had returned from the north. There is a persistent recollection of his dilemmas as a medical student being lured into poetry, since one of the most pressing questions addressed in *The Fall of Hyperion* is the running debate whether the poet can be as efficacious in healing as physicians,

> 'Who love their fellows even to the death;
> Who feel the giant agony of the world;
> And more, like slaves to poor humanity,
> Labour for mortal good ...'

> (I, 156–9)

Within the mythical narrative of the gods, the poet-persona undergoes a personal trial and a journey from one state of awareness to another, echoing Keats's epistolary discussions on psychological and experiential change such as those that liken the developing identity as moving through a mansion with three chambers and the paradigm of life as a vale of soul-making where the identity is 'schooled' to become a soul. The poet's first transitional state is relatively pleasant. Caused by drinking from 'a cool vessel of transparent juice, / Sipped by the wandered bee', he is left in a 'cloudy swoon' from which he awakens to a strange landscape littered with ruins of 'The superannuations of sunk realms' and old clothes, jewellery and metal objects. It seems to be an actualisation of 'the chamber of maiden thought', which the poet must leave for 'dark passages' of suffering already encountered by those from 'sunk realms' who have gone before. Approaching an image on an altar swathed in the soft smoke of incense which causes 'Forgetfulness of everything but bliss', he is challenged by the veiled figure to mount the steps in front of him, which becomes his second transition, and the effort feels like passing through death. The process of moving from a state of relative innocence to a more enlightened but distressing awareness of human suffering, is one that is painful and even violent, like an experience of dying and being spared just in time to move on to new life:

> Prodigious seemed the toil; the leaves were yet
> Burning – when suddenly a palsied chill
> Struck from the paved level up my limbs,
> And was ascending quick to put cold grasp
> Upon those streams that pulse beside the throat.

I shrieked; and the sharp anguish of my shriek
Stung my own ears – I strove hard to escape
The numbness, strove to gain the lowest step,
Slow, heavy, deadly was my pace: the cold
Grew stifling, suffocating, at the heart;
And when I clasped my hands I felt them not.
One minute before death, my iced foot touched
The lowest stair; and as it touched, life seemed
To pour in at the toes: I mounted up,
As once fair Angels on a ladder flew
From the green turf to Heaven.

So clinically precise and panic-stricken is this passage that it seems once again to have psychological sources in Keats's remembered experiences in the public wards of Guy's Hospital, or his terrible memory of witnessing death happening to his mother and his brother, or even more disturbingly, visualising in advance his own death. Moneta, 'the veiled shadow' informs the poet, 'Thou hast felt / What 'tis to die and live again before thy fated hour'. In considering the rival claims of different kinds of poets, the prophetess Moneta, whose alternative name Mnemosyne indicates her status as repository of memory in the world, can give her approval to none: 'But those to whom the miseries of the world / Are misery, and will not let them rest' (I, 148–9). Such people usually do not write poetry but are totally dedicated to 'the human face' and they 'think of the earth' rather than merely dreaming. However, Moneta acknowledges that amongst the active benefactors can be found some who write verse and that these are the true poets:

> ... – 'Art thou not of a dreamer tribe?
> The poet and the dreamer are distinct,
> Diverse, sheer opposites, antipodes.
> The one pours out a balm upon the world,
> The other vexes it.'
>
> (I, 198–202)

The poet-narrator, having 'died into life' and undergone a change in perceptions, is privileged to witness like an initiate the misery and suffering of Saturn. The 'benefit' (I, 167) which true poets can deliver to the world, then, is an ability to represent pain and suffering with compassion and humanist concern, a pattern recalling the sonnet 'On Sitting Down to Read *King Lear* Once Again'. The aspiring poet must live in the real world, must 'smell of mortality', and not hold out false hopes or delusions of other worlds.

However, the poet's capacity to change the world for the better is less confidently asserted. To be so determined not to use poetry as a vehicle for distracting from problems faced by people in the real world is to make a statement against 'aristocratic' art and values which seek self-centred pleasure, aesthetic adornment and escape into a 'golden' world with the effect of blinding people to their own condition. The ideas contribute to Keats's internal debate on the rival claims of dreaming and 'doing the world some good' which had been so central to the designs of *Endymion* and *Isabella* in particular. At the same time, the desire to be universally sympathetic to all who suffer, comprehending the feelings even of a failed ruler who is soon to be usurped, adds a qualification to any 'liberal side of the question' which would confine pain to one class of people. Keats is arguing for the 'disinterestedness' of the truly altruistic who 'Labour for mortal good' no matter where suffering occurs, analogous to a poet's Hippocratic Oath. He finds in himself powerful, conflicting feelings about the social utility of poetry, summed up in the respective conditions of the fallen Titans and Apollo: nostalgia and hope, stasis and process, despair and energy, evolution and revolution. As so often, instead of presenting these conflicts as stark oppositions, he prefers to see them together as part of a larger, paradoxical truth which is difficult to paraphrase in any simple way. His own struggling self-doubt about his ability to write such magnanimous poetry is clear.

However inconclusive it may be as a poem, *The Fall of Hyperion* has a consistent centre of attention which focuses on a debate turning on whether poetry can benefit the world. The work gives the impression of a mind struggling with ideas towards a clarity which never quite reveals itself, and admittedly it is confusing if judged as a formal argument or as a narrative originating in the war amongst the classical Titans. Given that Keats made so many attempts to restart the poem, and judging from his later unhappiness that Taylor decided to include the earlier 'Fragment' in the 1820 volume, it is certain that as author he still intended to wrestle the poem into unity and completion. We should bear in mind that both versions stand as fragments each of which is merely a fraction of an unwritten epic probably the length of *Endymion*, and remember that Keats did not intend to publish either in this state. In the face of its sometimes opaque reasoning and changes of direction, we can see the poet's own indecisions and problems in *The Fall*. It is like judging a draft of Dante's *Divine Comedy* on its first 500 lines, and the comparison is apt since Keats did have this poem in his mind as a model, having by this time consciously chosen to reject Milton's more straightforward narrative method as his model and to embrace Dante's method leading the poet and the reader into revealed mysteries. He had also come to see the language of *Paradise Lost* as inimitably eccentric and 'though so fine in itself [it] is a curruption [sic] of our Language – it should be kept as it is unique – a curiosity, a beautiful and grand Curiosity. The most remarkable Production of the world – A northern dialect accommodating itself to greek and latin inversions and intonations' (*JKL*, 2, 212). He was now concentrating on 'the purest english ... entirely uncorrupted of

Chaucer's gallicisms and still the old words are used' which he associated with Chatterton.

Since the fragment is all we have of *The Fall of Hyperion* we can at least respect the profundity of its humanist quest, and admire the splendour and intensity of its poetry which is amongst the most powerful Keats ever wrote. A more telling comparison might be with Michelangelo's extraordinary late, unfinished *Pietà* statues where figures emerge in rough relief from the lumps of unchiselled stone, the more vital and expressive for their not being fully realised, and where the sheer struggle with the medium itself is an overt and pressing concern of the artist. In fact, the description of the recumbent Saturn being comforted by Thea is perhaps the closest poetry can get to sculpture (from an author who had turned a Grecian urn into words) and it is presented as having the monumental qualities of 'fair statuary'. Observing from a spot 'Deep in the shady sadness of a vale, / Far sunken from the healthy breath of morn', the poet sees 'what first I thought an image huge, / Like to the image pedestalled so high / In Saturn's temple'. The scene is one of complete, statuesque stillness – 'where the dead leaf fell there did it rest' – as Thea comforts Saturn:

> Long, long those two were postured motionless,
> Like sculpture builded-up upon the grave
> Of their own power.

If one of the reasons – perhaps *the* reason – that Keats was to be so offended by his editors including the earlier *Fragment* of *Hyperion* in *Poems* (1820) was that he saw it as an admission he would write no more, then there are a set of deeper and more intrinsic reasons behind his sensitivity. He had begun and abandoned the poem several times, and even after discarding *The Fall* he intended to return to the project. He seems clearly to have had a 'career' pattern in mind, of alternating collections of short poems with a volume containing a single long poem, an epic. *Hyperion* was clearly intended to be next after his 1820 collection. He had forecast this intention in his preface to *Endymion*: 'I hope I have not in too late a day touched the beautiful mythology of Greece, and dulled its brightness; for I wish to try once more, before I bid it farewel.' Until he felt he had completed to his own satisfaction a long poem based on the Hyperion myth, he did not wish any version to be placed before the public, particularly since his use of the myth had changed radically even between the two fragmentary versions. *The Fall* strives to represent the mind in creation, the creative process itself, and as Helen Vendler suggests, it is a kind of tragic perspective on the more optimistic view of creativity adopted in 'Ode to Psyche'.[4] It is also a poem that we sense is 'reaching towards' something which Keats cannot yet say clearly enough for his own resolution. The dimly glimpsed destination of the thought is a new kind of poetry which incorporates all experience, and the fact that he describes it through the mouth of Apollo the poet, rather than the poetic persona, acknowledges it still lies in the future for the struggling writer:

> Knowledge enormous makes a God of me.
> Names, deeds, gray legends, dire events, rebellions,
> Majesties, sovran voices, agonies,
> Creations and destroyings, all at once
> Pour into the wide hollows of my brain,
> And deify me, as if some blithe wine
> Or bright elixir peerless I had drunk,
> And so become immortal.

(III, 11.13–20)

Such awesome 'disinterestedness' in Hazlitt's sense of felt social conscience had been associated by Keats with only three people in the whole of human history: Socrates, Jesus and Shakespeare (*JKL*, 2, 80, 101). The vision incorporates politics ('dire events, rebellions, Majesties'), and also the subjects usually termed religious, 'Creations and destroying'. It is the Yeatsian desire to 'cast a cold eye on life, on death' and to do so 'all at once', a simultaneous stance of impartial indifference to individual circumstances and yet empathetic compassion for all human suffering, the capacity to keep an unflinching eye even on the process of dying while comprehending the act of living as 'soul-making'. To achieve such an omniscient view of human experience and have the insight ultimately to 'heal' is the mark of one whose worldly works will be 'immortal' and in the face of such an awesome aspiration Keats is aware of his own inexperience and limitations. Once again Keats was to abandon temporarily the Hyperion project, this time with a feeling of having just about reached the end of his tether in his sense of needing to earn money 'by temporary writing in periodical works': 'I will write, on the liberal side of the question, for whoever will pay me...' (*JKL*, 2, 178).

Despite his frustration by now, Winchester gave to Keats, and to readers who are the beneficiaries of his poetry, one more precious gift. It came after the exhausting week spent in London prising some of the inheritance for George and himself from a pompously buoyant guardian (who now suggested without apparent facetiousness that Keats could make money by becoming a hatter, another of Abbey's own sidelines). He visited his sister and Mrs Wylie, George's mother-in-law, refused to visit Fanny Brawne in Hampstead which he thinks would be like 'venturing into a fire', instead trying to 'wean' himself from her, and attended a performance at Covent Garden. On Wednesday, 15 September he returned to Winchester by coach, sitting beside a cheerfully loquacious, 'good looking coachman'.

They ate their lunch together and talked. The subtleties of the season were on his mind after the enforced travel, and he wrote about the weather on Tuesday, 21 September to Reynolds who was staying with Woodhouse at Bath:

> How beautiful the season is now – How fine the air. A temperate sharpness about it. Really, without joking, chaste weather – Dian skies – I never lik'd stubble fields so much as now – Aye better than the chilly green of the spring. Somehow a stubble plain looks warm – in the same way that some pictures look warm – this struck me so much in my Sunday's walk that I composed upon it. I hope you are better employed than in gaping after the weather ... (*JKL*, 2, 167)

Writing on the same day to Woodhouse, he surmises that Bath is getting cool enough in the evenings for lighting fires:

> I should like a bit of fire to night – one likes a bit of fire – How glorious the Blacksmiths' shops look now – I stood to night before one till I was verry near listing for one. Yes I should like a bit of fire – at a distance about 4 feet 'not quite hob nob' – as wordsworth says ... (*JKL*, 2, 169)

The vignette brings us close to the uncanny intimacy of the moment so frequently met in Keats's letters as it is in Shakespeare's plays. In John Jones's suggestive words, the image 'bespeaks the deep sanity and peace of his imagination'.[5] The weather on Sunday, 19 September was very settled, according to the *Meteorological Journal*. It came in a fortnight of consistently 'Fine' weather and was on the day in London a minimum of 57 degrees and maximum 60, to rise on the Monday to an unusually clement 70 degrees, amongst the three warmest days in September that year. Keats then transcribes in his letter to Woodhouse three verses he had 'composed' on his walk on the Sunday. Here they are, reproduced exactly as he wrote them in this letter, inspired misprints and all, with the more familiar readings shown alongside:

> Season of Mists and mellow fruitfulness,
>   Close bosom friend of the maturing sun;
> Conspiring with him how to load and bless
>   The vines with fruit that round the thatch eves run;
> To bend with apples the moss'd cottage trees,
>   And fill all fruit with ripeness to the core;
>   To swell the gourd, and plump the hazle-shells
>   With a white* kernel; to set budding more,   sweet*
> And still more later flowers for the bees

Untill they think wam* days will never cease   warm*
For summer has o'er brimm'd their clammy Cells.

Who hath not seen thee oft, amid thy stores?
   Sometimes, whoever seeks abroad may find
Thee sitting careless on a granary floor,
    Thy hair soft-lifted by the winmowing* wind;   winnowing*
Or on a half-reap'd furrow sound asleep,
   Das'd* with the fume of poppies, while thy hook Drows'd*
    Spares the next swath and all its twined flowers;
And sometimes like a gleaner thou dost keep
   Stready* thy laden head across a brook;   Steady*
   Or by a Cyder press, with patient look,
Thou watchest the last oozings hours by hours –

Where are the songs of spring? Aye, Where are they?
   Think not of them, thou hast thy music too,
While barred clouds bloom the soft-dying day,
   And touch the stubble plains with rosy hue:
Then in a wailful quire* the small gnats mourn   choir*
   Among the river sallows, borne aloft
    Or sinking as the light wind lives and dies;
And full grown Lambs loud bleat from hilly bourne:
   Hedge crickets sing, and now with treble soft
   The Red breast whistles from a garden <g> Croft;
    And gather'd* Swallows twitter in the Skies –   gathering*

Although, as in the case of his other Odes, Keats gives no evidence of estimating 'To Autumn' especially highly as a poem, it has become one of the most familiar and best-loved poems in the English language, and by any measure it is extraordinarily accomplished. It is the poem in which he most nearly succeeds in achieving for himself the advice he gave to Shelley, to 'be more of an artist, and "load every rift" of [your] subject with ore' (*JKL*, 2, 323), and it is also the work about which he could most aptly say (as he had said of lines in the first *Hyperion*), 'for things which [I] do half at Random are afterwards confirmed by my judgment in a dozen features of Propriety –'. Among the 'features of Propriety' in this case are simultaneous imprintings of several dovetailing, temporal and intellectual patterns, which complement his other Odes in being reflections on multiple dimensions of time, space and art. At least four time schemes are unobtrusively superimposed. The first follows the hours of a single day, from the mists of morning 'maturing' into midday somnolence towards 'the last oozings hours by hours' from the cider-press, to evening when 'barred clouds bloom the soft-dying day', the time when gnats are at their most pestiferous in English warm weather. Secondly, the poem traces the characteristic sights, natural processes, sounds, and agricultural tasks belonging to the season of autumn in England: early growth of fruit and flowers; mid-season harvesting, winnowing and generally extracting; and post-harvest stubbled fields and 'full grown' lambs. The third time scheme places autumn in the organic cycle of the year as a whole in rural communities. Songs of spring are decentred ('Think not of them, thou hast thy music too') and autumn is placed as the central, transitional season from high summer in all its plenitude on one side and winter on the other when swallows have migrated to find warm weather elsewhere. Once again Keats's retentive memory may be harking back to his days reading the *Hospital Pupil's Guide* by 'Aesculapius':

> Though spring is the season of hope and novelty, to a naturalist more especially, yet the wise provisions and abundant resources of Nature, in the close of the year, will yield an observing mind no less pleasure, than the rich variety of her autumnal tints affords to the admirers of her external charms. (p. xviii)

The fourth time scheme which may not be obtrusive but has always been felt by most readers relates to the 'seasons' of a human life, from youth to maturity, and to at least an awareness of impending finality as the day is *soft-dying*, gnats *mourn* in 'wailful quires', 'the light wind lives *and dies*' and lambs are now '*full-grown*' and on the verge of being no longer lambs (a precise, farming observation by Keats as well as another moment of refraining from mentioning destined endings). The most impressive facet is the tact in which the final closure is not literalised but delicately implied, supporting a reading based on the special properties of art which, like the gathering swallows, can imaginatively guide the consciousness away from a frontal consciousness of death and back to the 'bosom' of the sunshine. The poem is reticent of death, shying away from gazing on it open-eyed, though its poised acceptance of transience and change suggests a broader, mortal acceptance that everything is right in its own time. For the migrating swallows who will return in spring, winter is evaded altogether, while yet remaining part of their natural cycle's routines: 'Let the fish philosophise the ice away from the Rivers in winter time and they shall be at continual play in the tepid delight of summer ...'

An even more subtly intangible pattern can be claimed, since the first stanza is purely a reflection of the natural world and denies human agency altogether as though the growth of the season operates organically from within, irrespective of human activities; the second details human activity and occupations, while the third creates the sense of a suspended dimension of art, both pictorial and musical as well as poetic, located in a specific time and place but also freed from these constraints as adroitly as 'Ode on a Grecian Urn' had achieved. 'Quires' can be sheets in a book, or poems, as well as a synonym for 'choirs', while 'gather'd' can apply not just to swallows and stooks but to groups of pages in a book, just as in Shakespeare's Sonnet 12 the 'summer's green, all girded up in sheaves' can refer not simply to bundles of wheat but also to bundles of papers and publications. Furthermore, through the pattern of thought in the poem we glimpse Keats's own repeated attempts – always in threesomes – to trace the 'allegory' of life as part of a humanistic, 'soul-making' sequence of life, visualised as moving through different chambers in a mansion towards enlightened individuality.[6] There are still more 'features of propriety' at the verbal level. Even the syntax changes subtly, from the continuous present in the first stanza, suggesting ongoing process alongside infinitives like 'to bend', 'to fill', as though the very origin of growth as a continuing process without past or future is pinpointed – Reuben Brower has found in the imagery of the first stanza 'an over-meaning, a tactile awareness of fruitioning'[7] – to the interrogatives of the second stanza drawing in the reader alongside a personified figure of autumn, and ending with present tenses, continuous and completed, as the whole process runs towards its conclusion. Practising poets and alert critics have always admired the apparent effortlessness and almost unanalysable 'word-music' in the language of 'To Autumn', as assonances and internal rhymes and half-rhymes knit complex patterns of sound through the language. Herbert Read points out that even in the early *Endymion* Keats's poetic language was 'experimental', pointing out that Bailey had later informed Lord Houghton 'that one of Keats's favourite topics of conversation was the principle of melody in verse, which he believed to consist in the adroit management of open and close vowels. He had a theory that vowels could be as skilfully combined and interchanged as differing notes of music...',[8] a 'theory' triumphantly realised in 'To Autumn'. Even the manuscript's hastily written misprints such as 'wam' and 'das'd' instead of 'warm' and 'daz'd', have a strange expressiveness and onomatopoeia, while 'winmowing' and 'stready' both uncannily create portmanteau coinages – winnow and mow, steady and ready – as though an even deeper part of Keats's verbal imagination is working to pack every word with maximum and multiple meanings. The poem is evidence also of his decisive shift away from 'Miltonic inversions' based on Latinate grammar and vocabulary when he abandoned *Hyperion* for the second time. Just as Keats considered Chatterton 'the purest writer in the English Language ... 'tis genuine English Idiom in English words ... English ought to be kept up' (*JKL*, 2, 167), so 'To Autumn' is Keats's own sustained homage to his mother tongue.

There is also a multiplicity of cultural sources and allusions half- or fully visible. Although 'To Autumn' seems personal, serenely self-assured, and stemming from direct observation of landscape (having no 'I' it is guided by an omniscient 'eye'), yet it is also a distillation of an almost astonishing number of identifiable literary sources, as if it is just as much a reflection on poetry as on nature. Robert Gittings picks up Keats's comment in his letter, 'I somehow always associate Chatterton with autumn', and notes strong verbal links with that poet's *Aella*.[9] Helen Vendler in *The Odes of John Keats* finds a density of sources remarkable for such a short poem, from Spenser's 'Mutability Cantos' in *The Faerie Queene*, Shakespeare's sonnets 'That time of year thou mayst in me behold' (73) and 'How like a winter hath my absence been' (97) and *The Tempest*, Milton's 'Il Penseroso' and his descriptions of Adam and Eve in Eden in *Paradise Lost*, Wordsworth's 'Ode on Intimations of Immortality', and a host of Keats's own earlier poems such as *Endymion* and *La Belle Dame*, as well as Coleridge's beautiful address to his sleeping baby at the end of 'Frost at Midnight' (published in 1798):

> Therefore all seasons shall be sweet to thee,
> Whether the summer clothe the general earth
> With greenness, or the redbreast sit and sing.
> Betwixt the tufts of snow on the bare branch
> Of mossy apple-tree, while the night thatch
> Smokes in the sun-thaw; whether the eave-drops fall
> Heard only in the trances of the blast,
> Or if the secret ministry of frost
> Shall hang them up in silent icicles,
> Quietly shining to the quiet Moon.

There are many more allusions from texts found or waiting to be found, such as Thomson's *Seasons*, Goldsmith's *The Deserted Village*, and at least for one verbal association, Collins's 'Ode to Evening': 'While *sallow* Autumn fills thy lap with leaves', which, incidentally, reminds us of one conventional sight of autumn which Keats has surprisingly *not* alluded to, the falling of dead leaves, as if even this is too insistently suggestive of closure for comfort. As well as the many verbal allusions, pictorial sources such as several of Poussin's paintings are also a part of the poem's memory, as Ian Jack has reminded us. In one of those ironies of coincidence, England's best-known painter of fleeting weather, John Constable, rented a house in Hampstead in that very year,[10] and he was later, in 1827, to live more permanently in Well Walk, Hampstead. Spaciousness is one of the poem's main impressions, and despite the concentration of such a range of overlapping echoes and sources, it is at no point crowded. Invoking one of Keats's mantra-like words, 'Intensity', the Ode embodies the paradox of being simultaneously intense, ripe and relaxed, so that the 'real' becomes 'ideal' while not losing the tactile impressionism of 'enacting' nature, so admired by F. R. Leavis.[11] Finally (though it is not even yet to exhaust the poem), critics have also seen 'To Autumn' as a political statement on the changing rural conditions in England at the time, Keats's equivalent of John Clare's moving evocations of a fast-diminishing agricultural harvest scene.[12] After all, the poem was written just a few days after Keats had returned from witnessing the political rally in London, and a sense of losing the agricultural basis of England through the effects of the Corn Laws, chronic grain shortages throughout Keats's life, collectivisation of common lands, and rural unemployment would have been all too evident around him. The subtext partly explains the gathering sense of nostalgia and of impending loss that pervades 'To Autumn'.

By Friday, 1 October Keats had resolved to leave Winchester and he asked Dilke to find him a cheap, quiet bed sitting-room in London. It was to be back to central London, this time at 25 College Street overlooking Westminster Abbey gardens. Brown, by now back in Winchester and on his way back to Wentworth Place, returned with Keats on the following Friday to Wentworth Place where Keats and Brown resumed living in late October. Under this arrangement Keats would not need to pay 'petty attentions to a diminutive housekeeping', and though he owed rent, at least Brown was an indulgent landlord. Joseph Severn saw him there and observed that Keats was 'well neither in mind nor in body', lacking 'the happy confidence and resolute bearing' which had previously marked his constitution. However, not all was bad news. He slotted back into his routine of visiting friends, prised a little money from Abbey while humouring his guardian's renewed suggestion of becoming a tea-merchant in his own company (an offer which Abbey did not follow up, instead suggesting bookselling as yet another suitable vocation). He began *King Stephen* and looked forward to a volume of new poetry, informing Taylor that he had decided 'not to publish any thing I have now ready written' but rather to write poems 'at home amongst Men and women' to 'nerve' him 'up to the writing of a few fine Plays' (*JKL*, 2, 238). He had changed his mind by 20 December and decided instead to accept Taylor's contractual option to publish his shorter poems in the spring. There was even a flutter of hope over *Otho the Great* which was accepted by Drury Lane, spurring Keats and Brown into thinking of revising the play and trying Covent Garden again with the hope of getting Macready to play the role, though none of these hopes actually eventuated. And it seems that on Christmas Day, the anniversary of his first 'understanding' with Fanny Brawne, their engagement was formalised though still not publicly acknowledged. 1819, Keats's year of extraordinary creativity despite its moments of despair and his continuing ill-health, ended on a note of creative fulfilment and high hopes.

12
Poems (1820)

In the last months of 1819 and January 1820 Keats was still visiting friends, dining out, and attending the theatre and Hazlitt's lectures. The arrival from America on 9 January of his brother George, set to tackle Abbey on the issue of the Keats inheritance now that he was financially desperate, stimulated the brothers into a round of visits to mutual friends. George did manage to extract from Abbey the legacy owed him, and also, as the brothers had agreed, most of the money remaining to John, but most of it was by then owed in debts. In turn, John passed over some of his own money to George to help him settle in America, and although apparently intended as repaying loans, this was leaving himself in an even more serious financial position than before. Charles Brown out of loyalty to John was to retain some residual sense of grievance against George, based on a misunderstanding which Fanny Brawne was later to describe to their sister. She was no friend of George since he disliked her, but she exonerates him from any fault except extravagance and careless selfishness (*FB*, 25). Brown's anger may have been exacerbated by the fact that George did in fact later become a very wealthy man through his investments in Louisville, and in fact he was perhaps 'Lousiville's first millionaire'.[1] This was all to lie in the future. George returned to America from Liverpool on 28 January. He would never see his brother again.

Brown was extremely worried about his companion who was 'dreadfully unhappy': 'He was too thoughtful, or too unquiet; and he began to be reckless of health', taking 'a few drops of laudanum to keep up his spirits' against Brown's advice (*KC*, 2, 72–3). A crisis came which Brown later recalled in his *Life of Keats*:

Not long after this, one night – (I have no record of the date, but it was either at the end of December or the beginning of January,) – one night, at eleven o'clock, he came into the house in a state that looked like <fearful> fierce intoxication. Such a state in him, I knew, was impossible; it therefore was the more fearful. I asked hurriedly, 'What is the matter, – you are fevered?' 'Yes, yes,' he answered, 'I was on the outside of the stage this bitter day till I was severely chilled, – but now I don't feel it. Fevered! – of course, a little.' He mildly and instantly yielded, a property in his nature towards any friend, to my request that he should go to bed. I followed with the best immediate remedy in my power. I entered his chamber as he leapt into bed. On entering the cold sheets, before his head was on the pillow, he slightly coughed, and I heard him say, – 'That is blood from my mouth.' I went towards him; he was examining a single drop of blood upon the sheet. 'Bring me the candle, Brown; and let me see this blood.' After regarding it steadfastly, he looked up in my face, with a calmness of countenance that I can never forget, <and> and said, – 'I know the colour of that blood; – it is arterial blood; – I cannot be deceived in that colour; – that drop of blood is my death-warrant; – I must die.' I ran for a surgeon; my friend was bled; and, at five in the morning, I left him after he had been, some time, in a quiet sleep. (*KC*, 2, 73–4)

We do in fact know the date, a freezing 3 February, 1820, when the minimum temperature was 35 degrees, the maximum just 36, which is 2 degrees Celsius. Keats had returned late to Hampstead from London, riding 'on the outside of the stage[-coach]' for thrift. Medical experts today tell me that 'arterial blood' is perceptibly darker than capillary and venous blood, but that in erosive tuberculosis an eruption into an artery would signal the very final stages and death would follow within days.[2] Since Keats was to last another year, this does not seem to have been the case and he may have been voicing his worst fear rather than an accurate observation. However, the stark facts were emerging for the former medical student who had witnessed the terminal stages of tuberculosis in three relatives, and the awful message was clear from other symptoms he had observed in his mother and brother. He was about a week later to describe the experience to Fanny Brawne as, 'so violent a rush of blood came to my Lungs that I felt I nearly suffocated' (*JKL*, 2, 254). His surgeon and physician (Mr Rodd and Dr Bree) concluded after this episode that his lungs were 'unimpaired' and that the problems lay in the stomach and the mind, but from this time onwards he knew that the persistent 'sore throat' had been a symptom of worse to come. On this occasion, as on later ones, Keats with his attachment to traditional medicine must have approved the treatment offered – phlebotomy or bloodletting. Despite being discredited by some thinkers since the seventeenth century, this was standard practice for fever, on the theory that a surplus of blood needed to be siphoned from the body. It is not entirely surprising that this did allay fever since it made the patient faint, but its regular use for sufferers from phthisis or lung diseases must have been disastrous.

February 1820 was a gruesome month for a man so sociable by temperament and so fond of travelling. Living with Brown at Wentworth Place in Hampstead, the bitter-sweet fact was that he was next door to Fanny Brawne to whom he had become formally engaged in December 1819 – sweet in proximity but bitter in his relative isolation from her. He had to write since he could see her for little more than brief visits or glimpse her in the garden, and he was left to imagine jealously her visits to others. On the day following his haemorrhage, he sent a brief message which sums up his feelings as he waits to hear her latch-key turn:

> Dearest Fanny, I shall send this the moment you return. They say I must remain confined to this room for some time. The consciousness that you love me will make a pleasant prison of the house next to yours. You must come and see me frequently: this evening, without fail – when you must not mind about my speaking in a low tone for I am ordered to do so though I *can* speak out.
>
> Yours ever
> Sweetest love. –
> J Keats (JKL, 2, 250)

The letters he writes almost daily to her in this month reveal a mind certainly in a 'prison' which was as much emotional as physical, and although his mind latches onto passages about female infidelity from *Troilus and Cressida* and *Othello*, the most apt reference in Shakespeare that comes to mind is his Sonnet 57:

> Being your slave, what should I do but tend
> Upon the hours and times of your desire?
> I have no precious time at all to spend,
> Nor services to do, till you require.
> Nor dare I chide the world-without-end hour
> Whilst I, my sovereign, watch the clock for you,
> Nor think the bitterness of absence sour
> When you have bid your servant once adieu;
> Nor dare I question with my jealous thought
> Where you may be, or your affairs suppose,
> But, like a sad slave, stay and think of nought
> Save, where you are how happy you make those.
> So true a fool is love that in your will,
> Though you do any thing, he thinks no ill.

All the helplessness, barely disguised jealousy and 'vassalage' Keats expresses in his letters at this time are encapsulated in Shakespeare's lines. The situation must have been just as stressful for Fanny, who at 20 was still young and was being invited to social events, her engagement to Keats kept secret from virtually everybody at Keats's choice. He is by turns elated and depressed, nagging, suspicious (even of her feelings for Brown), accusatory, pleading, apologetic for 'emprisoning' her yet feeling imprisoned himself in her love, and offering to release her from the engagement, philosophical, self-pitying, and sometimes resigned:

> I have been confined three weeks and am not yet well – this proves that there is something wrong about me which my constitution will either conquer or give way to – Let us hope for the best. Do you hear the Th[r]ush singing over the field? I think it is a sign of mild weather – so much the better for me. Like all Sinners now I am ill I philosophise aye out of my attachment to every thing, Trees, flowers, Thrushes Sp[r]ing, Summer, Claret &c &c aye [e]very thing but you — — my Sister would be glad of my company a little longer. That Thrush is a fine fellow I hope he was fortunate in his choice this year – Do not send any more of my Books home. I have a great pleasure in the thought of you looking on them.
>
> Ever yours
my sweet Fanny
J – K— (JKL, 2, 265)

Though he did give up meat for a while in his illness, at least Keats did not have to forgo drinking his beloved claret. A few months later on 'one hot July day, during his last summer in England, Horace Smith sent his carriage to pick up the invalid Keats ... One of the other guests, Thomas Hill, had brought from his cellars at Sydenham six bottles of "some undeniable Châteaux Margaux", which they spent the evening drinking in the open air.'[3] Châteaux Margaux is today a fine and expensive vintage, and even then would have been beyond Keats's own budget. His sense of humour had not deserted him in his letters to Fanny, but it could take a lugubrious turn: 'I fear I am too prudent for a dying kind of Lover. Yet, there is a great difference between going off in warm blood like Romeo and making one's exit like a frog in a frost ... Illness is a long lane, but I see you at the end of it, and shall mend my pace as well as possible' (*JKL*, 2, 281, 282). The perky thrush made another appearance in March: 'There's the Thrush again – I can't afford it – he'll run me up a pretty Bill for Music – besides he ought to know I deal at Clementi's' (*JKL*, 2, 278). Clementi's published sheet music and sold instruments from their shop in Cheapside, and the reference may reflect nostalgic recollections for Keats of more carefree days sharing music first with the Cowden Clarkes and later in Hunt's *soirées* with Novello. There is also a slightly enigmatic comment to Fanny: '... not intending that there shall be any interruption to our correspondence (which at some future time I propose offering to Murray) I write something!' (*JKL*, 2, 282). Murray was a publisher. Is Keats joking here, or are his letters, even these, written with such painfully conflicting feelings, in some way also written with a more studied eye to posterity? We cannot tell, but the mere possibility is intriguing.

From what we can deduce from his own rejoinders, Fanny was patient, tolerant of his erratic moods, tactful, and occasionally resistant and understandably fed up. Sometime in February during the anxious period in 1820, Fanny Brawne gave Keats a ring apparently inscribed with both their names, which he promised to treat 'like a sacred Chalice once consecrated and ever consecrate. I shall kiss your name and mine where your Lips have been ...' (*JKL*, 2, 270). He had already given her a ring too. In his misery, however, Keats continued to challenge her to relinquish him for her own sake, while making it clear this would destroy him emotionally. For all the disapprobation, squeamishness and sensationalising – censorious of either Keats or Fanny or both – fuelling critical attitudes to these distressing letters from Victorian times onwards, it has not always been conceded that Keats was still a very young man who was undergoing the greatest emotional division of his life at the very time he was clearly facing his own mortality. He was torn between his instincts of sexual desire and the equally strong motivation to protect Fanny and even unselfishly offering to release her from obligations of their engagement. For him she embodied a principle of beauty and a dream of his own future. Perhaps in flesh and blood she was not so beautiful to others as she was to him. She may have been inferior in beauty to Isabella Jones and the voluptuously 'eastern' Jane Cox, but she must have had the most precious property that can light up any face, youth. For Keats, so insistent in his poems on the impermanence of beauty, the principle which that fragile gift represents would, he knew, outlast the reality and also his own life. The truly moving quality in his premature death lies in the fact that, unlike many others who die young (like his admired Chatterton), he died in love.

In Keats's letters, desire overcomes the need to protect Fanny Brawne's feelings. By contrast, he was trying to shelter his sister Fanny from knowledge of the severity of his illness, constantly giving her encouraging news: '... I was resolved not to write till I should be on the mending hand: thank God, I am now so. From imprudently leaving off my great coat in the thaw I caught cold which flew to my Lungs. Every remedy that has been applied has taken the desired effect, and I have nothing now to do but stay within doors for some time' (*JKL*, 2, 251). He transfers his care from himself to her: 'You must be careful always to wear warm clothing not only in frost but in a Thaw ... Whenever you have an inflammatory fever never mind about eating. The day on which I was getting ill I felt this fever to a great height, and therefore almost entirely abstained from food the whole day. I have no doubt experienc'd a benefit from so doing ...' Otherwise he promises 'no news to tell you' except that 'the grass looks very dingy, the Celery is all gone, and there is nothing to enliven one but a few Cabbage stalks that seem fix'd on the superannuated List', and a few political snippets from 'the Papers'. His description of his situation and observations is so lively that full quotation might be justified, though again Keats is clearly protecting his sister with his tone, as with amusement he watches the world go by his window:

> I have a very pleasant room for a sick person. A Sopha bed is made up for me in the front Parlour which looks on to the grass plot as you remember Mrs Dilkes does. How much more comfortable than a dull room up stairs, where one gets tired of the pattern of the bed curtains. Besides I see all that passes – for instanc[e] now, this morning, if I had been in my own room I should not have seen the coals brought in. On sunday between the hours of twelve and one I descried a Pot boy. I conjectured it might be the one o'Clock beer – Old women with bobbins and red cloaks and unpresuming bonnets I see creeping about the heath. Gipseys after hare skins and silver spoons. Then goes by a fellow with a wooden clock<s> under his arm that strikes a hundred and more. Then comes the old french emigrant (who has been very well to do in france) whith his hands joined behind on his hips, and his face full of political schemes. Then passes Mr David Lewis a very goodnatured, goodlooking old gentleman whas been very kind to Tom and George and me. As for those fellows the Brickmakers they are always passing to and fro. I mus'n't forget the two old maiden Ladies in well walk who have a Lap dog between them, that they are very anxious about. It is a corpulent Little Beast whom it is necessary to coax along with an ivory-tipp'd cane. Carlo our Neighbour Mrs Brawne's dog and it meet sometimes. Lappy thinks Carlo a devil of a fellow and so do his Mistresses. Well they may – he would sweep 'em all down at a run; all for the Joke of it. (*JKL*, 2, 253–4)

The elderly Carlo, the Brawnes' dog, was later (after Keats's death) to bite Fanny on the hand quite badly, and within a day or two died of food poisoning, apparently unlamented in the household.[4] Brown, sharing the same house, was anxiously aware of the full situation, describing his own state to Taylor as 'wretchedly depressed' (*JKL*, 2, 274). Another friend to whom Keats was frank about his condition was Rice, who had lived with illness for many years himself, to whom Keats wrote:

> I may say that for 6 Months before I was taken ill I had not passed a tranquil day – Either that gloom overspred me or I was suffering under some passionate feeling, or if I turn'd to versify that acerbated the poison of either sensation. The Beauties of Nature had lost their power over me. How astonishingly ... does the chance of leaving the world impress a sense of its natural beauties on us. Like poor Falstaff, though I do not babble, I think of green fields ... I have seen foreign flowers in hothouses of the most beautiful nature, but I do not care a straw for them. The simple flowers of our sp[r]ing are what I want to see again. (*JKL*, 2, 260)

Keats did see the simple flowers of spring once more but his health continued to ebb and flow. During March and April he suffered from violent heart palpitations and declared to his sister Fanny, 'my health is tolerably well I am too nervous to enter into any discussion in which my heart is concerned' (*JKL*, 2, 285), but he was occupying himself with trying to find a home for her puppy. In his 'babylonish captivity' (*JKL*, 2, 286) while 'melting' in front of the fire, he longed to walk.

Brown decided to return to Scotland, partly in order to earn money by renting out his half of Wentworth Place as he did each summer, and unexpectedly the doctors approved Keats accompanying him, 'for change of exercise and air'. This was not to be and Brown went alone, but at least Keats could travel to London on 3 May, and he went to Gravesend to see Brown off in the 'scotch smack' on 7 May. Keats had to vacate while Brown was away and he moved temporarily to Kentish Town in order to be close to Leigh Hunt. His letters to Fanny Brawne became more substantial but also more disjointed and emotionally extreme. Now feeling distant from Wentworth Place in Hampstead he displays near paranoia, believing his friends (who at his choice were unaware of the romance) were belittling Fanny and laughing at her and gossiping: 'Your name never passes my Lips – do not let mine pass yours – Those People do not like me ...' (*JKL*, 2, 293). On 22 June he had a severe haemorrhage and continued to spit blood for several days, which made it necessary to move into Hunt's house in Mortimer Terrace in the Vale of Health, Hampstead in order to be cared for. He was in a bad way, and to some the inevitable end was coming into sight. To the eye of Maria Gisborne who visited in mid-July, he was 'under sentence of death from Dr Lamb. He never spoke and looks emaciated.'

Despite the advice of his friends and doctors to avoid poetry as too upsetting for his health, there were some flutters of literary activity during this period, which led at least to the publication of his final volume of poems. From time to time Keats took up again the Hyperion theme, and while still tinkering with this, towards the end of 1819, he had begun a work now known as *The Cap and Bells: Or, The Jealousies. A Faery Tale – Unfinished*. This marked a completely different direction into humorous fantasy and contemporary satire against, amongst many other things, the Prince Regent and government of the day as well as the Lake District poets. Written in Spenserian stanzas and reflecting a lightly allegorical 'faerie' apparatus, the tone suggests it was probably conceived as emulating Byron's new satiric stance. The first two stanzas of *Don Juan* had been published in 1819 and Keats was ambivalent and jealous of Byron, but that poem offered him a new model for contemporary, satirical poetry, incorporating in 'catch-all' fashion, as in *The Cap and Bells*, a range of targets, literary and political alike. Brown recounts that it was written without a plan, to be published under a pseudonym, Lucy Vaughan Lloyd, for the unashamed purpose of gaining popular success, adding a minor irony to Keats's earlier expressions of contempt for female readership. Brown reports that *The Jealousies*, as Keats wished it to be called, was written 'with the greatest facility', leaving its contradictions and false starts to be tidied up in a later revision. However, he was forced to give it up after his haemorrhage in February 1820, and its intention remains something of a puzzle. My own suggestion is that it may have something to do with the literary influence of Shelley's close friend and a loose member of the Leigh Hunt set whom Keats had met, Thomas Love Peacock, whose novel *Headlong Hall*, a satire on literary fashions among the Romantic poets in the Lake District as well as Shelley and gothic writers, was published in 1815/16, while *Nightmare Abbey* was published in 1818 and mocked the cult of melancholy made famous in Goethe's *The Sorrows of Werther*. Soon after the appearance of the first two cantos of *Childe Harold* Peacock had satirised Byron's early poetry in *Sir Hornbook, or Childe Launcelot's Expedition* (1813). His importance as a provocative catalyst for poets of the time has been rather neglected. Keats would have doubly appreciated the affectionate mockery of pretensions of poets he had himself felt excluded from on class grounds if he knew Peacock's works, as seems likely from his comic words in March 1818: '...West has damned – wholesale – Peacock has damned sattire...' (*JKL*, 1, 252). Peacock was able to trade on his friendships to puncture the egos of Shelley, Byron, Coleridge and their like, in ways that Keats must have been sorely tempted to do himself.

Commentators have emphasised as amongst the felicities of *The Jealousies* the wry social observation of central London:

> It was the time when wholesale houses close
> Their shutters with a moody sense of wealth,
> But retail dealers, diligent, let loose
> The gas (objected to on score of health),
> Conveyed in little soldered pipes by stealth,
> And make it flare in many a brilliant form
> That all the powers of darkness it repell'th,
> Which to the oil-trade doth great scathe and harm,
> And supersedeth quite the use of the glow-worm.

> (XXIV)

The context was that until the later eighteenth century oil lamps had been used for lighting but from the early 1790s onwards gas derived from coal was increasingly used in London streets and homes, much to the scepticism of locals who feared the dangers to health. In 1812 the Gas Light and Coke Company was given a charter, signalling its respectability which lasted up until the early twentieth century. Writing on such topical subjects may also have revived in Keats childhood memories and slang from the stables in the Swan and Hoop, when ostlers like his father were berated by well-to-do coach travellers (XXV–XXIX).

Far more psychologically revealing of Keats's emotional state than *The Jealousies* were two late love poems. 'To Fanny' was clearly a product of his feverish jealousy and makes reference to his ill-health, blood, and the exhaustion poetry causes him in 'the wintry air'. It is a poem of obsession in love:

> As when with ravished, aching, vassal eyes,
>   Lost in a soft amaze,
>   I gaze, I gaze!

but also of 'torturing jealousy' and crudely sexual fantasy:

> Let none profane my Holy See of Love,
>   Or with a rude hand break
>   The sacramental cake;
> Let none else touch the just new-budded flower;
>   If not – may my eyes close,
>   Love! on their last repose.

Despite valiant attempts by Susan J. Wolfson to argue that this and other 'late lyrics' show poetic experimentation and plans to develop in a new direction,[5] to most readers they seem driven, hectic and too close to the distressing events the poet was undergoing to have full artistic autonomy. Infinitely more artistically successful, however, is the sonnet whose opening phrase has given the title, *Bright Star*, to Jane Campion's film about Keats and Fanny (2009):

> Bright star! would I were steadfast as thou art –
>   Not in lone splendour hung aloft the night,
> And watching, with eternal lids apart,
>   Like Nature's patient sleepless Eremite,
> The moving waters at their priestlike task
>   Of pure ablution round earth's human shores,
> Or gazing on the new soft fallen mask
>   Of snow upon the mountains and the moors –
> No – yet still steadfast, still unchangeable,
>   Pillow'd upon my fair love's ripening breast,
> To feel for ever its soft fall and swell,
>   Awake for ever in a sweet unrest,
> Still, still to hear her tender-taken breath,
> And so live ever – or else swoon to death.

The dating of this poem is purely conjectural and it has been placed any time after 26 June 1818 (before he had met Fanny) or even earlier by Gittings who believes it was written not for Fanny Brawne but for Isabella Jones, while Severn, almost certainly mistakenly, said Keats wrote it on the later voyage to Italy. We do know that Keats recited or read it to Severn on the journey, and then copied it out in his Folio copy of Shakespeare on the page facing *A Lover's Complaint*, though Brown in offering a transcript later trusts his memory in recalling that it was first written in 1819. Touchingly, Fanny Brawne copied it into the copy of Cary's *Dante*, a gift to her from Keats, and its posthumous publication came in the *Plymouth and Devonport Weekly Journal* in September 1838. Despite the doubts about the intended recipient and its date, there is something about this beautiful sonnet which makes us *want* it to be addressed to Fanny and among his last poems, if not the last, and certainly in April 1819 both copied it into books, he into his Folio Shakespeare (slightly revised), she into the copy of Dante. It is one of Keats's most artistically controlled and serene tributes to femaleness, written in an other-centred spirit of negative capability which came infrequently in the last year of his life. It is no simple 'love poem' or impressionistic work of seascape, but a sustained contemplation of Keats's lifelong preoccupation with fusing eternity and the moment, the stars, the sea, and cycles of human life. Owing something to Florizel's lines to Perdita in *The Winters' Tale*, 'When you do dance, I wish you / A wave o'th'sea, that you might ever do / Nothing but that, move still, still so, / And own no other function' (4.4.140–3), and Helena's speech in *All's Well That Ends Well*, ''Twere all one / That I should love a bright particular star' (1.1.80ff.), the sonnet places side by side the image of the north star in the idea of permanence, 'still steadfast, still unchangeable' and signs of time like new-fallen snow, the rhythm of the heartbeat in the 'soft fall and swell' of his lover's breast and her 'sweet unrest'. The poem reaches towards an intersection between the timeless and time which will provide a point of living stasis which Wilson Knight describes as resolving 'the everlasting interplay of movement and stillness, liquid and solid'.[6]

The task that certainly occupied Keats's fitful attention in the first half of 1820 was supervised mainly by Taylor, editing poems for a third volume. Taylor was fully aware that he could not over-tax the poet's energy. If he needed proof he found it in Keats's spirited but exhausting refusal to have the climax of *The Eve of St Agnes* bowdlerised by having its sexual explicitness watered down for an imagined audience of fastidious 'ladies'. At least one decision was made very much against the author's wishes. *Hyperion. A Fragment* was included in the collection with responsibility being taken by the publishers, almost certainly Taylor himself:

Advertisement

If any apology be thought necessary for the appearance of the unfinished poem of HYPERION, the publishers beg to state that they alone are responsible, as it was printed at their particular request, and contrary to the wish of the author. The poem was intended to have been of equal length with ENDYMION, but the reception given to that work discouraged the author from proceeding.

Fleet Street, June 26 1820.

Keats in clear anger scored crosses over the 'Advertisement' in the first copy he received and wrote, 'This is none of my doing – I was ill at the time. This is a lie.' He may have been objecting to the suggestion that he was discouraged from continuing the poem because of the reception given to *Endymion* since, as we have seen, he made several attempts to continue the epic. But equally objectionable must have been the choice of the earlier and discarded *Hyperion. A Fragment* despite the existence of the later, more mature *The Fall of Hyperion: A Dream.* Even the latter was clearly not the end of Keats's aspiration since during 1820 he several times repeated his plan to continue and complete the poem about Hyperion. Epic was always his litmus test for greatness in non-dramatic poetry, and the form he aspired to. One can see his point. The publishers' decision, however well-meaning, looks like an anticipation that the poet would not live to publish a long poem in a single volume like *Endymion*, and however realistic this may have been, it can be seen as singularly insensitive, almost a prediction of his inevitable death.

None the less, despite his frustrations, Keats did have the satisfaction of seeing into print a new volume of his poems, containing mainly the fruit of his astonishing creative output in 1819, its title emphasising the romances:

Lamia, Isabella, the Eve of St Agnes, And Other Poems (1820)
Lamia
Isabella; or The Pot of Basil
The Eve of St Agnes

Ode to a Nightingale
Ode on a Grecian Urn
Ode to Psyche

Fancy
Ode ('Bards of passion and of mirth')
Lines on the Mermaid Tavern
Robin Hood

To Autumn
Ode on Melancholy

Hyperion [A Fragment]

The collection seems to have been placed in order by Keats, with the exception of the last, and there is a considered sequence. The first three poems, *Lamia, Isabella* and *The Eve of St Agnes* are his longer 'quest-romance' narratives turning on sexual desire. Then comes a group of odes which, if I am right about their spirit, are offered as relatively modest and intellectually teasing poems about art. 'Lines on the Mermaid Tavern' and 'Robin Hood' lighten the tone further as comic ballads with nostalgic refrains, 'dead and gone', 'No! those days are gone away' and 'Gone, the merry morris din ...' They are companion pieces, lamenting the loss of a poetic fraternity from the Elizabethan age (in the Mermaid Tavern associated with Ben Jonson) and earlier in the days of Robin Hood. The vision is inspired in part by Shakespeare's description in *As You Like It*:

> They say he is already in the forest of Ardenne, and a many merry men with him; and there they live like the old Robin Hood of England. They say many young gentlemen flock to him every day, and fleet the time carelessly, as they did in the golden world. (1.1.99–103)

Keats in his open avowal of nostalgia is confessing that his preference for Elizabethan poets over those of his own day is unrepentantly old-fashioned. It would make sense that 'To Autumn' and 'On Melancholy' were intended by Keats to end the volume on a more sombre and serious note reflecting his mood at the time of publication. Even without any presumed personal sensitivity, Keats could have felt an artistic impropriety in tacking *Hyperion. A Fragment* onto the carefully arranged sequence. It is completely different from the romances and odes in tone, mode of narration, sources and genre, and can be seen as undermining the autonomy of the collection and destroying the intended effect of it as a whole. It must have been clear to Keats that whatever form a future 'Hyperion' might take, it does not belong in this collection. His clear intention was that it should eventually be completed and published in its own single volume as an ambitious, serious epic to stand comparison with *Endymion* and perhaps even *Paradise Lost* and *The Divine Comedy*. The result as it stands would have been a disappointment to him, as well as a painfully blunt hint from his editors that they feared he would not live to see any future publication. In every other way, however, the 1820 volume is a sublime artistic success, comparable to *Lyrical Ballads* by Wordsworth and Coleridge in its significance for literary history. Far surpassing *Poems* (1817) and *Endymion* (1818) in poetic richness and accomplishment, it contains most of the poems from 1819 which have been accepted as Keats's most memorable poems and as amongst the greatest in the English language.

13
The Final Journey

Two years before, and in a more youthfully effervescent mood, Keats had observed proverbially to the Reynolds sisters, 'for a long day may be a short year' (*JKL*, 1, 151), and some similar paradox of relative time can emerge from the proportions of chapters in a biography. In any Literary Life attention to the 'Literary' will inevitably and perhaps cruelly outweigh the cluttered inconsequentiality of a 'Life'. It is understandable that childhood and youth, covering a span of fifteen years or so, can be packed into a single chapter because the 'literary' output has not begun, while other chapters can cover a concentrated period of only a month or two, like April and May in 1819, if they are rich in literary production. The poet's 'life' is just as crowded as anybody's with everyday activity, experiences and thoughts at all points between birth and death, but our concentration has necessarily been on the periods in Keats's life when he was intensely writing the poetry we now value. Rather unmercifully, this brief chapter will document a span of about eight months, for the energy that Keats had used to write poems, soon after the completion of 'To Autumn' and the publication of his poems in mid-1820, was required by him in the more primal struggle to continue living. This is not to deny that as it went on time could seem agonisingly slow to the suffering poet, and a day could seem like a year.

The volume of his poems was published in either the last week of June or the first in July 1820, but Keats was scarcely in a state to celebrate, having had another haemorrhage. In mid-July Severn reported to Haslam that 'Poor Keats has been still nearer the next world – a Fortnight back he ruptured a blood-vessel in the Chest' (*JKL*, 2, 306). He was tormented by jealousy in his irrational suspicion that Fanny was flirting with Brown and other men, and held only minimal hopes for the volume's success but he was still trusting to a longer life: 'My book is coming out with very low hopes, though not spirits on my part. This shall be my last trial; not succeeding, I shall try what I can do in the Apothecary line' (*JKL*, 2, 298). Severn describes in the uncharacteristically sombre poet 'such a deep thinking – determined – silent spirit ...' (*JKL*, 2, 307), which must have been disquieting to observe in his usually sociable and optimistic friend.

Keats was also becoming increasingly uneasy because medical opinion was gathering amongst his friends and had reached even George in America that his health would require a warmer winter: 'They talk of my going to Italy', he wrote to Fanny, adding ''Tis certain I shall never recover if I am to be so long separate from you ...' (*JKL*, 2, 303), while to Taylor he complained on 13 August, 'This journey to Italy wakes me at daylight every morning and haunts me horribly. I shall endeavour to go though it be with the sensation of marching up against a Battery.' Given his resistance, a letter from Shelley written on 27 July, rather than being read in a spirit of gratitude, must have sharpened his anxiety. Shelley rather tactlessly spells out the name of the disease which his friends had scrupulously avoided and which Keats himself denied (*JKL*, 2, 314) – 'This consumption is a disease particularly fond of people who write such good verses as you have done' (*JKL*, 2, 310) – continuing to joke in a way that was no doubt well meant but sounds callous. Shelley indeed seems incapable of quite adjusting his tone in the way Keats always could, since even a proffered compliment about the 'treasures of poetry' in *Endymion* is qualified by the critical comment that they are 'though treasures poured forth with indistinct profusion'. He went on to invite Keats to join him in Pisa but Keats declined the offer. It is one of the minor sadnesses of literary history that these two *wunderkinds* in Hunt's desired pantheon of poets never quite found a meeting of minds. Shelley was genuine in his admiration and affection and his *Adonais* is an elegy of true grief, but he never understood how significant were the differences between their personalities and backgrounds and he made no attempt to modify them. Keats for his part never overcame the class suspicion he had always harboured of the Eton-educated, disinherited aristocrat. Shelley was also too close for comfort to Byron, a man openly contemptuous of Keats, a feeling which Keats seemed to reciprocate out of mingled class jealousy and rivalry. The expensively educated Harrow boy seemed never to get over a prejudice that a graduate of a small, liberal school in Enfield for the sons of tradesmen could write apparently plausibly on Greek myths without being able to read Greek in the original. Even after Keats's death when Byron softened his attitude, there is a note of condescension that the young poet was apparently not 'manly' enough to get over the disappointment of a bad review:

> John Keats, who was killed off by one critique,
> Just as he really promised something great,
> If not intelligible, – without Greek
> Contrived to talk about the Gods of late,
> Much as they might have been supposed to speak.

Poor fellow! His was an untoward fate: –
'Tis strange the mind, that very fiery particle,
Would let itself be snuffed out by an Article.

(*Don Juan*, XI, 60)

Byron had conveniently forgotten his own earlier bruised feelings on receiving bad reviews. His comment about Keats being killed by reviewers was shared by Shelley though the latter showed genuine sympathy and affection. In writing *Adonais* he generalised the death to represent the fate of all misunderstood and persecuted young poets and a copy of Keats's 1820 volume was in his pocket when he drowned in May 1822. Five months after Keats's death Cowden Clarke in a letter to the *Morning Chronicle* signed merely 'Y' was to recall the almost suicidal 'sensative bitterness' Keats had felt over the reviews by Lockhart and Croker in 1818,[1] and even today many confirm that anxiety and stress can shorten the life of a victim of tuberculosis. Meanwhile, as John Goodridge shows, it is a tragedy that of all Keats's contemporary poets the one who never met him and yet unreservedly admired his poems and who would, one feels, have been personally compatible in many ways, was John Clare. Clare's poetry was deeply influenced by Keats and they shared the equally careful attention of Taylor who scrupulously kept Clare informed of the details of Keats's final days.[2]

Keats continued to resist the plan that was evolving around him, finding it 'almost impossible' to conceive that he should go to Italy. He still clung to the hope he could stay in England and close to Fanny, writing to her in a wounded spirit, 'If I cannot live with you I will live alone ... I should like to die. I am sickened at the brute world which you are smiling with. I hate men and women more. I see nothing but thorns for the future – wherever I may be next winter in Italy or nowhere ... the world is too brutal for me – I am glad there is such a thing as the grave – I am sure I shall never have any rest till I get there ...' (*JKL*, 2, 312). In his mood of anxiety bordering on panic, Keats at this time systematically alienated several of his friends such as Hunt, Haslam (over his marriage), Dilke, who was urging Italy upon him against his wishes and was known to disapprove of Fanny Brawne, and Haydon, who was persistently demanding back the copy of Chapman's *Homer* which he had lent Keats who had lost it. The sheer egotism of Haydon, and the signs of the mental illness that was to afflict the painter in later life and eventually lead to his suicide, had already irritated Keats and some rift was inevitable. Keats had become increasingly reserved with Reynolds who, influenced by his sisters who were no doubt jealous for their 'pet lamb versifier', also regarded Fanny Brawne in a very negative light. He continually suspected even Brown of flirting with Fanny although he was still in Scotland, and his hostile feelings were compounded by Brown's surreptitious and apparently sordid affair with their Irish maidservant Abigail O'Donoghue, which was to lead to her pregnancy, their secret marriage, and a son called Carlino. He sent Brown a letter which seems curt and cold in the light of their long and close relationship, informing him of the impending disembarkation to Italy and more or less saying goodbye: 'Do not, my dear Brown, tease yourself about me. You must fill up your time as well as you can, and as happily. You must think of my faults as lightly as you can' (*JKL*, 2, 321). Keats was in the kind of testy and choleric state which recalls the early descriptions of his schoolboy tendency to fight. This was not surprising given the emotional depths created by tuberculosis, the laudanum he was taking regularly, and a lifelong tendency to rapid changes of feelings and swings into the sharp depression of 'melancholy'. However, in his last letter to Brown written from Rome, he regrets things said and done to his friends 'from being so low in body and mind' and hopes 'If I recover, I will do all in my power to correct the mistakes made during sickness; and if I should not, all my faults will be forgiven.' In this contrite mood as quickly as he had broken his bridges to people he mended them, even buying a new copy of Chapman's *Homer* for Haydon and welcoming Haslam who almost accompanied him to Italy and certainly came to see him before the departure. He graciously thanked Shelley for his offer, giving him the copy of his book which Shelley took to his watery grave. With a slight edge of archness he recalled that Shelley had advised him not to publish his earlier volumes of poems, asserting that he had only published the recent volume 'to serve Mammon' in order to make money, and advising Shelley himself to exercise more 'discipline' in his own poetry, 'that you might curb your magnanimity and be more of an artist, and [quoting Spenser] "load every rift" of your subject with ore' (*JKL*, 2, 323). Keats also wrote again to Brown with his more characteristic familiarity and warmth, asking him to accompany him to Rome, something which he gives signs of coming to rely on since he mentioned it to both his sister and Haslam. It was fortunate that he extended the hand of reconciliation to the loyal Brown, and his last letters to him, though full of understated anguish, show the greatest trust that Keats ever invested in a friend.

Keats was still living in the Hunts' household where Mrs Marianne Hunt drew him in silhouette propped on a day-bed, and who much later in 1857 also died of tuberculosis. He confided later to Brown that he felt 'a prisoner' and that he 'used to keep [his] eyes fixed on Hampstead all day' (*JKL*, 2, 351), drawn not so much by the house as by the presence there of Fanny Brawne. In mid-August 'an accident of an unpleasant nature' forced him to decamp immediately which is what he had wanted to do anyway. A letter had arrived for Keats while he was asleep and through a disgruntled servant it was opened by Thornton Hunt, one of Hunt's many children and passed around the Hunt family. We do not know what the letter contained (one strongly suspects it was from Fanny Brawne about whom Keats was always secretive), but we do know the indiscretion was disproportionately upsetting, as Mrs Hunt is reported as saying 'Poor Keats was affected by this inconceivable circumstance beyond what can be imagined; he wept for several hours, and resolved, notwithstanding Hunt's intreaties, to leave the house; he went to Hampstead that same evening' (*JKL*, 2, 313 fn). It seems that it was a spirit of blind impulsiveness or instinct that drove him, on 12 August, still weeping and clearly very ill, to the door of the Brawnes at Wentworth Place. Mrs Brawne took him in and he was to stay for a month being nursed by the family. At long last he was now effectively living with Fanny Brawne, though for the sake of respectability he describes it formally to his sister as staying 'a short time with Mrs Brawne who lives in the House which was Mrs Dilke's'. After initially disapproving of the penurious young poet as a potential son-in-law, the widowed Frances Brawne ended up as one of his staunchest helpmeets and a beacon of light almost as bright for him as her daughter. Brown's house next door had been let out for the summer while he was in Scotland since he urgently needed the money from rental. The voyage to Italy now became more or less a foregone conclusion, a prospect which filled Keats with morbid dread although in his letters to his sister Fanny he characteristically protects her by suppressing his feelings and instead maintaining an air of brisk practicality. He later patched up the unpleasantness with the Hunts with a generous and affectionate note, which immensely gratified the loyal Hunt who had suffered over the years many rebuffs from his volatile young protégé.

While practicalities were handled by Woodhouse and Haslam, the financial arrangements for Italy were made largely by Taylor, who as publisher stood to be the beneficiary of Keats's book which had showed promising advance sales. In return, Keats, in a legal document dated 16 September 1820 assigned copyright of his books to the publishing firm of Taylor and Hessey (*JKL*, 2, 334–6). He had sent to Taylor on 14 August 1820 an undated 'Testament' on a 'scrap of Paper' (*JKL*, 2, 318–20) which as a will is at points jocular and minimalist in the extreme. He confirms his only estate 'consists in the hopes of the sale of books publish'd or unpublish'd' and nominates Brown and Taylor as 'the first paid Creditors – the rest is in nubibus – but in case it should shower pay my Taylor the few pounds I owe him'. 'My Chest of Books divide among my friends –'. He gave his most precious books, the facsimile of Shakespeare's Folio and editions of Spenser and Dante, to Fanny Brawne, who some time after his death passed them on to Fanny Keats. Before this, in a poignant touch, Fanny Brawne wrote in faint but still legible pencil alongside 'FINIS' at the end of *As You Like It* in the Folio text 'Fanny, April 17 1821'.

Keats did try to get some money from Abbey, whose reply is completely astonishing in the circumstances. He simply berated John for his folly in lending money to his own brother George, said casually that his own business was not doing well enough for him to spare any of his own money, and with gross bad taste cheerily ended on a feeble joke: 'It is therefore not in my power to lend you any thing ... When you are able to call I shall be glad to see you, as I should not like to see you want "maintenance *for* the day"' (*JKL*, 2, 331). Neither Keats nor Abbey was to know that the court case over

John Jennings would eventually be settled in favour of the Keats siblings, too late for John (or even, by that stage, George) to benefit, so Fanny inherited the whole estate, which by then had been diminished through legal fees to a still handsome amount of £4,500. In 1826 she was to marry Valentine Maria Llanos y Gutierrez who, despite his exotic name, was a slightly shady businessman and dull novelist whom Keats evidently met in Rome just three days before his death (*JKL* 1, 81).

With 'the assistance of a friend' – in fact Fanny Brawne, coyly described – Keats wrote what would be his last letter to his sister, dated 11 September. He feigns cheerfulness at leaving such a bad climate as England's and says his plan is to go to Naples and then to Rome 'where I shall find several friends or at least several acquaintances' (*JKL*, 2, 332). Since Brown had not replied to his letter, it was uncertain who would go with Keats since it was obvious he could not go alone. Haslam was prepared to go but he was recently married and could not leave England, and he hastily arranged instead for Severn to be the poet's last companion, an arrangement finalised less than a week before departure. Haslam had originally introduced the artist Joseph Severn to Keats in 1816, and he had been one of the artists' circle around Haydon. Reynolds, who had been much closer to Keats, confided his fears to Taylor after the boat had left that 'Severn ... is scarcely a resolute, intelligent or cheerful companion which a long voyage and a sickly frame so anxiously call for' (*KC*, 1, 157). Dr Clark in Rome later wrote to an unnamed friend: 'between you and I [he] is not the best suited for his companion, but I suppose poor fellow he had no choice' (*JKL*, 2, 358). Even Keats had his doubts about Severn's ability to endure 'other peoples illnesses' (*JKL*, 2, 349–50). Events showed that Severn rose to the task, but his presence does seem to have had a certain arbitrariness about it which clearly frustrated Keats. Although not a close friend by any means and not renowned for reliability, he was selected almost by default because nobody else could go. When he announced it to his family, his father struck and knocked him down, saying he was ruining his career as an artist. Ironically, this was exactly wrong, since Severn was to make his career out of that voyage, first by becoming known to posterity as the friend who accompanied Keats and later, staying in Italy and living a colourful and sometimes scandalous life as a painter, he rose to the position of British consul in Rome, through fortuitously meeting and courting English lords and 'superior persons' including Gladstone.[3] Though a friend of long standing he seemed no close confidant to Keats since, astoundingly, he did not even know just how close the poet was to Fanny Brawne until some sixty years later when he was shown their letters, and he then proceeded to blame her for accelerating his death. He arranged that when he died in 1879 his body would lie beside Keats's (not his wife's, buried in Marseille) and would bear the inscription 'Devoted friend and death-bed companion / of / JOHN KEATS', thus ensuring his own immortality for events that had happened over fifty years earlier.[4] However, Severn did in the event endure with unexpected stoicism the terrible assignment, and we are grateful for his detailed and harrowing descriptions of Keats's last weeks, days and hours.

It was in every way Brown who should have accompanied Keats on this journey. He was the friend to whom Keats had said 'You have been living for others more than any man I know.' The aftermath to Keats's invitation to him was tragic in the mode of the missed rendezvous in *Romeo and Juliet*. The reply Brown sent to Keats did not arrive in time so he did not know Brown was on his way. Brown did in fact come down from Scotland 'undeviatingly' and hastened to London at least to see Keats off and perhaps accompany him, but he arrived too late, a day after the boat had left. Keats was to write to him, 'I must have been at Bedhampton nearly at the time you were writing to me from Chichester – how unfortunate – and to pass on the river too! There was my star predominant!' (*JKL*, 2, 359). In fact, without their knowing, the respective boats lay side by side in Gravesend since Keats's left late. Keats continued to write to Brown from Italy, and here at least was one friend he could confide in about his greatest concern. He indicates that he hopes Brown will take care of Fanny Brawne after his death, and reveals how deeply he misses her: 'I can bear to die – I cannot bear to leave her. Oh God! God! God! Every thing I have in my trunks that reminds me of her goes through me like a spear. The silk lining she put in my travelling cap scalds my head. My imagination is horribly vivid about her – I see her – I hear her ...' (*JKL*, 2, 351). In his final weeks he could not bear to read her letters, and instructed Severn to leave them 'unopened'. Their contents a secret forever, they were buried with him. Fanny herself had never trusted Severn and she refused to meet him after Keats's death. Isabella Jones, the mysterious 'other woman' in Keats's life, was later openly contemptuous of Severn as the man she called 'Mr Egotist'. After reading his letters from Rome she threw them from her in disgust at his self-centredness. She remained deeply sceptical about Severn's motives in going with Keats to Rome, suspecting him of being self-seeking and insincere, and not the right person to accompany the poet at this time.[5] Perhaps we all make a subliminal choice about the one we wish to have as a companion in dying. By all accounts the shallow, frightened Severn was not the person Keats would have chosen.

Keats, Severn and Haslam departed on the *Maria Crowther* on 17 September, Leigh Hunt marking the poet's exodus from England in a touching article in the *Indicator* which glances at the final image in 'To Autumn': 'dear friend, as valued a one as thou art a poet, – John Keats, – we cannot, after all, find it in our hearts to be glad, now thou art gone away with the swallows to seek a kindlier clime'. Leaving Haslam at Gravesend, the boat proceeded out of the Thames to Portsmouth via Dungeness in Kent on the very southern tip of east England. Portsmouth was only seven miles from Bedhampton, and Keats took the opportunity of visiting his old friends the Snooks there. Unbeknownst to either, Brown was at that moment in Chichester harbour only about twenty miles directly east of where Keats was. Even such a short leg of the journey along the south coast of England was uncomfortable enough as the ship was alternately besieged by storms and furious gales to the point that water entered and the ship was becalmed. They had still not effectively left British soil until 2 October, and then took three weeks to reach Naples, only to be detained on the high seas in the ship for a week during the period of quarantine. Given the fact that there were several consumptives on the boat and that it was known to be an infectious disease (though not well understood), it is surprising they made it through quarantine. None the less, land they eventually did in Naples, by coincidence on 31 October, perhaps Keats's twenty-fifth birthday, or at the latest two days after it.

From the time they left London Severn wrote letters, mainly to Haslam, in the form of a journal and his account has become famous in its own right as the moving record of Keats's last months and days. There are images of Keats in Severn's account which are unutterably poignant and heroic, none more so than those of the dying poet tending the seasick on the tempestuous voyage.

> +19th Septr Tuesday off Dover Castle &c+
> I arose at day break to see the glorious – eastern gate – Keats slept till 7 – Miss C – was rather ill this Morn[ing] I prevailed on her to walk the deck with me at $^1/_2$ past 6 – she recovered much – Keats was still better this morn[ing] and Mrs Pidgeon looked and was the picture of health – but poor me! I began to feel a waltzing on my stomach at breakfast when I wrote the note to you I was going it most soundly – Miss Cotterell followed me – then Keats who did it in the most gentlemanly manner – and then the saucy Mrs Pidgeon who had been laughing at us – four faces bequeathing to the mighty deep their breakfasts – here I must change to a Minor Key – Miss C fainted – we soon recovered her – I was very ill – nothing but laying down would do for me – Keats assended his bed – from which he dictated surgically – like Esculapius of old in baso-relievo – through him – Miss C was recovered we had a cup of tea each and no more went to bed and slept until it was time to go to bed – we could not get up again – and slept in our cloths all night – Keats the King – not even looking pale — (*JKL*, 2, 342)

Severn may not have been quite conscious of the multiple layers of significance in this paragraph, for he adds them almost parenthetically in his sometimes clumsy attempts at humour. No wheel could come more satisfyingly and yet so dismayingly full circle for those who travel the life story of

Keats upon his poetry, his letters, and the idea of his fullest existence. Little touches: his being seasick in 'the most gentlemanly manner', his gallantry exhibited even in his distress, the more than half-hinted glimpse of a potential shipboard romance between Severn at least and a delicate, consumptive Miss Cotterell ('a very sweet girl about 18 but quite a martyr to the complaint – ' [*JKL*, 2, 339]) whose appearance, Severn elsewhere mentions, resembled Fanny Brawne's. The brilliant young poet was undergoing the 'final divorce' from the love of his own life, yet still finding a 'coterie', companionship, and his vocation for healing. There is the heroic shouldering aside of physical adversity as an embracing of transcendent, posthumous immortality etched in Severn's splendidly crass, hero-worshipping 'Keats the King – not even looking pale – '.

But what is most moving is that, with some strange instinct, Severn intimates Keats's return, whether reluctantly or with alacrity we shall never know, to his original vocation. Severn seems to realise his reader needs his memory jogging, for he first began to write the words 'he dictated professionally', and then more precisely wrote 'surgically' over it. Not only was he recalling the apparent false start of the successful medical qualification, but inadvertently also the precise vision that Keats had considered several times after his student days, becoming a ship's doctor. But the most breathtaking phrase is 'like Esculapius of old in baso-relievo', which is so rich in its nostalgic exactitude that the artist Severn could not have understood its full reference, and which may in fact be the reported words of Keats himself. Not only was that figure of the patron saint of doctors, now sadly in half-relief, an originary stimulus for Keats's initial choice of medicine, but also a particular 'Aesculapius', in the half-relief of an adopted *nom de plume*, was significant to the idealistic and healthy young student who entered Guy's Hospital on 1 October 1815, was examined on 25 July 1816, graduated as a qualified medical practitioner on 31 October 1816 and found himself exactly five years later, in effect waiting to die. In a way that is certainly ghostly, this very Aesculapius was Keats's own 'great presider', the writer of his medical textbook during his medical days.

Delayed still further by passport regulations and after an agonisingly uncomfortable rough coach journey from Naples during which Severn walked some of the way and gathered flowers for Keats, they finally reached Rome on 15 November. As previously arranged by Taylor, Keats was placed under the medical care of Dr Clark who had rented an apartment on the first floor of the Piazza di Spagna beside the imposing steps up to the Santa Trinità dei Monti church. To his own cost, Dr Clark was true to his promise to Taylor that Keats would not need to be troubled by financial considerations. He found an apartment for them in a block where the upper floors were regularly rented to foreign visitors who included English people on the Grand Tour. We can still visit Keats's final room, which is as narrow and disproportionately long as a corridor, just two metres wide and five metres long, and disturbingly claustrophobic despite its view over the 'Spanish Steps' and the Bernini Fountain. 'Like living in a violin' was how the Italian writer-composer Alberto Savinio was to describe it,[6] and although having a wonderful view from the window the increasingly invalid poet would have had to stare for many hours at its open-boarded ceiling painted lattice-like against sky blue 'large white flowers with golden centres', though another writer describes them as 'blue and white rosettes'.[7] Clark misdiagnosed Keats, which was surprising since his speciality was consumption and so many sufferers came to Rome to avoid the rigours of the English winter. Like all Keats's doctors he tended to believe the illness was partly a psychosomatic symptom of a highly strung poetic temperament, and that the very real blood he was vomiting came from a disorder of the stomach rather than the lungs. Perhaps he was concealing his honest diagnosis to maintain hope, and we should not be too quick to accuse him of a misdiagnosis. Clark's increasingly frank opinion was that Keats should never have left England since even then he was incurable, the change of air was far too late to help, and the difficult voyage had effectively shortened his life. It is significant that after his death the three women who had been closest to him, Fanny Brawne, Isabella Jones and Fanny Keats, were all to express deep regrets about the voyage which, in the event, turned out to be futile anyway. No doubt reflecting the social position of women at the time, unable even to be considered as potential travelling companions with a man, they all wished he had been allowed to die close to them in England, accessible to their care and company.

At first, however, there were some hopeful signs. Severn hired a piano into the tiny flat, and Dr Clark played Haydn's symphonies to please and distract the invalid. Keats was even able to walk and to ride a little, and to attend the theatre with the Cotterells. He managed a relatively cheerful letter to Brown on 30 November, in which he quips that 'Yet I ride the little horse, – and, at my worst, even in Quarantine, summoned up more puns, in a sort of desperation, in one week than in any year of my life' (*JKL*, 2, 360). Much of the *badinage* had been shared with Miss Cotterell, with whom Keats argued with a dark sense of humour about which of them was the more debilitated. She was assumed to be more advanced in illness but was to outlast him and die of consumption two years later. Although he was reading poetry and listening to Severn reading prose, Keats knew that writing would be an impossible strain:

> There is one thought enough to kill me – I have been well, healthy, alert, &c, walking with her – and now – the knowledge of contrast, feeling for light and shade, all that information (primitive sense) necessary for a poem are great enemies to the recovery of the stomach. (*JKL*, 2, 360)

The letter to Brown turned out to be his last and he signs off with unwittingly appropriate finality:

> Write to George as soon as you receive this, and tell him how I am, as far as you can guess; – and also a note to my sister – who walks about my imagination like a ghost – she is so like Tom. I can scarcely bid you good bye even in a letter. I always made an awkward bow.
>
> God bless you!
>
> John Keats.

On 9 December came a near fatal relapse when Keats, in the midst of rare good spirits, vomited nearly two cupfuls of blood, made worse by being deprived by Dr Clark of another eight ounces in bleeding him. Keats was suicidal and tried to take an overdose of laudanum but was restrained by Severn, motivated by his strong Christian beliefs not shared by Keats. He removed anything from the room that could be used to cause self-harm. A nurse was employed to watch when Severn could not. The next morning an equal amount of blood was lost, and another bout was let. Dr Clark searched Rome for a particular kind of fish supposed to be beneficial (possibly anchovy) which his wife 'delicately' prepared for Keats but he coughed more blood. After this Clark prescribed a starvation diet which not only made him delirious but put Severn in an impossible position since Keats kept demanding food. It seems a cruel miracle that the poet lasted in this kind of condition with little relief for another forty-six days, alternating between fever and calm, teeth chattering from cold, raving from starvation, denouncing angrily Severn's simple-minded Christian belief in providence, and sleeping only out of exhaustion after suffering for nights on end. Clark and the attentive Severn, who had to keep hiding the opium supply as well as razors and knives, were berated for keeping him alive against his wishes to live a 'posthumous life'. He even managed a lugubrious joke: 'Tell Taylor I shall soon be in a second edition – in sheets – and cold press.' Severn continues:

> Four days previous to his death – the change in him was so great that I passed each moment in dread – not knowing what the next would have – he was calm and firm at its approaches – to a most astonishing degree – he told [me] not to tremble for he did not think that he should be convulsed – he said – 'did you ever see any one die' no – 'well then I pity you poor Severn – what trouble and danger you have got into for me – now you must be firm for it will not last long – I shall soon be laid in the quiet grave – thank God for the quiet grave – O! I can feel the cold earth upon me – the daises growing over me – O for this quiet – it will be my first' – when the morning light came and still found him alive – O how bitterly he grieved – I cannot bear his cries – (*JKL*, 2, 378)

Behind his question to Severn lay his own all too familiar acquaintance with the process of dying witnessed not only in his family but in his medical training. Amongst his final words were whispered 'don't breathe on me – it comes like Ice'.

At 11 p.m. on 23 February, Keats died in Severn's arms aged 25. Severn specifies this date and time in the 'English style' though, as with his birth date there is a complex argument about the dates of his death and burial. Rollins summarises in this way: 'According to the Roman method of reckoning time, whereby one day ended and another began at 6 p.m., Keats did die on February 24 at 5 o'clock, so that the date given in the cemetery register, as well as later on the gravestone and the Keats House in Rome, is correct' (*KC*, 1, 225–7, fn). The next day death-casts were made of his face, hand and foot. An autopsy revealed 'the worst possible Consumption – the lungs were intirely destroyed – the cells were quite gone ...' (*JKL*, 2, 379). Police came: 'The furniture, the walls, the floor, every thing must be destroyed by order of the law' because it was considered that infectious tuberculosis would leave its traces, and the landlady expected the extravagantly inflated costs to be met from Keats's virtually empty estate. In the end the figure was revised downwards and was paid by Taylor.

On Monday, 26 February at daybreak, since Protestants in Rome could not be buried on either Sunday or during the day time, Keats was buried in the place he had chosen, the Protestant cemetery in Rome a few yards from Byron's daughter Allegra. 'Many English requested to follow him ... the good-hearted Doctor made the men put turfs of daisies upon the grave – he – said – "this would be poor Keats's wish – could he know it" – ' (*JKL*, 2, 379). The only sounds in the graveyard were 'a few simple sheep and goats with their tinkling bells'. Severn later designed the headstone, a lyre 'with only half the strings – to show his classical genius cut off by death before its maturity'. Keats's wish was that no name would appear, simply the words 'Here lies one whose name was writ in water', perhaps a reference to the fountain playing continuously outside his window on the 'Spanish Steps' or perhaps in pessimistic evaluation of his poetic reputation. When the headstone eventually was engraved and placed in 1822 Brown insisted on the addition of a prolix introduction to the enigmatic phrase. Rapidly word went round, to Brown, Taylor, Haslam, Hunt, Rice, Dilke and Reynolds – all those whom Fanny Brawne said had been drawn to Keats by a 'spell' of his friendship – and to others like John Clare (through Taylor) who had found the spell to lie in the poetry. Shelley set about writing *Adonais* which was intended to speak for all poets, assuming that the young poet had been killed by hostile reviews. An extract from this poem was to be recited on 5 July 1969 in London's Hyde Park by a modern Cockney minstrel dressed in white frills, Mick Jagger, to mark the recent death of his fellow Rolling Stone who had died young, Brian Jones.[8] Severn wrote, 'the [unopened] letters I put into the coffin with my own hand'. Fanny Brawne reported that a locket of her hair was also buried with him. We do have the letters she started writing to Fanny Keats after John's death, and they show her in a very affectionate and genuinely grieving light.

> – all his friends have forgotten him, they have got over the first shock, and that with them is all. They think I have done the same, which I do not wonder at, for I [have] taken care never to trouble them with any feelings of mine, but I can tell you who next to me (I must say *next* to me) loved him best, that I have not got over it and never shall – (*FB*, 25)

Fanny Brawne did not marry until twelve years after his death, at the age of 33, which at that time was quite advanced for a woman. She mourned publicly for about five years. She had insisted that her mother tell her the news as soon as Keats died, adding 'I am not a fool!' The friendship between the two Fannys blossomed in their letters to each other after Keats's death. They exchanged news and views on dressmaking and on rearing pigeons, one of Fanny Keats's interests – even the merits of opium in the form of laudanum to dull the pain of toothache – and Brawne provided strong moral support in the constant struggle with Mr and Mrs Abbey until Fanny Keats came of age in June 1824 and could at last with enormous relief leave their guardianship. Even when her inheritance finally became available Abbey procrastinated for a year in paying it, apparently on the grounds that he had spent much of his own money in acting as her guardian (*FB*, 73), or taking advantage of Fanny's own mistaken belief that she had been born not in 1803 but in 1804. Abbey in fact had to be sued by Dilke and Rice to extract the full amount of Fanny's inheritance which now included Tom's and John's shares.[9]

The thrush had stopped singing, the nightingale had fled into the next valley, gathering swallows no longer twittered but had migrated to warmer climes in that final winter. But the songs persist in the words John Keats has given us, returning like the seasons on every re-reading.

> But this is human life: the war, the deeds,
> The disappointment, the anxiety,
> Imagination's struggles, far and nigh,
> All human; bearing in themselves this good,
> That they are still the air, the subtle food,
> To make us feel existence, and to shew
> How quiet death is.
>
> (*Endymion*, Book II, 153–9)

On 10 June 1954, John Masefield as Poet Laureate unveiled a memorial to Keats in Poets' Corner at Westminster Abbey. It had first been proposed to the Dean and Chapter of Westminster in March 1939 but there was a postponement due to the war. There is a small stone oval[10] and at the top of it is a lyre with a swag of carved flowers linking it to an identical tablet for Shelley. The inscription below reads simply 'John Keats 1795–1821'. The stone is placed above the memorial statue to Shakespeare – 'a High Power ... a good Genius' ... 'Is it too daring to Fancy Shakespeare this Presider?'[11] As he had predicted, John Keats after his death was at last among the English Poets.

Notes

1. 'He could not quiet be'

1. Maurice Whelan, *In the Company of William Hazlitt: Thoughts for the 21st Century* (Melbourne: Australian Scholarly Publishing, 2003), ch. 5.
2. William Stroup, 'The Romantic Child', *Literature Compass*, 1 (2004) RO 078, 1–5, referring to M. J. Daunton, *Progress and Poverty: An Economic and Social History of Britain 1700–1850* (Oxford: Oxford University Press, 1995), 412.
3. A facsimile of these records can be seen at the *JSTOR* website: http://www.jstor.org.
4. For a very detailed history of these years, see John Barrell, *Imagining the King's Death: Figurative Treason, Fantasies of Regicide, 1793–1796* (Oxford: Oxford University Press, 2000).
5. Robert Gittings, *The Keats Inheritance* (London: Heinemann, 1964).
6. Andrew Motion, *Keats* (London: Faber and Faber, 1997), 31.
7. See Tom Bates, 'John Clare and Boximania', *John Clare Society Journal* (1994), 5–18, which presents valuable information about the sport, some drawn from J. Ford, *Prizefighting: The Age of Regency Boximania* (Newton Abbot: David and Charles, 1971).
8. Stanley Plumly, *Posthumous Keats: A Personal Biography* (New York, W. W. Norton, 2008), 155.
9. Nicholas Roe, *John Keats and the Culture of Dissent* (Oxford: Clarendon Press, 1997).
10. John Barnard, 'Charles Cowden Clarke's "Cockney" Commonplace Book', in Nicholas Roe (ed.), *Keats and History* (Cambridge: Cambridge University Press, 1995), 65–87, 66.
11. John Nyren, *The Young Cricketer's Tutor ... The whole collected and edited by Charles Cowden Clarke* (repr. London: Davis-Poynter, 1974).
12. An appreciative chapter on Nyren's book and Clarke's contribution to it appears in Edmund Blunden's *Cricket Country* (London: The Imprint Society, 1945), ch. X. Since Blunden had written a book on Keats, he naturally notes the links. For a history of the Hambledon Club, placed in the context of public sport in London, see David Underdown, *Start of Play: Cricket and Culture in Eighteenth-Century England* (Harmondsworth: Penguin Books, 2000).
13. David Jesson Dibley (ed.), *Leigh Hunt: Selected Writings* (Manchester: Carcanet Press, 1990), 104–5.

2. 'Aesculapius'

1. Hillas Smith, *Keats and Medicine* (Newport, Isle of Wight: Cross Publishing, 1995), 35.
2. Robert Gittings, *John Keats* (Harmondsworth: Penguin Books, 1968), Appendix 2, 642–9. Gittings argues from physical likenesses. See also Susan C. Lawrence, *Charitable Knowledge: Hospital Pupils and Practitioners in Eighteenth-Century London*

(Cambridge: Cambridge University Press, 1996), 137 fn 89 and 139 fn 98; though Lawrence does not mention any possible connection with John Keats. For more general information on the profession at that time, see also W. F. Bynum and Roy Porter (eds), *William Hunter and the Eighteenth-Century Medical World* (Cambridge: Cambridge University Press, 1985), which contains incidentally an essay which indirectly relates to Keats, Joan Lane's 'The Role of Apprenticeship in Eighteenth-Century Medical Education in England', 57–104.

3. Nicholas Roe, *John Keats and the Culture of Dissent* (Oxford: Clarendon Press, 1997), 171–2.
4. Ibid., 172.
5. For the controversy over dating, see Robert Gittings, 'John Keats, Physician and Poet', *Journal of the American Medical Association*, 224, 2 (April 1973), 51–5.
6. 'Recollections of Keats', 125, quoted by Roe, *Culture of Dissent*, 163.
7. Hermione de Almeida, *Romantic Medicine and John Keats* (New York: Oxford University Press, 1991), 25.
8. Sir Sidney Colvin, *John Keats: His Life and Poetry, His Friends, Critics, and After-Fame* (London: Macmillan, 1917), 27–8.
9. Donald C. Goellnicht, *The Poet-Physician: Keats and Medical Science* (Pittsburgh: University of Pittsburgh Press, 1984), 37.
10. Goellnicht confirms the importance of this position and its appointment on merit, and adds that 'We know from South that the great Astley Cooper himself took an interest in Keats soon after Keats arrived at Guys'; ibid., 39.
11. Lawrence, *Charitable Knowledge*, 100 and 337.
12. I am extremely grateful to an archivist at Guy's Hospital library for mentioning this to me in 1992, and to the Wellcome Institute in London for allowing me to inspect it in their wonderful library. Page numbers are absorbed into the text.
13. *The London Medical and Physical Journal*, 36, 214 (December, 1816), 508.
14. Lawrence, *Charitable Knowledge*, 123.
15. Ibid., 71.
16. Ibid., 134.
17. Quoted without reference by Andrew Motion, *Keats* (London: Faber and Faber, 1997), 87.
18. Goellnicht, *The Poet-Physician*, 29 and 40.
19. James Paget, quoted by Roy Porter, *The Greatest Benefit to Mankind: A Medical History of Humanity from Antiquity to the Present* (London: HarperCollins, 1997), 316. See also Guy Williams, *The Age of Miracles: Medicine and Surgery in the Nineteenth Century* (Chicago: Academy Chicago Publishers, 1987), and Roy Porter, *Flesh in the Age of Reason: The Modern Foundations of Body and Soul* (Harmondsworth: Penguin Books, 2003).
20. Maurice Buxton Forman (ed.), *John Keats's Anatomical and Physiological Note Book* (Oxford: Oxford University Press, 1934).
21. Gustave Flaubert, *Madame Bovary*, trans. Alan Russell (Harmondsworth: Penguin Books, 1950), 189.
22. Smith, *Keats and Medicine*, 52.
23. Lawrence, *Charitable Knowledge*, 25.
24. See Sharon Ruston, *Shelley and Vitality* (Basingstoke: Palgrave Macmillan, 2005).
25. Stuart M. Sperry, *Keats the Poet* (Princeton, NJ: Princeton University Press, 1973).
26. De Almeida, *Romantic Medicine*, 157–62.
27. Goellnicht, *The Poet-Physician*, 34.

28. Agnes Arber, *Herbals: Their Origin and Evolution: a Chapter in the History of Botany, 1470–1670* (3rd edn, Cambridge: Cambridge University Press, 1938), 7.
29. Cooper, *Lectures* (1830), 439–40, quoted in de Almeida, *Romantic Medicine*, 150.
30. I am using the third edition, London, 1814.
31. Birmingham, 1812.
32. I have worked from the third edition (London, 1832).
33. Keats initially wrote 'henbane' but changed it no doubt because the wolf's associations are more menacing than the domestic hen's.
34. Laura E. Campbell, 'Unnecessary Compromise: Publisher Changes to "Ode to Psyche"', *English Language Notes*, 33 (1995), 53–8.
35. Motion, *Keats*, 364 and elsewhere.
36. Rachel P. Maines, *The Technology of Orgasm: 'Hysteria', the Vibrator, and Women's Sexual Satisfaction* (Baltimore and London: Johns Hopkins University Press, 1999).
37. William Cullen, *First Lines of the Practice of Physic* (Edinburgh: Bell, Bradfute, 1791), vol. 4, 105 and vol. 3, 46–7, quoted in Maines, *The Technology of Orgasm*, 53.
38. See *JKL* 2, 70, 2, 111, 2, 113. For the kind of life Keats could have expected on an 'Indiaman', see Robin Haines, *Doctors at Sea: Emigrant Voyages to Colonial Australia* (Basingstoke: Palgrave Macmillan, 2005).
39. See Goellnicht, *The Poet-Physician*, 227.
40. *Endymion*, Book II, ll. 481–4.

3. 'Was there a Poet born?'

1. See *Thomas Chatterton: Selected Poems*, ed. Grevel Lindop (Manchester: Carcanet Press, 1972).
2. See Edmund Blunden (ed.), *Leigh Hunt's 'Examiner' Examined* (1928, repr. Hamden, CT: Archon Books, 1967), 31ff.
3. Nicholas Roe, *Fiery Heart: The First Life of Leigh Hunt* (London: Pimlico, 2005), 225.
4. Jeffrey N. Cox, *Poetry and Politics in the Cockney School* (Cambridge: Cambridge University Press, 1998), 95.
5. See Bill Overton, *The Eighteenth-Century British Verse Epistle* (Basingstoke: Palgrave Macmillan, 2007).
6. Cox, *Poetry and Politics*, 101.
7. W. J. Bate, *John Keats* (Cambridge, MA: Harvard University Press, 1972), 51.
8. For full details, or what little we know of them in this period, see John Barnard, '"The Busy Time": Keats's Duties at Guy's Hospital from Autumn 1816 to March 1817', *Romanticism*, 13 (2007), 199–218.
9. Cox, *Poetry and Politics*, 84.
10. Roe, *John Keats and the Culture of Dissent*, 57–8.
11. Hunt, quoted in Blunden (ed.), *Leigh Hunt's 'Examiner' Examined*, xi.
12. Cox, *Poetry and Politics*, 88, 87.
13. Jack Stillinger, *Romantic Complexity: Keats, Coleridge and Wordsworth* (Urbana, IL: University of Illinois Press, 2006), 556.
14. Cox, *Poetry and Politics*, 121.

4. 'Fraternal souls' and *Poems* (1817)

1. *The Keats Circle: Letters and Papers and More Letters and Poems of the Keats Circle*, second edition (Cambridge, MA: Harvard University Press, 2 vols, 1965).

2. See Sarah Wootton, *Consuming Keats: Nineteenth-Century Representations in Art and Literature* (Basingstoke: Palgrave Macmillan, 2006).

3. See, for example, Gillian Russell and Clara Tuite (eds), *Romantic Sociability: Social Networks and Literary Culture in Britain, 1770–1840* (Cambridge: Cambridge University Press, 2002); Jeffrey N. Cox, *Poetry and Politics in the Cockney School: Keats, Shelley, Hunt and their Circle* (Cambridge: Cambridge University Press, 1998); and Felicity James, *Charles Lamb, Coleridge, Wordsworth: Reading Friendship in the 1790s* (Basingstoke: Palgrave Macmillan, 2008).

4. Cox, *Poetry and Politics*, ch. 3, 'John Keats, Coterie Poet'.

5. Quoted in Vera Cacciatore, *A Room in Rome* (Rome: The Keats-Shelley Memorial Association, 1970), 10.

6. Nicholas Roe, *Fiery Heart: The First Life of Leigh Hunt* (London: Pimlico, 2005).

7. See R. S. White, *Pacifism and English Literature* (Basingstoke: Palgrave Macmillan, 2008), 190–4.

8. See Duncan Wu, 'Leigh Hunt's "Cockney" Aesthetics', *The Keats-Shelley Review*, 10 (1996), 77–97.

9. Leigh Hunt, 'Poems by John Keats', *The Examiner*, 6 and 13 July 1817.

10. Leigh Hunt, 'On Young Poets', *The Examiner*, 1 December 1816.

11. A selection of Reynolds's poems can be found in *John Hamilton Reynolds: 'The Garden of Florence', 'The Press', 'Odes and Addresses to Great People'*, ed. Donald H. Reiman (New York and London: Garland Publishing, 1978).

12. For a detailed biography of Reynolds, see the Introduction to *The Letters of John Hamilton Reynolds*, ed. Leonidas M. Jones (Lincoln: University of Nebraska Press, 1973).

13. Mary Cowden Clarke, *The Life and Labours of Vincent Novello* (London: Novello and Co., 1862), 13–14. See Daisy Hay, 'Musical Evenings in the Hunt Circle', *The Keats-Shelley Review*, 21 (2007), 122–34.

14. From a letter by Haydon reprinted in Stanley Jones, 'B. R. Haydon on Some Contemporaries: A New Letter', *Review of English Studies*, NS 26 (1975), 183–9. For further details about Haydon's attitudes to Hazlitt and Wordsworth, see Stanley Jones, *Hazlitt: A Life From Winterslow to Frith Street* (Oxford: Oxford University Press, 1989) and David Blayney Brown, Robert Woof and Stephen Hebron, *Benjamin Robert Haydon: 1786–1846: Painter and Writer, Friend of Wordsworth and Keats* (Grasmere: The Wordsworth Trust, 1996).

15. *Letters*, 1, 118–19 fn.

16. Ibid., 120.

17. Roe, *Fiery Heart*, 154. For a fuller account of the affair, see Theresa M. Kelley, 'Keats, Ekphrasis, and History', in Nicholas Roe (ed.), *Keats and History* (Cambridge: Cambridge University Press, 1995), 212–37.

18. See R. S. White, *Keats as a Reader of Shakespeare* (London: Athlone Press, 1987), ch. II.

19. 'On Gusto', *The Examiner*, 26 May 1816, repr. in *The Round Table*. See R. S. White (ed.), *Hazlitt's Criticism of Shakespeare* (Lampeter: Edwin Mellen Press, 1996), 36–7 and *passim*.

20. See Wootton, *Consuming Keats*.

21. John Barnard, 'First Fruits or "First Blights": A New Account of the Publishing History of Keats's *Poems* (1817)', *Romanticism*, 12 (2006), 71–101.

22. See the details of this uncertainty in Susan J. Wolfson (ed.), *The Cambridge Companion to Keats* (Cambridge: Cambridge University Press, 2001), 2.

23. See Edmund Blunden (ed.), *Leigh Hunt's 'Examiner' Examined* (New York: Archon Books, 1967), 129–40.

24. Reproduced in G. M. Matthews (ed.), *Keats: The Critical Heritage* (London: Routledge, 1971), 71–4.

25. See Reynolds's letter in *The Letters of John Hamilton Reynolds*, ed. Leonidas M. Jones (Lincoln: University of Nebraska Press, 1973), 18–20.

26. See Richard Marggraf Turley, *Bright Stars: John Keats, 'Barry Cornwall' and Romantic Literary Culture* (Liverpool: Liverpool University Press, 2009).

27. Barnard, 'First Fruits or "First Blights"', 92.

28. Quoted by Walter Jackson Bate, *John Keats* (Cambridge, MA: Harvard University Press, 1963), 151.

29. See John Goodridge, *John Clare: Poetry and Society* (Cambridge: Cambridge University Press, forthcoming).

5. 'That which is creative must create itself': 1817 and *Endymion*

1. See John Barnard, 'Keats's Letters', in Susan Wolfson (ed.), *The Cambridge Companion to Keats* (Cambridge: Cambridge University Press, 2001), 120–34, and Nichola Deane, 'Keats's Lover's Discourse and the Letters to Fanny Brawne', *The Keats-Shelley Review*, 13 (1999), 105–14.

2. For criticism of the poem see Michael Ferber, '*Alastor*', in *Critical Studies: The Poetry of Shelley* (New York: Penguin Books, 1993), 23–33, repr. in Donald H. Reiman and Neil Fraistat (eds), *Shelley's Poetry and Prose: Authoritative Texts [and] Criticism* (2nd edn, New York: W. W. Norton & Company, 2002), 654–63 and Earl R. Wasserman, *Shelley: A Critical Reading* (Baltimore, MD: Johns Hopkins University Press, 1971).

3. *The Excursion* (1814), 687–756, 840–1; see Barnard, *Complete Poems*, Appendix 1.

4. For a very thorough and absorbing account of Pantheism, see Michael P. Levine, *Pantheism: A Non-Theistic Concept of Deity* (London and New York: Routledge, 1994).

5. The process of revision and correction is traced in detail by Margaret Ketchum Powell in 'Keats and His Editor: The Manuscript of *Endymion*', *The Library*, 6 (1984), 139–52. More generally, see also Zachary Leader, *Revision and Romantic Authorship* (Oxford: Oxford University Press, 1999), chapters 5 and 6.

6. This and the subsequent reviews are reprinted in the excellent collection edited by G. M. Matthews, *Keats: The Critical Heritage* (London: Routledge & Kegan Paul, 1971), 75–156.

7. See Richard Marggraf Turley, '"Slippery steps of the temple of fame": Barry Cornwall and Keats's Reputation', *The Keats-Shelley Review*, 22 (2008), 64–81.

8. Edmund Blunden (ed.), *Leigh Hunt's 'Examiner' Examined* (New York: Archon Books, 1967), 173.

9. Christopher Ricks, *Keats and Embarrassment* (Oxford: Clarendon Press, 1974) and Marjorie Levinson, *Keats's Life of Allegory: The Origins of a Style* (Oxford: Basil Blackwell, 1988).

10. A whole book has been written on this literary gathering and its contexts: Penelope Hughes-Hallett, *The Immortal Dinner: A Famous Evening of Genius and Laughter in Literary London, 1817* (Harmondsworth: Penguin Books, 2000).

11. Benjamin Haydon, *The Memoirs and Autobiography of Benjamin Robert Haydon* (London: Peter Davies, 1926), 316–17.

12. Haydon, *Journals*, 4 May 1821, quoted in Robert Woof and Stephen Hebron, *Benjamin Robert Haydon: 1786–1846: Painter and Writer, Friend of Wordsworth and Keats* (Grasmere: The Wordsworth Trust, 1996), 78.

6. 'Dark passages': 1818, January to June

1. Miriam Allott (ed.), *Keats: The Complete Poems* (London: Longman, 1970), 285, headnote.
2. See Ian Jack, *Keats and the Mirror of Art* (Oxford: Clarendon Press, 1967) and more particularly Michael Levey, '"The Enchanted Castle" by Claude: Subject, Significance and Interpretation', *The Burlington Magazine*, 130 (1988), 812–20.
3. See Levey, '"The Enchanted Castle"', 818 and 820.
4. A close reading of the poem alongside Boccaccio's account is offered by Eva Leoff in *A Study of John Keats's Isabella* (Salzburg: Salzburg Studies in English Literature, Salzburg University, 1972).
5. Jeffrey N. Cox, '*Lamia, Isabella*, and *The Eve of St. Agnes*: Eros and "Romance"', in Susan J. Wolfson (ed.), *The Cambridge Companion to Keats* (Cambridge and New York: Cambridge University Press, 2001), 53–68, 56.
6. See R. S. White, *Natural Rights and the Birth of Romanticism of the 1790s* (Basingstoke: Palgrave Macmillan, 2005), chapter 6.
7. Miriam Allott, after quoting from the passage, concludes that 'The "thought" underlying such passages is never fully worked out ...', *John Keats: A Reassessment* (Liverpool: Liverpool University Press, 1959), 53. John Jones does not mention the passage in his otherwise detailed analysis of the poem in *John Keats's Dream of Truth* (London: Chatto & Windus, 1969).
8. Essay on 'The Meaning of "Hyperion"', in Allott, *John Keats: A Reassessment*, 103.
9. See Lucy Newlyn, '*Paradise Lost*' and the Romantic Reader (Oxford: Clarendon Press, 1993).

7. Walking North and the Death of Tom: 1818, July to December

1. *The Letters of Charles Armitage Brown*, ed. J. Stillinger (Cambridge, MA: Harvard University Press, 1966). For details of his life, see the biography, E. H. McCormick, *The Friend of Keats: A Life of Charles Armitage Brown* (Wellington: Victoria University Press, 1989).
2. Quoted in Carol Kyros Walker, *Walking North With Keats* (New Haven and London: Yale University Press, 1992), 9.
3. Nelson S. Bushnell, *A Walk After John Keats* (New York: Farrar and Rinehart, 1936); see Walker, *Walking North*, 17, for information and some problems with this conjecture. Walker works from the sixth edition (1814) while I have had access only to the fifth edition: *The Traveller's Guide through Scotland and its Islands: illustrated by maps, sketches of pleasure-tours, views of remarkable buildings, and a plan of the lakes of Cumberland* (5th edition, Edinburgh: J. Thomson, Jun. and Co., 1811).
4. Repr. John Clare, *The Journal, Essays, The Journey from Essex*, ed. Anne Tibble (Manchester: Carcanet Press, 1980).
5. John Thelwall, *The Peripatetic*, ed. Judith Thompson (Detroit: Wayne State University Press, 2001), 252. See especially Thompson's Introduction, 34–5.

6. Robin Jarvis, *Romantic Writing and Pedestrian Travel* (Basingstoke: Macmillan, 1997), 196–206.
7. Gillian Russell, 'Keats, Popular Culture and the Sociability of Theatre', in *British Romanticism and Popular Culture*, ed. Philip O'Connell and Nigel Leask (Cambridge: Cambridge University Press, 2008), 415–59, 440.
8. Claire Lamont, 'Meg the Gipsy in Scott and Keats', *English*, 36 (1987), 137–45.
9. Stanley Plumly, *Posthumous Keats: A Personal Biography* (New York: W.W. Norton & Co., 2008), 149.
10. See Robert Gittings, *John Keats*, Appendix 3, 642–9, who points out that 'the invention of the syphilis interpretation was entirely Miss [Amy] Lowell's own. She then proceeded to refute her own invention, and was followed by Hewlett and Bate' (643). Gittings favours the idea that Keats caught a gonorrhoeal infection just before he went to Oxford to see Bailey, but he offers little material evidence and his reasoning seems slender.
11. See E. A. Wrigley, *The Population History of England, 1541–1871: A Reconstruction* (Cambridge, MA: Harvard University Press, 1981).
12. Quoted in Donald Goellnicht, *The Poet-Physician: Keats and Medical Science* (Pittsburgh: University of Pittsburgh Press, 1984), 201.
13. Nicholas Roe, *Fiery Heart: The First Life of Leigh Hunt* (London: Pimlico, 2005), 150.

8. 'A gordian complication of feelings': Love, Women and Romance

1. All that we know about Isabella Jones, which is not much, is summarised by Robert Gittings, *John Keats: The Living Year* (London: Heinemann, 1954), Appendix D.
2. Ibid., chapter 6.
3. See Elizabeth Fay, *Romantic Medievalism: History and the Romantic Literary Ideal* (Basingstoke: Palgrave Macmillan, 2002), 113–15.
4. Despite a complex textual situation, the text quoted here, following Barnard's edition, is the one Keats published in 1820.
5. Gittings, *John Keats: The Living Year*, chapters 7 and 8.
6. Zachary Leader, *Revision and Romantic Authorship* (Oxford: Oxford University Press, 1996), 301–7.
7. Margaret Homans, 'Keats Reading Women, Women Reading Keats', *Studies in Romanticism*, 29 (1990), 341–70.
8. Jack Stillinger, *The Hoodwinking of Madeline and other Essays on Keats's Poetry* (Urbana: University of Illinois Press, 1971).
9. John Barnard, *John Keats* (Cambridge: Cambridge University Press, 1987), 90.
10. William Empson in *Seven Types of Ambiguity*, 214–17, notes the intensity of sensations concentrated into contrasts of imagery, in *The Eve* and also the 'Ode on Melancholy'.
11. Jerome J. McGann, *The Beauty of Inflections: Literary Investigations in Historical Method and Theory* (Oxford: Oxford University Press, 1985). Chris Jones in 'Knight or Wight in Keats's "La Belle Dame"? An Ancient Ditty Reconsidered', *The Keats-Shelley Review*, 19 (2005), 39–49, suggests the plural textual tradition should be respected, citing medieval poems as precedents.
12. Walter Jackson Bate, *John Keats* (Cambridge, MA: The Belknap Press of Harvard University Press, 1963), 312–14.

13. Sarah Wootton, *Consuming Keats: Nineteenth-Century Representations in Art and Literature* (Basingstoke: Palgrave Macmillan, 2006), chapter 4, 'Keats's Belle Dame as *Femme Fatale*', 109.
14. Fay, *Romantic Medievalism*, 122.
15. For a summary of Keats's complex attitude to contemporary science, see Alan Richardson, 'Keats and Romantic Science', in *The Cambridge Companion to Keats*, ed. Susan J. Wolfson (Cambridge: Cambridge University Press, 2001), 230–45.
16. *The Diary of B. R. Haydon*, ed. W. B. Pope (Cambridge, MA: Harvard University Press, 1960), 2, 72.
17. Edmund Blunden (ed.), *Leigh Hunt's 'Examiner' Examined* (1928, repr. Hamden, CT: Archon Books, 1967, 141–8.
18. *Studies in Romanticism*, 29 (1990), 341–70.
19. Anne K. Mellor, 'Keats and the Complexities of Gender', in *The Cambridge Companion to Keats*, ed. Susan J. Wolfson (Cambridge: Cambridge University Press, 2001), 214–29, 216.
20. See Jon Mee, 'Keats and Women' in Mee's revision of Robert Gittings (ed.), *John Keats: Selected Letters* (Oxford: Oxford World's Classics, Oxford University Press, 2002), xxx–xxxii.
21. See also *JKL*, 2, 78–9: 'In this state of effeminacy the fibres of the brain are relaxed in common with the rest of the body, and to such a happy degree that pleasure has no show of enticement and pain no unbearable frown.'

9. 'Tease us out of thought': May 1819, Odes

1. A book on Keats and philosophy is yet to be written, but one that broaches the subject is by Laurence S. Lockridge, *The Ethics of Romanticism* (Cambridge: Cambridge University Press, 1989); see 'Keats and the Ethics of Immanence', 380–402.
2. For information about Keats's reading of Robertson's various books, see Greg Kucich, 'Keats's Literary Tradition and the Politics of Historiographical Invention', in Nicholas Roe, *Keats and History* (Cambridge: Cambridge University Press, 1995), 238–61; and Roe's 'Introduction', 12.
3. See Jeffrey Smitten, 'Impartiality in Robertson's *History of America*', *Eighteenth-Century Studies*, 19 (1985), 56–77.
4. See, for example, John Hick, 'Soul-Making and Suffering', in Marilyn McCord Adams and Robert M. Adams, *The Problem of Evil* (Oxford: Oxford University Press, 1990), 168–88, cited in Michael P. Levine, *Pantheism: A Non-theistic Concept of Deity* (London and New York: Routledge, 1994).
5. Lemprière, *A Classical Dictionary*, 510.
6. Mary Tighe, *Psyche or, the Legend of Love* (repr. New York: Garland Publishing Inc., 1978), 97.
7. Ian Jack, *Keats and the Mirror of Art* (Oxford: Oxford University Press, 1967).
8. Earl R. Wasserman builds his argument upon oxymorons in *The Finer Tone: Keats's Major Poems* (Baltimore: Johns Hopkins University Press, 1953), chapter 2.
9. See also Sonnet 101.
10. Sidney, *Astrophil and Stella*, Sonnet 1.
11. See Rosalie Colie, *Paradoxia Epidemica: The Renaissance Tradition of Paradox* (Hamden, CT: Archon Books, 1966).
12. For the tortuous textual arguments concerning who speaks and to whom, see the notes to the various editions by Allott, Barnard and Stillinger.

13. Stillinger's text is quoted. Barnard's reads:
    'Beauty is truth, truth beauty, – that is all
    Ye know on earth, and all ye need to know.'
    A range of meanings opens up, depending on where we end the quotation marks. The version printed in *Annals of the Fine Arts* has no quotation marks, but the one published in Keats's *Poems Published in 1820* contains them as followed by Stillinger and here.
14. The most comprehensive study of Keats and music is by John A. Minahan, *Word Like a Bell: John Keats, Music and the Romantic Poet* (Kent, OH: Kent State University Press, 1992). Amongst other themes, Minahan writes on 'Music as Organizational Principle in Keats's Poetry'.
15. Helen Vendler, *The Odes of John Keats* (Cambridge, MA: Harvard University Press, 1983), 81.
16. See Albert R. Chandler, 'The Nightingale in Greek and Latin Poetry', *The Classical Journal*, 30 (1934), 78–84.
17. Robert Gittings, *John Keats: The Living Year: 21 September 1818 to 21 September 1819* (London: Heinemann Educational Books, 1954), chapter 14.
18. Chandler, 'The Nightingale in Greek and Latin Poetry', 78, referring to Pliny, *Natural History*, X, 43.
19. Miriam Allott (ed.), *John Keats: The Poems* (London: Longman, 1970, rpt. 1995), 541 fn.

10. Playwright

1. For more details on Keats and the theatre of his day, see Harry R. Beaudry, *The English Theatre of John Keats* (Salzburg: Salzburg Studies in English Literature, 1973), Bernice Slote, *Keats and the Dramatic Principle* (Lincoln, NE: University of Nebraska Press, 1958), Jonathan Mulrooney, 'Keats in the Company of Kean', *Studies in Romanticism*, 42 (2003), 227–50, and Gillian Russell, 'Keats, Popular Culture, and the Sociability of Theatre', in *British Romanticism and Popular Culture*, ed. Philip O'Connell and Nigel Leask (Cambridge: Cambridge University Press, 2008).
2. For more detail, see Jane Moody, *Illegitimate Theatre in London, 1770–1840* (Cambridge: Cambridge University Press, 2000) and Gillian Russell, *The Theatres of War: Performance, Politics and Society, 1793–1815* (Oxford: Oxford University Press, 1995).
3. David Underdown, *Start of Play: Cricket and Culture in Eighteenth-Century England* (Harmondsworth: Penguin Books, 2000), 80.
4. On the development of animal rights in the period, see the references cited in R. S. White, *Natural Rights and the Birth of Romanticism of the 1790s* (Basingstoke: Palgrave Macmillan, 2005), 224–31.
5. For an entertaining biography, see Harold Newcomb Hillebrand, *Edmund Kean* (New York: AMS Press, 1966).
6. The review is most conveniently reprinted in John Barnard (ed.), *John Keats: The Complete Poems* (Harmondsworth: Penguin Books, 1977), 527–9.
7. R. S. White, *Hazlitt's Criticism of Shakespeare* (Lampeter: Edwin Mellen Press, 1996), 36–7.
8. See ibid., 52.
9. R. S. White, *Keats as a Reader of Shakespeare* (London: Athlone, 1987), 88–90.
10. Anonymous, *Helvetic Liberty, An Opera in three Acts by a Kentish Bowman*, quoted in Jeffrey N. Cox, 'Re-viewing Romantic Drama', *Literature Compass*, 1 (2004), 1–27, 9.

11. The following descriptions of *Otho* are revised from my book, *Keats as a Reader of Shakespeare*, chapter 8.
12. Thomas McFarland, *The Masks of Keats: The Endeavour of a Poet* (Oxford: Oxford University Press, 2000), 176.

11. Autumn in Winchester

1. Ilse Cornwall Ross, *A Season of Mellow Fruitfulness: John Keats in Winchester 1819* (Winchester: Ilex Terrace Press, 1995), 51.
2. For an analysis of Keats's report and its intersection with 'Ode to Autumn', see James Chandler, *England in 1819: The Politics of Literary Culture and the Case of Romantic Historicism* (Chicago and London: University of Chicago Press, 1998), 425–31.
3. Vincent Newey, 'Hyperion, The Fall of Hyperion, and Keats's Epic Ambitions', in *The Cambridge Companion to Keats*, ed. Susan J. Wolfson (Cambridge: Cambridge University Press, 2001), 69–85.
4. Helen Vendler, *The Odes of John Keats* (Cambridge, MA: Harvard University Press, 1983), chapter 6.
5. John Jones, *John Keats's Dream of Truth* (London: Chatto & Windus, 1969), 262.
6. For readings that stress the more political and subversive subtext of 'To Autumn' see Nicholas Roe, 'Keats's Commonwealth' in Roe (ed.), *Keats and History* (Cambridge: Cambridge University Press, 1995), 194–211 and in the Odes more generally, Daniel P. Watkins, *Keats's Poetry and the Politics of the Imagination* (Rutherford, NJ: Fairleigh Dickinson University Press, 1989).
7. Reuben Arthur Brower, *The Fields of Light: An Experiment in Critical Reading* (Oxford: Oxford University Press, 1951), 39.
8. Herbert Read, *The True Voice of Feeling: Studies in English Romantic Poetry* (London: Faber and Faber, 1968), 56.
9. Robert Gittings, *John Keats: The Living Year: 21 September 1818 to 21 September 1819* (London: Heinemann Educational Books, 1954), 187. This reference is expanded upon, and the list of sources augmented by literally dozens more, by H. Neville Davies, 'Keats, Winchester, and the Marriage Psalm', *The Keats-Shelley Review*, 4 (1989), 31–60.
10. Stanley Plumly, *Posthumous Keats: A Personal Biography* (New York: W.W. Norton & Co., 2008), 271–2.
11. F. R. Leavis, 'Keats', *Revaluation* (London: Chatto & Windus, 1936), chapter 7.
12. Clare, writing from a more native, rustic point of view, was in fact critical of Keats's poetry of nature, though he was probably thinking of the early poems like 'I stood tip-toe' and 'Sleep and Poetry': 'In spite of all this his descriptions of scenery are often very fine but as it is the case with other inhabitants of great cities he often described nature as she appeared to his fancies & not as he would have described her had he witnessed the things he describes ...' (*Heritage*, 156).

12. *Poems* (1820)

1. Mark Willis, 'In Search of *Mr Keats*', *The Keats-Shelley Review*, 17 (2003), 136–45, 141, quoting an article by John Briney in [*Louisville*] *Courier-Journal*, 6 December 1957.

2. I have benefited from the advice of Bruce Robinson and Peter Underwood, Professors of Medicine at the University of Western Australia.
3. Angus Graham-Campbell, '"O for a draught of vintage": Keats, Food and Wine', *The Keats-Shelley Review*, 17 (2003), 42–60, 47–8.
4. The son born to Brown and Abigail was to be named Charles after his father, but was always known as Carlino, whether with reference to the Brawnes' dog Carlo is unknown.
5. Susan J. Wolfson, 'Late Lyrics: Form and Discontent', in *The Cambridge Companion to Keats*, ed. Susan J. Wolfson (Cambridge: Cambridge University Press, 2001), 102–19.
6. G. Wilson Knight, *The Starlit Dome: On the Poetry of Wordsworth, Coleridge, Shelley and Keats* (London: Methuen, 1959), 305.

13. The Final Journey

1. John Barnard, 'Who Killed John Keats?' *Times Literary Supplement*, 2 December 2009.
2. John Goodridge, 'Junkets and Clarissimus: The Untold Story of John Clare and John Keats', *Romanticism* (forthcoming).
3. See *Joseph Severn: Letters and Memoirs*, ed. Grant F. Scott (Aldershot: Ashgate, 2005).
4. See Grant F. Scott's Introduction' to Severn's *Letters*, 2.
5. See her letter to Taylor, 14 April 1821, repr. in *Severn: Letters*, 149–51.
6. Quoted in Vera Cacciatore, *A Room in Rome* (Rome: The Keats-Shelley Memorial Association, 1970), 10.
7. Compare Sally Brown, 'Suppose me in Rome', in *Keats and Italy: A History of the Keats-Shelley House in Rome* (Rome: Edizioni Il Labirinto, 2005), 27, and Richard Haslam, 'An Echo and a Light unto Eternity: The Founding of the Keats-Shelley House', ibid., 79.
8. The reading can be viewed online on YouTube.
9. Worried that Mrs Abbey seemed to think her younger than she was, Fanny took the precaution of acquiring her birth certificate, with help from Fanny Brawne and Dilke. Abbey tried to avoid giving her the inheritance when she reached 21, but eventually she did receive not only her own portion but also John's and Tom's. Fanny Brawne introduced Fanny Keats to her future husband, a Spanish refugee and an author, Valentine Maria Llanos y Gutierrez. They married in 1826.
10. Sculpted by Frank Dobson.
11. I am grateful to Christine Reynolds, Assistant Keeper of Muniments in the Library at Westminster Abbey for these details.

Select Bibliography

The endnotes to this book indicate detailed works of scholarship, leaving this list to cover only essential reference books and useful or historically important critical works.

Editions and reference works (in chronological order)

John Keats: The Letters, ed. M. Buxton Forman. 4th rev. edn, Oxford: Oxford University Press, 1952.

John Keats: Poetical Works, ed. H. W. Garrod. Oxford English Texts, 2nd rev. edn, Oxford: Oxford University Press, 1958.

John Keats: The Letters, 1814–1821, ed. H. E. Rollins. 2 vols, Cambridge, MA: Harvard University Press, 1958.

John Keats: Selected Poems and Letters, ed. Douglas Bush. Boston: Houghton Mifflin Company, 1959.

The Diary of Benjamin Robert Haydon, ed. Willard Bissell Pope. Cambridge, MA: Harvard University Press, 1960.

The Keats Circle: Letters and Papers and More Letters and Poems of the Keats Circle, 2nd edn, 2 vols, Cambridge, MA: Harvard University Press, 1965.

The Letters of Charles Armitage Brown, ed. J. Stillinger. Cambridge, MA: Harvard University Press, 1966.

John Keats, The Odes of Keats and their Earliest Known Manuscripts, ed. Robert Gittings. London: Heinemann, 1970.

Letters of John Keats: A New Selection, ed. Robert Gittings. Oxford: Oxford University Press, 1970 and regularly reprinted.

Keats: The Critical Heritage, ed. G. M. Matthews. London: Routledge & Kegan Paul, 1971.

The Letters of John Hamilton Reynolds, ed. Leonidas M. Jones. Lincoln: University of Nebraska Press, 1977.

John Keats: The Complete Poems, ed. John Barnard. Penguin English Poets, 3rd rev. edn, Harmondsworth, Middlesex: Penguin Books, second edn, 1977.

The Poems of John Keats, ed. Jack Stillinger. London: Heinemann, 1978.

Complete Poems and Selected Letters of John Keats, ed. Edward Hirsch. New York: Random House, 1994.

John Keats: The Poems, ed. Miriam Allott. Longman Annotated English Poets, London: Longman, 1970, reprinted, 1995.

John Keats: Selected Letters, ed. Robert Gittings, rev. Jon Mee. Oxford: Oxford University Press, 2002.

Joseph Severn: Letters and Memoirs, ed. Grant F. Scott. Aldershot: Asghate Publishing, 2005.

Biography (in chronological order)

Brown, Charles Armitage, *Life of John Keats* [written 1836], ed. Dorothy Hyde Bodurtha and Willard B. Pope. London: Oxford University Press, 1937.

Clarke, Charles and Mary Cowden, *Recollections of Writers*. Repr. Fontwell, Sussex: Centaur Press, 1969.

Letters of Fanny Brawne to Fanny Keats [1820–1824], ed. Fred Edgcumbe. Oxford: Oxford University Press, 1936.

Houghton, Lord Richard Monckton Milnes, *The Life, Letters and Literary Remains of John Keats*. London, 1848, repr. London: J. M. Dent & Sons, 1927.

Colvin, Sir Sidney, *John Keats: His Life and Poetry, His Friends, Critics and After-fame*. London: Macmillan, 1917.

Lowell, Amy, *John Keats*. 2 vols, Boston: Houghton Mifflin, 1925.

Hewlett, Dorothy, *Adonais: A Life of John Keats*. London: Hurst and Blackett, 1937.

Adami, Marie, *Fanny Keats*. London: J. Murray, 1937.

Blunden, Edmund, *Keats's Publisher*. Oxford: Oxford University Press, 1940.

Richardson, Joanna, *Fanny Brawne*. London: Thames & Hudson, 1952.

Gittings, Robert, *John Keats: The Living Year: 21 September 1818 to 21 September 1819*. London: Heinemann Educational Books, 1954.

Bate, Walter Jackson, *John Keats*. Cambridge, MA: The Belknap Press of Harvard University Press, 1963.

Ward, Aileen, *John Keats: The Making of a Poet*. New York: Viking Press, 1963.

Gittings, Robert, *The Keats Inheritance*. London: Heinemann, 1964.

Gittings, Robert, *John Keats*. London: Heinemann Educational Books, 1968.

Owings, Frank N., Jr., *The Keats Library: A Descriptive Catalogue*. London, [1978?].

Richardson, Joanna, *The Life and Letters of John Keats*. London: The Folio Society, 1981.

Becker, Michael G., *A Concordance to the Poems of John Keats*. New York: Garland, 1981.

McCormick, E. H., *The Friend of Keats: A Life of Charles Armitage Brown*. Wellington: Victoria University Press, 1989.

Pinion, F. B., *A Keats Chronology*. London: Macmillan, 1992.

Woof, Robert and Stephen Hebron, *John Keats*. Grasmere: The Wordsworth Trust, 1995.

Coote, Stephen, *John Keats: A Life*. London: Hodder & Stoughton, 1995.

Benjamin Robert Haydon 1786–1846, ed. David Blayney Brown, Robert Woof and Stephen Hebron. Grasmere: The Wordsworth Trust, 1996.

Motion, Andrew, *Keats*. London: Faber and Faber, 1997.

Roe, Nicholas, *John Keats and the Culture of Dissent*. Oxford: Oxford University Press, 1997.

Hughes-Hallett, Penelope, *The Immortal Dinner: A Famous Evening of Genius and Laughter in Literary London, 1817*. London: Penguin Books, 2000.

Mee, Jon, Thomas Keymer and Clara Tuite, eds, *The Cambridge Companion to English Literature, 1740–1830*. Cambridge: Cambridge University Press, 2004.

Everest, Kelvin, 'John Keats', *Dictionary of National Biography*. Oxford: Oxford University Press, online, 2004–6.

Keats and Italy: A History of the Keats-Shelley House in Rome. Rome: Edizioni Il Labirinto, 2005.

Spellbound by Rome [Incantati da Roma]: The Anglo-American Community in Rome and the Founding of the Keats-Shelley House. Rome: Palombi Editori, 2005.

Plumly, Stanley, *Posthumous Keats: A Personal Biography*. New York: W. W. Norton and Co., 2008.

Brown, Sue, *Jospeh Severn, A Life: The Rewards of Friendship* Oxford: Oxford University Press, 2009.

Crutcher, Lawrence M., *The Keats Family*, Louisville: Kentucky, 2009.

Criticism

Obviously a huge amount of valuable material can be found in journals, particularly those specialising in Keats and in the Romantics, such as the *Keats-Shelley Journal*, *Keats-Shelley Review* and *Romanticism*, and more recently *Romanticism on the Net*, an electronic journal, and *Voice of the Shuttle: The Romantics*, a comprehensive internet search engine. Below are listed a small number of useful works.

Aske, Martin, *Keats and Hellenism: An Essay*. Cambridge: Cambridge University Press, 1985.

Barnard, John, *John Keats*. Cambridge: Cambridge University Press, 1987.

Bate, Jonathan, *Shakespeare and the Romantic Imagination*. Oxford: Clarendon Press, 1986.

Bayley, John, 'Keats and Reality', *Proceedings of the British Academy*. 1962, repr. *English Poets: British Academy Chatterton Lectures*. Oxford, 1988, pp. 184–222.

Bennett, Andrew, *Keats, Narrative and Audience: The Posthumous Life of Writing*. Cambridge: Cambridge University Press, 1994.

Bewell, Alan J., 'The Political Implications of Keats's Classicist Aesthetics', *Studies in Romanticism*, 25 (1986): 220–9.

Braida, Antonella, *Dante and the Romantics*. Basingstoke and New York: Palgrave Macmillan, 2004.

Bromwich, David, *Hazlitt: The Mind of a Critic*. Oxford: Oxford University Press, 1983.

Brooks, Cleanth, *The Well-Wrought Urn: Studies in the Structure of Poetry*. New York: Harcourt Brace Jovanovich, 1975 [1947].

Bush, Douglas, *John Keats: His Life and Writings*. New York: Macmillan, 1966.

Chandler, James, *England in 1819: The Politics of Literary Culture and the Case of Romantic Historicism*. Chicago and London: University of Chicago Press, 1998.

Colvin, Sidney, *John Keats*. London: Macmillan, 1917.

Cox, Jeffrey N., *Poetry and Politics in the Cockney School*. Cambridge: Cambridge University Press, 1998.

De Almeida, Hermione, *Critical Essays on John Keats*. Boston: G. K. Hall, 1990.

De Almeida, Hermione, *Romantic Medicine and John Keats*. New York: Oxford University Press, 1991.

Dickstein, Morris, *Keats and His Poetry: A Study in Development*. Chicago: University of Chicago Press, 1971.

Erberle-Sinatra, Michael, *Leigh Hunt and the London Literary Scene*. London and New York: Routledge, 2005.

Fay, Elizabeth A., *A Feminist Introduction to Romanticism*. Oxford: Blackwell, 1998.

Fay, Elizabeth A., *Romantic Medievalism: History and the Romantic Literary Ideal*. Basingstoke and New York: Palgrave Macmillan, 2002.

Fermanis, Porscha, *John Keats and the Ideas of the Enlightenment*. Edinburgh: Edinburgh University Press, 2009.

Finney, Claude Lee, *The Evolution of Keats's Poetry*. 2 vols, New York: Russell & Russell, 1963 [1936].

Fogle, R. H., *The Imagery of Keats and Shelley: A Comparative Study*. Chapel Hill, NC: University of Carolina Press, 1947.

Gallant, Christine, *Keats and Celticism*. Basingstoke and New York: Palgrave Macmillan, 2005.

Garrod, H. W., *Keats*. Oxford: Oxford University Press, 1926.

Gittings, Robert, *The Nature of Biography*. London: Heinemann, 1978.

Goellnicht, Donald, *The Poet-Physician: Keats and Medical Science*. Pittsburgh: University of Pittsburgh Press, 1984.

Goldberg, M. A., *The Poetics of Romanticism: Towards a Reading of John Keats*. Yellow Springs, OH: Antioch Press, 1969.

Goslee, Nancy M., *Uriel's Eye: Miltonic Stationing and Statuary in Blake, Keats, and Shelley*. Alabama: University of Alabama Press, 1985.

Hartman, Geoffrey, 'Poem and Ideology: A Study of Keats's "To Autumn"', in *The Fate of Reading*, Chicago: Chicago University Press, 1975, 124–46.

Haskell, Dennis, *The Poetry of John Keats*. Sydney: Oxford University Press, 1991.

Hillebrand, Harold Newcomb, *Edmund Kean*. New York: AMS Press, 1966.

Jack, Ian, *Keats and the Mirror of Art*. Oxford: Clarendon Press, 1967.

Jones, John, *John Keats's Dream of Truth*. London: Chatto & Windus, 1969.

Knight, G. Wilson, *The Starlit Dome: On the Poetry of Wordsworth, Coleridge, Shelley and Keats*. London: Methuen, 1959.

Kucich, Greg, 'John Keats', in *Literature of the Romantic Period: A Bibliographic Guide*, ed. Michael O'Neill. Oxford: Clarendon Press, 1998, 143–66.

Levinson, Marjorie, *Keats's Life of Allegory: The Origins of a Style*. Oxford: Blackwell, 1990 [1988].

Marggraf, Richard Turley, *Keats's Boyish Imagination*. London and New York: Routledge, 2004.

McFarland, Thomas, *The Masks of Keats: The Endeavour of a Poet*. Oxford: Oxford University Press, 2000.

McGann, Jerome J., 'Keats and Historical Method', in *The Beauty of Inflections: Literary Investigations in Historical Method and Theory*. Oxford: Oxford University Press, 1985.

Murry, John Middleton, *Keats and Shakespeare*. Westport, CT: Greenwood Press, 1978 [1926].

Newlyn, Lucy, *'Paradise Lost' and the Romantic Reader*. Oxford: Clarendon Press, 1993.

O'Neill, Michael, *Keats: Bicentenary Readings*. Edinburgh: Edinburgh University Press, 1997.

O'Neill, Michael, 'Writing and History in *Hyperion* and *The Fall of Hyperion*', in *Romanticism and the Self-Conscious Poem*. Oxford: Oxford University Press, 1997, 210–34.

O'Neill, Michael, 'Keats and the "Poetical Character"', in *Placing and Displacing Romanticism*, ed. Peter Kitson. Aldershot and Burlington, VT: Ashgate, 2001, 157–65.

O'Neill, Michael, ed., *Literature of the Romantic Period: A Bibliographical Guide*. Oxford: Oxford University Press, 1998 and reprinted.

Richardson, Alan, *British Romanticism and the Science of the Mind*. Cambridge: Cambridge University Press, 2001.

Ricks, Christopher, *Keats and Embarrassment*. Oxford: Clarendon Press, 1974.

Ridley, M. R., *Keats's Craftsmanship: A Study in Development and Growth*. Lincoln, Nebraska: University of Nebraska Press, 1963 [1933].

Roe, Nicholas, *John Keats and the Culture of Dissent*. Oxford: Clarendon Press, 1997.

Roe, Nicholas, *Leigh Hunt: Life, Poetics, Politics*. London and New York: Routledge, 2003.

Roe, Nicholas, *Fiery Heart: The First Life of Leigh Hunt*. London: Pimlico, 2005.

Roe, Nicholas, ed., *Keats and History*. Cambridge: Cambridge University Press 1995.

Roe, Nicholas, ed., *Romanticism: An Oxford Guide*. Oxford: Oxford University Press, 2005.

Ryan, Robert M., *Keats: The Religious Sense*. Princeton, NJ: Princeton University Press, 1976.

Sandy, Mark, 'Twentieth- and Twenty-first Century Keats Criticism', *Literature Compass*, 3/6 (2006): 1320–33.

Scott, Grant F., *The Sculpted Word: Keats, Ekphrasis, and the Visual Arts*. Hanover, NH: University Press of New Hampshire, 1994.

Sharp, Ronald A., *Keats, Skepticism, and the Religion of Beauty*. Athens, GA: University of Georgia Press, 1979.

Sperry, Stuart M., *Keats the Poet*. Princeton, NJ: Princeton University Press, 1973.

Spurgeon, Caroline, *Keats's Shakespeare: A Descriptive Study Based on New Material*. Oxford: Oxford University Press, 1966 [1928].

Stillinger, Jack, *The Hoodwinking of Madeline and Other Essays*. Urbana: University of Illinois Press, 1971.

Stillinger, Jack, *Romantic Complexity: Keats, Coleridge, and Wordsworth*. Urbana: University of Illinois Press, 2006.

Thorpe, Clarence Dewitt, *The Mind of John Keats*. New York: Oxford University Press, 1926.

Turley, Richard Marggraf, *Keats's Boyish Imagination*. London: Routledge, 2004.

Turley, Richard Marggraf, *Bright Stars: John Keats, 'Barry Cornwall' and Romantic Literary Culture*. Liverpool: Liverpool University Press, 2009.

Vendler, Helen, *The Odes of John Keats*. Cambridge, MA: Harvard University Press, 1983.

Wasserman, Earl R., *The Finer Tone: Keats's Major Poems*. Baltimore: Johns Hopkins University Press, 1967 [1953].

Watkins, Daniel P., *Keats's Poetry and the Politics of Imagination*. Rutherford, NJ: Associated University Presses, 1989.

Whale, John, *John Keats*. Basingstoke and New York: Palgrave Macmillan, 2005.

Whelan, Maurice, *In the Company of William Hazlitt: Thoughts for the 21st Century*. Melbourne: Australian Scholarly Publishing, 2003.

White, R. S., *Keats as a Reader of Shakespeare*. London: Athlone Press, 1987.

White, R. S., *Hazlitt's Criticism of Shakespeare*. Lampeter: Edwin Mellen Press, 1996.

White, R. S., *Natural Rights and the Birth of Romanticism of the 1790s*. Basingstoke: Palgrave Macmillan, 2005.

Wolfson, Susan, *Formal Charges: The Shaping of Poetry in British Romanticism*. Stanford, CA: Stanford University Press, 1997.

Wolfson, Susan, ed., *The Cambridge Companion to Keats*. Cambridge and New York: Cambridge University Press, 2001.

Wootton, Sarah, *Consuming Keats: Nineteenth-Century Representations in Art and Literature*. Basingstoke: Palgrave Macmillan, 2006.

Index